TORPEDO

TORPEDO

The Complete History of the World's Most Revolutionary Naval Weapon

ROGER BRANFILL-COOK

Seaforth
PUBLISHING

FRONTISPIECE: The Battle of Pachoca, 6 May 1877, the first time a locomotive torpedo was fired in anger: launched by the British ironclad frigate *Shah*, the torpedo missed its target, the rebel Peruvian turret ship *Huáscar* (see page 170).

Copyright © Roger Branfill-Cook 2014

First published in Great Britain in 2014 by
Seaforth Publishing
An imprint of Pen & Sword Books Ltd
47 Church Street, Barnsley
S Yorkshire S70 2AS

www.seaforthpublishing.com
Email info@seaforthpublishing.com

British Library Cataloguing in Publication Data
A CIP data record for this book is available from the British Library

ISBN 978 1 84832 215 8

Typeset and designed by Ian Hughes, Mousemat Design Limited
Printed and bound in China

Contents

Acknowledgements

Wherever possible the illustrations included in this book are credited to their originators or to the institutions which hold them for future generations. I have been collecting and reading books on naval subjects for over fifty years, which means that many of the authors whose works I quote left us many years ago. Others are still alive, but not even the editors of their last works can trace them.

When information has been discovered on the Internet, and the original source is either not stated or was unknown, I have not hesitated to reproduce the appropriate illustrations, lest they be lost to our common pool of knowledge with the disappearance of the website. If any of the authors and artists whom I have been unable to contact, even after extensive enquiries, see their work included in this book, it is with the aim of giving them full credit, and referring readers to find and browse their books with the same pleasure that they have given me.

I must record my sincere thanks and appreciation to the following who have aided me in putting together this encyclopedia. Without their contributions the work would have been the poorer.

Hallvard Aasdalen, Bjørn Bakkhe and Kjell J Glosli for help with the Oscarsborg torpedo battery.
Dennis Andrews for permission to use his painting of the wreck of the *Kursk*.
Scotia Ashley of the National Library of Australia and Anastasia Symeoides of Fairfax Media Syndication for help on the *Kempenfelt* accident.
Scott Belcher of Chatham Historical Dockyard, for access to HMS *Gannet* and HMS *Ocelot*.
Martin Bellamy of the Society for Nautical Research for help re the lithograph of HMS *Shah* and *Huascár*.
Sophia Brothers of the Science Museum, for permission to use the photo of the *TB 17* and TBD *Tartar*.
Andrew Choong of the National Maritime Museum, Greenwich, for help in searching the archives.
Debbie Corner, George Malcolmson and Alex Geary at the RN Submarine Museum.
Martin Dean of adusDEEPOCEAN and Andy Liddell of SalMO for permission to use the sonar scan of the wreck of HMS *Royal Oak*.
Terry Dickens of World Naval Ships Forum, for permission to use his photo of *Maillé Brézé*.
Dan Dowdey of the Friends of the *Hunley*, for permission to use his painting of the CSS *Hunley*.
Jeff Dykes and Brian Hodder for details of the *Sidon* disaster.
Mr Robert Elder of the National Museum of the Pacific War, Fredericksburg, for the photo of the USN pentad mount.
Peter Enne and Thomas Ilming of the Military History Museum, Vienna, for photos of the *Viribus Unitis* model and torpedoes in the museum's collection.
Maciej Florek, 'snakedoc', of www.ubootwaffe.pl, for permission to reproduce photo and information on U-boat torpedo tubes of WW2.
Francesco Franchi for his drawing and photos of the Mignatta and of his diorama.
Paul Freshney of *Model Boats* magazine, for permission to reproduce the painting of HMS *Khartoum*.
John Gidusko for his help and advice re the USS *Liberty* incident.
Captain Tim Johnson for permission to reproduce his painting of a *Daphné*-class submarine.
Lauren Jones of the Royal Engineers Museum, Chatham, for access to the Brennan collection.
Fritz Koopman for permission to use the photo of his model of *PT 109* shot by Matt Grzybinski.
John Lambert and Al Ross for permission to use their range of drawings.
Anthony Lovell of the Dreadnought project, for advice re the *Königsberg* explosion.
Jerry Mason of uboatarchive.net, for help with Kriegsmarine torpedoes and submarine tubes.
Michael Mohr of navsource.org, for the photo of USS *Florida*.
David Moore, for permission to use his drawing of the Brennan launch sequence.
Jean Moulin and Stéphane Gallois for help with the Simonot device.
The staff of The National Archives reading room, Kew.
Yvonne Oliver of the Imperial War Museum, for help in sourcing photos.

Dick Osseman for allowing me to use his photo of a Turkish Gatling gun.

Richard Pekelney of the San Francisco Maritime National Park, for permission to use the naval documents available on their website.

Mark Postlethwaite at www.posart.com, for permission to reproduce his painting of the *Blücher* under attack.

Nancy Richards of the USS *Bowfin* Submarine Museum and Park, Hawaii, for photos of the Mark 27 Mod 4 'Cutie'.

John Roberts, John Coker and Marc Farrance of Explosion, for access to the collection and their advice.

Peter Schupita for permission to include his drawings of Austro-Hungarian Whiteheads.

Tim Short of gracesguide.co.uk, for permission to reproduce the drawing of TB *Kotaka*.

Erwin Sieche for permission to use his drawings of *Szent István*, for the information on Rizzo's torpedoes, and much other valuable help.

Günther Sollinger of Riga, Latvia, for help on the German FL-boats.

Mme Souvignet of the Musée de la Marine, Paris, for permission to reproduce the painting of the *Vauban*.

Mark Stewart, ASAA, for permission to use his painting of the Last Dam Busters.

David M Sullivan for sourcing a back edition of *Warship International* and for help with contacts.

Tom Tanner of Lothian, Maryland, of BB_Ops.tripod.com for his help on Imperial German Navy torpedo tubes.

Conrad Waters for help on modern torpedoes.

Ross Watton for permission to use his painting of *Norge* and *Eidsvold*.

Oliver Weiss of Waldenfont.com, for the view of his firm's model of USS *Alarm*.

Dr Frank Wittendorfer of the Siemens Archives, for the photos of the FL-boats.

Jenny Wraight, Royal Navy Admiralty Librarian, Portsmouth, for guidance.

And my especial thanks go to my editor, Robert Gardiner, for his help and encouragement.

Roger Branfill-Cook,

Ivoiry

Introduction

The torpedo was the great leveller of the age of the ironclad, and the principal weapon of the U-boat forces that nearly secured victory for Germany in both world wars. Winston Churchill said that during the whole of the Second World War the only threat he really feared was the U-boat offensive in the Atlantic. In the Pacific, the torpedo was the weapon used by the US Navy to sink the majority of Imperial Japan's warships and virtually all of her merchant fleet between 1941 and 1945, isolating her island garrisons and strangling the Home Islands themselves. It was torpedoes which sealed the fate of the *Bismarck*, crippled the Italian battle fleet at Taranto, sank most of the battleship casualties at Pearl Harbor and finally put down the largest dreadnoughts ever built.

For all the immense investment in large-calibre guns and thick armour, apart from the three British battlecruiser losses at Jutland (which were almost certainly the result of poor ammunition-handling procedures), of all the dreadnought battleships and battlecruisers, only *Hood* and *Kirishima* were sunk by heavy gunfire alone. Ironically, both were British battlecruiser designs. On the other hand, in both world wars, torpedoes launched either by the enemy or by their own side – to scuttle them – sank no less than twenty dreadnoughts. They were, in order of sinking: *Lützow* (scuttled), *Svobodnaya Rossiya* (scuttled), *Szent István*, *Royal Oak*, *Conte di Cavour*, *Littorio*, *Caio Duilio*, *Barham*, *Oklahoma*, *West Virginia*, *California*, *Repulse*, *Prince of Wales*, *Hiei* (scuttled), *Scharnhorst*, *Musashi*, *Fuso*, *Yamashiro*, *Kongo* and *Yamato*.

Up until the dramatic introduction of the Fritz-X guided armour-piercing bomb which sank the *Roma*, bombers had the ability to damage a capital ship on the high seas, free to manoeuvre and able to defend itself, but not sink it. Only the torpedo could guarantee immobilising and even sinking a battleship at sea. But despite the introduction of anti-ship guided missiles in the latter part of the Second World War, and their modern descendants today, the torpedo remained, and still remains, the ship-killer par excellence.

Hundreds of warships and tens of thousands of merchant ships have been sunk by torpedoes, or were so severely damaged that they were knocked out of action for months, if not years. In the modern age, the torpedo continues to be the major arbiter of potential naval actions worldwide, some 150 years after Robert Whitehead's invention first took to the water.

When my publisher asked me to compile this encyclopedia of the torpedo, my first reaction was that the subject matter is immense. To tell the whole story in all its minor details would take a multi-volume work running to several thousand pages, which few would purchase and even fewer read in its entirety.

As I began collating information, I quickly came to realise that a large amount of technical and historical detail is already available, if one only knows where to search. The detailed technical history of torpedo development has been well covered by those authors to whom I pay due acknowledgement. In addition, a vast store of technical, historical and photographic information is salted away in the various national and naval archives, truly an Aladdin's cave for those who wish to delve deeply into the specifications of any particular model of torpedo. I must pay tribute to the dedicated and often underfunded archivists and museum curators, who are the guardians of knowledge for present and future generations.

Then there is that universal trove of knowledge, the Web. Here one can browse long into the night, lured by links which lead off into hitherto unknown territories. But the Web is to be treated with caution: the amateur nature of the Web means that all too often contributors repeat the errors of authors who should have known better, not having had the time or the opportunity to return to the original sources. Web articles are often contradictory, and sometimes downright incorrect. What saves the Web is that with the presence of a site moderator one can correct such errors by quoting original sources. But the biggest weakness of the Web is its transitory nature: when the webmaster passes on, or loses interest, the information disappears. That is why I have used details published on certain specialist websites in my encyclopedia, with the aim of not only preserving the information, but also recognising the unpaid efforts of these enthusiasts.

Wherever possible, I have used current photographs to illustrate certain items, preferring even shots taken through display cases to official photographic records from archives. My aim is to encourage readers to visit every museum and heritage site they can, from the surviving ships themselves to the magnificent artefacts such as the huge cutaway model of the Austro-Hungarian battleship *Viribus Unitis* in the Vienna Military Museum.

Because of the wide scope of the subject, I have deliberately restricted myself to the mobile, fish or automobile torpedo and its derivatives. The original definition of a 'torpedo' was applied to an underwater explosive device for coast defence, which became the naval mine; this is in itself a vast subject, which lies outside the scope of this work, although the hybrid Mark 24 'mine' and the hybrid Mark 60 Captor will, however, be found here.

I have included several photographs and drawings of torpedoes, but the examples are far from exhaustive. There are hundreds of different types, but in reality they all share certain basic characteristics: a metal cylinder, of varying length and diameter, made of steel or bronze; an early pointed nose, changing to a less acute point, then a blunt rounded shape, finally ending with a metaplat (flattened nose) in the most modern types; whiskers and exploder can be found protruding from the nose of many types, and although practice heads did not, of course, carry exploders, divers must beware of later torpedoes, which carried an inertia exploder internally, in the upper or lower part of the nose; at the opposite end, first one, then two propellers, initially two-bladed but then increasing to three, four and six blades, before disappearing completely. The earliest stabilising fins ran along the top and bottom of the cylinder, but these soon disappeared, leaving two horizontal tail fins and two vertical: the Whitehead Fiume factory put the tail fins behind the propellers, the Royal Laboratories ('RL') version had them before the propellers.

There are very few divergences. If you come across a torpedo with an oval cross-section instead of round, you have a Brennan. If the torpedo has two propellers set side by side at the tail, it is almost certain to be a Howell.

Due to the large number of different torpedoes, specifications are generally omitted from the narrative, so readers who require technical details of a particular model of torpedo or a range of torpedoes from, say, a specific country, should look in the tables in Part V.

In my research, I found very little published information on the wide variety of torpedo delivery vehicles and launch systems, and I have done my best to provide what I freely admit is a basic introduction to this topic. Again, the issue of anti-torpedo defence has been previously addressed here and there, but I have tried to tie up the various threads of a struggle which is still ongoing.

In bringing the whole story together, I have tried to give a broad, yet still detailed, overview of this important subject, to serve as a general reference work for naval enthusiasts and historians.

In conclusion, I must pay tribute to the work of the late Edwyn Gray, the undisputed expert on early torpedo development. Gray spent years tracking down the most obscure inventor and the most unfeasible patent application, in order to write his two major reference works listed in the Bibliography. After his death his extensive research files were donated by his widow to the RN Submarine Museum in Gosport. In compiling this encyclopedia, I have surfed widely in his books for my précis of the early development of the fish torpedo, but I wholeheartedly refer the reader to the works of Edwyn Gray for fuller details.

Part I

The Inventors and their Torpedoes, Successful and Imaginative

CHAPTER 1

Robert Fulton and his Infernal Devices, 1804–1813

In the nineteenth century the name of Robert Whitehead was generally synonymous with that of his invention: in the press of the day, torpedoes were referred to not by their designation or manufacturer, but as 'Whiteheads'. However, the story of the torpedo itself does not begin with Robert Whitehead, but instead with that prolific genius, Robert Fulton, some sixty years earlier.

In the course of his short but fruitful career, Robert Fulton designed canal dredging equipment, a steamboat tested on the Seine on 9 August 1803, and the *North River Steamboat*, the first successful passenger-carrying steam vessel, in 1807. During the Anglo-American War of 1812, he designed the first steam warship, *Demologos*, which was not completed until after his death, and was then renamed *Fulton* in his honour. Before he died, he had proposed a submerged cannon which he christened the *Columbiad*, designed to fire projectiles into the vulnerable underwater hull of an enemy vessel. He was, of course, conversant with the attempt by his fellow American, Bushnell, to destroy British warships using his primitive submarine boat the *Turtle* during the Revolutionary War. He was also aware of the reasons why Bushnell had failed. And he took up the name 'torpedo', which Bushnell had used to describe his explosive devices.

And so it was, during a visit to France, that he decided to offer his services to the French government. In December 1799 Napoleon had returned to Paris from his triumphs in Italy, and he immediately began planning an attack on England. It was on the 12th of the same month that Fulton proposed to the French to build a submarine to help them in their war effort. His offer was refused but he built the submarine anyway, named it the *Nautilus* and successfully tested it in the Seine on 13 June 1800. However, the problem of designing a suitable weapon for his submarine – the same as had put an end to Bushnell's experiment – led Fulton to concentrate instead on underwater explosive devices.

In 1803 he showed his steam launch to Napoleon; this would, if developed, have given the French a major advantage in launching a cross-Channel invasion. However, the innovative Fulton fell foul of one major obstacle: in military matters Napoleon was at heart a conservative. He had even rejected the first practical breech-loading rifles firing self-contained cartridges offered by Pauly of Paris, preferring to put his faith in the old-fashioned muzzle-loading flintlocks. He would never

be prepared to risk sending his army to sea based on unproven schemes by Fulton. Disappointed by the attitude of the French, Fulton did what every self-respecting armament salesman would do, and crossed to the other side.

The British were aware that at sea they had the upper hand, but the margins were slim, for at any moment adverse weather or faulty strategy might allow the French army to debouch onto the beaches of southeast England. In such a scenario the British were none too confident of success; far better to prevent the invasion before it could be launched. By 1804 Napoleon was amassing his '*Grande Armée*' on the heights above Boulogne, and the French navy was busy building invasion barges. The British tried without success to stop them using conventional tactics and technology, but the coastline was difficult to approach and French defence works were just too strong. They needed an advantage, an edge, and Fulton proposed to give them just that.

Although Fulton later claimed that the British response was lukewarm at best, in fact he was supported

The French defences facing the British in October 1804: a line of British warships moored bow to stern prepares to bombard the port. The Grand Army is camped on the heights, and the principal target, the boats of the invasion fleet, are moored against the shoreline, covered by guns and mortars ashore. (© National Maritime Museum, Greenwich, London, PZ6989)

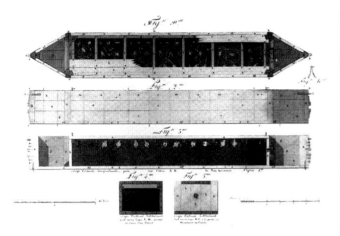

Here is what appears to be one of the 'large coffers'. It measured around 21ft (6.4m) long. At the right-hand end in the drawing is an attachment to enable it to be towed into action.

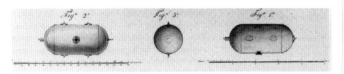

The second drawing shows what appear to be copper casks. These are probably the 'small coffers'. Fulton had used copper as the external skin of his submarine *Nautilus*, and also for constructing 'submarine bombs' during his stay in France.

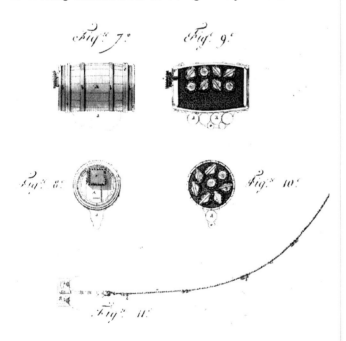

Here we have the 'hogsheads'. They are described as being the size of a forty-gallon cask. They have weights, probably iron cannonballs, attached to their underneath to ensure that they float one way up, otherwise the priming powder could fall from the pan in the fuse. The drawing at the bottom presumably shows a hogshead being towed into position.

by the highest echelons of government, who ensured that considerable resources were put at his disposal. He was given the cover name of 'Mr Francis' and some of the Royal Navy's most enterprising officers were seconded to the enterprise.

Following on from his experiments in France, he designed several novel devices for attacking the invasion barges, which like many unconventional weapons before them were generically dubbed 'infernal devices'. For the first planned attack on Boulogne in August 1804, Fulton produced '5 large coffers, 5 small, and 10 hogsheads'. Happily, a folder exists in the National Maritime Museum containing drawings of his inventions, ironically drafted by a Frenchman, a certain Monsieur Garriguer, who sent them to Monsieur Guillemard, navy engineer at Rochefort. The artist would appear to have had first-hand access to some of Fulton's devices, which had failed to explode as planned.

These 'infernal devices' were packed with 'incendiary balls' and the space between them filled with gunpowder. They were to be exploded by means of a clockwork delay fuse which tripped a flintlock action, all contained in a waterproof box. The prewound and cocked fuses were to be activated by withdrawing a pin, and the operators were tasked with returning each pin as proof that the devices had been correctly armed.

It appears that Fulton had designed what, in modern terms, are designated sub-munitions. As the shock from exploding black powder would usually be effective only within a limited radius, the sub-munitions could spread mayhem over a wide area, setting fire to sail and cordage and timber alike. One can only hope that Fulton had tested these devices before sending men into combat to risk their lives with them. One basic drawback would appear to be

One of the intricate clockwork fuses. One has to wonder why the original used as the basis of the drawing had not actually tripped. Perhaps it was a trifle too complex for 100 per cent operational reliability.

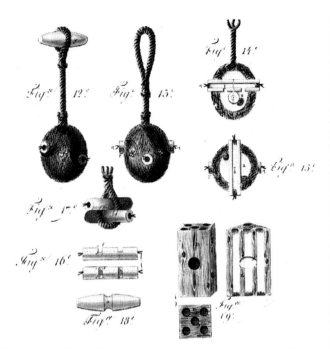

Here are the 'incendiary balls' contained in the gunpowder filling.

ensuring that the incendiary balls actually caught fire as they were ejected, and were not simply blown to pieces.

To deliver his 'infernals' into the ranks of the French, Fulton conceived a stealth craft, a small catamaran to be sculled by a crew of two, dressed in black and wearing masks (like the current image of a ninja). It is unlikely that Fulton himself designed these, but in trials they proved 'barely discernable at 25 fathoms (46m) and invisible at 35 (64m) even from halfway up the rigging'. The payload was to be carried on the gratings fore and aft. Since these flimsy craft would be completely incapable, in any tideway, of towing the large coffers and even the hogsheads by the efforts of only two men, their weapons must have been the small copper cylinders. That would leave the large coffers and the hogsheads to be towed into release position by oared cutters, allowing them to drift down, joined together in pairs, under wind and current towards their intended victims.

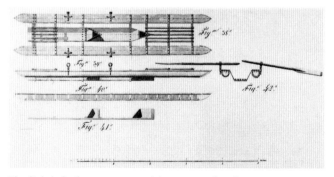

The lightly-built catamaran, with supports for the two rowers, and two pairs of sculls.

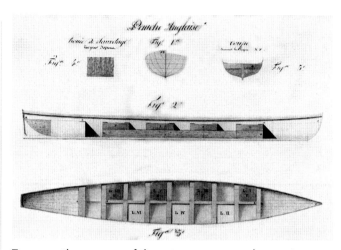

To ensure the recovery of the catamaran teams, there was even a lifeboat, with extra buoyancy from compartments filled with cork, to enable them to survive under small-arms fire from the defenders.

With such emphasis on stealth, it is disappointing to note that the British attack, when it went in against Boulogne on the night of 2 October 1804, was clearly anticipated by French Rear Admiral Lacrosse. To add to the lack of subtlety, the British sent in no less than four fireships, towed by armed launches. Into the middle of all this, Fulton's stealth teams paddled their catamarans at a snail's pace. Despite the considerable efforts expended, the results were disappointing. Only one French pinnace was sunk, her crew of fourteen men being killed in the explosion of a fireship they were boarding. There were no casualties on the British side, so the lifeboats appear to have worked as planned.

On 8 December an attempt was made to destroy Fort Rouge, guarding the entrance to the port of Calais, using one fireship and two catamarans, one of which missed the fort and the other of which failed to explode. This time there were no casualties on either side. A third attack was launched, against Boulogne, on 1 October 1805, but this time employing improved versions of Congreve's incendiary rockets (which were to produce the 'rockets' red glare' over Baltimore seven years later), and this time the French were taken by surprise and fires started ashore.

Fulton's fiendish devices were towed into action by Captain Seccombe in a boat rowed by eight men, plus the coxswain, who placed the devices so as to lie on port and starboard sides of a French gun brig anchored in Boulogne Roads. A boat from HMS *Immortalité* commanded by Lieutenant Payne did the same. On withdrawing, the two officers were disappointed to see that the explosions on each side of their two target vessels appeared to have had no effect. The next morning Fulton was at a loss to explain why the infernal devices had not, as intended, destroyed

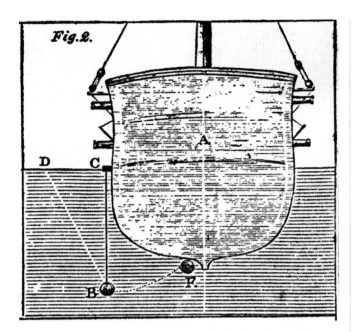

Fulton's explanatory drawing of the under-keel explosion from his treatise *Torpedo War and Submarine Explosions.*

the French brigs. Later reports in French newspapers confirmed that the explosions had only produced a shock effect and canted the vessels to one side, without damaging them.

Fulton set his analytical mind to work, and realised that if the explosion took place alongside the hull, the blast effect would rise vertically beside the ship. What was needed was a means of ensuring that the explosion took place under the keel. He envisaged the shock wave of a solid body of water being displaced upwards against a

small part of the ship's bottom, which would give way, the explosion having the same effect as if the vessel had been thrown bodily upwards some 20 or 30ft (6 or 9m), and then dropped back down onto a rock 3–4ft (90–120cm) in diameter. He had invented the modern ship-breaking under-keel explosion almost 140 years before it was first used in action.

Nevertheless, he still had to work out how to ensure that his torpedo passed beneath the bottom of the ship to finish up next to the keel instead of merely lying alongside. He kept to his original plan of towing two torpedoes joined together, then releasing them either side of the target vessel's anchor chain. However, instead of simply attaching the joining rope to the centre of the torpedo tail as at 'A' in the above drawing, he arranged the rope so that each torpedo was attached at an angle by a bridle, as in 'B' and 'C'. The action of the tide, represented by the arrow 'D', could then be used to swing one or both torpedoes

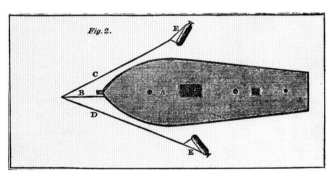

The modified torpedoes as they were deployed against the *Dorothea.* 'B' is the anchor cable.

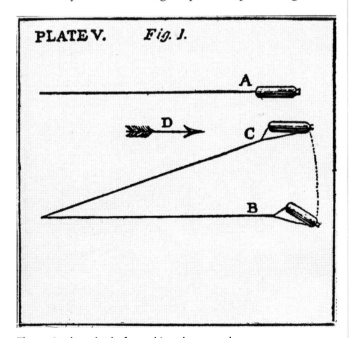

The revised method of attaching the torpedoes.

The spectacular end of the *Dorothea*, the very first vessel to be destroyed by an underwater explosive device.

towards the ship and draw it up against the bottom of the hull, where the clockwork fuse would detonate it.

Back in England, to maintain confidence in his towed torpedoes, Fulton put on a demonstration on 15 October 1805 using his new bridle torpedo attachments, in which an old brig, the 200-ton *Dorothea*, was attacked by rowboats towing two of his modified devices, one of which was filled with 180 pounds (lbs) (82kg) of powder, to be set off by an eighteen-minute delay fuse. After the boats' crews had practised the operation several times, the real attack went in, and the two torpedoes, joined by 70ft (21.3m) of rope, were released to catch on the *Dorothea*'s anchor cable. During this manoeuvre one of the observers, Captain Kingston, was heard to declare – presumably on the basis of Fulton's failure at Boulogne – that if the torpedo were placed under his cabin while he was at dinner, he should feel no concern for the consequences.

Twenty minutes later, just as Fulton had planned, the explosion beneath her keel lifted the brig bodily some 6ft (2m); she broke in half, and both halves rapidly sank. Fulton described the result as 'in twenty seconds, nothing was to be seen of her except floating fragments'. One is left to imagine that the demonstration drastically changed Captain Kingston's opinion. The one hundred Royal Navy officers and the government officials present were suitably impressed, but just a week later Napoleon's hopes of invasion were dashed at Trafalgar. With the threat removed, there was no further employment for Fulton, and he returned home to the States.

On 20 July 1807 he sank a 200-ton brig off Governor's Island, New York, in front of an audience of some two thousand spectators. He had once more modified the torpedoes, suspending them from floats to keep them several feet below the waterline of the victim. Even so, it took three attempts. On the first, the fuse became inverted, and the priming powder in the flintlock pan fell out, so it did not go off. On the second attempt, the towed torpedoes missed the ship's cable completely, and blew up 100yds (90m) past her, throwing up an impressive column of water 60 or 70ft (18 to 20m) high. On the third attempt, no doubt to everyone's delight, the brig was blown up and broke in two, just like the *Dorothea*.

To make absolutely certain that in future his torpedoes would not miss the target, Fulton proposed a new method of attack. This was described in his treatise on *Torpedo War and Submarine Explosions* published in New York in 1810 (and from which Fulton's drawings in this section are taken). He imagined a clinker-built rowboat some 27ft (8.3m) long, with a beam of 6ft (1.8m), single-banked, with six long oars. For self-defence the boat was to be armed with four blunderbusses, mounted one on each quarter (for reasons of clarity they are omitted from the drawing below). Fulton had read a report in a French newspaper of how back in 1805 the blunderbuss in Captain Seccombe's boat had not only protected them from French musket fire from their intended victim, but had caused the only French casualties in the attack at Boulogne. On the stern of the rowboat was attached a platform, extending out above the rudder and carrying a fifth blunderbuss, but this one was to be loaded with an iron harpoon half an inch (12.7mm) in diameter and 2ft (61cm) long.

Fulton's torpedo-boat design of 1810.

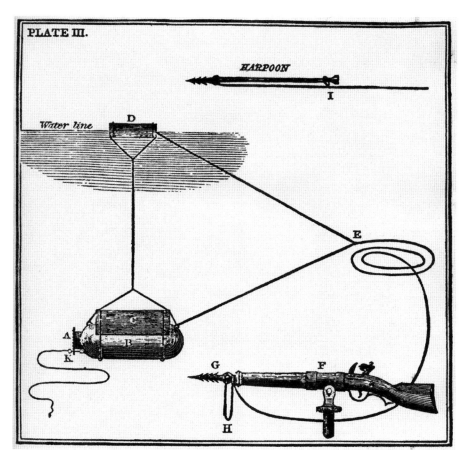

PLATE III.

HARPOON

Water line

The details of Fulton's harpoon float torpedo.

A greased rope was attached to the harpoon's nose, and also to a ring ('I' in the drawing above) which, when the harpoon was fired, was free to slide backwards along the shaft, coming to rest in front of a base cup. Fulton designed this arrangement to act as a stabiliser for the harpoon, as a result of up to twenty trial shots, in which he claimed to have never missed a target 6ft square (1.8m x 1.8m) set up at between 30ft and 50ft (9–15m) from the gun. Each time, the head of the harpoon was driven clean through timber 3in (76mm) thick.

On firing the harpoon at an enemy ship's timber hull, the greased rope would uncoil, and pull the torpedo body after it. The torpedo was to be armed automatically: a separate rope attached to the deck ('E' in the drawing of the torpedo boat) would be pulled from the torpedo fuse, setting the clockwork delay mechanism in motion. The torpedo itself was to be suspended beneath the surface from a float cork, and the length of the suspension rope was to be adjusted so as to take into account the draught of the vessel being attacked, to ensure the torpedo finished up underneath the keel. Fulton had invented a simple torpedo depth setting.

All this was described in his 1810 treatise, together with elaborate calculations of how much money would be

saved by flotillas of his harpoon torpedo boats, compared with the price of building and manning just one 80-gun ship of the line. It was evident from his writing which attacking naval power he intended to protect the United States against, presumably because they had not proceeded with his torpedo designs.

But then he turned his attention away from towed torpedoes, and harpoon torpedoes, and set out plans for moored observation mines. He even devised an automatic system whereby at preset intervals each mine would set its arming lever to 'safe', and would return to the surface for routine maintenance.

Having launched the first successful steam passenger vessel in history, Fulton later turned his attention to helping his country to fend off British coastal attacks during the War of 1812, proposing the use of the spar torpedo – which was actually used in action against British ships – and designing the steam-powered floating battery *Demologos*, to be armed with a battery of underwater cannons. Then, at the young age of forty-nine, he died suddenly as the result of catching pneumonia after saving a friend who had fallen through the ice on the Hudson River. It would be in another American conflict, and almost fifty years later, before his spar torpedo went into action again.

CHAPTER 2

Fulton's Legacy

THE SPAR TORPEDO

Although Robert Fulton never actually built a spar torpedo, on 4 September 1813 he had described to Captain Stephen Decatur a new method of torpedo attack he had devised. Fulton proceeded to draw a diagram showing a boat supporting two torpedoes on long spars which projected below the level of its keel, and which were to be exploded against the underwater hull of an enemy ship. Since he had acted in an advisory capacity during the war with Britain, it is conceivable that his ideas had been put into practice by others. It is on record, for instance, that HMS *Ramillies* captured and sank a spar torpedo boat off Long Island in 1813, and there is evidence of their use on the Great Lakes.

The first effective spar torpedo attack had to wait another fifty years, when Confederate Lieutenant William T Glassell, commanding a 'David' semi-submersible torpedo boat, exploded his spar torpedo against the Union frigate USS *New Ironsides* on 5 October 1863. His victim did not sink, but was badly damaged.

The first successful submarine attack was the *H L Hunley*'s sinking of the USS *Housatonic* on the night of 17 February 1864, again using a spar torpedo. The little submersible was a desperate measure by the Confederates to break the stranglehold of the Union navy's blockade of the port of Charleston. Prior to her successful action, she had already drowned most of the men of two of her crews, and following the attack she disappeared. Her wreck was discovered buried in silt and sand not far off Charleston Harbour in 2000. The Friends of the *Hunley*, the association which raised and is working to preserve her, has full details of this pioneer vessel on their website www.hunley.org.

Historians had always assumed that the *Hunley*'s commander would attempt to ram the spar torpedo into the hull of his target like one of Fulton's harpoons, then withdraw, leaving the weapon impaled in the victim. The charge would be detonated at a safe distance by pulling on a cord attached to the torpedo. Study of the tip of *Hunley*'s spar, however, has revealed the remains of the copper casing of the torpedo, meaning that it was detonated when still attached to the spar. A Singer drawing of the torpedo in The National Archives has been used to calculate that it

An illustration of the *H L Hunley* by Daniel Dowdey, showing her spar torpedo. (Friends of the *Hunley*)

Daniel Dowdey 2013

contained a charge of up to 135lbs (61kg) of black powder. As the spar is only 16ft (4.9m) long, detonating this large charge at such a short distance could well have knocked several crew members unconscious. We know the *Hunley* survived the explosion, since the commander of Fort Moultrie saw the prearranged blue magnesium light signal to indicate the mission had succeeded, a blue light also seen by survivors of the *Housatonic*. She may have been damaged by the blast in such close proximity, but the fact that her wreck was eventually discovered not far off Charleston Harbour and safety, has forced historians to revise their notions that the spar torpedo was basically a suicide weapon, as dangerous to the assailant as the victim.

Spar torpedoes were fitted to other Confederate vessels, in particular the ironclad CSS *Richmond*, which carried a spar torpedo projecting from her bow underwater. When taken up by the Union side, a significant change was made. Whereas the *Hunley*, in order to approach her target unseen until the very last moment, had been designed as a submersible, and was therefore vulnerable to even a small amount of damage caused by the underwater shockwave, the Union spar torpedo crews used surface boats to bring their torpedo into contact with the underwater part of the enemy's hull, just as Fulton had intended. If their boats were sturdy enough, they would have their bows lifted by the underwater explosion but with luck they would survive. The enemy vessel, holed below the waterline by even the modest charges of the day, and with no internal subdivision, would head for the bottom.

The Union's spar torpedo boats claimed their first victim under the command of the young daredevil Lieutenant William Barker Cushing. At the age of three he had run away to sea, falling off the end of a jetty while pursuing a departing ship. Saved from drowning by a nearby sailor, he had decided a year later to depart to see the world on one of his father's horses. Attempting to shoe it himself, the four-year-old had been kicked senseless by the indignant horse. Dropped from the naval academy because of endless pranks, he answered his nation's call when civil war broke out, and managed to have himself reinstated into the navy. The attack on the troublesome rebel ironclad *Albemarle* was Cushing's idea. With the help of John Lay, he rigged up two steam launches as spar torpedo boats and set off for the *Albemarle*'s lair on the Roanoke River. One launch sank en route, but on the night of 27 October 1864 the attack went in. Finding his prey protected by a boom of floating logs, Cushing circled some way off, then called for full steam to enable his launch to leap the slime-covered log boom. Having crossed this barrier, he manipulated Lay's four lanyards, one attached to each of his hands and feet, to deploy the torpedo head underneath the hull of *Albemarle* and then detonate it. The explosion swamped his launch, forcing Cushing and his crew to abandon it and try to escape as best they could. The *Albemarle*, despite the efforts of her commander, Lieutenant Warley and his crew, sank to the river bottom with a hole blown in her bows. Cushing was eight days short of his twenty-second birthday.

The relative effectiveness of the spar torpedo led all other naval powers to adopt it in one form or another. Following the end of the American Civil War, the next use of the spar torpedo in anger was by the Russians on the Danube and in the Black Sea during the Russo-Turkish war of 1877–78, and then by the French against the Chinese seven years later (for details see Part IV).

Inspired, no doubt, by their countrymen's pioneering use of the spar torpedo, and bolstered by Russian and French successes in the years since the end of the civil war, the Torpedo Station was still issuing detailed *Spar-Torpedo Instructions for the United States Navy* as late as 1890. According to these instructions the standard outfit of Service spar torpedoes comprised a set of twenty-four, with twelve for use on board ship and twelve for the ship's boats.

Each Service spar torpedo measured 12in (30.5cm) long by 9in (22.9cm) square, all inside measurements. They were fabricated from sheet iron tinned inside and out, the inside surfaces being shellacked and the exterior asphalted. The empty case weighed about 15lbs (6.8kg), and the charge was equivalent to 34lbs (15.4kg) of dry gun-cotton, including the primer. The latter was fired by electricity, rubber grommets being arranged in the top of the case. Exercise torpedoes were also available, slightly longer than the Service type but only a third of the width and depth, and shellacked inside and outside. The Exercise torpedo weighed 3lbs (1.4kg) and its charge of dry gun-cotton added another 4lbs (1.8kg). The firing circuit was to be made up by cutting and connecting suitable lengths of insulated double cable from the 300ft-long (91.4m) reel supplied.

The Service spar torpedo for boat use would be attached to a spar made up of two steel tubes 18ft and 15ft long which telescoped one inside the other with an overlap of 2ft (9.45m total length), held in place in the bow of the boat by a complex system of yokes and gearing, to permit accurate placing of the torpedo. The boat torpedo was to be immersed to a depth of at least 10ft, and could safely be exploded 22ft away horizontally (3m deep by 6.7m distant).

Interestingly, the Service spar torpedoes for ship's use were to be attached to the ends of 45ft-long (13.7m) wooden spars braced out from the sides of the ship, one on either side of the foremast and one on either side of the mizzen. Ship's torpedoes were also to be immersed to a depth of at least 10ft, but to ensure the safety of the attacking ship had to be exploded at a distance of at least 35ft (10.7m) from her hull. For the Exercise torpedo, an immersion of 5ft at a range of 20ft was suitable for firing from both a boat and the ship (1.5m depth at 6.1m distance). Instructions were also provided for converting the Service torpedo to a contact exploder, and for constructing improvised spar torpedoes from wooden kegs or casks, caulked on the outside to make them watertight, and charged with black powder.

For its part, the Royal Navy also continued with the spar torpedo up to and beyond the end of the nineteenth century. One design comprised a metal cage enclosing a ring of six TNT cylinders placed around a seventh cylinder, to which was attached an electrical primer and lead to a battery on the launch. Firing was initiated by a pair of contact horns protruding from the head of the torpedo.

The surviving early film sequence shot by Alfred West in around 1898 shows Royal Navy spar torpedo exercises, probably in Fraser Lake, which was part of Portsmouth Harbour. In the full sequence, when the huge water plume has subsided, the steam pinnace setting off the spar torpedo explosion appears unharmed.

THE 'CROUCHING DRAGONS'

The final manifestation of the spar torpedo concept were the 'Crouching Dragons', or 'Fukuryu', the weapon of a brave and dedicated group of young men of the Imperial Japanese navy's Special Service Corps in 1945. As seen in the illustration on the next page, here we have an explosive device on the end of a long pole, intended to sink a vessel by exploding against its underwater hull. To all appearances, this is a classic spar torpedo – and conceived as a desperate last resort against a vastly superior naval power, as was the very first spar torpedo.

Unbelievable as it may sound, these sailors were trained as suicide frogmen, prepared to wade out from the invasion beaches, or hole up in diving chambers hidden off the coast in wrecked ships or underwater caves, in order to thrust their spar torpedo into the hull of an Allied landing craft heading for the shores of Japan.

A surviving Fukuryu trainee, Mr Shimizu Kazuro, was interviewed by a journalist at his home in Nagano prefecture in the course of 2013. He described how conditions for the Japanese in 1945 were becoming desperate. As a young naval trainee of just sixteen he was drafted to the 'Tokkotai', the Special Service Corps who made up the kamikaze units. From an initial total of 300 trainees, all firstborn sons, only children, and boys with no father were drafted out, then the trainees thought to be of

Discovered in the Solent, a dinner plate, possibly from RN mess No 20 attached to the torpedo school at HMS *Vernon*, was decorated with a spar torpedo and its successor, a very early Whitehead, but both evidently in use at one and the same time. The Latin inscriptions translate as 'Great perils lurk' and '*Vernon* is always strong'.

An indistinct still from a very early film, shot by Alfred West in around 1898, showing spar torpedo and mine explosions. The original, one of a six-frame fragment, was attached by West to documents to prove his copyright, and is now held at The National Archives, Kew.

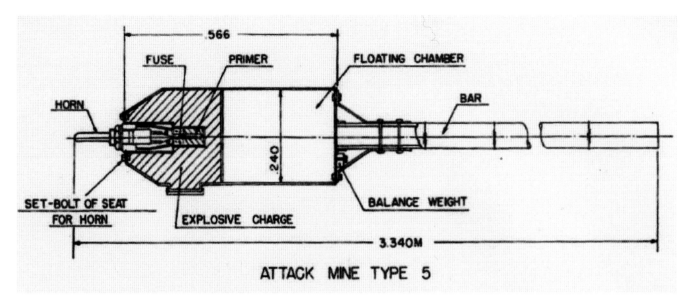

ATTACK MINE TYPE 5

Above: Drawing from the January 1946 report by the Naval Technical Mission to Japan, index no S-91(N): The Fukuryu Special Harbor Defense and Underwater Attack Unit – Tokyo Bay.

Below: Next door to the Yasukuni shrine in Japan is the Yushukan Museum of the Heroes. Thanks to the efforts of survivors such as Shimizu Kazuro, a statue was placed in the museum to honour the lost Fukuryu trainees, the 'human spar torpedoes', so many of whom lost their lives not in action, but in training.

above-average intelligence were separated and sent away, and the 100 left were the kamikaze recruits.

The Crouching Dragons wore rubber diving suits, and breathed recycled air through a simple arrangement using caustic lye. However, if they forgot to breathe in using their nostrils and exhale though the mouth, they could accidentally inhale caustic lye and quickly lose consciousness. Training consisted of jumping from boats and practising descending to their operating depth, and then they would practise walking on the seabed, guided from a boat by an officer pulling on guide ropes. All too often the trainees would be dragged down by their equipment, which out of the water weighed more than they did, or they would mix up their breathing procedure and suffocate, or the defective brazing on the breathing gear would fail and let in water with disastrous results, or they would simply become entangled in weeds and drown.

Mr Kazuro recalled how at least fifty of his comrades died in this appalling manner. There were too many to cremate in a religious ceremony at the local shrine, so their bodies were simply piled on fires lit along the shore.

Reference works often state that the Fukuryu units were disbanded before hostilities ended because of these appalling casualties. But that was not so. After the news of the Hiroshima and Nagasaki atomic bombs, and the emperor's radio broadcast, the officers ordered all the equipment and documents to be gathered up and burnt. The Fukuryu were to have remained a closely-guarded secret. It was only after many years that the survivors revived the memory of their lost comrades, and arranged for the small commemorative statue to be made and placed in the Yushukan Museum.

THE TOWED TORPEDO

Robert Fulton had conceived the idea of a towed torpedo back in 1804 for the attack on Boulogne, when pairs of large coffers and pairs of hogsheads were towed to where they were left to drift down onto the French ships under the action of wind and tide. When he sank the *Dorothea* off the Downs in October 1805 he had used the same type of arrangement. He modified this idea in 1807 for the demonstration when he sank the old brig at New York, keeping his charges underwater, suspended from floats. And there the idea rested.

Several years before the appearance of Mr Harvey's kite or towed torpedo, the CSS *Hunley* was originally intended to tow behind her a 90lb (41kg) explosive charge. Diving under the hull of the target, she was to tow the charge into contact with the ship on the side from which she had commenced her run, when it would be detonated. The target's hull was intended to cushion the little submersible from the blast.

Because of difficulties with towing a large charge by a slow-moving submersible, with the ever-constant danger of their own charge coming into contact with *Hunley* and sinking her, the plan was changed to the definitive spar torpedo design which she used with success against the *Housatonic*.

The Harvey kite torpedo

In 1871 Captain John Harvey, Royal Navy (retired), wrote in a letter that he had been working on the idea of a towed torpedo for some 'quarter of a century', which would mean that he had begun in or around 1846, but that his nephew Commander Frederick Harvey had brought it to the stage where it could be deployed operationally. The idea took up from where Fulton left off. The explosive charge was contained in an otter board, of the type used by fishermen to keep open the mouth of their trawl net. It was towed beneath the surface suspended from a cork float. The towing cable was kept at an angle of 45 degrees to the course of the attacking vessel by a second line controlled by brakemen.

The principle was simple but daring. The attacking vessel streamed its Harvey torpedo, and at a safe distance the firing key was activated, to avoid the risk of the tow cable becoming entangled in the ship's propeller, pulling the device into one's own ship. The attacker passed to one side of the target vessel, so as to bring the Harvey into contact with the victim's hull. A pair of firing levers was then depressed, exploding the charge. It was simple, it worked, and it was much less expensive than a Whitehead torpedo, of which the Harvey was a contemporary, all factors designed to ensure its popularity with the Admiralty and the Treasury. And it must be said that although there were certain risks, faced with the slow-firing big guns of the day, it was much safer than the even cheaper alternative, the spar torpedo.

Just as with fishermen's otter boards, those of the Harvey were shaped so as to be handed port and starboard. This meant that their firing levers also had to be handed, those for the port torpedo being fitted on the right and vice versa for the starboard torpedo, as can be seen in the drawings. These and all others in this description are taken from Frederick Harvey's *Instructions for the Management of Harvey's Sea Torpedo*, which he wrote in 1871. The torpedoes themselves were constructed of seasoned elm $1\frac{1}{2}$in (38mm) thick, reinforced by external iron strapping. An internal case containing the explosive bolt was made of thick copper sheet. The torpedoes in the illustration are the 'large' model.

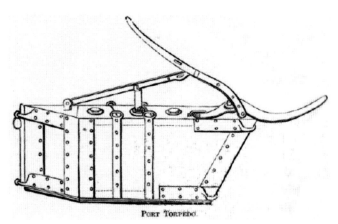

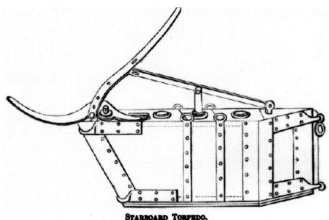

On the left: the port torpedo. *On the right:* the starboard torpedo.

Coming into action by passing astern of the target vessel. The starboard torpedo is hoisted on the lower yard, its safety bolt still in place. The port torpedo has struck the target ship's hull to starboard. Although not clear, it is likely that the charge will have detonated on the other (i.e. port) side, or indeed under her keel.

Even the large model was of modest size, being 5ft long x 6^1/$_8$in wide x 1ft 8^3/$_4$in deep (1.524m x 155.6mm x 527mm). The exploding bolt could contain, among other explosives, either 60lbs (27.2kg) of compressed gun-cotton, 76lbs (34.5kg) of black powder, or 100lbs (45.4kg) of dynamite. For the more impecunious, Harvey also offered a 'small' model, the dimensions being 3ft 8in x 5in x 1ft 6in (1012m x 127mm x 457mm). It could carry up to 22lbs (10kg) of compressed gun-cotton, 27lbs (12.25kg) of black powder, or 35lbs (15.9kg) of dynamite.

The Harvey was tested against the turret ironclad HMS *Royal Sovereign*, and the results were excellent. For the first trials the target was anchored, and blank-fired her turret guns to verify how many shots she could loose off before the torpedo hit. With a towline of 300ft (91.4m), the steam paddle-wheel tug *Camel* scored ten hits out of ten, all below the waterline. With *Royal Sovereign* manoeuvring at between 8 and 9 knots, and *Camel* towing at 10–11 knots, again all six torpedoes streamed scored hits.

Despite these excellent results, the British Admiralty were reluctant to purchase large numbers of Harvey torpedoes, despite the vigorous support of Fisher. The reason was clear: the Whitehead was proving its effectiveness, and the fish torpedo was in a different class altogether. Nonetheless, the Royal Navy did purchase Harvey torpedoes and kept them on the establishment for over forty years. They could be fitted with electrical firing primers invented by Captain McEvoy in 1871.

The Russians tried a copy of the Harvey in action against the Turks, also with an electric primer, invented by Captain Menzing, a German. It appears that their towed torpedoes made contact with their targets, but that the electrical firing key failed every time.

The French adopted the Harvey, but considerably modified it at Boyardville after 1872, presumably in order to avoid paying royalties to Harvey. According to instructions first issued in 1875, practice in the French navy was to stream the torpedo closely behind the towing ship, then extend the control spar and draw the torpedo out on the beam when the enemy was in range, a curious arrangement which risked fouling the ship's propeller. It was the favourite weapon for squadron action, and every large ironclad was equipped with a towed torpedo on each beam. It was felt that if an enemy vessel avoided an attempt to ram her, then one or other of the towed torpedoes would strike. The French discovered that the towed torpedo worked even better if the target vessel was under way, rather than moored, as her own motion drew the torpedo into contact with her hull.

By 1877 the French torpedo tactics had been brought

The torpedo salesman's dream scenario: an ironclad fleet surprised at night by a formation of torpedo boats towing Harvey torpedoes.

to such a high level of efficiency that the commander-in-chief of the French navy commented that the ram and the towed torpedo 'tended to neutralize each other; [the towed torpedo] is destined effectively to hold at bay any enemy who desires to use his ram.' They kept them in front-line service longer than most navies. The Americans experimented with the Harvey, but did not retain them for long.

The Harvey was useful if employed as a complement to the ram when fighting heavily armoured ships. If you missed with the ram, which was more than likely, then one or other Harvey had a good chance of striking a mortal blow to the target. A stealthy attack at night, on an anchored or slow-moving blockading ship, also had a good chance of success.

Of course, in daylight, unless your own vessel was heavily armoured, to close to ramming distance or towed torpedo range was suicidal. And in a daylight fleet action, with numerous vessels manoeuvring to bring guns to bear or effect a ramming, to stream two volatile explosive devices, ready armed and primed, on each beam of your own vessel was highly hazardous. If your vessel was disabled, or lost steering, then it was just possible that a Harvey might be drawn against your own hull, with the exploder levers towards your ship.

In retrospect, the Harvey was a workable weapon system, but it had the misfortune to arrive on the scene at the same time as the much superior Whitehead.

STEALTH WEAPONS: MIGNATTA, BARCHINO SALTATORE, SLC MAIALE, CHARIOT, NEGER AND KAITEN

Fulton had finally been forced to abandon the concept of a stealth attack weapon, lacking the necessary power source to guarantee mobility and accurate delivery of the warhead. Instead he turned to relatively complicated fixed mines for coastal defence. But a century later, inventive minds revived his stealth weapon concept, and brought new power sources to bear to make them a practical proposition.

In 1909, Lieutenant Godfrey Herbert of the Royal Navy, former second-in-command of Nasmith's submarine *A 4*, and serving in surface ships before returning to submarines, patented the idea of a manned torpedo. The Admiralty of the day dismissed it as impractical and unsafe. His idea was to see form in the hands of the Italian navy.

Mignatta

In 1918 the first 'human torpedo' arrived on the scene in a dramatic manner, operated by two Italian naval officers. Major of Naval Engineers Raffaele Rossetti had designed a 'Mignatta' (Italian for 'leech'), using components from a standard Italian Navy B57 Model 14in torpedo.

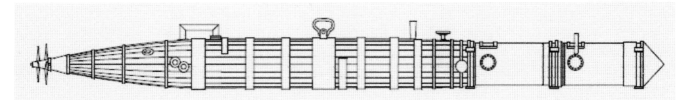

The drawing above and the following photos of the Mignatta are courtesy of Francesco Franchi.

At the same time Physician Sub Lieutenant Raffaele Paolucci had conceived the idea of walking on the seabed into an enemy anchorage, dragging behind him an explosive charge. He trained for such an action, walking long distances on the seabed wearing a diving suit and dragging behind him a length of iron to represent the charge.

Bringing these two ideas together, Rossetti conceived and built the definitive Mignatta, which ended up 8m

The tail of the Mignatta, showing the wooden construction held together with brass hoops.

(26ft) long with a diameter of 600mm (24in). Powered by compressed air, it was driven by two four-bladed contra-rotating propellers at a slow speed of 2 knots, for a maximum distance of 16km (10 miles). There was no mechanical means of steering: the crew had to direct it by extending their arms and legs. Without breathing apparatus they were obliged to keep their heads above water. The warhead was composed of two detachable charges, each one containing 175kg of explosive and provided with clockwork fuses giving a delay of up to six hours.

The scale drawing of the Mignatta shows the two detachable explosive charges. When the second charge has been detached, in front of the central air flask was a second streamlined nose cone, to allow the operators to use the Mignatta to make good their escape. Inside the tail unit are the mechanical parts of the 14in torpedo, with the three-cylinder engine and propeller shaft to the contra-rotating gears in the tail. Note the complete lack of rudders and horizontal tail planes. What appears to be a handhold at the top rear is in fact the compressed air pipe to the engine, carried outside the hull to impart some heating from the surrounding seawater.

Despite the apparent crude nature of the Mignatta, against all expectations Rossetti and Paolucci succeeded in entering Pola harbour on the night of 1 November 1918, even dragging their Mignatta over the harbour defence boom and then over a protective gate. Having attached one of the charges to the Austro-Hungarian flagship *Viribus Unitis*, they were spotted and were forced to scuttle their Mignatta. Taken on board the target vessel as prisoners, they were surprised to learn that the very day they had set

A fine model of Rossetti's Mignatta, built in 2011 by Francesco Franchi.

out on their mission, the *Viribus Unitis* had been handed over to the newly formed Yugoslav National Council and renamed *Jugoslavia*. The change of nationality did not save the ill-fated vessel, and when the charge exploded she capsized and sank to the harbour bottom.

Barchino saltatore

A very different kind of stealth weapon had already been tried out by the Italian navy, with their '*barchino saltatore*', or 'jumping boat', also known as the sea tank from its pair of caterpillar tracks. Driven by electric motors, these assault boats were intended to climb the Austro-Hungarian net boom harbour defences to attack their fleet at anchor, with the two 450mm torpedoes carried in drop collars. The 16m long boats could proceed at a speed of 4 knots for up to 30 nautical miles. With a crew of four, they were carried to the chosen target by mother craft.

Designed by Attilio Bisio of the SVAN Company that built them, a total of four were commissioned by the Italian navy in March 1918. *Cavalletta* and *Pulce* were scuttled during an abortive attack on Pola on 13 April 1918. A month later, the third boat *Grillo* attempted to enter Pola harbour but was spotted and fired upon. Abandoned by her crew, she sank, but was recovered by the Austrians. The latter were so impressed by the Italian boat that they planned to build a close copy and carry out attacks of their own on Italian bases. The war ended before they could put this plan into operation. The fourth '*barchino*', *Locusta*, saw no action and was scrapped in 1921.

SLC Maiale and Chariot

During the late 1930s two captains in the Genio Navale (the Italian navy's engineering corps), took up Rossetti's Mignatta and redesigned it to produce the SLC ('*silura lenta corse*', or 'slow-speed torpedo'). In the hands of the famous elite unit Decima MAS (literally, the 10th Motor

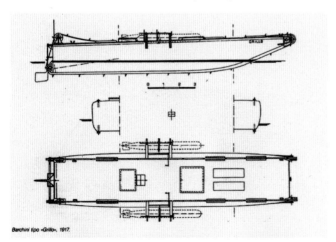

Barchino saltatore *Grillo* of 1917.

Torpedo Squadron), the whole balance of naval power in the Mediterranean was altered by these tiny units when SLCs put out of action the rebuilt Royal Navy battleships *Queen Elizabeth* and *Valiant* in Alexandria harbour on the night of 19 December 1941.

They were, however, extremely difficult to control, having a tendency to roll, and the crews' exertions were not helped by the clumsy suits and breathing gear. These problems were carried over into the British copy of the SLC, the Chariot. A detailed description of the Chariot, plus the construction of a working replica, can be found on the website, www.divingheritage.com/torpedo.htm, hosted by Phil Nussle.

In October 1943 the Regia Marina had built three examples of a much larger SLC, the SSB ('*siluro San Bartolomeo*'), which they planned to use in an attack against shipping in Gibraltar, but the plan was overtaken by the Italian surrender. Instead of riding astride the torpedo, the crew now sat in a cockpit area well furnished with controls and instruments. A surviving example of a San Bartolomeo can be seen today in store at Explosion, the Museum of Naval Firepower in Gosport, and a second one is on display at the Historic Ship *Nautilus* and Submarine Force Museum, Groton, Connecticut.

Neger

The German Kriegsmarine went further than the Italians and the British, in producing the 'Neger', a form of human torpedo which transported and launched a second torpedo, the pilot then hopefully returning to his base. In reality, his chances of surviving an attack on an Allied invasion fleet – their intended target – were at best slim: the clumsy combination was difficult to control, and the pilot's vision was extremely limited as the Neger lacked even the simplest of periscopes. To navigate he had therefore to keep the Perspex dome surrounding his head and shoulders above water, which made his craft easy to detect by enemy lookouts. The tiny cockpit cannot have helped.

Kaiten

The name 'Kaiten' comes from the Japanese '*kaiten igyo*' which means 'a great undertaking'. Given the desperate situation of Japan in 1944–45, faced by the overwhelming strength of the US Navy and threatened with invasion of the home islands, the Imperial Japanese navy (IJN) turned to extreme measures. The airborne kamikaze pilots are well known, but if there were not enough aircraft and not sufficient trainers, the young Japanese recruits were drafted into other branches of the suicide corps.

The lethal performance of the 24in Type 93 torpedo was legend. The problem now was how to bring sufficient

An SLC of the type used with great success by Decima MAS of the Regia Marina, especially at Alexandria and Gibraltar.

Type 93s to bear to have a significant effect. Traditional Japanese submarine training had stressed the need to attack enemy warships, in order to whittle away the severe numerical disadvantage under which Japan fought. Now the stress was to be on sinking attack transports headed for invasion beaches. But Japanese submarines were all too easily detected and sunk by the Americans whenever they put in an attack. The answer seemed to be to put a pilot in the Type 93 torpedo, to guide it to its target. The pilot was initially given the option of baling out of his craft when its fuel ran out, but since the thought of being captured was felt to bring dishonour, many Japanese chose suicide when approached by would-be American rescuers. In later sorties, the entry hatch was bolted shut from the outside.

Many casualties also occurred during training. The trainees would be carried in a motorboat at speed, having to acclimatise themselves by peering through the type of periscope which they would use in their Kaiten. Once proficient in navigating using this primitive aid, they would begin training on a Kaiten fitted with an exercise head. This had an automatic blowing device if the trainee dived below a preset depth. The final part of their course involved ramming the Kaiten into a target vessel. Unfortunately, all too often the shock of impact not only badly damaged the Kaiten but also seriously injured its trainee pilot.

Kaiten were intended to be launched either by carrier submarine, from cruisers and destroyers via a rear ramp, or from a ramp or slip on land. Only the former system was ever used operationally.

The British copy of the SLC, the Chariot, being hoisted aboard.

American GIs examine an abandoned Neger washed up on Peter Beach at Anzio on 2 August 1944. The seventeen-year-old pilot was taken prisoner. It is doubtful if any of the sturdy Americans in the photo would have fitted inside. (US National Archives)

Kaiten Type 1 Specifications:
Length: 14.5m (45ft)
Diameter: 1m (3.05ft)
Payload: 1550kg (3410lbs) HE
Total weight: 8 tonnes (8.05 long tons)

Speed/Range:
78,000m (85,332yds) at 12 knots
43,000m (47,042yds) at 20 knots
23,000m (25,162yds) at 30 knots

The Kaiten Type 1 was the only type used in actual combat. It was produced by the simple expedient of bolting the Type 93 Model 3 torpedo, less warhead but with larger fins and rudders, into the rear of a new one-metre (39in) diameter forward section, comprising the cockpit and warhead. A conical section faired the connection. The warhead held 3410lbs (1550kg) of explosive and was capable of inflicting devastating damage. The pilot held in his hand the pistol handle for the electric detonator. At the moment of impact with the target his weight was thrown forward, closing the switch.

The torpedo was fitted with an electric gyroscope which was preset by the navigator of the carrier submarine, to despatch the pilot in the direction of a previously detected enemy vessel. Control was extremely difficult. At over 5 knots the pilot's view was obscured by spray, so a special fuel reduction valve had to be installed to produce a minimum speed of 5 knots. But then as the oxygen fuel was used up, the weight of the torpedo decreased, control became more difficult and it was impossible to submerge. So the pilot had to be provided with manual means of introducing and purging water ballast to maintain his chosen depth and trim. Normally the Kaiten ran at a nose-down angle of between 1 and 3 degrees.

The Kaiten would be carried on wooden blocks on the deck of the mother submarine, secured by a clamp ring. A tube connected the Kaiten's cockpit with the interior of the submarine, through which the pilot would pass, after which the hatch would be bolted shut.

The mother submarine at periscope depth of 9m (30ft), gave final target instructions to the pilot by telephone. At between 6000 and 7000m (6500–7700yds) from the target, the Kaiten was then released. If carried forward of the conning tower, the pilot started his engine before release to avoid being run down by the submarine. The Kaiten's gyro automatically followed the set course, at 6m (20ft) depth for a predetermined period of time before surfacing, bringing the target to about 1000m (1100yds) range. The pilot took over control from the gyro, adjusted his course to strike the target amidships, and set the depth according to his estimate of the ship's draught. After running the 1000m, if he missed he could turn and come in again for a second attempt.

Many attacks had to be called off when the mother submarine was within launch range, because the Kaiten was found to be unserviceable. When in enemy-dominated waters, the mother submarine remained submerged during the day at depths of 30–40m (100–130ft), and since the Type 93 had not been designed to operate for long periods at such pressures, its engine compartment became waterlogged. Leaks also occurred at the body join, and around the entry hatch.

A total of 130 Kaiten pilots died in action, and a further fifteen in training accidents. In addition, over six hundred crewmen died in eight mother submarines sunk during Kaiten operations. In exchange for these heavy casualties, Kaiten scored only two confirmed sinkings, plus several ships damaged. On 20 November 1944, fleet tanker USS *Mississinewa* was struck by a Kaiten, probably launched from submarine *I 47* in Ulithi anchorage; sixty-three men were lost in the sinking. (A colour photo of her on fire is at NHCC, photo ref K-5510. For nearly sixty years the wreck lay on the bottom, posing a considerable environmental hazard, until in February 2003 a US Navy salvage team recovered nearly two million US gallons of oil.) On 24 July 1945 the destroyer escort USS *Underhill* was escorting a convoy to Leyte when several sonar contacts were reported. *PC 804* claimed a successful

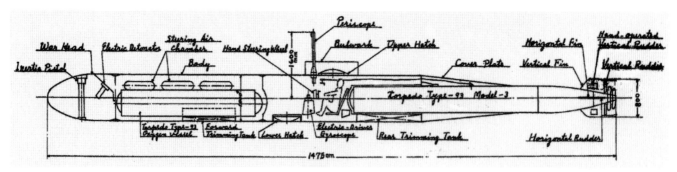

Type 1 Kaiten.

A surviving Type 1 Kaiten in the Yushukan Museum.

depth-charge attack on a submarine, but her depth charges had blown to the surface two Kaiten, close aboard on either side of *Underhill*. Her captain shaped to ram the Kaiten to port, when *Underhill* was blown in two by massive explosions, killing 112 officers and men.

The Type 2 Kaiten was an attempt to gain more range and speed with a larger payload, using hydrogen peroxide as fuel. Benefiting from German technical advice, the IJN experimented for some time with this dangerous fuel, achieving an engine output of 1500bhp, from a double-bank engine layout of two sets of four cylinders side by side, with two crankshafts geared together at the rear. Accepting that there would be insufficient time left to complete this ambitious project, it was abandoned in March 1944. The work done was not wasted, however, since the basic hull layout and engine were adopted for the Kaiten Type 4.

The Kaiten Type 4 followed on from the abandoned Type 2, and used the same basic hull design, engine and payload. Instead of hydrogen peroxide, its engine ran on pure oxygen. Engineers estimated that the oxygen consumption of this unit, in reaching 40 knots, would be extremely high, severely limiting its range, and in this they were proved correct. In the event, no Kaiten Type 4 was ever issued for combat use. In trials its maximum sea speed was only 25 knots. Interestingly, for training purposes, by removing several of the oxygen tanks room was found to accommodate up to four men.

Kaiten Type 4 Specifications:
Length: 16.5m (50.32ft)
Diameter: 1.35m (4.12ft)
Payload: 1800kg (3960lbs) HE
Total weight: 18.17 tonnes (17.87 long tons)

Speed/Range:
62,000m (67,828yds) at 20 knots
50,000m (41,572yds) at 30 knots
27,000m (29,538yds) at 40 knots
(Performance figures as per the original estimates)

Captured Type 4 Kaiten can be viewed in the Washington Naval Yard, at the *Bowfin* Museum in Honolulu, and in Gosport, England.

Since there was a surplus of Type 92 electric torpedoes, it was decided to convert them to Kaiten Type 10. The torpedo was divided into two halves, and a centre section with cockpit was welded on, with a streamlined fairing to cover the joins. Since the Type 10 was intended for use from land bases, only a top hatch was fitted.

The area of the control surfaces was increased, and these were under the direct control of the pilot. When the motor stopped, the Kaiten rose to the surface, and when restarted, the pilot controlled the immersion using the diving rudders. He was supplied with one periscope of the type used in the midget submarines, but it was fixed. Fewer than six Kaiten Type 10 were produced before the war ended, and none were used operationally.

Kaiten Type 10 Specifications:
Length: 9m (29.5ft)
Diameter: 53cm (20.64in)
Payload: 300kg (600 lbs) HE
Total weight: 3.05 tonnes (3 long tons)

Speed/Range:
35,000m (38,290yds) at 9 knots

A surviving example of the Type 10 Kaiten can be seen in the Yamato Museum in Kure.

Post-war Human Torpedoes
Inspired by the SLC and Chariot, the armed forces of many countries have designed different types of 'human torpedo' since the Second World War, for covert missions. The popular growth of tourist scuba-diving has also led to their development for peaceful recreational use. The introduction of modern scuba diving gear has also greatly simplified the operators' task, compared with wartime breathing apparatus.

CHAPTER 3

Der Küstenbrander, the inspiration for Whitehead, and others

In the 1860s there appeared an invention with the germ of a good idea, even though the initial form would prove completely unworkable. In around 1860, retired Fregattenkapitän Giovanni de Luppis of the Austrian navy was shown papers produced by an unnamed Austrian officer in the marine artillery, for an exploding boat which could be brought into contact with an enemy ship. De Luppis thought this would be a good idea, and spent several years developing it, eventually coming up with a prototype model of what he called his 'Küstenbrander'.

'Küstenbrander' in English translates as 'coastal fireship'. Fireships had been used in naval warfare for centuries. Their most notable exploit had been the scattering of the Spanish Armada off Calais in 1588, which led to the disintegration of the fleet and thwarted the invasion of England. In the days of wooden ships with tarred decks and vast spreads of canvas, the approach of a fireship loaded with combustible materials and gunpowder was viewed with dread. They were most profitably used in attacking a fleet at anchor or in harbour, for the vagaries of wind and waves worked against their employment on the high seas.

At about the same time as Luppis was constructing his first feasibility model, the name Küstenbrander was also used by the submarine pioneer Wilhelm Bauer for his third submersible project, offered to the Royal Prussian war and naval ministry at the end of 1864. For his third essay, Bauer proposed armament, but no torpedoes. His project was not taken up. Both Küstenbrander designs used the principle of the fireship but tried to employ them in the opposite sense, to defend a coastline against a hostile fleet.

Unlike Bauer, Luppis actually produced his Küstenbrander. The working model was built of wood, and powered by a clockwork motor. (Bauer had planned to power his version of the Küstenbrander with an ingenious closed-circuit engine, a kind of gas turbine using paraffin and oxygen generated from manganese dioxide.) The power plant of Luppis's design is often criticised as the main limiting factor, but at that time powerful, wound spring-operated mechanisms were becoming commonplace in large clocks for ecclesiastical and public buildings. They were capable of reliably storing and releasing energy. They would suffice for the reduced scale demonstration model. What they would not be capable of was high-speed propulsion in the full-sized device.

The weapon aspect was workable enough, as far as it went: an explosive payload detonated by a percussion pistol coming into contact with the waterline of the target vessel. De Luppis appears to have completely ignored the fact that line-of-battle ships would henceforth be clad with thick plates of armour at the waterline. To arrange for the necessary contact to take place, de Luppis proposed to steer his boat from the shore by means of tiller ropes.

He offered his model to the navy officials in Vienna, who felt that he had the basis of a good idea, but that at that moment it was unworkable. They suggested he co-operate with an established marine engineer to develop it further. Since the foremost marine engineer in the Austrian empire at that time was Robert Whitehead, de Luppis visited him at Fiume and they set up a partnership to develop de Luppis's brainchild.

Whitehead was bitten by the bug of this new idea, and spent considerable time trying to increase the power output and improve the complicated steering arrangements. But however hard he tried, he realised that he would never be able to overcome the two fatal drawbacks of the Küstenbrander. First, it ran on the surface at slow speed. It remained visible to its intended victim, whose crew could either fire at it, steer clear of it or, because of the Küstenbrander's pathetic lack of power, simply fend it off as it came near. Second, it lacked a realistic radius of action, because of its source of motive power. Having explained this to de Luppis, Whitehead ended their partnership.

The following description makes use of the model in the Vienna Military Museum and a second model built for an exhibition in

A very old photo showing de Luppis's strange design.

Rijeka in 2008. The Küstenbrander has a mast, for auxiliary sail power. On either side of the hull are fastened strange bolsters much like the fenders on tugboats. Probably they are cork-filled buoyancy aids to keep it afloat in the face of defensive gunfire. The propeller is not clearly visible in this photo, but from another old photo it appears to have had two broad blades. Behind the propeller is a fixed keel board, and hinged at the rear of this is a curious V-plan rudder in the form of two vertical boards joined at their front faces, worked by tiller cables on the transom connected to the shore. The arming mechanism is worked by a third tiller rope from the shore, passing along the top of the hull to the curious fitting behind the prow, which has a lever weighted by a ball to set the exploder by some devious means. The curved vertical arm has to be the exploder striker. To either side of amidships outrigger arms extend, braced to the bow by wires. Their only obvious purpose would be to try to ensure that if the little vessel struck its target at an angle, the outriggers would attempt to swing it round so the bow striker could come into contact. There is a large handle on the starboard side between the outrigger and the stern, which would have been used to wind the clockwork mechanism. The whole arrangement appears amateurish in the extreme, and one can only wonder at the patience of Whitehead, an experienced marine engineer, faced with this contraption.

Robert Whitehead continued to gain official favour, building the steam engines that powered the *Ferdinand Max* to victory at Lissa, and making them robust enough to stand up to the shock of ramming. And all the time his fertile mind turned over the idea of de Luppis' device, analysing its drawbacks and working out solutions, as we shall see in Chapter 4.

THE LEGACY OF THE KÜSTENBRANDER

De Luppis may have died a disappointed man, believing that Whitehead had taken his idea and turned it into something completely different, but the idea of the Küstenbrander lived on. In particular, later inventors seized on the one aspect of de Luppis's idea that Whitehead had ignored when building his own fish torpedo: the attempt to direct it throughout its trajectory by remote control.

Nikola Tesla

The renowned inventor Nikola Tesla patented radio control in 1898, and used it to direct his remote control boat, which he called the 'Telautomaton', which was 6ft (1.83m) long, built of iron and powered by an electric

Working model of Tesla's 'Telautomaton' boat in the Tesla Museum, Belgrade.

FL-boat *FL 1* being unloaded from a railcar. The radio masts are not yet fitted, but she seems to be equipped with a searchlight, perhaps for trials in night attacks. (Photo courtesy of the Siemens Archives)

motor driven by two batteries. Tesla demonstrated its potential on an artificial lake in Madison Square Garden just after the end of the Spanish-American War.

He claimed he could build a larger version with an explosive warhead, to attack enemy ships. Not surprisingly, there were no takers. As a surface runner, the Telautomaton would have needed high speed, first to catch an alert target ship, and second, to rapidly run the gauntlet of the intended victim's defensive fire.

Siemens-Schuckert Fernlenkboot

On 28 October 1917 the Royal Navy monitor HMS *Erebus* was attacked off the coast of Flanders by explosive German motorboat *FL 12*, directed by radio and spotted by an aircraft: the '*Fernlenkboot*', or FL-boat, built by

FL 1 at high speed, with a crew on board for the tests. The white-painted decking and the bow wave would have given away their approach, but their small size and speed of closing made for a difficult target. The radio-antenna masts are raised, and the rear mast is higher than the first, to take account of the bow rising at speed. The antenna cable descends from the front mast. (Photo courtesy of the Siemens Archives)

An MT-boat captured and tested by the British at Malta (photo by E D Wooley, from the article by J Caruana in *Warship International* (1991), No 2)

Siemens-Schuckertwerke blew a 50ft-long hole in the anti-torpedo bulge, but *Erebus* survived the attack.

Previous attacks had failed, the first when an FL-boat hit the mole at Nieuport, and then when a smaller monitor destroyed another FL-boat with gunfire. It is often reported that the FL-boats were spotted by aircraft but controlled from the shore by cables. The Siemens Archive photos show that in fact the FL-boats were directed from the spotter aircraft by radio control, as evidenced by their high radio-antenna masts fore and aft. The top of the hull was painted white to aid the observer in the controlling aircraft. With a length of 17m, they carried a 700kg explosive charge, and were propelled by a petrol engine at speeds of up to 30 knots.

Decima MAS

Then in the Second World War, the Italians developed and used with some degree of success their '*barchino esplosivo*' Type MT. This 'exploding motorboat' was operated by the famous Decima MAS, a cover name for the stealth units of the Regia Marina.

The method of operation was simple, but extremely hazardous. Carried to the scene of action by a mother craft, the MT-boat's pilot steered directly for his target, set the charge to explode on contact, locked the controls and threw himself backward into the water, cradling in his arms his large, folded, back-rest cushion. The cushion floated, and he hauled himself up out of the water and onto his tiny raft, in order to escape the shock wave of the imminent explosion.

The immensely brave and dedicated pilots succeeded

in crippling the British heavy cruiser HMS *York* in Suda Bay, Crete, on 25 March 1941 and sinking an oiler. The cruiser was beached with her engines out of action, and despite desperate efforts to repair her, she was wrecked by Stuka dive-bombers and scuttled.

On 26 July 1941 Decima MAS attempted a major attack on Malta's Grand Harbour, which failed disastrously, through British early warning radar and the rapid-firing twin 6pdr guns of the coastal defences, and the unit's leaders were killed.

Linse explosive motorboats

'*Linse*' in German means 'lentil', an appropriate name for the tiny, skimming explosive motorboats with which the *Kleinkampfverband*, or 'small battle units', were supposed to stop the Allied invasion of Fortress Europe – alongside the Neger, Molch and Seehund midget submarines. Of all the special attack units, the Linse seemed, even to its operators, to be the most suicidal. No doubt inspired by their Italian allies' success with the MT-boat, the Germans decided to copy the idea but go one stage further, combining raw courage with more advanced technology.

The Linse was a small wooden motorboat powered by the ubiquitous Ford V-8 petrol engine, with a reliable output of 95bhp. That was sufficient to propel these 1.8-ton 5.75m (18ft 10in) long x 1.75m (5ft 9in) wide boats at a top speed of 35 knots. In the stern compartment was a 300kg (660lbs) explosive charge, with a 7-second delay fuse. The charge in later boats was increased to 400kg (880lbs). They were intended to be used in groups of three, two filled with explosive and steered by one man, and a third control boat, with a crew of three in a large rear compartment: the helmsman and two radio operators each directing an explosive Linse.

The explosive-boat pilots, who were less likely to be volunteers, but rather, picked from a penal battalion, would head at full speed for their chosen target. At the last moment they would illuminate red and green lights fitted to the stern of their Linse, and bale out into the water, hoping to be picked up by the following control boat. The crew of the latter would, however, already have their hands full, using the red and green lights to direct the two Linse by radio control during the final part of their attack run. The radio system used was that taken from the Goliath remote control demolition tank, and was well-proven.

If all went well, each Linse would impact on the hull of the target vessel, when a metal framework around the bow would compress and fire a small explosive charge. This would blow off the bow section, leaving the rear section carrying the main charge to sink below the waterline of the victim. After 7 seconds the delayed action fuse would operate and blow the main charge. At that moment it was to be hoped that the crew of the control boat had faithfully followed their pilots and recovered them out of the water. Lacking the large floating cushion of the Decima MAS pilots, they would be at fearful risk of concussion from the blast.

All this adrenalin-fuelled action, of course, would be framed in the gun-sights of the target vessel, which would be firing with every weapon that could bear. No wonder the Linse attacks were referred to by their operators as '*Opferkämpfer*', or 'suicide missions'.

Despite the drawbacks, these devices were actually taken into action. Their first recorded use was during an attack on the Anzio beachhead in April 1944 in conjunction with Neger units. That attack was a complete failure. However, it appears that Linse operators sank the Hunt-class destroyer HMS *Quorn* off the Normandy beaches on 3 August 1944, with the loss of 130 officers and men.

The final fling for the Linse occurred at Split on 12 February 1945, when six motorboats crossed the defensive boom and entered the harbour. They attacked the AA cruiser HMS *Delhi* and were engaged by the ship's 20mm Oerlikons. They missed *Delhi* but one hit *LCF 8* (landing craft flak) lying alongside and blew up. The resultant blast seriously damaged one of *Delhi's* propeller shaft brackets and jammed her rudder. She had to be towed to Malta, and after surveying back at Chatham, she was deemed to be beyond economic repair.

It was suggested that perhaps the Linse units could also act as lifeboats for Neger pilots who had got into difficulty. Another scheme was to employ them to lay down smokescreens off the beaches. But finally, a degree of sanity prevailed and these extra tasks were dropped.

Shinyo and Maru-ni

Towards the end of the Second World War the Japanese, faced with the overwhelming naval and air superiority of the Americans, turned to individual heroism and self-sacrifice with their suicide weapons, and one of these was to be the explosive motorboat.

The Imperial Japanese navy and army remained rivals throughout the Second World War, going to the extreme lengths of building their own aircraft production factories. The army even built and operated its own submarines to supply its far-flung island garrisons. So it is not surprising that both services produced their own type of small attack boat.

The navy version was the 'Shinyo' ('sea quake'), intended as a suicide weapon to be rammed into enemy ships, and carrying a large explosive charge in the bow. Speed was around 23 knots, falling to only 18 knots when the explosive charge was in place.

The Japanese army shied away from asking its men to crew suicide craft, and their version, the 'Maru-ni', was normally intended to carry two depth charges. The pilot would run alongside the target ship and release the depth charges, set to shallow, then attempt to escape at speed in the 6 seconds before they exploded. The firepower of his American opponents meant that in fact his mission was virtually a one-way trip.

Cheap to build out of wood, with automobile engines, and simple to operate, the Japanese built over six thousand Shinyo and around three thousand Maru-ni boats. They were intended to be hidden in caves and camouflaged lairs all around the coasts of the Japanese islands, to sortie en masse and fall upon the American invasion fleet. Unfortunately for the Japanese, complete units of attack motorboats, along with their pilots and support teams, were to be lost en route to their intended bases when their transport ships were sunk by American submarines.

Of those units that did get into action, they succeeded in sinking *LCI(M) 974*, sub-chaser *PC 1129*, *LCS(L)(3) 26*, *LCS(L)(3) 7*, *LCS(L)(3) 49*, *LSM 12* and *LCI(G) 82*. Seriously damaged were attack transport USS *War Hawk*, *LCI(G) 365*, *LST 925*, *LST 1028*, *LCS(L)(3) 27*, DD USS *Badger*, *YMS 331*, DD USS *Hutchins*, VC2-S-AP3 *Bozeman Victory* and USS *Carina* (AK 74).

One has to ponder on the mayhem which could have been caused by the four thousand Shinyo and Maru-ni retained in the Japanese home islands to await the expected Allied invasion.

Shinyo Type 1 captured by the Americans, outside its typical cave lair. The central engine cover has been removed. At either side of the stern can be seen the racks for the 120mm RO-SA rockets, fitted to increase speed during the final run in to the target or as a means of back-up propulsion in the event of engine failure. The Shinyo on the right has been marked with the word 'Danger', to avoid the unsuspecting from tampering with its lethal contents. (US Army photo)

USS *Cole* secured to the deck of the heavy lift ship MV *Blue Marlin*, showing the 40ft hole blown in her side by the suicide bombers.

USS *Cole*

An *Arleigh Burke*-class guided-missile destroyer, 505ft (124m) long, displacing 8900 long tons at full load, and capable of a speed of 30 knots, *Cole* was the target of a suicide attack by al-Qaeda terrorists on 12 October 2000.

Earlier, on 3 January 2000, al-Qaeda operatives had planned to attack the destroyer USS *The Sullivans* with a boat loaded with explosives, while she was anchored at Aden. The plot failed when the terrorists so overloaded their boat that it sank. The group convened in Kuala Lumpur to discuss what had gone wrong and to relaunch the attempt to destroy another American warship.

Their chance came on the morning of 12 October when the USS *Cole* called at Aden for a routine refuelling stopover. She had completed mooring by 0930, and commenced refuelling an hour later. At 1118 local time a small boat loaded with between 400 and 700lbs of high explosive (200–300kg) approached the *Cole*'s port side and rammed into the ship's hull amidships. The suicide

bombers detonated their explosive charge, and blew a 40ft wide hole in the side of the *Cole*. The blast impacted on the ship's galley where crew members were lining up for lunch; seventeen were killed and a further thirty-nine others injured.

First rescue ship on the scene was the Royal Navy frigate HMS *Marlborough*, whose crew provided medical and damage-control assistance. A quick-response force was airlifted in to secure both the damaged *Cole* and the US embassy. In the following days, seven US warships arrived to provide assistance to the crew of the *Cole*. Divers confirmed that her keel was undamaged, and she was towed to the heavy lift ship MV *Blue Marlin*, which transported her back to the States for repairs. USS *Cole* was taken in hand by Northrop Grumman Ship Services in Pascagoula, and transported overland to a construction bay near to where she had been built five years earlier. Refloated in September 2001, *Cole* rejoined the fleet on 19 April 2002.

A Japanese painting showing a night attack by army Maru-ni boats armed with depth charges. The chaotic scene is well representative of the rare massed attacks by explosive motorboats. (US Army)

CHAPTER 4

Whitehead and the Copies

Having jumped ahead to consider the legacy of de Luppis' Küstenbrander, we must now return to the main protagonist of the torpedo saga, Robert Whitehead.

Robert Whitehead was a thorough engineer, capable of taking a problem and working on it relentlessly until he had hammered out a solution. That he did not continue to develop Luppis's idea of the Küstenbrander is therefore intriguing.

Later engineers took up the idea, as we have seen in the previous chapter, and made it work. Whitehead could have replaced the 'clockwork' power source by a compressed air motor, as he fitted to his prototype torpedo. But as a highly visible surface-runner that would have been vulnerable to gunfire from the target vessel, and a one-inch Nordenfelt round could certainly pierce the air flask wall.

He could have explored the float torpedo option, using flotation devices such as Fulton had employed to sink the brig at New York. Filling the float with cork would have rendered it virtually unsinkable. The float torpedo configuration would also have furnished him with his desired aim of striking the target not on its armoured waterline, but at its most vulnerable spot, the underwater hull.

The continuous controllability was another aspect he discarded. It is likely that Luppis's arrangement of tiller ropes added drag and complication. They also risked entangling the propeller. Piano wire could have been a viable alternative, as later used by Brennan.

It is probable that the single most compelling reason why he discarded the notion of the Küstenbrander was the invisibility aspect. If he could succeed in making an underwater explosive device travel in the direction he sent it, and if it would continue to keep to the depth he selected to do the most harm to the target, then the invisibility/surprise factor would seem to take priority. After all, it was the very opposite of the brave but extremely hazardous spar torpedo which was making the news in the 1860s.

In fact, what Whitehead did was not to continue to develop an existing idea, but to take a great leap forward, with the results we know so well. The Whitehead story has already been described in great detail by the late Edwyn Gray, so here we will only examine the salient features in the unfolding of the saga.

A photo Gray included in his book on Whitehead, *The Devil's Device*, wondering if it showed Whitehead with the lost prototype, is almost certainly of something completely different (see Chapter 21 for details). No authenticated photo of the 1866 prototype has come down to us, and this is perhaps indicative of Whitehead's thoroughness. He was a hard-headed businessman, not a romantic. Why preserve as a cherished memento a primitive version when the next model was so superior?

The prototype Whitehead built and tested in 1866 is known only from eyewitness descriptions. It was said to have a blunt nose like a dolphin, with fins extending for virtually the entire length of the body. It is evident that the onlookers were kept at a considerable distance. A more detailed and probably more accurate description is given by Fregattenkapitän Theodor Braun in the November 1935 issue of *Marine-Rundschau* magazine:

'The "Torpedo" was made of steel sheets with a length of 3.4m (11ft 1³/₄in), a diameter of 0.36m (14in) and a weight of 136kg (300lbs). Two vertical fins extended from this diameter a further 25mm (1in) upwards and downwards, joining at the stern and leaving a cutout for a two-bladed propeller, with a vertical rudder that could be fixed. In the centre of the body there were two guide strakes also extending 25mm beyond the full diameter. The internal layout was kept secret from the inspecting committee. The nose contained a simple percussion detonator, followed by the payload of 8kg (17.6lbs) of gun cotton. The next section contained the 'depth control' consisting of a plate responding to water pressure and an arrangement for transmitting the plate's movements via simple external wires to a pair of fins.'

Braun also reported that the prototype was set in motion inside a 'launching cage' suspended beneath an anchored boat, hence the need for the guide strakes. The two-cylinder engine was driven by compressed air at a pressure of 370psi through a regulating valve to ensure a constant speed, which was around 6.5 knots over a distance of 200yds; it then travelled on for another 100yds at a lower speed. It is clear that Whitehead was still thinking at this stage of a close-range coastal weapon to defend harbours and anchorages.

Azimuth control was achieved by means of a preset rudder mounted behind the propeller, regulated after trial and error on the Fiume range. This procedure would be retained for decades as a means of testing and then adjusting each individual torpedo over the many years of its active service life. Depth control was by a hydrostatic

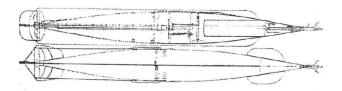

A technical drawing of a very early Whitehead reproduced by Fregattenkapitän Theodor Braun in *Marine-Rundschau* magazine, November 1935. (Drawing courtesy of Erwin Sieche)

pressure valve acting on horizontal tail planes, and on the first model this was extremely erratic. The eyewitness account of its resemblance to a dolphin was perhaps derived from the prototype's behaviour as much as its appearance.

In the drawing reproduced in Braun's article, all the features of the 1866 prototype are present, plus a pair of horizontal stabilisers fitted on either side of the nose. In addition, the two-bladed propeller is enclosed in a shroud. However, the device shown behind the warhead is clearly the pendulum, regulating the hydrostatic valve fitted amidships, so it is probable that this drawing shows the revised prototype of 1868 incorporating Whitehead's 'Secret'. Movement of the depth-keeping gear appears to be transmitted via *external* horizontal wires to the tail planes, via rocking levers. These small planes are fitted in front of the propeller shroud. Probably the horizontal stabilisers were fitted to the nose while Whitehead mastered the adjustment of the pendulum. The vertical rudder appears to be braced by diagonal wires to the propeller shroud, and lengthening or shortening these wires would give the required steerage.

A photograph from Count Hoyos's collection shows an early Whitehead torpedo (displayed inverted), and today we can find this very same torpedo mounted on the wall in the Vienna Military Museum.

Contrary to the plan drawing, the Vienna torpedo now has a three-bladed propeller, similar to other early Whiteheads with shrouded propellers in the Split maritime

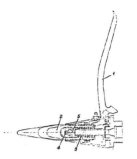

ACCIARINO DEL PRIMO SILURO WHITEHEAD

Att urto la leva 1 lascia libera la massa 2 che, spinta dalla molla 3, ora compressa, urta contro la capsula 4 che così detona e comunica l'accensione attraverso il forettino 5.

Here is a cutaway drawing of the first type of Whitehead exploder, again from Fregattenkapitän Theodor Braun in *Marine-Rundschau* magazine, November 1935. (Drawing courtesy of Erwin Sieche)

museum. The adjustable vertical rudder which would be fastened to the propeller shroud is missing, as are the movable horizontal tail planes. The external control wires to the tail are not present, but the central horizontal strakes are there. What appears to be a sliding regulator set in the top part of the vertical fin also corresponds precisely with the drawing. The long exploder is missing from the nose, but the four holes, two either side of the nose, are clearly the positions of the attachments for the bow stabilisers. This in fact could be the relic of the second prototype of 1868, because no other Whitehead has been seen with these fixed bow planes.

Note the considerable keel surface offered by the rearward extensions of the top and bottom fins, aiding directional stability. It was likely that with the slow speed of the prototypes, the torque rolling moment from their single propeller was not excessive, and the vertical strakes could control it. After all, slow-speed full-size ships with only one propeller do not suffer noticeably from torque rolling. When the torpedo speed was upped considerably, it would become necessary to fit the contra-rotating

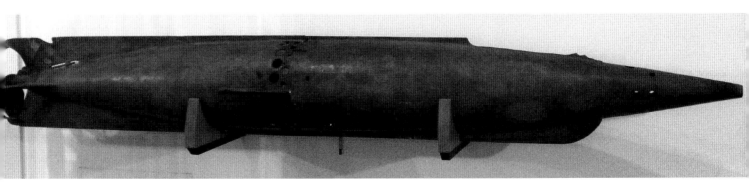

Early Whitehead torpedo at the Vienna Military Museum. (Photo courtesy of Mr Peter Enne)

propeller arrangement.

The drawing of Whitehead's first exploder model shows the rearward inclination of the long arming lever. When lever '1' is thrown rearwards on leaving the launch cradle, the exploder cap '2' is free to operate on contact with the target. It moves to the rear, overcoming the pressure of the spring '3' and hits the percussion cap '4', firing the exploder '5' into the main charge. On later torpedoes the arming lever would be inclined forward. This long lever also formed a useful safety feature for anyone brave enough to retrieve a fired live torpedo which has missed its target. By pushing the lever forward the exploder is disarmed.

Note that in the drawing of the complete torpedo 'of 1868' the vertical lever is missing (although this could be due to the poor quality of the drawing), but that three horns now project from the exploder, to ensure detonation even from a glancing blow.

The success of the 1868 prototypes was guaranteed by incorporation of Whitehead's 'Secret' which controlled the depth-keeping. Put in simple terms, to even out the

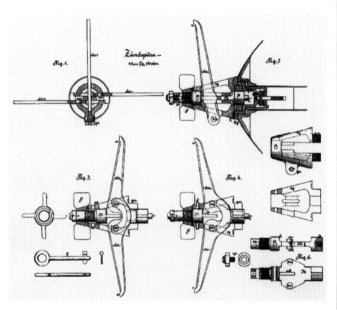

Here, in a plan from the 1908 Austro-Hungarian navy maintenance manual, is the mechanism for the exploder 'whiskers'. Not shown is a small rectangular plate on a lever which fits into the circular lug on the underside of the cone. On leaving the tube this plate strikes a projection, and arms the exploder mechanism. It is still set to safe, however, until the flat paddle blades have been screwed backwards along the central thread. In so doing, they push on the pivots of the two pairs of 'whiskers', bringing them forward where they will set off the exploder, even if the torpedo strikes a glancing blow. At the same time, the central firing pin can now move backwards when its nose hits the target. (Drawing courtesy of Erwin Sieche)

varying depth responses obtained from the hydrostatic pressure sensor, he had interposed a vertical pendulum. When the valve called for a reduction in depth, too rapid a reaction could cause the torpedo to broach, followed by a corrective signal, causing it to dive. The pendulum sensed the change in inclination of the torpedo and imposed a corrective force of its own, thus dampening down the over-rapid signals from the depth-keeper. Variations in

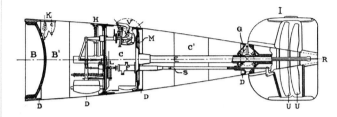

The tail of a US Navy 18in Whitehead torpedo of 1898, showing the hydrostatic depth valve 'V' and the pendulum 'D', together forming Robert Whitehead's 'Secret'. (From the Bureau of Ordnance 1898 handbook)

depth were thereby reduced from several feet to just a few inches. All that was now required would be to await the arrival of the Obry device – but that is getting ahead of the story.

Robert Whitehead's 1868 models were tested by the Austrians and approved for use by their navy, but as a result of the financial crisis in the Austrian empire following the Seven Weeks War with Prussia they were unable to purchase exclusive rights, and Whitehead was free to launch his invention on the world stage.

The next year Royal Navy representatives visited Fiume, and Whitehead travelled to England to demonstrate his 14in and 16in models. The British government paid him the paltry sum of £15,000 to purchase the 'Secret', and also for the right to begin manufacturing their own versions of the Whitehead in the Royal Laboratories (RL) at Woolwich. A fortuitous clause in the contract allowed for improvements made by the engineers in Woolwich to be shared with the Fiume factory, and vice versa.

Robert Whitehead purchased the bankrupt Fiume factory in 1872 and renamed it the Silurifico Whitehead, and events moved rapidly forward. In 1874 the Royal Laboratories engineers fitted contra-rotating two-bladed propellers, which took away the need for the stabilising fins top and bottom, the torque from one propeller counteracting that from the other. Naturally, they shared their work with Fiume, who immediately adopted the same arrangement. In the meantime, Fiume had experimented with a pair of two-bladed propellers set side by side with a

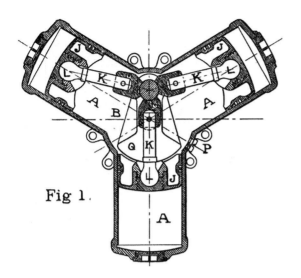

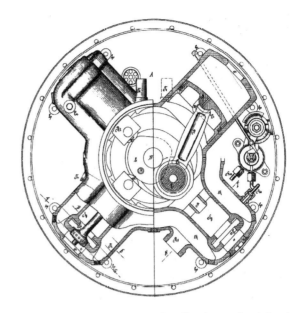

On the left, the Brotherhood three-cylinder engine in a USN 18in Whitehead (Bureau of Ordnance 1898 handbook); on the right, the four-cylinder engine of an Austrian 18in Fiume torpedo of 1908. (Plan courtesy of Erwin Sieche)

horizontal control surface set between them. (This experimental design is displayed in the museum in Split.) But the RL design was clearly superior, and the twin tandem propeller system was dropped. The next year saw the change to a three-cylinder radial engine designed by Peter Brotherhood, and this design would have an extremely long life.

A strange development by the Royal Laboratories changed the position of the vertical and horizontal control surfaces, moving them to the conical rear body, ahead of the propellers. From detailed examination of the contemporary plans, it is clear that this move was carried out in order to simplify production, and especially the control connections which no longer had to pass around the propellers. It would also have significantly reduced the cost of production. Fiume was reluctant to copy this move, and it is a reliable recognition feature to determine from which factory subsequent models originated. Hydrodynamically, the Fiume arrangement of control surfaces positioned behind the propellers was more efficient.

By 1882 the pressure contained in the air flasks had reached at least 1500psi, and other countries which had obtained a manufacturing licence for the Whitehead found it extremely difficult to produce air vessels able to withstand such pressures. The Whitehead factories accordingly supplied the air vessels. This problem was particularly acute in the United States in the last quarter of the nineteenth century, with no manufacturer capable of undertaking this work. The Fiume air flasks of the period prior to the Great War were formed from straight tubes, with internal end caps screwed in front and rear.

In 1883 Dr Froude's work on hydrodynamics led to the introduction of a semi-rounded nose replacing the sharply tapered cone. This not only allowed the carrying of a larger warhead, but also surprised everyone by adding at least one knot to the torpedo's speed, much in the way that the bulbous bow aids surface ships. The Split Museum holds a strange Whitehead torpedo head that is bulb-shaped, probably an attempt to increase the payload without increasing the overall length. It might be thought this could have improved the speed, but since it was not proceeded with, it obviously did not.

Five years later the first 18in torpedo appeared, which would prove to be a popular size over many decades. Then in 1890 Robert Whitehead opened his own factory in Weymouth in southern England, and a third factory at St

A Whitehead in the Vienna Military Museum. (Photo courtesy of Mr Peter Enne)

Tropez in France. Back in England in 1893 the manufacture of the British versions of the Whitehead was transferred from the Royal Laboratories to the Royal Gun Factory. The same year three-bladed contra-rotating propellers were introduced, followed in 1897 by the four-bladed variety.

In the meantime, in 1895 Whitehead introduced a startling new innovation: the gyroscope patented by Obry and designed to control a torpedo in azimuth. At a stroke, this application produced two major improvements. First, the torpedo's steering would no longer depend on preset rudder adjustments based on empirical practice with each individual torpedo. Now every production torpedo had the ability to keep on a straight course under the control of its gyroscope. Second, the gyroscopic control could itself be preset to continue straight ahead for a short distance after launch, and then to take up another course for the torpedo at the angle fed into the device prior to launch. The Whitehead was now controlled automatically and continuously in both the vertical and horizontal planes.

In 1900 the Obry itself was further improved by the introduction of servo actuation of its control impulses, thereby preserving the energy in the spinning gyro right out to the torpedo's maximum range, avoiding the risk of it toppling. Later models were started by air blast, running up to operating speed within a fraction of a second, which avoided the brief delay in the gyro taking over control of the torpedo's direction, sometimes the cause of deviations when fired from broadside tubes of a vessel at speed.

The Royal Navy Submarine Museum in Gosport holds 18in Whitehead torpedo No 1274. The body of the

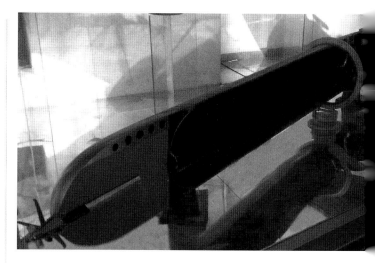

An 18in sectioned Whitehead from 1905 with blunt nose, in the Vienna Military Museum. Note the eccentric filling of the warhead, to lower the centre of gravity and help keep the weapon upright. (Photo courtesy of Mr Peter Enne)

torpedo is in phosphor-bronze, which shows that not only Schwartzkopff torpedoes were manufactured in that material: it was a slightly more expensive option in the Fiume catalogue.

In around 1900 Fiume completed an order from the Japanese government for a massive 27.5in torpedo, and then in 1905 they ordered a series of 24in torpedoes for coastal defence installations such as those situated at Go-Saki and Ko-Saki on Tsushima. These large Fiume

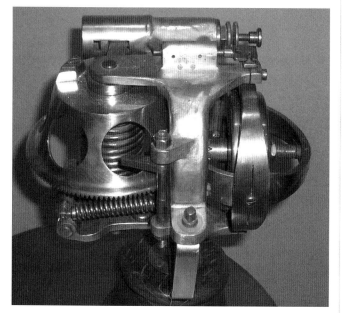

An early spring-operated Obry gyroscope on display in Rijeka. (Photo courtesy of Erwin Sieche)

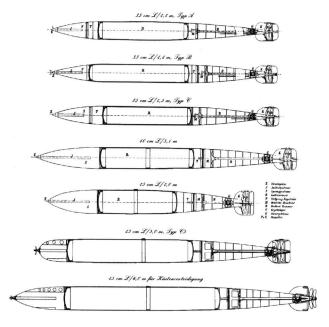

A range of Austro-Hungarian Whitehead torpedoes built at Fiume, up to a 6m model for coastal defence batteries – note the Royal Laboratories-style tail on the latter. (Drawing courtesy of Mr Peter Schupita)

The Fiume factory in full production towards the end of the nineteenth century. (Photo courtesy of Erwin Sieche)

Another view inside the Fiume factory about 1905. The gentleman in a frock coat, centre left, is almost certainly a Japanese client, come to view the 24in torpedoes Japan ordered from Fiume for coastal defence. The warhead on the left can be compared with the standard 18in model in the centre. The huge torpedo body itself can be seen on the bench to the right.

Schwartzkopff torpedo on display at Explosion. (Photo by the author, courtesy of Explosion, the Museum of Naval Firepower)

torpedoes were the first of a series of 24in heavyweight torpedoes such as the naval versions of 1919, part of a development trend which would lead to the Type 93, popularly known as the 'Long Lance'.

The next major improvement had to wait until 1905 when the first 'heater' torpedo was introduced. Engineers had long known of the beneficial effects of using the surrounding seawater to avoid the compressed air freezing as it was fed to the motor. Applying this principle to burning a fuel with the injected compressed air vastly improved the motor's efficiency, giving startling increases in torpedo range and speed. Three years later the first 21in torpedo was introduced, still a popular size today, as it allows for a large capacity warhead. The modern torpedo had arrived in time for the Great War.

Meanwhile, Robert Whitehead had passed away in 1905, at the age of eighty-two. The weapon he had perfected was about to prove its worth in dramatic ways.

SCHWARTZKOPFF

The Schwartzkopff torpedo was indubitably a copy, and a pirated one at that. It must have amused Tirpitz to have chosen a German engineer whose name in German translates as 'Blackhead' to copy the Whitehead. The French were playing the same game at the same time, refusing to pay royalties to Mr Snider in England for copying his breech-loading conversion of a muzzle-loading rifle, claiming that their own almost identical version had been designed at the very same time by a 'Monsieur Schneider'.

However, at the time when the set of plans of one of the latest Whitehead models disappeared from the Fiume draughting office – when by coincidence a respected Berlin industrialist named Herr Louis Schwartzkopff just happened to be staying as a guest at the Whitehead family home – Robert Whitehead had still not patented any of his inventions.

A year after his visit Schwartzkopff began to manufacture his own torpedoes which, in the opinion of one contemporary British observer, were a very close copy of the Whitehead. To be fair, anyone who wanted to produce a workable torpedo at that time would have been obliged to build one which closely resembled the extremely successful Whitehead. There was one obvious difference: the body of the Schwartzkopff was made from phosphor-bronze, and whereas a Whitehead made of steel required careful cleaning after each test run to avoid rusting, the phosphor-bronze body of the Schwartzkopff did not rust. This advantage did not last long, because very soon the enterprising Mr Whitehead was offering in his sales catalogue versions of his popular models in steel or phosphor-bronze. On the other hand a Schwartzkopff cost significantly more than a Whitehead. They were listed at £450 when the current Whitehead model retailed at £320. It was no wonder that Tirpitz did not allow the German navy to be tied to just one private supplier, but decided to set up a state torpedo factory.

In the annual report of the torpedo school for 1884 there was an interesting article on the Schwartzkopff. Lieutenant Egerton of HMS *Vernon* and Mr Marston, chief engineer at the torpedo school, had paid a visit to the works in Berlin and seen tests of new torpedoes. The brand new torpedoes were first charged to an air pressure of 50 atmospheres (735psi), and were run for 200m (218yds) at a depth of 3m (10ft). They were recovered, recharged to 50 atmospheres and their rudders realigned for a second run under the same conditions. For the third run they were charged to 80 atmospheres (1175psi) and set to run at a target at 400m (436yds) range, following which their rudders were once more adjusted. For the fourth run, the air vessels were taken to their normal pressure of 90 atmospheres (1323psi), and once again the torpedo was

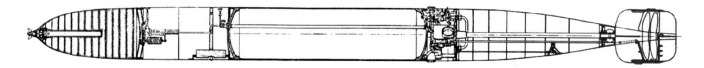

General section and plan view of the US Navy's Schwartzkopff model of 1898. (From the maintenance manual issued in 1903)

aimed at the 400m target.

Before delivery to the customer, each Schwartzkopff torpedo would have been test run between fourteen and eighteen times. In the tests observed by the visitors, the Schwartzkopff torpedoes kept to a uniform depth, scarcely varying more than a decimetre (4in) above or below the set depth.

Even the Royal Navy purchased a batch of Schwartzkopffs when the Fiume and British factories were temporarily unable to meet their requirements. It is likely the fine example on display in the torpedo gallery at Explosion came from this batch.

In 1898 the US Navy purchased twelve Schwartzkopff torpedoes to compare them with the contemporary Whitehead models being produced under licence by Bliss. A manual was issued in 1903 but, significantly, no further orders were forthcoming.

From the sectioned drawing of the US Navy Schwartzkopff, it is clear that the torpedo has all the items one would expect to find in a Whitehead of the period, but arranged differently. The nose whiskers of the exploder, for example, do not unscrew as the torpedo passes through the water in order to arm the exploder; they are merely contact horns, and the safety device is an internal shear pin. Furthermore, Schwartzkopff had not yet copied Whitehead's revised layout with the depth-keeping mechanism behind the air flask, avoiding the need to run the control connections through the flask. The gyro used on the Schwartzkopff was a model invented by Kaselowski, but it worked in a similar way to Obry's gyro.

BLISS-LEAVITT

The American firm of E W Bliss Company was licensed by Whitehead to produce his torpedoes for the US Navy. Between 1896 and 1904 they manufactured 438, 18in Whiteheads in five different models in two different lengths, namely the 3.55m (11ft 7¾in) Marks 1, 2 and 3, and the 5m (16ft 4¾in) Marks 1 and 2. The 3.55m Mark 3 and the 5m Marks 1 and 2 had the Obry gear. In addition, the US Navy purchased a batch of some fifty Mark 1a torpedoes directly from Whitehead.

In 1898 Howell sued Bliss for infringement of his patent of 1871, part of which mentioned the gyroscopic

effect the flywheel drive had on azimuth control of the torpedo. The court decided that Whitehead's and therefore Bliss' use of the Obry gear did not infringe on Howell's patent and the case was thrown out.

At about the same time, Bliss began to introduce improvements that would eventually lead to a torpedo of their own design. One significant change was the air-blast gyroscope, in which the wheel was spun up to 10,000rpm in around a third of a second, avoiding the slight delay in the gyro taking over control of the torpedo as it entered the water, which had led to some irregular running.

In 1904 one of the Bliss Company's engineers, Frank McDowell Leavitt, developed his own 21in torpedo design, based loosely on the Whitehead, but using a two-stage single-wheel Curtis turbine in place of the Brotherhood-type reciprocating engine. As this drove a single propeller, the initial model suffered from rolling. Leavitt soon modified his design to incorporate two counter-rotating turbine wheels, each connected to a propeller, thus balancing out the torque and curing the rolling tendency. The design of this double unit was credited to Lieutenant Gregory Davidson, USN.

The Bliss-Leavitt torpedoes, apart from being 21in, differed from the Whiteheads by having larger warheads and a much longer range, 4000yds (3,658m) at 27 knots for the Bliss-Leavitt Mark 1, compared with 1500yds (1372m) at 28.5 knots for the fastest USN Whitehead, the 5m Mark 2. This was not quite the end of the Whitehead in US Navy service, however, as in 1908 the newly created torpedo factory was asked to produce twenty Whitehead Mark 5s, and even more were ordered at the same time from Vickers Limited in England. Between 1904 and 1906 Bliss produced about 750 Bliss-Leavitt torpedoes of Marks 1 to 3. These remained in service throughout the Great War, and were not declared obsolete until 1922.

Bliss reverted to the 18in diameter for contemporary submarines, torpedo boats and early destroyers. The Bliss-Leavitt Mark 4 was similar to the 21in Mark 3, but was intended for submarines. (The Mark 5 was the Whitehead mentioned above.) The Bliss-Leavitt Mark 6 of 1911 altered the turbine wheels to rotate in the horizontal plane, as in all following US turbine torpedo designs.

With the Mark 7, 18in submarine model first introduced into fleet service in 1912, the company launched the 'steam' torpedo, in which a spray of water was introduced into the combustion chamber at the same time as the compressed air and fuel. The water cooled the gases and in turning to steam increased the gas volume. The result was a torpedo capable of running 6000yds (5486m) at 35 knots. The companion 21in model was the Mark 8, which would arm the flush-decker destroyers ordered during the Great War.

The Mark 9, 21in 'steam' torpedo, a special short model for the underwater torpedo tubes of US dreadnoughts, was the last model manufactured by Bliss-Leavitt, and the last torpedo to be designed by them would be the Mark 10, but this would be manufactured instead by the Newport torpedo station. Orders from Bliss-Leavitt were stopped in the post-Great War economy drive, but the firm's products would continue in naval service for many years.

A scene on board USS *Olympia* around the turn of the nineteenth century showing crewmen carrying out maintenance on her torpedoes. The original caption says these are 18in Whitehead torpedoes, but by their diameter it is clear they are 21in Bliss–Leavitts. (Photo by Frances Benjamin Johnston, Library of Congress)

CHAPTER 5

The Serious Rivals, the Dead Ends, the Hopefuls and the Hopeless

VON SCHELIHA

At first sight it may appear strange that Colonel Victor von Scheliha, a German officer who had served the Confederacy in the American Civil War and was well known as a railway engineer, might be considered a serious rival to Robert Whitehead. He offered a torpedo design for consideration by the British Admiralty's torpedo committee which met for the first time in May 1873, and he persuaded a nephew of the Duke of Wellington to register on his behalf a British patent on his torpedo design. The nephew, Frederick Arthur Wellesley, had met von Scheliha in Saint Petersburg when Wellesley was acting as military attaché at the British Embassy in the Russian capital. Wellesley had in fact observed trials of a prototype torpedo, built to von Scheliha's plans, on the River Neva, and he described its performance as being most satisfactory.

From his British patent it is clear that von Scheliha had at an early stage grasped the essential principles required to build a workable torpedo:

- he controlled its depth through a system of a 'suspended weight' and a 'spring and diaphragm', in other words, a hydrostatic valve damped by a pendulum, the basis of Whitehead's 'Secret';
- he proposed to power it with a three-cylinder radial engine at a time when Whitehead's early models still had a V-twin engine;
- he had discovered that a significant increase in performance could be attained by introducing a heater device to raise the temperature of the compressed air as it was fed to the engine – an improvement which was not 'rediscovered' for another thirty years;
- he succeeded in controlling his torpedo in azimuth, long the main criticism of the 'fire and forget' Whitehead torpedo, by electrical impulses passed to the torpedo by a reel of insulated wire it deployed behind it as it ran. These signals could also be used to vary its depth by opening valves to change the amount of water ballast or air in buoyancy bags.

If such a device had been constructed by a professional naval engineer in Britain, it could have been made to work. Unfortunately for von Scheliha, possessing no venture capital of his own, he had passed the plans of his torpedo to the Russian government for them to construct and test. They had encouraged the colonel to take up lodgings at an expensive St Petersburg hotel to wine and dine influential guests and persuade them to support his project.

There was one basic flaw with his torpedo design, which was that he did not intend it to explode on impact with a target, but to carry multiple warheads which could be released on electrical signals – similar to the MRV (multiple re-entry vehicle) arrangement on a ballistic missile of the Cold War. By this he claimed to be able to sink a whole fleet. But by so doing he overreached the possibilities of the design, and the Russians lost interest. Having no means to pay for his lavish entertainment, von Scheliha was condemned to a debtors' prison, and disappeared from history, along with his torpedo.

BRENNAN

Luppis had the germ of a good idea in wanting to control his Küstenbrander from the shore. If an attacker knows that you can launch a weapon which will unerringly follow his every move as he tries to evade it, he may be discouraged from attacking in the first place. And the bolder souls who keep coming anyway will be simply blown out of the water. Luppis' guided boat hit at the waterline; Whitehead's unguided torpedo hit the underwater hull. Combining these two aspects, Irish inventor Louis Brennan produced his torpedo, which became the first truly practicable guided missile.

The only surviving example of a Brennan torpedo extant today is in the Royal Engineers Museum in Gillingham, Kent. All the photos in this section are by the author, with the kind assistance of Lauren Jones of the museum. The Royal Engineers were involved with the Brennan instead of the Royal Navy because it was the sappers who were responsible for submarine mining, the laying and operating of controlled electrically-detonated minefields to defend harbours and anchorages in the United Kingdom and around the empire. The Engineers would also be more at ease with the elaborate means designed to protect and operate the Brennan, as its complicated and extensive launch stations were usually installed inside existing coastal fortifications, also built and maintained by the Royal Engineers. The section of 7in-gauge bullhead rails in the museum, down which the torpedo would be launched, was recovered from the

Brennan station in Fort Albert on the Isle of Wight.

The operating principle of the Brennan is simple in concept, but extremely sophisticated in application. Basically, each of two propellers was driven by a drum, on which was wound a long length of thin wire. When the torpedo was launched down its ramp, the wires were pulled from the torpedo by a winch in the launch station, powered by a steam engine. There was therefore no power source contained within the torpedo body as this was all positioned on land. The torpedo simply contained the transmission system. The two drums were rotated in opposite directions and this caused the propellers also to rotate in opposite directions, without the need for contra-rotating gears as in the contemporary Whitehead. The presence of two drums was also used to guide the torpedo. By operating a complex system of pulleys in the shore station, differential tension could be applied to the two drums. A sensing mechanism then applied this to the bow and stern rudders, changing the direction of the torpedo.

Depth-keeping had originally been a problem, as Brennan had relied on fixing the bow planes at a suitable angle of attack to keep the torpedo running at the desired depth, the rear horizontal planes being non-movable. Not surprisingly, this had not worked as expected, and some of the early testing required that Brennan prove his device by allowing it to operate as a surface runner, while he worked on perfecting the depth control. He accordingly added a hydrostatic depth-control device, as on the very first Whitehead. Again this caused erratic depth-keeping, and again Brennan returned to the workbench. Finally his efforts paid off, and the Brennan's depth-keeping was described in a report by Major Sale, RE, in November 1886 as 'a wholly novel and strikingly ingenious apparatus for meeting conditions far more complex than are met by the corresponding apparatus in the Whitehead torpedo.'

Examination of the internals of the sole surviving Brennan in Gillingham do not reveal the presence of a depth-control pendulum, which formed the essential part of Whitehead's 'Secret'. What is present is a rectangular box, power-driven from the rear wired drum, with levers connected to the hydrostatic valve and, presumably, to the bow depth planes (although the latter connection is missing). The depth mechanism is a sealed unit, which was not kept in the body of the torpedo but in a locked safe in the launch station, only being retrieved and inserted in the torpedo shortly before launch. This formed part of Brennan's almost pathological fear that his ideas would be pirated and freely copied – not unreasonable in view of the espionage and skulduggery that surrounded Robert Whitehead and his 'Secret'. But unlike Whitehead, who sold the 'Secret' to any and all comers with the ready cash,

On the left is Brennan dirigible (guided) torpedo No 18 in its display case. The oval body of the Brennan can be seen here. To left and right of the nose are the depth planes. Above and below are the bow rudders. The holes are for the hydrostatic depth-keeping valve. The arrowhead is a towing lug for recovering the torpedo after a practice launch.

Brennan, who signed an exclusivity deal with the British government, managed to retain the secret of his successful depth mechanism so well that, even today, we have very little idea of how it worked in practice.

The depth mechanism box obviously acted as a servo mechanism for operating the non-balanced bow planes against the considerable resistance of water pressure. There must be some means of damping over-reactions

To the left of the production torpedo is a wooden model believed to represent the very first type described in Brennan's British patent of 1877.

from the hydrostatic valve, working to the same end as the large Whitehead pendulum – perhaps a weight sliding on a rod. But the box is compact, and unless and until it is either opened or X-rayed, it seems Brennan succeeded in taking *his* 'Secret' to the grave with him, when he was knocked down by a car in his eightieth year. It would be fascinating to delve into the genius of the man who invented a monorail gyro-stabilised railway train, and an early helicopter, amongst his other innovations.

The 1877 full-size prototype torpedo was stated to have been 9ft long, rectangular in section and boat-shaped in plan view, which corresponds with the shape of the small model in the photo. A year later, having proved that the propulsion system worked as intended, Brennan developed the concept into a cigar-shaped torpedo stabilised by long tail fins at top and bottom, with contra-rotating propellers and a hump on top to provide for the wire take-offs. The final production model led the two wires through the centre of the concentric propeller shafts, avoiding fouling the propellers. Brennan then added an ingenious device which at intervals released rings from the rear of the propeller shafts, to hold the two driving wires together and prevent them from separating in the water.

The openings in the bronze torpedo body are, from left to right: a rectangular access hole for the steering and depth mechanisms, used to insert the depth mechanism sealed box shortly prior to launch; then the large openings for the wire drums; next the access to the reciprocating mechanisms which moved pulleys back and forth as the wires unrolled, ensuring that they always came off the drums at right angles; finally, the hatch to insert a calcium phosphide canister for practice runs. This latter device gave off smoke to mark the position of the torpedo for recovery at the end of its run. Not visible in the photo is the very first access cover, on the warhead in the nose, allowing the launch operators to cock the inertia pistol, which would arm itself after a set number of propeller revolutions, when well away from the launch station. On top of the body is the folded mast, which would be propped into an upright position before launching the torpedo, carrying a small pennant to mark its course to the observer controlling the steering mechanism.

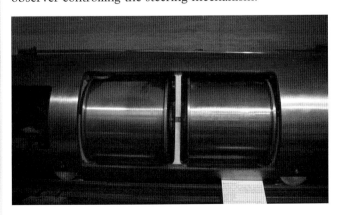

Here are the two wire drums (devoid of their wires) rotating in different directions and each connected to a propeller.

Top left of the left-hand drum is part of one of the reciprocating pulleys which took the wire off its drum at right angles, moving back and forth as the reel unwound. The reason why the torpedo body is oval in section was to provide room above the drums for these take-off pulleys, and below the drums for the steering connection to the vertical tail rudder. Under the body are the four wheels on which the torpedo ran down the launch rails into the water. Not visible inside them at the bottom of the torpedo body are the four fixed guide projections, which ran inside the rail edges to keep the torpedo on a straight path. The Royal Engineers collection contains a small-scale silver-plated demonstration model some 20cm long. Pulling on the cork attached to the wire emerging from the propeller shafts revolves the drum.

The perfected torpedo entered service in around 1890. The surviving example is some 22ft long, weighing just over one ton. The operator could steer it by observing its extended mast which was the only projection above water. Using 2000yds (1830m) of the thicker wire (0.07in gauge/1.8mm) introduced in 1894 it could reach a top speed of 24 to 25 knots over short distances, 21 to 22 knots over 1000yds (914m), and 19 to 20 knots over 1600yds (1463m). Maximum range was around 2000yds (1830m). Carrying a 220lb (100kg) charge of wet gun-cotton, the Brennan was a reliable and effective close-range defence weapon. Cost was stated as around £300 in February 1887, to which, of course, must be added the considerable costs of building and equipping the launch station.

Effective as it may have been, by 1906 the whole system was deemed to be obsolete and no longer cost-effective. Long-planned extensions to the existing stations were cancelled. What had happened in the meantime? First, it was hardly a rapid-reaction defence weapon, needing a head of steam to operate the winding drums in the launch station. Given the vast investment in the launch sites, the machinery could have been upgraded to run on internal combustion engines or electric motors. But there were more significant drawbacks.

Its large locations were impossible to conceal and would therefore have all been known to a potential enemy. On the other hand, this would still have a deterrent effect. When launched, the steering flag gave away its course and position to the target. But then knowing it was on the way was different from being able to avoid it, as the Brennan would unerringly follow the target's evasive manoeuvres. The launch rails, overhead girder and trolleys (see Chapter 18) and the torpedo itself running down the rails could be bombarded by QF guns on an attacking ship. They offered a small target but were easily damaged.

But, finally, the few existing launch stations had involved a significant investment in masonry, armoured lookout positions and machinery, for what was essentially a comparatively small short-range weapon, especially compared to the price of a fixed torpedo tube installation for Whiteheads. And in the intervening years the Whitehead torpedo itself had developed out of all recognition.

THE HOWELL TORPEDO

The Brennan being tied to coastal defence by its use of heavy winches and launch girders, the most serious competitor to the early Whitehead at sea was the American Howell torpedo. A serving US Navy officer, Lieutenant Commander John Howell spent his spare time designing and perfecting a torpedo of his own, which used a completely different mode of propulsion.

Rather than using compressed air and a reciprocating engine to drive his torpedo, Howell settled on a large internal flywheel. This added one unavoidable complication – the need for an external power source to spin the flywheel up to speed. Howell used a steam turbine attached to the starboard side of the launch tube, working through clutches in the torpedo body, to spin the 131lb (60kg) steel flywheel up to launch speed. One slight drawback was that the turbine and flywheel, when at full speed, did produce a certain amount of noise, which might give away a torpedo boat on a stealthy approach – rather like the sound made by the submarine *Nautilus* in the 1954 movie *20,000 Leagues under the Sea*.

There were compensations, however. When the flywheel had reached 10,000rpm, on pulling the firing lever, first the drive clutches were withdrawn, then the torpedo stop latch which held it in the tube was released and, finally, the propulsion charge of black powder was fired, launching the torpedo. The horizontal rudders and the propeller speed regulator were locked for the initial few metres, then the torpedo set off at its preset depth and aimed course.

Howell had discovered that the large flywheel acted like a gyroscope, tending to stabilise the course of his

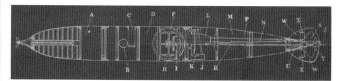

Side view of the sectioned Howell torpedo. The plates showing details of the Howell torpedo are taken from the Bureau of Ordnance general description of the Howell torpedo 14.2in, Mark I, prepared by the Naval Torpedo Station in 1896.

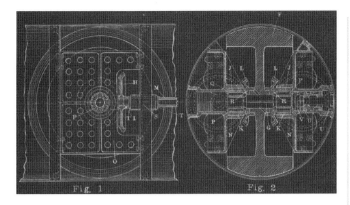

The heart of the torpedo, its steel flywheel 'F', weighing 131lbs (60kg), seen from the side (Fig 1) and in section (Fig 2), which was spun up through the clutch (U) to 10,000rpm prior to launch.

torpedo. If a contemporary Whitehead encountered a strong wave coming from one side, it would tend to be deflected from its aimed course. The Howell, on the other hand, would not be deflected but would be rolled by the wave, a roll which was relatively simple to correct by the swing of the vertical rudder pendulum. So strong was the gyroscopic effect that Howell patented it as representing a major improvement in torpedo control. (As noted earlier, when Whitehead later adopted the idea of the gyroscope, Howell sued him for copyright infringement.) And, of course, the flywheel drive left no wake to give warning of the torpedo's course and allow the target to take avoiding action.

One idea that was common to both designers was Whitehead's 'Secret', the pendulum to regulate for over-rapid compensation of the hydrostatic depth-keeping device. But the Howell had one more unique feature. To avoid the need for contra-rotating screws, he had used twin inward-turning propellers set horizontally. As the flywheel slowed down in the course of the torpedo's run, the speed regulator automatically adjusted the pitch of both propellers, to ensure that the Howell maintained a steady speed. Both speed regulator and horizontal rudders were locked out of operation for the initial period of the run, to avoid upsetting the regulating devices on impact with the water.

The warhead nose contained the contact exploder and the safety mechanism. This consisted of a steel four-bladed screw-fan, normally held in the rearward position on the threaded body of the exploder by a shear pin of lead. When the torpedo entered the water, the shear pin broke under the impetus of the screw turning in the water flow, the screw-fan screwed itself forward until it reached a section with no further screw thread, when it was free to revolve without undue resistance to the water flow. The exploder body was now free to move backwards on striking the

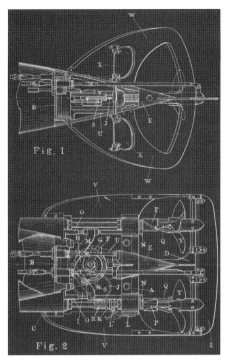

The twin propellers, geared down to 8/10ths of the flywheel speed at launch (8000rpm). Also shown is the speed regulator arrangement, which adjusts the pitch of the inward revolving propeller blades, to maintain a steady speed even as the flywheel slows down. The horizontal tail plane (Z) is quite large, for control of the depth-keeping, but the small vertical rudders (X) appear more like the trim tabs on aircraft control surfaces, such was the strong directional effect of the flywheel.

target, activating the primer and the main charge.

In the event of a miss with a war shot, soluble paper covers dissolved and let water enter two holes plugged by soap. When the soap dissolved in turn, water entered the dry primer and rendered it inert. The practice head, filled with seawater to the same weight as the warhead, had an identical screw-fan nose fixture, to duplicate the characteristics of the warhead. At the end of its run, a soluble cover would allow seawater to enter a pocket containing a cylinder of calcium phosphide. This would emit smoke enabling the position of the torpedo to be spotted for recovery. A depth register recorded the depths attained by the torpedo during its practice run.

From the above, it is clear that the Howell was a workable device with good accuracy. Unfortunately for Lt Cdr Howell, his naval duties did not permit him to fully devote his time to the perfection of his idea. He seems to have begun experimenting in 1870, with an initial model driven by a propeller at both ends. But it was not until thirteen years later, in 1883, during the competition organised at the behest of Congress by the US Navy in order to find a suitable design of torpedo, that his design was virtually finalised. Three years later, Lt Cdr Barber of the Bureau of Ordnance testified before the Senate committee on ordnance and warships to the effect that the Howell's 'principal advantages over the Whitehead are directive force, its size and its cost. Its remarkable power for maintaining the direction in which it is pointed, when acted upon by a deflecting force, makes it possible to launch it with accuracy from the broadside of a vessel in rapid motion.'

In 1888, after the navy had selected the Howell for issue, the inventor sold the rights to the Hotchkiss Ordnance Company, which proceeded to produce fifty Howell Mark I torpedoes. They were fitted on battleships, cruisers and torpedo boats. But when the decision was taken to fit underwater tubes to battleships and cruisers, the Howell lost out to the Whitehead, and no further orders were forthcoming after the first fifty.

This would appear to be a great shame. The Howell Mark I, 14.2in (36cm) in diameter and 11ft (3.35m) long with a body made from rolled brass 1/16in (1.60mm) thick, weighed 518lbs (235kg) with either warhead or exercise head. It could carry an explosive charge of some 100lbs (45kg) of wet gun-cotton at a speed of 25 knots for a distance of 400yds (366m), although a *New York Times* article on the first test firing from the cruiser USS *Detroit* reported a run of 900yds (823m). Even after the adoption by the rival Whitehead of Howell's gyroscopic principle, the large mass of the flywheel in the latter's torpedo, compared with the separate smaller gyroscope in the Whitehead, would have guaranteed greater accuracy; and also far less risk of a circular run, plus no danger of torpedo air flask rupture which was to cause several warship casualties.

A larger diameter than 14.2in would have meant a much larger flywheel, or perhaps even two in a 21in Howell, with a significant increase in range. But presumably the need to equip the launch tube with a high-speed turbine to spin up the flywheel weighed heavily against the Howell. After all was taken into consideration, it has to be admitted that the Whitehead was much simpler to launch.

Finally, due to its prolonged gestation period, by the time the Howell entered general service, the Whitehead offered a much superior performance, plus a gyroscope of its own. The 400yd operational range of the Howell was suicidally close for a torpedo boat of the 1890s, and use of the Howell by battleships and cruisers at that range could only be justified by the need to administer the *coup de grâce* to an armoured opponent battered into silence by gunfire.

There is a tailpiece to the Howell story. In May 2013 several newspapers reported the discovery of the mid-section and tail of a Howell Mark I torpedo on the seabed off San Diego. Two Navy dolphins named Ten and Spetz were being trained to search for lost naval ordnance on the sea bottom. First one, then the other, returned to the surface to butt their nose against the divers' boat, indicating that they had found something interesting. Their trainers were amazed to find that the dolphins had discovered a lost Howell torpedo. It was missing its practice head, due to the corrosive effect of the mixed metals on the screws holding it in place, but the mid-section and tail, including the variable-pitch propellers and both sets of rudders, were in very good condition. The relic has been restored in a chemical bath to make it suitable for display. The restorers found it was marked as Torpedo # 24, and on searching navy records it was discovered that the battleship USS *Idaho*, conducting torpedo practice off San Diego on 20 December 1899, had in fact recorded the loss of Howell Mk I # 24.

The nineteenth century saw not only the successful Whitehead torpedo and its derivatives, but also a vast collection of strange and wonderful torpedo designs, some of which were built and tested, and others which, thankfully, remained on the drawing board or in the patent descriptions or, sometimes, never escaped the highly imaginative minds of their inventors. To fully describe them all would take a complete book, and that is just what the late Edwyn Gray produced under the title of *19th Century Torpedoes and Their Inventors*. The following, therefore, is merely an attempt to classify these weapons according to their type, and to highlight certain features which, although applied to an unworkable design, still held a certain merit.

THE ROCKET TORPEDO

Surprisingly, the most popular designs involved rocket propulsion, no less than fourteen being patented between 1864 and 1893. The first example, patented by Andrew Alexander in 1864, featured spiral vanes attached to the torpedo's body, to screw it through the water, apparently in the hope of achieving a certain degree of accuracy, always a problem with the early unguided rockets. He was followed the same year by the rocket-propelled float torpedo invented by James D Willoughby, which also featured an explosive fixed to a spar, thus combining rocket, float and spar torpedo elements.

In rapid succession came the rocket torpedoes of Robert Weir (1870), George Quick (with a claimed top speed, underwater, of 135 miles an hour, 1871), Miles Callender (with a cleverly designed warhead which pivoted down and forward to strike the hull bottom of the victim, also 1871), Reverend Charles Mead Ramus (which was a rocket-propelled float torpedo, 1873), William H Mallory (optimistically powered by charges of compressed gunpowder, 1878), William Giese (with a harpoon nose to stick in its target's hull, 1879), Asa Weeks (an amazing twin rocket surface-runner plus spar, 1883), a disappointing example from the Royal Laboratories (1883), Washington Irvine Chambers (which was an awash runner, 1885), and Timothy Sullivan and Ernest Etheridge (the torpedo body in two sections to be steered by four central fins, 1887).

Appropriately, the nineteenth-century rocket torpedo designs ended with a bang, when in 1893 disgruntled inventor Patrick Cunningham, whose rocket torpedo design had been rejected by the US Navy, launched it down the main street of his home town, with incendiary results. What, of course, all these inventors lacked was a reliable propellant, still several years in the future, and also a means of controlling the depth and direction of their high-speed underwater missiles, which would be many more years in the making.

The Russians still favour rocket propulsion, and their modern designs are described in the appropriate chapters.

THE FLOAT TORPEDO

The second most popular configuration was that of the float torpedo, with no less than eight designs, plus the two rocket-propelled floats already mentioned above. As its name suggests, this was an underwater explosive device carried to its target by a surface float, thus avoiding the thorny problem of regulating the depth of the weapon, a device so closely guarded by Robert Whitehead as his 'Secret'.

There was one main advantage to the float torpedo – which was also its Achilles' heel. It was dirigible, or steerable, because it was visible to the operator. At the same time, it was also highly visible to its intended victim, whose crew would be rapidly taking evasive action and firing at the float with all the guns that would bear. Recognising this fatal drawback, several designers stressed the high survivability of their particular design of float.

In order to turn a drawback into an advantage, the inventors often stressed the fear expressed in the press of uncontrolled Whiteheads running amok among friendly ships. Unfortunately, during this early period it appeared simpler to bring the locomotive torpedo under directional control than it was to guarantee the steering of the dirigible – as was embarrassingly demonstrated on numerous occasions, including in action.

In 1862 the float torpedo invented by Warsop & Brental was actually tested by the Royal Navy. Powered by compressed air at a pressure slightly higher than that of the first Whitehead, it was steerable by tiller ropes like the Küstenbrander. However, it was propelled not by a screw but by an old-fashioned feathering paddle wheel, which was hardly guaranteed to produce any worthwhile velocity, and this was almost certainly the reason for the rejection of an otherwise promising weapon.

Henry Knapp's curious float torpedo (1875) used a bow propeller, only surpassed in eccentricity by Hugh Nealy's float-supported clockwork-powered torpedo moved by means of its screw-shaped body (1887). Three float torpedoes made use of electricity: Henry Julius Smith (1872) employed it to steer, but ingeniously proposed using it to heat the compressed air for propulsion; Nordenfelt (1883), who tested a dirigible powered by batteries; as did Sims (1889) with the Sims-Edison. Alfred P S Miller (1887) proposed a torpedo shaped like a later Zeppelin gondola, and Patrick (1888) proposed a 24in float torpedo no less than 42ft (12.8m) long.

Gabet's 'torpille radio-automatique' of 1909 was the swansong of the float torpedo. On 24 December 1909 French inventor Gustave Gabet tested his radio-controlled torpedo in the Seine near Paris. A journalist described it as a dirigible (or steerable) torpedo, with a length of some 30ft (9m). It was of the float torpedo type, the lower cylinder containing the electric batteries and 200hp motor being suspended from a smaller upper cylinder which carried two lamps set on pillars of different heights. The proposed warhead was to comprise no less than 1980lbs (900kg) of dynamite. The powerful electric motor was hoped to give the torpedo a top speed of 20 knots. Gabet claimed to be able to control his torpedo out to a maximum radio range of 14,000yds (13,000m), but it was certain that the batteries would not suffice to drive the torpedo at 20 knots for this distance. He stated his torpedo would cost around £3000, which was a substantial sum in 1909.

The trial run seems to have succeeded. The *torpille radio-automatique* appeared to be a workable vehicle, but of course it suffered from the lack of a stealthy approach common to all float torpedoes. Added to this major tactical drawback, its large size meant it was extremely expensive, and therefore it is no surprise Gabet's invention was never followed up. It has to be said that 20 knots, while a respectable speed for a torpedo of the 1870s, was nowhere near fast enough to catch any worthwhile prey forty years later.

Another journalist, writing in the *Reading Eagle* of Tuesday, 4 January 1910, appeared to be confused over the torpedo's motive power, claiming that the batteries were only fitted to work a system of signal lamps –

The huge *torpille radio-automatique* being launched. (Gallica Bibliothèque Numérique)

described as 'acetylene' lamps by the previous correspondent – and that the torpedo was to be driven by a 200hp petrol engine! Since he also reported that the propeller was readily reversible, and one cannot envisage a gearbox operated by remote control at that date, the reference to a petrol engine has to be an error.

Apparently, the lights served as signals to the controller, since as Monsieur Gabet related, 'It does not suffice to direct a torpedo boat, one must also know what is happening inside. For that reason the lights undergo eclipses [*sic*], which reveal to the operator placed on shore the nature of the command received by the torpedo boat. He is thus informed a couple of seconds ahead when such and such a manoeuvre is going to be made, and thanks to this optical control he can intervene to correct an error or to annul a disturbing wave.'

Wisely, before building his torpedo Gabet had filed a US Patent, No 907488A, describing himself as a 'professor' (schoolteacher) living in Rochefort-sur-Mer. The patent specified an apparatus 'whereby it is possible to operate from a distance by luminous and electrical waves an engine, rudder, a dirigible torpedo, a signal or any other mechanism.'

The Ericsson torpedo seen dumped unceremoniously behind the Torpedo Development Station building in around 1890. (NHHC, photo # NH 82828)

THE SURFACE-RUNNER

The third category was the surface- or awash-runner, which had the same advantages and disadvantages as the float torpedo. These were designs from Ericsson (1870), Lay (1872), George H Reynolds (1881) and Berdan (1883) and, although each one ultimately failed, they did exhibit certain notable features.

The most significant of the hopefuls predates Brennan. It was that prolific inventor Ericsson, designer of the USS *Monitor*, who tested his steerable pneumatic torpedo in around 1872. A large, clumsy device which ran on the surface, controlled by varying the pressure in the air hose it trailed out behind it, the Ericsson torpedo was remarkable for one major innovation, the contra-rotating two-bladed propellers, the first to be used in a practical application, although the torpedo they drove was a signal failure.

The Ericsson pneumatic torpedo consisted of a rectangular box constructed of iron plates riveted together, 8ft 6in in length by 20in wide and 30in deep (2.6m x 0.5m x 0.76m). It weighed in at 2000lbs (907kg), of which 400lbs (181kg) was the nitroglycerine warhead. Its clumsy shape meant that it could not be launched from a torpedo tube, but had to be lowered into the water by ship's davits. The use of the highly volatile nitroglycerine would not have endeared it to potential users.

One thing the Ericsson had was a certain turn of speed, for its two-cylinder oscillating engine, powered from a distance by a trailing air hose, drove it along at 10 knots, or slightly more than the contemporary Whitehead, and to a maximum range of around 880yds (804m). However, the need to drag behind it the unrolling air hose rendered it virtually uncontrollable when approaching its maximum range. As Edwyn Gray so succinctly noted, the Ericsson was a typical Victorian monstrosity, especially when compared with the sleek Whitehead which, in much modified form, is still with us today.

John Louis Lay came to fame through his invention of the spar torpedo used by Lieutenant Cushing to sink the *Albemarle*. Unfortunately, when he turned his hand to dirigible torpedoes, his designs showed a high degree of complexity, but a disappointing lack of effectiveness. An awash-runner, his torpedo had a warhead of 500lbs (227kg), almost five times the size of that in the contemporary Whitehead, necessary because his weapon would strike an enemy ironclad at its least vulnerable spot, on the waterline armour belt.

Various dimensions have been quoted for Lay torpedoes, but at between 3ft and 3ft 6in in diameter (914mm to 1067mm) and between 23 and 25ft long (7m to 7.62m), they were certainly impressive. Powered by carbolic gas which was prevented from freezing by running the feed pipes external to the torpedo body, it was demonstrated as capable of a speed of 9 knots over a distance of 3000yds (2745m) and more. A dirigible torpedo, it was steered from the shore or a launch vessel by electric cables from a highly complicated control box.

Lay's giant torpedo made a good impression – except on its Peruvian customers as noted in Part IV – but the British Admiralty summed up its main drawback: a price tag of £2200, or more than seven times the price of the rival Whitehead.

Reynolds' patent (1881) described an awash torpedo controllable in depth as well as direction from the shore by insulated cable, and was notable for using the heating properties of the surrounding seawater.

In complete contrast, Hiram Berdan (1882), well-known for his Sharpshooters regiment in the US civil war and later work in cartridge and rifle development, seemed to have gone adrift with his proposal for a surface-runner torpedo, propelled by powder charges, steered by tiller ropes, and towing behind it a second torpedo carrying the warhead.

WEIRD AND WONDERFUL

In this last category, the prolific Ericsson proposed a surface cannon firing a projectile which would continue to its target underwater (the 'hydrostatic javelin', the predecessor of ASROC), and three inventors, Philip Braham (1868), Lord Milton (1878) and Ericsson again (1886), proposed underwater cannon firing projectile torpedoes. Two designed dart-like weapons, William H Mallory (1878) with a coil-spring propulsion system, and Captain McEvoy (1885) with a clockwork-powered version.

More sensibly, Androvsky (1869) was a potential rival for Whitehead, but just too late: by the time his designs were ready, the Russian Admiralty had already taken delivery of their first models from Fiume. Ottmar B Gern (1872) proposed a 6-ton monster torpedo to be transported slung beneath the submarine he was developing. Paulson (1880) suggested a steam-powered torpedo steered by a compass with electrical connections to the rudder. J S Williams (1884) proposed an electric battery-powered torpedo steerable by electric cable from a shore or floating station, a kind of electrified Brennan, and Hiram Maxim's brother Hudson (1885) proposed a straight copy of the Brennan but could not perfect the steering mechanism.

CHAPTER 6

The Torpedo Comes of Age

TORPEDO DEVELOPMENT DURING THE GREAT WAR

The torpedo now entered a stage of maturity, and concomitantly left behind the great named individuals who had imagined it, conceived it, and brought it to this maturity. From here on the developments would be driven by conflict, and the engineers were simply cogs in the machine. The notable names in this new stage would be those of the users, not the makers. There is the name of just one last designer to retain: on the eve of the Great War Lieutenant F H Sandford invented the pattern-runner. Its introduction, however, would have to wait until the following world war. Also, just before the outbreak of war, the production of British torpedoes was again moved, this time to the Royal Naval Torpedo Factory (RNTF) at Greenock, Scotland.

During the war great use was made of the popular 18in and the newer 21in torpedoes – the latter introduced in 1910 – the smaller sizes being mostly obsolete, and used only for ships' boats in cutting-out expeditions, such as the attempts to destroy the stranded submarine *E 15* in the Dardanelles. However, early RN and German submarines did retain the latest 14in models and, of course, they were the first torpedoes used successfully in drops from aircraft. The German navy introduced an interim calibre, the 50cm, which was 19.7in diameter.

The Allied blockade of Germany resulted in major non-ferric metal shortages, leading to the German occupying troops scavenging lead, brass and copper from houses in Belgium and northern France. This led them to introduce short-term expedients such as the use of cast iron instead of copper for the piping runs of their U-boat diesel engines: confiscated submarines and diesel engines in Allied hands after the Great War would cause their new owners significant problems. Despite this, the Germans concentrated on producing high-quality torpedoes, probably by taking shortcuts elsewhere, as they believed that the submarine torpedo was the decisive weapon that would help them win the war. One side effect, of course, was that they would not be producing Schwartzkopff torpedoes with phosphor-bronze bodies. Bronze would, however, continue to be used to produce U-boat torpedo tubes.

For a similar reason, having designed a stable warhead explosive in hexanite, a mixture of TNT and hexanitrodiphenylamine, the Germans continued with its production to the end of the war. This contrasted with the attitude of the British, who in 1917 were forced to dilute TNT with ammonium nitrate to produce amatol, a slightly inferior quality explosive, due to TNT being required elsewhere.

The fear of the surface torpedo was probably greater than the actual physical damage inflicted on the battle fleets. A far more dangerous development was the sinking of thousands of merchant ships by German U-boats, the majority by the torpedo.

On the Royal Navy side there were many submarine torpedo successes, but doubly galling in view of the relative scarcity of German ship targets, far too many torpedo failures. These were tracked down to inefficient exploders. Fisher became enraged, and declared he would have Assistant Director of Torpedoes Charlton 'blown from a gun'. The reasons were the same as would reappear in the US Navy nearly thirty years later: a failure to expend expensive torpedoes in live-firing exercises involving the use of warheads against hard targets, as opposed to the standard practice of substituting a practice head. The exploders sometimes failed to go off, and it took a considerable time to find and eradicate the problem.

Thus it was infuriating for the crew of the only 'K'-class steam submarine which ever drew a bead on a U-boat, to actually hit it with an 18in torpedo, but have it fail to explode. This class thereby failed to kill a single enemy, although accounting for a good number of RN deaths through accidents.

Again, the small, fast and highly manoeuvrable 'R' class, the first true hunter-killer submarines, might have made more of an impact, and promoted the future use of this new breed of submarine, had exactly the same thing not happened to one of them, seeing their torpedo hit a U-boat without exploding.

The Germans, for their part, experimented with a very large torpedo of 600mm diameter (23.6in) which they intended as the future armament of their last super-dreadnoughts and cruisers, plus the very large prototype destroyers. Very few were produced, and there is no record of their combat use. There was a proposal for an even larger torpedo, the 70cm (27.6in) J9. They did, however, make considerable advances, introducing remote control of exploding motorboats by radio, and of aerial torpedoes by wire, and they even introduced a magnetic influence exploder, which again would come to maturity late in the following world war.

In 1917 the Germans designed an electric torpedo, capable of a speed of 28 knots over 2000yds. Despite its slow speed, it had several advantages over the thermal-engined types. It was wakeless, giving escort vessels no indication of the location of the U-boat which had fired it. It did not change its mass, as did thermal torpedoes as their air and fuel were used up, so trim remained the same throughout its run. Finally, in an economy geared for war production, the electric torpedo did not require the same amount of highly-skilled man-hours in its construction as did the thermal type: it could be built by less specialised firms. Fortunately, the Armistice intervened before any electric torpedoes were fired in anger by the U-boat fleet.

The Americans produced a small experimental electric torpedo only $7^{1}/4$in in diameter and some 6ft long, and followed it by a full-size 18in weapon in 1919. Then they lost interest in electric torpedoes for over twenty years. When the USA entered the war in 1917, large numbers of flush-decker destroyers were ordered, and to equip them the firm of Bliss-Leavitt produced over three thousand of their 21in Mark 8 'steam' torpedoes, a production record at the time. These would remain in service with the flush-deckers through to 1945, and many would cross the Atlantic to join the Royal Navy when fifty of these veteran destroyers were delivered to Britain in 1940.

BETWEEN THE WARS

In the early 1920s the USN decided to withdraw the underwater tubes from its battleships, followed by the removal of their above-water tubes, deemed too dangerous in a big-gun battle. Above-water torpedo tubes remained standard fittings on all new cruiser designs, but except for the *Omaha*-class ships – which could be used in the role of destroyer flotilla leaders as in the IJN – the tubes were removed from all US cruisers in the mid 1930s. This move was not the result of a desire to reduce top-weight, as all the early Treaty cruisers came in under weight, but on the grounds that their tactical deployment did not require them, cruisers being reserved for gunfire support of destroyer flotillas.

Meanwhile, major moves were made in terms of the propulsion units. By the end of the Great War the standard British torpedo engine was a wet-heater four-cylinder radial made of bronze, with integral cylinder barrels and heads as in contemporary automobile practice. Because of the increasing weight of the air flask, required to withstand ever higher pressures, experiments were made with hydrogen peroxide, which needed a lighter containment vessel, to produce oxygen via a catalyst. These developments were shelved by the British, but taken up by the Germans, the Japanese and the Americans in the latter part of the Second World War.

To obtain more power from existing pressure vessels, thought was given to using air enriched with oxygen – up to 57 per cent by weight, or even pure oxygen. The British 21in Mark VII of 1928 was the Royal Navy's first enriched air torpedo, carried by the *London*-class heavy cruisers, and this led to the 24.5in Mark 1 installed in the *Nelson* and *Rodney*. Before the outbreak of the Second World War, however, due to corrosion problems with the air vessels, both enriched air models were changed to run on normal compressed air.

At around the same time, the British were perfecting the burner-cycle reciprocating engine, which retained the classic four-cylinder radial layout. The bore/stroke ratio of these compact radial units bore little resemblance to the contemporary automobile long-stroke inline reciprocating engine, with its inherent disadvantages of piston friction and heavy, out of balance, reciprocating weights. The radial engine could thus continue to rival the American preference for the turbine engine. The first British torpedo to use the burner-cycle engine was the long-lived Mark VIII for submarine use. It was a modernised model of the Mark VIII which would be fired against the *General Belgrano* fifty-five years later. The corresponding torpedo for surface ships was the Mark IX.

The Brotherhood burner-cycle engine was fed with compressed air at around 840psi. A small amount of paraffin was atomised in the air and burned. The resultant gas was fed into the cylinders at a temperature of 1000°C, and additional fuel was injected just before the piston reached top dead-centre. The compression caused the fuel mixture to detonate, driving the piston down as in a diesel engine. The exhaust gas was evacuated through ports in the cylinder, but there were also two auxiliary exhaust ports in the piston crown. By 1945 this impressive power unit would have been tuned to produce up to 465bhp, sufficient to propel a 21in torpedo at 50 knots. Plans to run a version of this engine on nitric acid promised to produce 750bhp, but the outbreak of war meant that it was never built.

In 1923 German experiments with electric torpedoes continued in secret in Sweden, and the design was finalised six years later. Since the Versailles treaty banned Germany from possessing submarines, the electric torpedo was held in readiness until Hitler came to power and began repudiating the terms of Versailles.

Magnetic influence exploders had been developed during the Great War, and the Duplex exploder was fitted to Royal Navy torpedoes from 1938. But the old problem of insufficient live-firing tests cropped up, and was to seriously affect their performances. The only navy to carry out large-scale live torpedo firing was the Imperial Japanese navy, which had expended many obsolete warships in tests in the lead-up to the Second World War. The Japanese saw in the torpedo the weapon they needed to give them an edge over the numerically superior US fleet in the Pacific. Japanese war strategy involved wearing down the US Navy in a series of actions across the Pacific Ocean until parity had been reached with the Japanese battle line, when the dreadnoughts would move in for the decisive final battle. A major part of this strategy depended on the torpedo: they set to work to produce the best in the world, and in this they succeeded.

Japanese development of an electric torpedo for submarines began in 1921, inspired by the model the Germans had introduced to their U-boats just prior to the Armistice. The design was finalised by 1925. The 21in torpedo was powered by two 54-cell lead-acid batteries feeding a 95ehp motor. It could run at 28 to 30 knots out to 7000m (7660yds), carrying a 300kg (660lbs) warhead. It became the Type 92 in 1934, but manufacture was suspended, ready for mass production in the event of war.

The Imperial Japanese navy studied other German late war developments, including the 600cm 23.6in torpedo. They had previously tried out the 27.5in Fiume torpedo produced in around 1900, and in 1905 they had ordered 24in torpedoes from Fiume for coastal defence. Now they decided to produce a heavyweight torpedo of their own for the anticipated conflict with the Americans. The result was the 24in Year 8 torpedo of 1919, capable of 38 knots over 10,000m (11,000yds) and carrying a 345kg (759lbs) warhead. Ten years later the 24in Type 90 appeared, capable of 46 knots over 7000m (7660yds) with an explosive charge of 375kg (825lbs).

They had briefly tested oxygen-enriched torpedoes in 1917. Future Admiral Oyagi, during the two years (1926–27) he spent at the Whitehead factory in England, heard rumours that the Royal Navy was fitting oxygen-fuelled 24.5in torpedoes in *Rodney* and *Nelson*. In fact the 24.5in Mark 1 originally ran on oxygen-enriched air, but on his return to Japan, Oyagi headed up a team to work on producing a version of the Japanese 24in torpedo to run on 100 per cent oxygen.

There were severe problems to overcome. The oxygen had to be prevented from coming into contact with any of the lubricants in the torpedo mechanism, to avoid the risk of explosion. More serious were the explosions which occurred in the engine combustion chambers as soon as the oxygen and kerosene fuel were injected. The design team overcame this hazard by starting the torpedo on compressed air, stored in a 'first air bottle' and only then gradually changing over to pure oxygen. They succeeded in producing a working torpedo, which was designated the Type 93, from the year 2593 in the Japanese calendar when the design was finalised.

The Type 93 oxygen-fuelled engine produced 520 horsepower at 1200rpm, compared with the 240hp of the British 24.5in and the 320hp of the initial Mark VIII. It could run at 49 knots for 20,000m (22,000yds), an exceptional performance. At 36 knots it would reach out to a phenomenal 40,000m (44,000yds). It carried a 490kg (1078lbs) warhead, capable of inflicting devastating damage. And it was practically wakeless. To profit fully from its deadly characteristics the IJN introduced power-reloading gear to their large fleet destroyers, following the provision of multiple reloads on board their cruisers.

Since the Japanese had previously had difficulty in forging the air vessels required for their licence-built Whiteheads, they constructed a special 4000-ton press to forge the body and after end of the flasks for the Type 93 out of steel billets. The air flask forward end cover was fixed with a large copper washer, the internal pressure keeping the joint gas-tight, and the arrangement proved extremely satisfactory.

The Type 93 was too large to be carried in submarines, so a smaller 21in oxygen torpedo was designed for them in 1935, the Type 95. It could run at 49 knots for 9000m (9840yds) and at 45 knots it reached out to 12,000m (13,000yds). The Type 95 carried a 405kg (891lbs) warhead. In 1943 the Model 2 would carry a warhead of 550kg (1210lbs). The Type 95 first air bottles often leaked, and while in the tubes on cruisers and destroyers it was a simple matter to verify the pressure of their oxygen-fuelled torpedoes at regular intervals and, if necessary, top it up, in a submarine this was not so easy, a factor leading to the electric Type 92 being resuscitated.

In 1937 the Japanese designed their third oxygen-fuelled torpedo, this time an even smaller 18in model, the Type 97, designed for midget submarines. It carried a 350kg (770lbs) charge at 45 knots over 5500m (6000yds). The original Type 97 would see action only once, during the attack on Pearl Harbor, as its leaky first air bottles were impossible to check and recharge, since the torpedoes were muzzle-loaded into the tubes before the start of a mission, and the crew had no access to the torpedoes when under way.

The Japanese pre-war torpedo arsenal was completed by the excellent Type 91 aircraft torpedo, and this is fully described in Chapter 8. They experimented with high-speed torpedoes for destroyers, the two built reaching 56 knots, and also with turbine torpedo engines, but neither

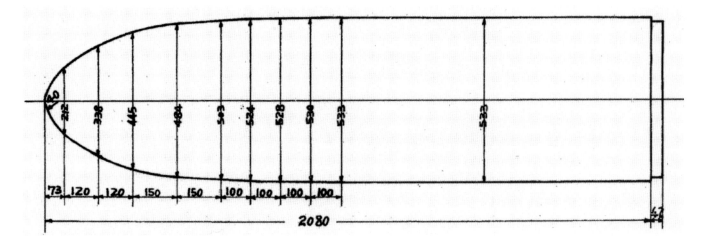

The Italian-designed streamlined nose introduced from 1940 on Japanese torpedo types. The dimensions are in millimetres. (Drawing from US Naval Technical Mission to Japan, *Japanese Torpedoes and Tubes*, Article 1, 'Ship and Kaiten Torpedoes', April 1946)

development was pursued. Up until 1940 they used round-nosed torpedo heads, but in that year the Italian streamlined torpedo head was introduced and used on all types, with a claimed increase in speed of around 2 knots, with no increase in engine power.

The US Navy produced three new torpedo designs in the 1930s, which would continue to serve throughout the Second World War. The Mark 14 submarine torpedo was designed in 1931, and was a development of the previous Bliss-Leavitt designs. The destroyer version was the Mark 15, which was longer with a larger warhead, but otherwise differed in minor details only. The wartime experiences with these two types will be described in Part IV. The Mark 13 aerial torpedo is described in Chapter 8.

The US Navy had begun experiments with alternative fuels as early as 1915, and in 1929 had started a research programme at the Naval Research Laboratory. By 1934 they had produced 'navol', a concentrated solution of hydrogen peroxide in water to provide an oxygen source, burning alcohol as fuel. The projected Mark 17 Navol torpedo for destroyers was interrupted by the attack on Pearl Harbor and the urgent need to produce torpedoes of the existing types.

After February 1924, when Fiume became part of the Kingdom of Italy, the Italians constructed a torpedo testing tower beside the torpedo factory. This is its reinforced concrete structure photographed in 2003. The lower level had two torpedo frames which could be lowered for underwater launches; the next level up carried out deck-level launches; and the third level simulated aircraft launches. The wooden structures on top contained measuring instruments and observers. (Photo courtesy of Erwin Sieche)

THE SECOND WORLD WAR

As in the early days of the Great War, German submariners quickly began to score successes against their Royal Navy adversaries. Divers sent down to examine the wreck of HMS *Royal Oak*, sunk in Scapa Flow by Prien, discovered parts of a G7e electric torpedo. A complete example, which had luckily failed to explode, was recovered embedded in the hull of the child refugee ship SS *Volendam*, and more G7e torpedoes were found on board *U 570* when she surrendered to British forces in 1941. But the British had no tactical requirement for a slow torpedo, and high speed was their priority in view of the paucity of German warship targets.

When, tardily, it was appreciated that Royal Navy submarines in the Mediterranean could well profit from the use of wakeless torpedoes, development of a British electric torpedo was begun, but with a low priority. The weapons were eventually produced too late for use in the Mediterranean, and when they were despatched to the Pacific theatre they were never fired in anger before the war ended. They would, however, be used as the starting point for the successful post-war British electric torpedoes described in the following chapters.

Meanwhile, the German U-boat crews began to suffer the first of a series of frustrating failures. In the battle for Norway, U-boat torpedoes set to run under their target failed to explode, or detonated prematurely some distance from the ship. The deep running was eventually traced to faulty design of the depth mechanisms, which were subject to derangement if the air pressure inside the U-boat was higher than normal, for example after venting air into the interior. The designers of the magnetic influence exploders had failed to take into account the different properties of the Earth's magnetic field in the northerly waters off Norway.

These combined failures saved many British warships from destruction, and in at least one case, led directly to the loss of the U-boat: on 14 September 1939 Gerhard Glattes in *U 39* fired three torpedoes at the carrier HMS *Ark Royal*, only to have them explode prematurely. Alerted by the prematures, *Ark Royal*'s escorting destroyers hunted down and sank *U 39*, the first boat to be lost during the Second World War. This and other catastrophic failures off Norway had a devastating effect on the morale of the German crews. Dönitz, the commander of the U-boats, designated Rear Admiral Kummetz to investigate, and several officers responsible for the faulty designs were court-martialled.

British duplex exploders, incorporating contact detonators as well as magnetic influence devices, were prone to the same problems. This was fortunate for the crew of the cruiser HMS *Sheffield*, engaged in shadowing the German battleship *Bismarck* in May 1941. When she was attacked in error by Swordfish torpedo bombers whose crews had mistaken her for the *Bismarck*, she was saved when several magnetic influence exploders went off prematurely.

In the Pacific the IJN made no such mistakes with their torpedoes, beginning with the excellent Type 91 aircraft torpedoes described in detail in Chapter 7. By contrast the Allies long remained completely unaware of the oxygen-fuelled Type 93, 24in torpedoes fired from cruisers and destroyers. It left no wake, and in early surface battles such as in the Java Sea was often fired in salvoes at very long range. When their ships were sunk or seriously damaged by devastating underwater explosions, the Allied crews put the damage down to mines, or nearby Japanese submarines working in conjunction with their surface forces – as the British had tried to do in the Great War.

In later actions in narrow waters such as the seas around Guadalcanal, the crews of the Japanese cruisers and destroyers profited from the high speed of the wakeless Type 93s, typically 48 knots out to 20,000m. And when a Type 93 hit its unsuspecting victim, the explosive effect of its 490kg (1078lbs) warhead was devastating.

The smallest of the oxygen-fuelled torpedoes, the 18in Type 97, designed for use by midget submarines, still carried an effective warhead. One of these Type 97s may even have struck USS *Oklahoma* at Pearl Harbor, hastening her sinking and ensuring she capsized instead of ending up on an even keel like the other torpedoed battleships at Pearl (see Chapter 22). The Type 97 Model 2 was used from 1942 with an important modification. Because of the impossibility of recharging the first air bottles when the torpedoes were loaded in the tubes of the midget submarine, the torpedoes were modified to run on oxygen-enriched air, with 38 per cent oxygen instead of 100 per cent. This meant that the problematic first air bottles could be eliminated, the 38 per cent oxygen mixture being safe to use for engine starting. A minor advantage was that the engine slide valves could now be coated in lubricant to prolong their working lives. In all the pure oxygen models no lubrication could be used on the valves, which typically had to be changed after only three practice runs. The modified Type 97s went into action against Allied ships in Madagascar and in Sydney Harbour. Examination of a Type 97 which had missed its target at Sydney revealed the old problem of maintenance when loaded externally – the gimbals of the gyro had rusted and caused the torpedo to deviate off course.

In 1942 production of the Type 92 electric 21in torpedo for submarines was restarted. It was slower than the oxygen-fuelled Type 95 but still capable of a respectable 30 knots out to 7000m (7655yds). This would form the basis of the Type 10 Kaiten human torpedo, following the example of the use of the Type 93 power unit in the Type 1 Kaiten already described in Chapter 2.

The Type 93 was redesigned to start on an oxygen–kerosene fuel mixture, inhibited from exploding by the injection of carbon tetrachloride. The internal rearrangement, which omitted the first air bottle, allowed the fitting of a much larger warhead with 780kg (1716lbs) of explosive. Luckily for the Allies, none of these Type 93 Model 3 torpedoes would go into service before the war ended. Examples of the extensive damage caused by the warhead of a standard Type 93 torpedo can be seen in Part IV.

Compared with the successes scored by the surface ships, the results obtained by the Japanese submarine force were disappointing, not from any fault with the torpedoes, but because of their tactical deployment. Japanese submariners were ordered to sink heavily escorted warships, in order to reduce Japan's numerical inferiority, instead of concentrating on troop transports and supply ships. Despite valiant efforts, and crippling losses, during the entire Pacific conflict the large fleet of Japanese submarines succeeded in sinking only two carriers (one of which was the already crippled *Yorktown*), one light carrier and one escort carrier, one heavy cruiser (the unescorted *Indianapolis*) and one light cruiser, two destroyers and two destroyer escorts, and four submarines. These relatively modest results were doomed to make little impression on the overwhelming US Navy forces deployed against Japan.

At the same time, the development of homing torpedoes and magnetic influence exploders, both of which would have been extremely valuable in combating escort vessels, was begun but abandoned. As with their ambitious aircraft production plans, the Japanese empire was simply not producing sufficient numbers of trained engineers to carry these projects through to completion. By the time they realised that their tactics of prioritising attacks on warships had allowed the Americans to tighten the noose around the home islands, it was too late to do anything but prepare to die heroically in suicide aircraft, exploding motor boats and human torpedoes.

The US Navy's great torpedo scandal

When the USA entered the Second World War there was a severe shortage of modern torpedoes for submarines. Even in 1942 many boats sailed from Pearl outfitted with old Mark 10 torpedoes, or with destroyer Mark 15s fitted with shorter warheads and muzzle-loaded into their rear torpedo tubes.

As a reaction to the attack on Pearl Harbor the US submarine fleet was immediately launched into an unrestricted war on Japanese warships and merchant ships. The sixty-six live torpedoes fired by US submarines during the month of December 1941 alone compares with the eleven fired against U-boats in the Great War and a very small number expended in live test firings. The latter was one of the causes of the severe problems which would plague the US submarine fleet well into the summer of 1943.

Submarine commanders returning from patrols began to report that their Mark 14 (and even the older Mark 10) torpedoes were clearly seen to be running straight and true, but they had passed well below the target vessel, meaning they were running much deeper than the depths set into the control mechanism. The Mark 14s with their top-secret influence exploder more often than not failed to go off, even when the torpedo passed beneath the target's keel, and some even exploded prematurely.

Even more disconcerting were the reports that when a torpedo ran straight and true and struck the target, far too often the warhead would fail to explode. The worst example was an attack by the USS *Tinosa* on a Japanese whaler, the *Tonan Maru 3*. Torpedo after torpedo was launched, up to fifteen in total, and all were observed to hit, but not one exploded. Some were seen to rebound from the target's hull and leap into the air. It is estimated that of all US torpedoes fired up to the summer of 1943, 70 per cent were duds.

When such disastrous results were passed on up the line, the reaction from the ordnance establishment (BuOrd) was that there was no problem with the torpedoes; therefore, the fault had to lie with the submarine crews. This blinkered attitude contributed to the disappointing performance of US submarines during the whole of 1942 and the first half of 1943. If the 70 per cent of duds had actually exploded, the rapid advance of the Japanese invasion forces might have been slowed or curtailed, and the Pacific War significantly shortened.

The first problem was with depth control. On 5 January BuOrd advised that the Mark 10 torpedo, dating from the Great War period and still in use in 'S'-class boats, appeared to be running some 4ft deeper than set. It seems that this discrepancy was caused by the difference in weight between practice heads and warheads, an unbelievable situation when one thinks that all practice heads used for training and, in particular, calibrating the running of service torpedoes should have had the exact same hydrodynamic characteristics as the warhead which would replace them in action. Otherwise the training exercise was meaningless. In addition, it is true that the age of the Mark 10s, the oldest of which had entered service in

1915, might have been a contributing factor, with the springs in the depth mechanisms losing tension over the years. However, realistic testing, including the use of catcher nets, would quickly have identified such problems. Net testing was never carried out prior to the Second World War.

The higher speed Mark 14 suffered from a separate problem, in that the positioning of the water inlet of the hydrostatic depth-keeper valve in the torpedo meant it was adversely affected by the high-speed water flow over the torpedo casing. To make things worse, the depth recorder device was affected by the same problem, and registered a correct depth even when the torpedo ran too low. When finally this problem had been identified, the hydrostatic valve was repositioned inside the free-flooding rear balance chamber, which resolved the problem. Again, if the problem had been accepted in early 1942, rapid redesign measures could have been implemented.

The BuOrd began by accepting that perhaps the Mark 14s were running 4ft lower than set, based on their findings with the old Mark 10. Submarine commanders continued to report deep runners passing under their target, and it was not until the operational units carried out their own impromptu tests with catcher nets at Frenchman's Bay in Australia on 20 June 1942 that it was proved the Mark 14s were running as much as 11ft deeper than set, not 4ft. The BuOrd still refused to accept these results, and it took the personal intervention of Admiral King in August 1942 to oblige BuOrd to investigate, when they found the Mark 14 ran 10ft deeper than planned. Modification kits were sent out, and the torpedoes so modified were identified by the suffix 'A', as in the Mark 14 Mod 3A.

The deep running having been identified and action having been initiated to rectify it, the next problem to be examined concerned the Mark 6 magnetic influence exploder. The British and German navies had already experienced difficulties with this type of exploder, and both had deactivated them. The design object was to initiate warhead explosion beneath the keel of the target ship by using the difference in the Earth's magnetic field caused by the ferrous metal of the ship overhead. The difficulty arose because these differences varied according to latitude, and also because warships in particular were being degaussed following the introduction of the magnetic mine early in the Second World War. Because the Commander of Submarines for the Southwest Pacific, Captain Ralph Christie, had been involved with the development of the Mark 6 exploder and implicitly believed in its advantages, it was not until late 1943 that instructions were sent out to deactivate the magnetic influence aspect of the exploder.

Long before then, submarine commanders had been reporting the third major fault, that even when the torpedo struck fair and square it failed to explode. Again the BuOrd would not acknowledge this failing, until Vice Admiral Charles Lockwood authorised trial firing of live torpedoes against a cliff on Hawaii. Of three torpedoes fired, one failed to explode, and after a dangerous recovery operation the exploder was dismantled, and was found to have distorted on impact, jamming the firing pin. The same type of impact exploder that had functioned satisfactorily in the 33.5-knot Mark 13 aerial torpedo was not strong enough to withstand impacts at the 46.3 knots of the Mark 14. Again, realistic test launches, or even the simulation of live launches using live exploders, had simply not been carried out during the cash-strapped 1930s. Fixes were applied, and the Mark 14s began the systematic destruction of Japanese naval and merchant ships at an impressive rate.

It was suspected that identical failures had occurred in the destroyer Mark 15 torpedo, which was virtually identical apart from a larger warhead. Due to the nature of high-speed destroyer surface torpedo attacks, such as the night actions around Guadalcanal, more misses were to be expected than with the slow, calculated submarine approach. Nevertheless, the same modifications that had been implemented for the Mark 14 were also applied to the Mark 15. By the time they went into effect, the US destroyer force would have few remaining opportunities to use their torpedoes. But a major success came in the Surigao Strait in 1944, as related in Chapter 22.

USN developments

Three important torpedo developments during the Second World War implemented by the US Navy were the electric torpedo, the homing torpedo and the hydrogen peroxide torpedo.

Following their abortive essay in the Great War, the electric Mark 18 torpedo was finally developed as a result of studies of captured German G7e torpedoes. The basic problem to be solved was producing an electric motor of high power, yet small enough to fit inside the shell of a torpedo. To do this, traditional construction requirements were relaxed, accepting temporary overheating and sparking commutators, not fatal in view of the intended short run to the target. Practice runs would involve refurbishment or replacement of the motor. By these means the motor weight was reduced from between 500lbs and 1000lbs (227–454kg) down to only 250lbs (113kg), the same weight as the electric motor in the

German G7e used as a model. Although slow, it was cheap to produce and accurate, and left no wake to lead escorts back to the firing point. Introduced in 1943, some 9000 would be produced, and the Mark 18 would go on to sink around a million tons of Japanese shipping before the war ended.

A modification of the Mark 24 mine (see Chapter 8) for submarine use, with wooden strakes running along its sides to allow for launching the 19in torpedo from standard tubes, resulted in the homing torpedo Mark 27, popularly known as the 'Cutie'. One basic change incorporated a 'floor switch' instead of a 'ceiling switch'. The latter prevented the Mark 24 from attacking surface ships, the former prevented the Cutie from attacking its own launch submarine. Of the 106 fired against enemy escorts, thirty-three hit, and twenty-four of these sank the target, the other nine being damaged.

A full 21in diameter homing torpedo used before the end of the Second World War by the US Navy was the Mark 28, with a 585lb (265kg) warhead; fourteen were launched against escorts, and four hit.

Being at the receiving end of the Japanese Type 93 torpedo spurred the navy into resuscitating its pre-war plans for production of the Navol torpedo, and in addition to the planned destroyer Mark 17, a new Mark 16 was developed for submarines. As a result of the savings in weight of propulsion components, allowing for a larger warhead, and the higher efficiency of the fuel, the Navol

Mark 16 Mod 1 achieved a range of 11,000yds (10,058m) at 46.2 knots compared with 4500yds (4115m) for the Mark 14. Several hundred of each mark were produced before the war ended but none were fired in anger.

One development shared by the British and the Americans was the introduction of a powerful new explosive for warheads. Torpex, introduced in 1943, was a mixture of 42 per cent RDX (cyclonite), 40 per cent TNT and 18 per cent powdered aluminium. Its use in torpedoes was desirable because the addition of aluminium increased the duration of the explosive pulse, enhancing the destructive underwater effect.

German torpedoes

In 1939 the standard German torpedo used by U-boats, surface ships and S-boats was the 21in G7a, developed from the G7 of the Great War. It differed from the torpedoes of most other navies by burning decalin (dec-ahydronaphthalene) instead of kerosene. It was fitted with the 'Fiume' tail. The early models had four-bladed propellers but later models had six-bladed. Starting in 1938, the initial production of the G7a or 'Ato' required about 3730 man-hours. By 1943 the process had been streamlined, and production took just 1707 man-hours. Similarly, between 1939 and 1943 the Germans managed to reduce the amount of non-ferrous metals used in the G7a as follows: copper reduced from 370kg to 169kg; tin from 61kg to 22kg, and nickel from 46kg to just 2kg.

The G7a formed the basis for the G7e electric torpedo. This was similar in shape except for an 'RL' form of tail. Compared with the 2300 G7a thermal torpedoes fired by the Kriegsmarine (including surface ships and S-boats) up to the end of January 1945, 7000 electric G7e models had been fired, mostly by U-boats, showing the importance of this wakeless model. It was, of course, much cheaper to produce, using materials and labour not normally required for torpedo production. It did, however, have one special requirement: while the boat was on patrol,

The tail of a 'Cutie' showing the wooden strakes. (Photo courtesy of Nancy Richards of the USS *Bowfin* Submarine Museum and Park, Hawaii)

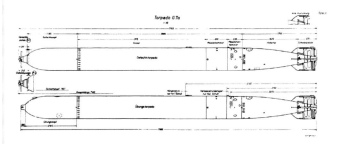

The standard thermal-engined G7a torpedo of the Second World War, above with warhead, below with exercise head.

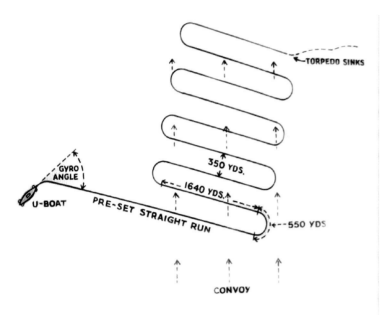

A typical FAT pattern. (Drawing from 'The Admiralty's appreciation of the German U-boat force', June 1944)

the batteries needed constant heating to 30°C, otherwise the range performance was seriously affected. Because of this, the G7e could not be carried in the upper deck storage compartments of U-boats. Both types could be preset to run a pattern course, but on the G7e the battery was changed from 93 amp/hours to 125 amp/hours. This gave it a range of 8200yds (7500m) at 30 knots.

The FAT ('*Federapparattorpedo*' or 'spring-operated torpedo') version was a pattern-runner introduced in 1942 to attack dense convoy formations; it ran a wandering course with regular 180-degree turns. It was best suited for beam firing rather than from dead ahead. The U-boat crew would input the chosen pattern using a control panel. From the end of 1942 onwards it was manufactured at the rate of roughly one hundred per month.

LUT ('*Lagenunabhangigertorpedo*' or 'torpedo independent of target inclination') was a more sophisticated version of the FAT, introduced in early 1944, with more variable patterns, but was only used operationally towards the end of the war. Some sources mention problems with input spindles refusing to detach on launch, leading to hot running in the tube.

The introduction of a homing torpedo had been expected by the Allies, but nevertheless its effect was a great shock. The G7e electric torpedo was virtually silent compared with the thermal-engined type, and it was this feature which permitted the successful development of passive acoustic homing. Experiments in Germany had begun in 1935, and the first homing torpedo, T4 'Falke' ('falcon') was issued to the Kriegsmarine in January 1943.

Of around a hundred produced, some thirty were used. It was soon replaced by the superior T5 'Zaunkönig' ('wren'), known to the Allies as the GNAT (German naval acoustic torpedo). The T5 was designed for use against escort vessels moving at between 12 and 19 knots, the preferred speed for an Asdic search. The T5 carried four hydrophones in a flat-nosed version, or two behind a round-nosed Bakelite cap. The cap was filled with glycerine and ethylene glycol to ensure good acoustic transmissions to the hydrophones. After launching, the U-boat usually went deep and silent, to avoid attracting its own T5. Although two U-boats were suspected of having been sunk by their T5s, post-war analysis revealed that in fact they had been sunk by Allied surface and air forces.

It is believed that a total of 640 T5s were fired during the Second World War, achieving a hit rate of 6 per cent, owing to the widespread introduction of countermeasures by the escorts. Towards the end of the war an improved version, the Zaunkönig *2* was introduced, with variable settings intended to bypass escorts and strike at slower merchant ships, plus resistance to countermeasures. Only one boat was equipped before the war ended, and none were fired.

German projects

During the war the German navy was involved in over fifty torpedo research projects, which represented a huge investment in scarce time and resources. Among the projects which never went into production, but which would form the basis for many post-war developments were the following.

'Lerche' was a system of torpedo control using hydrophones in the torpedo that relayed the sounds via wires to a controller in the launch submarine. He could differentiate between the propeller sounds of a target and the noise produced by a Foxer decoy, and steer his torpedo accordingly.

'Boie' was a system using active sonar pinging instead of passive hydrophones. The Germans conducted a great deal of research into differentiating between different echoes, such as those from the surface. Its successor was 'Geier' ('vulture'), with active sonar, ranging to 280yds (256m).

'Ibis' was a wake-follower homing torpedo, as was 'Fasen' ('pheasant') which detected the echoes from a ship's wake but then went into a preset search pattern. 'Marchen' was a magnetic homing torpedo. Finally, in 1944 the Germans built and tested a tandem body torpedo propelled, not by a conventional propeller, but by a 'flapping wing' carried between the two hulls. It worked well in trials, but obviously could not be launched from a

U-boat, although air-dropping was a possibility.

In a different class altogether was the 'Ingolin' range of torpedoes using hydrogen peroxide as a source of oxygen, based on research by Dr Walther. The 'Steinwall' powered by a turbine engine reached the long range of 24,000yds (22,000m) and was intended for use with anti-convoy LUT programming.

The largest German torpedo design was the Junkers M5, using a closed-circuit oxygen power source. It was 29.6in diameter with a length of 36ft. The engine produced around 600bhp, but every test model sank, and the project was abandoned.

In the Atlantic, the balance had swung in completely the opposite direction to the Pacific: in the latter part of the Second World War, the surface escorts and patrol aircraft had come to dominate the German submarines. Despite their homing torpedoes, they had been driven from the

Atlantic by superior Allied ASW technology, supported by carrier- and shore-based aircraft. The true submarine boats, the fast schnörkel-equipped Type XXIs, were coming into service at the very end of the war in Europe, when it was far too late to affect the outcome.

A G7a late model with two six-bladed propellers shown alongside the Biber preserved in Gosport. (Photo by the author, courtesy of the Royal Navy Submarine Museum, Gosport)

CHAPTER 7

Aerial Torpedoes

Under the impetus of total war, by the end of the conflict of 1914–1918 the early, primitive, flimsy aircraft had developed out of all recognition. The types of torpedo bomber will be described in the following part, but here we will examine the actual torpedoes they carried into action.

The first requirement was for light weight, so the Short seaplanes sent to the Dardanelles by the British in 1915 could at first only carry the RGF Mark X 14in model. These had been made in 1897, and they were of the older, non-heater type, but still adequate for aircraft dropping. Even so, the planes found it difficult to take off from water carrying a torpedo, and the observer/rear gunner was often left behind. With more powerful engines in later models, the 18in RGF Mark IX could be carried aloft, and its much larger warhead did more damage; 18in was to remain the standard aerial torpedo size through to the end of the Second World War.

For their part the Germans experimented with torpedo-dropping planes, and designed special stand-off weapons to be carried by Zeppelins (see Part III).

In 1919 the US Navy began experimenting with torpedo planes, the first trials using the 18in Bliss-Leavitt Mark 7 Type D short torpedo designed to fit the tubes on older submarines. In May 1920 they experimented with the normal length Mark 7 Mod 5 torpedoes, dropped at 50–55 knots. One torpedo dropped from a height of 18ft (5m) was undamaged while another dropped from 30ft (9m) suffered severe damage. The Mark 7s were accordingly strengthened to survive the shock of water entry. They were also fitted with an exploder safety pin that was pulled out on dropping.

Mark 7 Mod 1A torpedoes were used in the mass torpedo practice run conducted against the battleship *Arkansas* on 22 September 1922. Attacking from both sides over a twenty-five-minute period, the aircraft dropped seventeen torpedoes at ranges between 500 and 1000yds (450 to 900m), and scored eight hits. In 1924, trials showed that the Mark 7 could be successfully dropped at an airspeed of 95 knots and a height of 32ft (10m).

The following year the US Navy began development of a torpedo which would gain fame in the Second World War, the 22.4in Mark 13. Designed specifically for use from aircraft, because of its increased diameter the Mark 13 could not be launched from the standard 21in

torpedo tube. Later in the Second World War, however, it would be fitted to PT-boats, launching from a roll-off rack (see Part III).

On the outbreak of war in 1939, the 18in torpedo was standard in the air forces of Britain (Mark XII), Germany (LF5), Italy (Fiume model), Norway, and Japan (Type 91). The French alone opted for a smaller model, the 15.7in aerial torpedo Model 1926.

Similar to the Japanese, and to a lesser extent the British, the Germans were bedevilled by disruptive inter-service rivalries. The most serious was that between the Luftwaffe and the Kriegsmarine. The nascent German navy had no requirement for torpedoes smaller than 21in, but the Luftwaffe did. The latter were obliged to turn to the Norwegians for the design of the 18in torpedo they would use in the coming conflict. In 1934 they purchased torpedoes from the Hørten factory, and set up a modest production facility for them. They also sought Italian aircraft torpedoes, and in 1942 Hitler gave priority to the production of aircraft torpedoes. By 1945 some ten thousand had been produced, but in 1939 only the Norwegian 18in design was in service.

Both the British and the Japanese practised torpedo dropping in shallow water, to attack an enemy fleet at anchor. For the Taranto raid, the Fleet Air Arm knew they would have problems because of the shallow harbour, so they arranged a wire drum under the nose of the Swordfish, the wire being attached to the nose of the torpedo, pulling it up as it was launched, so that the torpedo hit the water in a belly flop rather than a nose dive. To stabilise it further they had used breakaway wooden tail fins.

The Japanese Assistant Naval Attaché in Berlin, Lieutenant Commander Takeshi Naito flew to Taranto to assess the raid, and later discussed his findings with Commander Fuchida, who would go on to lead the attack on Pearl Harbor.

THE JAPANESE TYPE 91 TORPEDO
'Type 91' refers to the date when the design was started, '91' being the Japanese year 2591, or 1931 AD. When in 1944 (Japanese year 2604) the Type 91 was simplified for ease of production and strengthened, the new model was known as the Type 4.

The Type 91 aircraft torpedo was the model which sank or disabled a large number of US ships at Pearl

A salvaged 18in Type 91 torpedo used in the attack on Pearl Harbor under examination. (US Navy photo)

Harbor. The Japanese claimed that just seven Type 91s had been used to sink HMS *Prince of Wales*, and seventeen were thought to have struck HMS *Repulse*, explaining why the latter vessel, dating from the Great War, sank so quickly. Some were of the original type with an explosive charge of 330lbs (150kg), and some the Modification 2, with a charge of 450lbs (204kg).

In 1942 the Mod 3 carried an increased charge of 528lbs (240kg), the Mod 4 (Strong –see below) of 1944, 675lbs (306kg), and the final Modification 7 (Strong) brought the charge to 920lbs (417kg), or almost three times the explosive charge of December 1941. The explosive used was Type 97, being 60 per cent TNT and 40 per cent hexyl. The exploder was an inertia type fitted in the top centre-line of the torpedo, and armed by water travel.

The following US battle damage report of the torpedo

hits on USS *Houston* shows the kind of damage inflicted by these 18in aircraft torpedoes.

On 14 October 1944 off Formosa, at 1641 the 10,000-ton *Cleveland* class cruiser USS *Houston* was heeling to port to make a high speed turn to starboard when she was hit amidships by an aircraft torpedo, which detonated in contact with the bottom. Her No 1 propeller shaft was broken, and the drag on the propeller pulled the broken shaft 5$\frac{1}{2}$ft [1.7m] towards the stern, damaging the bulkheads and flooding an engine room. *Houston* took on a 15-degree list to starboard, and her main deck was awash when she rolled. Some 6400 tons of seawater had entered the hull.

By midday on 16 October her crew had successfully undertaken damage control measures and reduced her list to 8 degrees. They had succeeded in pumping out 1700 tons of water, and the main deck was no longer under water when she rolled. Unfortunately, at 1348 a second Japanese aerial torpedo hit her, this time in the stern. *Houston* took in another 1100 tons of seawater, but her list to starboard was slightly counteracted and reduced to 6 degrees.

She was towed to Ulithi for temporary repairs, where blankets and lifejackets were stuffed into the gap made by the propeller shaft tube, allowing the flooded engine room to be pumped out. Critical bulkheads were shored up, wooden cofferdams were placed around hatch coamings, and a patch was welded over the hole in the hangar floor. She then proceeded to a dry dock at Manus where she was sufficiently patched up to return to the States.

In 1944, in order to punch through the multi-layer torpedo defence system (TDS) fitted to US capital ships, the Japanese introduced the 'V' warhead, which was a shaped charge type. They tested it against a multiple compartment TDS of the type fitted to the US *Colorado*-class battleships, and the charge punched completely through all layers of the TDS. However, only three of these 'V' heads were used in combat before the war ended.

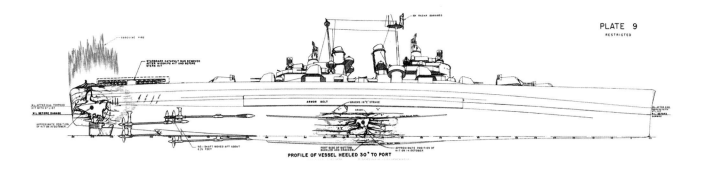

PLATE 9
RESTRICTED

PROFILE OF VESSEL HEELED 30° TO PORT

The damage to the hull bottom and the stern area of *Houston*, showing where the aircraft fuel in the hangar had started a major fire aft.

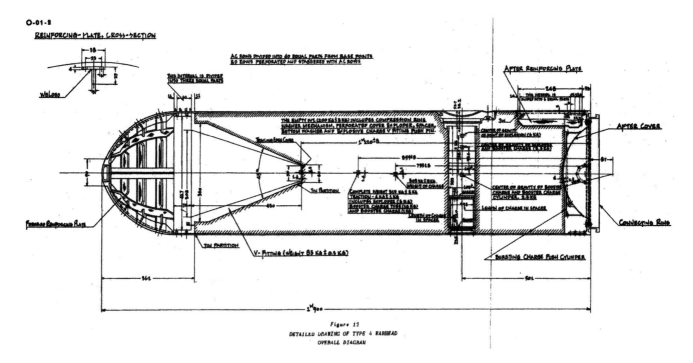

Figure 12
DETAILED DRAWING OF TYPE 4 WARHEAD
OVERALL DIAGRAM

All Type 91 and Type 4 torpedoes were powered by an eight-cylinder radial engine, producing 210bhp and a non-adjustable speed of 41 or 42 knots depending on the model. Cylinders were of phosphor-bronze and the pistons of bronze. The contra-rotating propellers had four blades. To prevent damage to the warhead on dropping, approximately the first 24in (600mm) of the torpedo nose were covered with a rubber sheath 0.4in (10mm) thick, which would shatter into small fragments when it hit the water. They had captured and examined several US Mark 13s with the wooden nose shroud fitted, but Rear Admiral Shoji Naruse, head of the team which designed the Type

The hollow charge 'V' warhead for the Type 91. This type would reappear during the Cold War to combat double-hulled Soviet nuclear submarines. (Drawing from US Naval Technical Mission to Japan, *Japanese Torpedoes and Tubes*, Article 2, 'Aircraft Torpedoes')

91, told American interrogators in 1945 that he did not approve of such a fitting.

The Japanese preferred a length/diameter ratio of 11 or 12:1, and they considered the US Mark 13 to have a relatively poor shape for good underwater stability. They had the experience of testing the very large 27.5in torpedo

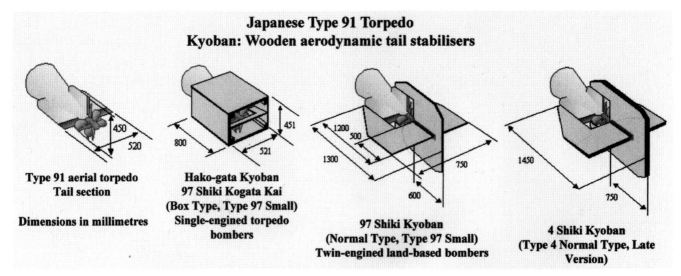

The Type 91 wooden tail fins. (Modified from the original Wikipedia article produced by user 'Shun Zero', the web name of a talented young software engineer in Japan)

manufactured for them in around 1900 by Whitehead in Fiume, which had suffered from poor underwater stability due to the same problem.

They had tested Type 91 torpedoes with eight tail fins, which gave steadier water travel characteristics than the four-fin tail, but they discovered that recovery from the initial dive took too long. From 1940 the Japanese had fitted small anti-roll flippers to the sides of their aerial torpedoes, controlled by the second gyro, and reported they were a success. Before this innovation, they had been forced to try to counter rolling by only partially filling the warhead space, to keep the centre of gravity as low as possible. With the anti-rolling stabilisers they could now fill the warhead with explosives, which greatly increased its destructive effect.

The wooden tail appendages were added to stabilise the torpedo after release from the aircraft. They also reduced the risk of the torpedo entering the water rolled slightly to one side, when the horizontal control surfaces would act as rudders and deviate the torpedo from its course. The plywood structure was offered to the tail diagonally, passed over and in front of the fins then pulled back into place, being held by air pressure. For aircraft that carried their torpedo internally, a smaller frame was used.

On water entry, the weak points of the aerial torpedo were the warhead joint, and the torpedo body shell of the engine room/buoyancy chamber. If the entry angle was reduced because of a high-speed/low-altitude drop, the Type 91 risked buckling in the area of the engine/buoyancy chamber. The Modification 3 (Improved) strengthened this area with T-section longitudinal ribs. In Modification 3 (Strong) these reinforcing ribs were changed from T-section to I-section. When the revised Type 4 went into production, it was again reinforced, and maximum launch speed was increased to 400 knots. All the Type 91 and Type 4 torpedoes were controlled by two air-blast, air-sustained gyros. One controlled the steering and the other the anti-roll stabilisers.

The launching procedure was as follows: a gear wheel moved by a rack on the aircraft on release opened a small air valve to start the gyros, then on water entry a flap opened a second larger valve admitting air to the engine; the horizontal stabilisers were locked in the 'up' position for the first 10m of the water run, after which they were freed off to move normally; to prevent damage on water entry, both propellers could freewheel until engine power was applied.

The IJN experimented with an oxygen-fuelled aircraft torpedo, the Type 94, with a 250bhp engine and a speed of 45 knots. It was discontinued when they realised that the main advantage of using oxygen, with all the attendant inconveniences, was extreme long range, and this was not required of an aircraft torpedo. They also built three prototypes of a large 23in diameter aircraft torpedo, the Type M, but dropped development when the new aircraft intended to carry it did not materialise in numbers.

Late in the war the IJN experimented with the Type QR, a standard Type 91 torpedo modified for attacks on submerged submarines. On water entry it was designed to circle and descend at the same time. The initial diameter of the spiral was about 300yds (290m), and the torpedo could continue this down to some 320ft (100m); fifty were made in 1945 and some issued to units but no record of their use has survived.

Another two anti-submarine spiral attack types were tested, the Model 6 and the Model 7, both unpowered, the first with a steel warhead and wooden body, the second with an all-steel lengthened body. Both had full-length wooden wings glued the full length of the body. Detonation was to be by proximity fuse. Testing was incomplete at the war's end.

US NAVY MARK 13 TORPEDO

In common with the Japanese, the US Navy had retained full control over its air arm. The Mark 13 torpedo was to become a devastating weapon carried into action by the highly trained US Navy torpedo bomber pilots. But in the early days it acquired a bad reputation for erratic running or simply sinking without reason. One Grumman TBF pilot described it as apt to run 'like a wild hippopotamus with its head above water'. After being far too often on the receiving end of the Japanese Type 91 which could be, and was, dropped fast and high, the US Navy settled down to devise solutions.

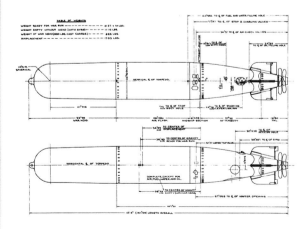

General arrangement drawing of the torpedo Mark 13-2. (From *Ordnance Pamphlet No 629(A)*, US Naval Torpedo Station)

The modifications are shown in Part II, Chapter 14. A plywood drag ring was fixed around the warhead by a piece of wood wedged horizontally through the nose ring. It was an internally braced plywood tube, intended to increase air penetration and reduce the water entry shock by up to 40 per cent. The plywood structure broke away on water impact. It was this construction that Japanese Rear Admiral Naruse criticised, as the wood fragments risked being sucked into the propellers. A shroud ring around the tail helped prevent 'hook' or veering on water entry. In addition, a plywood rectangular box around the torpedo tail was held in place by wooden dowels, which sheared on water impact, shedding the plywood.

On leaving the plane, the starter mechanism began to run up the gyro and start the engine on compressed air only, to avoid the risk of the engine turbines overheating and burning out during the long air travel. A water delay valve prevented the fuel from reaching the engine. It was wired shut with copper wire on loading the torpedo underneath the aircraft. On impact with the water, the wire was broken and the main engine combustion cycle started. Similarly, the exploder was armed by a water impeller. To avoid the slipstream turning the impeller in the air, it too was wired shut with annealed soft copper wire, designed to shear on water impact.

By 1944/45 the optimum torpedo drop point was from 800ft at a speed of 260 knots, a huge improvement over the early war low and slow approach which was so dangerous for the aircrews. The US Navy made a training film in 1945, and the guidance it contained is described in Part IV.

PENTANE

Mark 21 Pentane was an experimental British air-dropped electric torpedo for anti-submarine work. The design was started 1947, after the collapse of the futuristic 'Z-weapons' programme, and by the mid 1950s had produced a working weapon system. Unfortunately, as a standard-sized 21in torpedo it had been designed for torpedo bombers, which had been phased out of service by the time it appeared. Helicopters of the era were not powerful enough to carry it, so Pentane was dropped in favour of the lightweight American Marks 43 and 44 anti-submarine torpedoes. One example survives in store at Explosion in Gosport.

For later developments, the lightweight homing torpedoes launched from fixed wing and rotary wing aircraft, and drones, as well as from surface ships, see Chapter 8.

Pentane's tail unit. (Photo by the author, courtesy of Explosion, the Museum of Naval Firepower)

The Modern Torpedo Post-Second World War

Just as the aircraft carrier came to supplant the battleship as the decisive capital ship during the course of the Second World War, so in the latter half of the twentieth century the submarine came to threaten the place of the aircraft carrier in its turn. And the principal weapon associated with the submarine is, of course, the torpedo.

The post-war period was to see the struggle between submarines and surface ships (plus aircraft) continue at a frenetic pace, without ever the two elements having had the chance to put their tactics and technologies to the ultimate test. The two sinkings by submarine in 1971 and 1982 were classic encounters in the Second World War style, initiated by modern submarines against obsolescent opponents. The American and Russian nuclear undersea and above-water fleets may have played their dangerous cat-and-mouse game throughout the Cold War, but they never fired on each other – as far as they admit.

The 1940s and 1950s saw a great deal of development work, building on the experience of designs which had first seen action during the Second World War, and this work has continued into the present century.

BRITISH EXPERIMENTAL TORPEDOES
Heyday

This was an experimental streamlined torpedo designed by Dr Barnes Wallis, inventor of the wartime 'dam-buster' bouncing bomb. The Heyday prototype was powered by a rocket motor fuelled by hydrogen peroxide and compressed air, constructed by a German scientist working at Vickers Armstrong. Laminar flow was a relatively new technique used during the war in the aircraft industry, and Wallis, one of its proponents, attempted to apply it to hydrodynamic research. With a standard torpedo shape of the 1950s, laminar flow could only be achieved around the curved nose section. The parallel body sides created turbulent flow. Barnes Wallis attempted to produce an experimental shape with a greatly increased area subject to laminar flow and therefore less skin friction, allowing a higher speed. The most he managed to achieve was laminar flow over just 28 per cent of the body, which in itself was a remarkable result.

Meanwhile, American studies revealed that laminar flow was extremely difficult to achieve and that the

The sectioned hull of Mark 12 Fancy, the hydrogen peroxide experimental torpedo copied from German models of the Second World War. (Photo by the author, courtesy of Explosion, the Museum of Naval Firepower)

slightest blemish or fixture ruined the effect. In addition, the exaggerated egg-like profile of Heyday made it completely impossible to launch from a submarine's torpedo tube and extremely difficult from the deck of a ship. Possibly it could have been used for air-launched torpedoes, but this was not pursued and the project lapsed. By good fortune Dr Wallis's original test vehicle has survived, and is on display in the torpedo gallery at Explosion in Gosport.

Examination of modern torpedo nose designs will reveal the extreme care used to ensure maximum laminar flow.

Fancy

This was the codename given to a British version of the wartime German Ingolin torpedoes fuelled by hydrogen peroxide. Instead of building a new torpedo designed to incorporate the special requirements of this highly volatile fuel, British scientists attempted to modify the existing Mark 8 torpedo, substituting the HTP tank and catalyst system for the air flask, to produce the Mark 12.

This make-do-and-mend approach inevitably led to disaster. Following the sinking of HM Submarine *Sidon*, and a second Mark 12 explosion on the firing range, the project was cancelled. Other countries that took a more innovative approach to the problem succeeded in producing workable HTP torpedoes, and they entered service with the Swedish and Russian navies – although it

is to be feared that the loss of *Kursk* may have resulted from the latest HTP incident. One example of Fancy is stored in the Aladdin's cave that is Explosion in Gosport.

Bidder

After the unfortunate Fancy affair, it is refreshing to describe a British success story. The Royal Navy began work in 1947 on a new homing torpedo based on captured German wartime examples. The electric battery-powered Bidder went into submarine and surface ship service as the Mark 20.

Grog

Harking back to the Brennan, and inspired by captured information on the German Spinne T10 torpedoes, the Royal Navy added a jettisonable wire spool to the tail of Bidder, and produced Grog, a wire-guided 21in submarine torpedo which went into service with the Royal Navy in 1966 as the Mark 23.

HEAVYWEIGHTS – NOVEL GUIDANCE AND PROPULSION SYSTEMS
Mark 45 (USN) ASTOR

Wire control was also used on the American Mark 45 torpedo, which first went into service in 1963, but for a different reason.

A cutaway demonstration model of the Mark 20 Bidder has been carefully restored by John Coker at Explosion in Gosport, and this photo shows the work nearing completion. (Photo by the author, courtesy of Explosion, the Museum of Naval Firepower)

A Mark 45 torpedo on display in Aiea, Hawaii. (Photo courtesy of Cliff, uploaded from flickr.com/photo/2856782503/2861264268)

Profiting from German wartime designs, the Cold War-era Russian nuclear boats were displaying high speed, allied to deep diving abilities. They were, however, noisy boats and could be detected and tracked by their US Navy shadows, but sonar bearings alone were insufficiently accurate to ensure a kill with conventional torpedoes of the day. The Mark 45 was therefore armed with a W34 low-yield (11 kilotons) tactical nuclear warhead, designed to ensure destruction of the enemy boat by a proximity detonation. To ensure that full control was kept over the release of the nuclear weapon, wire control was added to carry out the detonation. Target guidance signals could also be sent via the wire connection, but ASTOR had no onboard homing ability.

The Mark 45 was 19in (483mm) in diameter, and was launched silently from a standard 21in tube by allowing it to swim out. It was 227in (5.8m) long and weighed 2400lbs (1100kg). Powered by a seawater battery and a 160ehp electric motor, it could reach 40 knots and had a maximum range of 15,000yds (13,650m), uncomfortably close for any vessel launching a nuclear weapon.

In 1976 the Mark 45 was replaced in service by the Mark 48, which is still the current USN submarine torpedo. The nuclear warheads were removed from the Mark 45s and a conventional warhead fitted by Westinghouse. These so-called 'Freedom' torpedoes were offered for foreign sale without much success.

Tigerfish

The Royal Navy's Mark 24 Tigerfish was a 21in heavy torpedo powered by chloride silver/zinc oxide batteries, for a top speed of 35 knots for final run in to target and a maximum range of 22 nautical miles (39,000m) at low speed. Wire-guided to the point of the launch submarine's sonar target acquisition, it then used passive terminal sonar homing. A signal could be sent down the wire to make the Tigerfish switch between passive and active homing. It entered service in 1979.

Despite its ambitious capabilities, Tigerfish never lived up to expectations. Its guidance systems were hopelessly unreliable, and when HMS *Conqueror* was ordered to attack the *General Belgrano* in 1982, her commander opted to use the old traditional unguided Mark 8 torpedoes instead of his Tigerfish (see Part IV). Hampered by a lack of ultra-deep diving capability, Tigerfish was withdrawn in February 2004.

Propulsion systems

High-speed targets called for faster torpedoes, the rule of thumb requiring that the torpedo needs to possess a 50 per cent margin over the speed of the submarine it is attacking. Electric torpedoes were adequate for tracking down diesel-powered boats capable of 20 knots underwater, but nuclear boats running at 30 knots called for new propulsion systems.

An important innovation was the introduction of a new fuel for existing internal combustion torpedo engines, invented by Dr Otto Reitlinger, and accordingly called Otto fuel II. It has nothing in common with the 'Otto cycle' used to describe internal combustion engines, and is a powerful monopropellant. Otto fuel II is composed of the following synthetic chemicals (approximate percentages by weight): 76 per cent is a nitrated ester explosive propellant, propylene glycol dinitrate (PGDN); 1.5 per cent is a stabiliser, 2-nitrodiphenylamine; 22.5 per cent is a desensitiser, dibutyl sebacate.

A reddish-orange liquid, Otto fuel II is stable, not volatile, and needs no oxygen to initiate combustion: its three components will react among themselves when vaporised and heated. Its fuel energy density far surpasses that of the comparable-sized electric storage battery.

Mark 48 (USN)

One of the major torpedoes to use Otto fuel II is the long-lived Mark 48. It entered service in 1972, replacing the Mark 14 and Mark 37 torpedoes in the USN submarine fleet. Designed to combat the fast and deep-diving Soviet Alpha class, the Mark 48 has been continually developed and upgraded to keep it in the front line. Its swashplate piston engine is powered by Otto fuel II and operates a pump-jet propulsor. The Mod 6 variant of the 1990s significantly reduced the noise level of the engine, making the Mark 48 more difficult to detect by its target. The destruction potential of the warhead, which is exploded by a proximity fuse, is augmented by the explosion of remaining fuel.

Performance details of the latest ADCAP (advanced capabilities) version are classified, but it is rumoured to have a maximum diving depth of 800m (2625ft) and a top speed of around 55 knots. The Mark 48 can be wire-guided, and has onboard active and passive common broadband advanced sonar system (CBASS). The most recent upgrade was intended to equip it for operation in littoral waters. The pump jet minimises vibrations emanating from the propeller wash undulations impacting the torpedo fins. The pump-jet propulsion is used in modern hunter-killer submarines for the very same reason.

The current Russian heavyweight torpedoes include the propeller-driven HTP-fuelled 25.6in calibre Type 65, designed to attack US nuclear aircraft carriers and large merchant ships such as supertankers. It is reported that the explosion of one of the latter types was responsible for the loss of the *Kursk*.

Spearfish

This is the current Royal Navy heavyweight torpedo for anti-submarine and anti-ship use. Spearfish is a 21in torpedo 23ft (7m) long, weighing 4075lbs (1850kg). Powered by a Hamilton Sundstrand 21TP04 gas turbine engine driving a pump jet, Spearfish can reach a top speed of 80 knots over short distances, or run out to 30 nautical miles (54,000m) at low speed. Its Otto fuel II is mixed with hydroxyl ammonium perchlorate, which acts as an

An artist's impression of Spearfish underwater. (Image courtesy of BAE Systems)

A close-up of the tail section of a Spearfish, with its pump-jet propulsion unit. (Photo courtesy of BAE Systems)

oxidiser and improves the specific energy of the fuel. It is guided by wire from the launch submarine, then homes using active or passive onboard sonar, analysing the results in its own microprocessor which allows the torpedo to take autonomous tactical decisions.

Wake-following

Modern homing torpedoes with an anti-surface ship capability use wake-following to acquire and hit their ship target. Sensors in the head of the torpedo, which can be electronically directed upwards, are attuned to detect the edge of a ship's wake passing overhead, and to recognise the other edge of the wake, where the torpedo is programmed to execute a turn to follow the wake in a

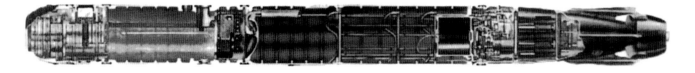

A sectioned view of the Mark 48 Mod ADCAP.

sinuous course, biased to the direction where it is narrower – that is, towards the stern of the target ship – until it is close enough to home onto the hull itself and pass beneath the keel to detonate. Other models have been developed which follow the wake directly, and these are the hardest to counter, because of the reduced closing time. A modern example of a wake-follower is the Russian 21in USGT pump-jet torpedo.

To counter wake-followers, defensive anti-torpedo torpedoes have been developed which launch from the target vessel's fantail (see Part III).

Shkval

The Russian VA-111 'Shkval' ('squall') rocket-propelled torpedo is an interesting development, but its supposed employment raises questions. After ejection from a normal 21in torpedo tube, Shkval quickly accelerates to its underwater cruising speed of some 200 knots. It can do this because the Russians have taken the problem of cavitation suffered by high-speed propellers, and turned it literally on its head, using a bubble carpet system first used on boat-hulled hovercraft in the 1960s and 1970s. By creating and ejecting from its nose a stream of supercavitating bubbles, the Shkval travels in this relatively frictionless medium, and is therefore capable of reaching speeds up to four times faster than older conventional torpedoes.

Touted as a rapid-reaction anti-torpedo defence, at a time when noisy Russian submarines were at risk of attack from the stealthier US Navy boats, it is clear the Shkval can be an effective rapid-response weapon to attack an enemy submarine which its launch boat has detected.

It was originally claimed to be designed to intercept an incoming torpedo and explode it well outside danger range. However, this would seem to be a misinterpretation of its capabilities. Assuming an accurate sonar fix, it could strike an enemy submarine before the latter could manoeuvre out of its way or launch against its own boat, but the very speed that is touted as an advantage is also its principal weakness. At 200 knots, it has no means of homing actively or passively. With even the best current sonar ranging allowing up to 15 degrees leeway, at the Shkval's maximum range of 12,000yds (11,000m) it

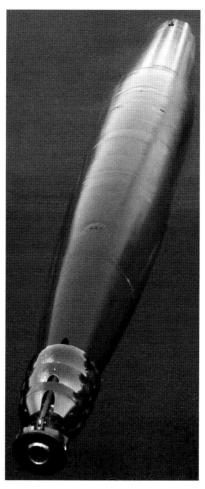

Shkval showing the special nose

would miss by 500yds (450m). The original Russian version had a nuclear warhead, which could still take out a target at that distance. However, how would the Russians have planned to trigger the warhead? For years it has been reported that they have produced a later version which, having reached the vicinity of an enemy submarine at high speed, will of necessity slow down to begin hunting. Of course, once it has acquired its target, there is always the possibility that it will then close at its original high speed to ensure a kill. But this is basically an anti-submarine employment, and the homing version has yet to make an appearance.

Anti-torpedo ability would need precision homing or guidance which the Shkval does not have during its high-speed run. The only way of ensuring destruction of an incoming torpedo at long range would be to provide Shkval with a small nuclear warhead, when the high-speed run is of advantage in distancing the launch submarine from the nuclear blast. Otherwise any modern high-speed torpedo with a nuclear warhead would do the job almost as well, and with the benefit of guidance.

It is thought to use spring-out stabiliser fins, which would need to project beyond the stream of bubbles to have

Shkval's main rocket orifice and its peripheral steering nozzles. On top is the guide bar and the gap for the torpedo stop. At the 5 o'clock position is the electronic socket for target information update and launch initiation.

any effect. In the photo of the tail nozzles, the tips of these fins can be seen retracted into the body. At the speed at which it travels through the water, Shkval needs a highly sophisticated rapid-reaction depth control system, as a slight up or down angle could quickly lead it to broach the surface or dive to crush depth. One further drawback is that the supercavitating action is extremely noisy and the Shkval can be detected from long range, allowing the target to launch hard-kill countermeasures and attempt to take evasive action.

LIGHTWEIGHT ANTI-SUBMARINE TORPEDOES

Although all the modern lightweight 12.75in anti-submarine torpedoes have a relatively small warhead, the ability to hit and hole a submarine which has gone deep is likely to prove fatal. And Sting Ray, MU90 and the US Mark 50 have shaped-charge warheads to punch through the spaced double-hulls of Russian boats. Most 12.75in torpedoes are powered by electric batteries, but the US Mark 46 uses an Otto fuel II reciprocating external combustion engine, and the Mark 50 Barracuda has a lithium/sulphur hexafluoride closed-cycle system which is shared with the Japanese GRX-4. The Russians, however, prefer the use of a solid-fuel rocket, for example in their APR-2E anti-submarine torpedo.

The MU90 has been sold to the navies of France, Germany, Italy, Denmark, Poland and Australia. It is the modern 12.75in diameter to fit the NATO standard launch tubes, and is 112in long (2.85m). Capable of diving to 1000m (3280ft), it has active or passive homing. Its electric batteries powering a pump jet enable it to sprint at up to 50 knots. It has an onboard profiling capability which allows it to scan and detect bottomed diesel-powered submarines. EuroTorp has begun development of an anti-torpedo hard-kill version.

The EuroTorp MU90 anti-submarine homing torpedo.

The EuroTorp MU90 anti-submarine homing torpedo.

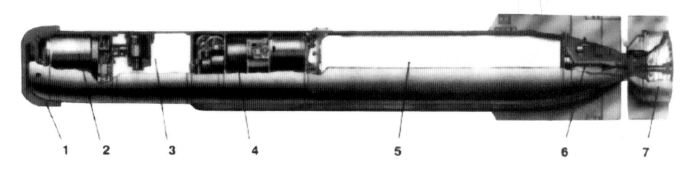

Russian APR-2E torpedo

1 = Protective fairing
2 = Homing system electronics
3 = Warhead
4 = Control system electronics
5 = Propulsion system
6 = Control surfaces mechanisms
7 = Brake parachute system

An artist's impression of Sting Ray underwater, launched from a helicopter. (Image courtesy of BAE Systems)

Sting Ray

Sting Ray is a lightweight anti-submarine homing torpedo to the standard 12.75in calibre, which entered service with the Royal Navy, the Royal Air Force, the Norwegian and the Thai navies. Powered by magnesium/silver chloride batteries driving a pump jet, it is capable of speeds up to 45 knots, and homes using active and passive sonar.

Mark 54 Mako LHT (USN)

The US Navy called for this latest homing torpedo to resolve problems with the older Mark 50, which had been given high performance (at high unit cost), to pursue deep-diving rapid Soviet submarines during the Cold War period, and the Mark 46, which was unsuitable for use in the shallow water environment of the littoral actions the US Navy sees as one of its primary roles in future.

By combining the homing systems and hollow-charge warhead of the Mark 50 Barracuda with the Otto fuel II propulsion system from the older Mark 46, Raytheon produced the Mark 54 Mako, originally known as the lightweight homing torpedo (LHT), at a relatively low unit cost compared with small production run European rivals. It has a top speed of 40 knots, which is adequate to hunt the diesel-powered submarines the US Navy is likely to encounter in coastal waters. Nuclear boats are too large to hide there, and cannot bottom in shallow water like the diesel boats, because of fears of blocking vital cooling

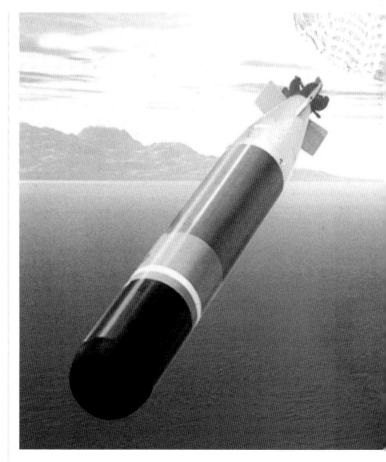

Mark 54 Mako. (Courtesy of Raytheon)

water inlets with seabed sediment. The Mark 54 shares with the latest Mark 48 ADCAP heavyweight a sophisticated software and hardware package built around a PowerPC 603e chip.

Mark 60 CAPTOR mine

With this weapon Robert Fulton's ideas of the mine and the torpedo came full circle. Fulton had envisaged his moored mines returning to the surface at preset intervals for routine maintenance. The Mark 60 'enCAPsulated TORpedo' could be laid by plane, ship or submarine at depths down to 3000ft (910m) where it would lie in wait for the signature of a passing submarine. The aluminium casing would then open and deploy a standard Mark 46 homing torpedo which would begin hunting the target submarine.

Technicians load a Mark 60 CAPTOR into a B-52G at Loring AFB in 1989. (USAF, photo # DF-ST-90-11649)

Part II
Torpedo Launchers and Delivery Systems

CHAPTER 9

Spar Torpedo Boats, Drop Collars, Launch Troughs and Rails

SPAR TORPEDO BOATS

Spar torpedoes were first carried into action during the War of 1812, but they had to wait fifty years before scoring their first successes, during the American Civil War. They were fitted to Confederate semi-submersible torpedo boats known as 'Davids', intended to take on and defeat a new Goliath, and then to the submersible *H L Hunley*, as described in Part I.

A spar torpedo consisted of a bomb on a long pole or spar, carried by a small, fast, low-lying boat. Under the cover of night or fog the torpedo boat stealthily approached an enemy ship and detonated the bomb close to the vulnerable underwater hull. This sounded simple enough in theory, but experience had shown these missions to be suicidal under the best of circumstances. Once detected, the little torpedo boats were highly vulnerable, and even if the torpedo was deployed correctly, its charge was often too small to cause any significant damage. Spar torpedo boats were, in the eyes of one American observer, little more than 'a waste of good men'.

USS *Spyten Dyvil*

Stung into retaliation by the Confederate successes, the Union decided to build a large spar torpedo boat. Originally called *Stromboli*, on 19 November 1864 she was renamed *Spyten Dyvil* after the district of that name in New York. Displacing 207 long tons, the vessel was constructed of wood with the deck and hull sides covered in iron armour. Her engines propelled her at a maximum speed of 5 knots, she carried a crew of twenty-three officers and men, and her sole armament was a retractable spar for placing torpedoes containing 60lbs of fine black powder.

The bow was fitted with a pair of iron clam-shell doors. Inside these doors was a sluice gate leading to a square iron tank which could be pumped dry by a centrifugal pump. At the rear of the tank was a spherical bearing carrying the torpedo-positioning shaft, which could be raised and lowered in order to correctly place the torpedo according to the chosen target.

The attack sequence was as follows. The manhole in the top of the iron tank was opened to allow loading of the torpedo head in its holder at the front end of the placing spar. The manhole would be closed. Then the bow flaps, followed by the sluice gate, were opened, allowing water to flood the tank. The spar would be run out beneath the target vessel, and raised or lowered to ensure that the torpedo head was placed beneath the target's hull. The spar would be retracted, leaving the torpedo in place. Retracting the spar would activate the fuse, exploding the torpedo at the usual distance of 20ft. The bow flaps would be closed, the sluice gate shut, and the iron tank pumped

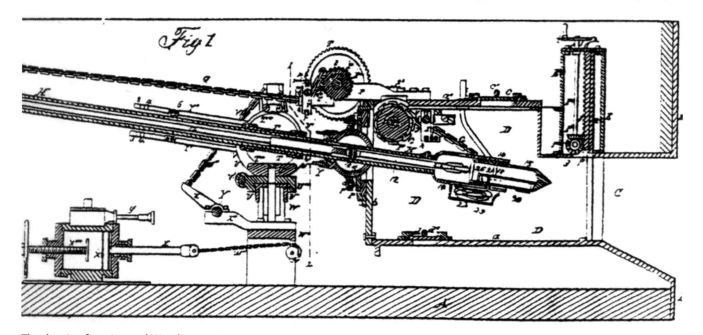

The drawing from Lay and Wood's patent.

dry, ready to reload a following torpedo.

This machinery appeared to work extremely well, and *Spyten Dyvil* used it to clear obstructions in the James River. She lasted up until 1880, when she was scrapped.

USS *Alarm*

The excellent model of USS *Alarm* from the Walden Model Co, available at www.waldenmodels.com, showing what her extreme ram contained. (Photo courtesy of Oliver Weiss)

On 17 October 1870 David Dixon Porter became Chief of the Bureau of Navigation of the US Navy, and decided to move on from the 'monitor' era of the Civil War. Monitors, he felt, were poor sea boats, and despite their heavy armour they remained vulnerable to spar torpedoes attacking their unprotected underwater hulls. Impressed by the Confederate spar torpedo boats and the Union's own *Spyten Dyvil*, Porter decided to continue to develop the spar torpedo boat concept in defiance of the 'monitor' supporters and the reluctance of Congress to fund new warships in the post-war period.

He wanted double-hull torpedo boats built of iron with watertight compartments to minimise damage, especially from the explosion of their own torpedo at relatively close range. The spar itself would copy the successful mechanism patented by William Wood and John L Lay for the *Spyten Dyvil*. Porter intended his torpedo boat to fight bows-on, so he included a 15in Dahlgren gun behind hatches in the bow. Ahead of the Dahlgren extended an enormous ram 24ft long, containing the steam operating gear for the spar and ending in a valve through which the spar and torpedo would pass, to project a further 30ft. Gatling guns were mounted on the bulwarks. The double hull could be flooded to lower the vessel when attacking, the deck structures were kept to a minimum, and the funnel was arranged to telescope to half its height, to increase the stealth capability of the boat.

To enable her to make use of her ram if the spar torpedo failed to deal a fatal blow, *Alarm* was propelled by

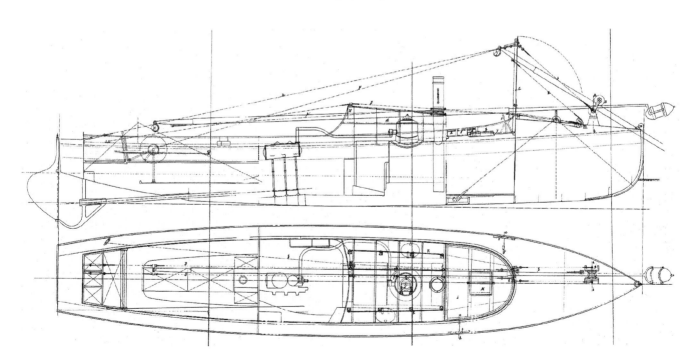

French steam pinnace of 1889 rigged to deploy a spar torpedo. Note the extensive rig of post, blocks, rope and chain needed to accurately position the torpedo – carried slightly offset to port – but which had a minimum effect on displacement. The same type of steam pinnace would later be fitted with collars to launch Whiteheads, but the added weight of these would cause the boat to sit much lower in the water. (Châtellerault Archives, plan no CAN TOR 1889PL 42)

a Fowler wheel, a kind of horizontal paddle wheel with pivoting blades, which offered the possibility for her to make extremely rapid turns, essential for a torpedo ram. The same Fowler wheel, however, proved to be her Achilles' heel, reducing her top speed to a pitiful 9 knots, which completely negated her value as a ram ship. Despite efforts to improve on her speed, irrespective of the efficiency or otherwise of her torpedo equipment, as a ship she proved a failure. Used for experiments, she was laid up in 1874, and finally scrapped in 1898.

DROP COLLARS

For ships' boats and the early small torpedo boats (rated second-class), the weight of a torpedo tube and its compressed-air launch system posed severe weight problems. The lightweight drop collar seemed to provide the answer. This seemingly simple solution had two drawbacks: the early drop collars give the impression of being very flimsy devices, considering the weight of the torpedoes and the lively motion of these small craft; second, before the introduction of the gyro, to start the motor of an early torpedo and drop it in the water was a somewhat hit-and-miss affair, compared with giving it a healthy push out of a launch tube in the direction you hoped it would continue to run. The drop collar would, however, survive to be carried into action in two world wars.

Italian drop collars were much more substantially-constructed devices. Drop collars were mounted on the *barchino saltatore*. On *MAS 15* the system allowed Rizzo to carry out a successful stealth attack on the Austro-Hungarian dreadnought *Szent István*. With no flash from a powder charge the Austrians remained unaware of his attack until it was too late.

The armed drop collars still fitted to Rizzo's *MAS 15*, preserved as an exhibit in the Museo Sacrario delle Bandiere delle Forze Armate al Vittoriano beneath the Victor Emmanuel monument in Rome. (Photo from website: forum.valka.cz)

PT-boats and MTBs

The early Second World War British MTBs and US Navy PT-boats were fitted with lightweight torpedo tubes. Even so, the weight of the tubes limited the other armament they could carry, so roll-off racks were substituted. In mid 1943, on US PT-boats the Mark 8 torpedoes and the Mark 18 tubes were replaced by four lightweight 22.5in Mark 13 torpedoes, carried on lightweight Mark 1 roll-off torpedo launching racks. They were then able to carry four shorter torpedoes as well as a heavy gun armament of 20mm, 37mm and 40mm cannon in addition to their original armament of .50-cal machine guns. As with the Italian MAS boats, the racks had the added advantage of requiring no black powder launch charge, thus avoiding giving away the boat's position at the moment of launch.

A view on board a Royal Navy second-class torpedo boat with the torpedoes loaded into the drop collars. (© National Maritime Museum, Greenwich, London, 59-2057)

Restored *PT 658* showing her four Mark 13 torpedoes on roll-off racks, and her armament of a 37mm forward, a Bofors aft and two twin .50-cal amidships. (Photo by Jerry Gilmartin, May 2011)

LAUNCH TROUGHS AND RAILS

As torpedoes grew bigger and heavier, and their speed increased dramatically, designers searched for ways to launch them effectively from small craft. As early as the 1880s the *Polyphemus* was at risk of running down a torpedo launched from her bow tube – after all, once in the water the torpedo motor had to accelerate the weapon up to its set speed. In the Great War period, the internal combustion motor and hydrodynamic developments in hull design were producing torpedo-capable boats of modest dimensions but able to reach 40 knots or more.

The solution was to carry the torpedo in a trough located at the rear of the torpedo boat, using a pusher rod to throw it backwards into the water. Even travelling at high speed, the motorboat would then have to take immediate avoiding action to escape from the path of its own torpedo. The system was brought to a state of operational efficiency and went to war in the CMBs, or coastal motorboats, built by Thornycroft.

Simple and efficient as the launch system was, it had one fatal drawback. A small motor torpedo boat, built of wood and loaded with petrol, was extremely vulnerable to defensive fire from its intended target. The best chance of success lay in being able to approach the victim unseen and unheard, preferably at a modest speed to avoid creating a bow wave. At the moment of launch, the throttles were opened full, the motors accelerated with a deafening noise, and the boat created the unwanted bow wave. She was thus revealed, and exposed, and the enemy could not only open fire but also commence avoiding action.

Despite these drawbacks, the economy of the arrangements meant that Thornycroft's designs continued to be built up until the Second World War, and they were the direct inspiration for the Soviet G5s, usually depicted dashing at high speed in formation.

Q-boats

In 1935 the government of the Philippines decided to form an offshore patrol squadron of fast motorboats, controlled by the army as an element of coast defence. Thornycroft delivered one 65ft CMB which was numbered *Q 111*, armed with two 21in torpedo tubes mounted at either side of the wheelhouse. A further boat, *Q 112*, was delivered in sections and re-erected in the Philippines. This second boat was a 55-footer, armed with two 21in torpedoes in stern troughs in the classic CMB configuration. Faced with an embargo on further sales, due to the onset of the Second World War, the Philippine

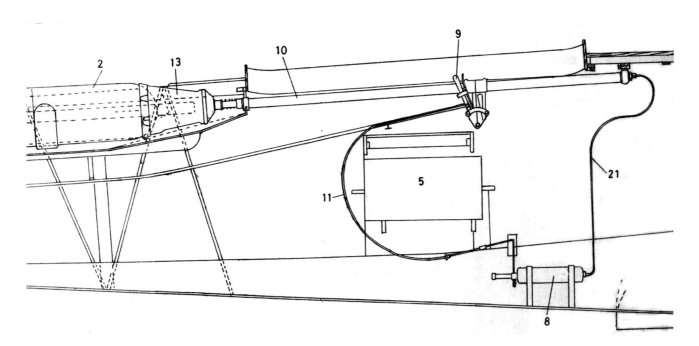

The torpedo launch mechanism of the Thornycroft 55-footer CMB, showing the cordite-powered ram. The screw clamps holding the torpedo in the trough are loosened slightly, then the operating lever (9) is pulled. This fires the cordite charge in the vessel (8) and the gas is led through tube (21) to the ram rod (10). This is driven backwards, and the cap (13) fitted to the rear of the ram and which surrounds the head of the torpedo, pushes the weapon (2) rearwards at high speed. Note that there is no warning flash to give away the firing boat. (Drawing courtesy of John Lambert)

The three Philippine army Q-boats alongside. Note the three different types of mast carried: *Q 113* on the left has an inverted V-shaped mast similar to American PT-boats (the ladder construction behind the mast is a dockyard crane); *Q 112* is in the centre, with *Q 111* to the right. Note the fixed torpedo tubes on this larger boat.

army copied the design of the 55-footer and built a third boat, *Q 113*. All three Q-boats took part in the struggle against the Japanese invasion forces, and on one occasion they shot down three Mitsubishi Zero fighters attempting to strafe them (a real-life exploit similar to the opening action scene in the John Ford movie *They were Expendable*).

Soviet CMBs

Having suffered from the attentions of the Thornycroft CMBs in the Baltic, it was only natural that the young Soviet navy should turn to this type of torpedo craft. They had captured or salvaged several examples, and the Tupolev aircraft design bureau undertook to improve on the basic Thornycroft design. The G5 (G for

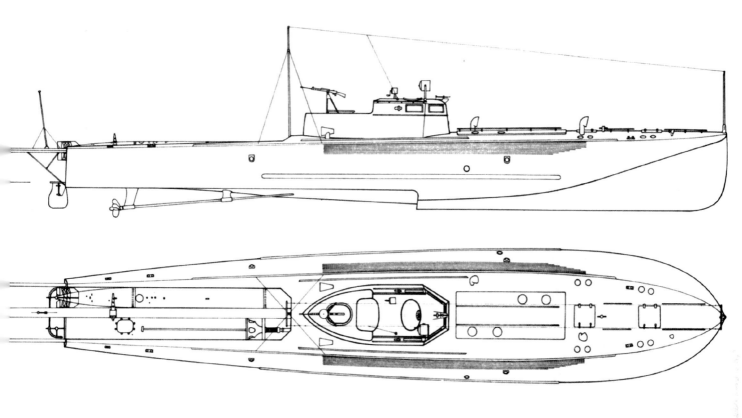

Early G5 of Series 7, armed with one 7.62mm Degtyarev MG. The launch ram in the starboard tube is shown at maximum extension after having launched a torpedo. (Drawing by Przemyslaw Budzbon in *Warship*, No 8, courtesy of Conway Maritime Press)

Glissiryuschchy, or hydroplane) was designed in 1933, and built of aluminium. Armed with two 21in torpedoes in stern troughs, production boats were capable of speeds of up to 56 knots, depending on the type of engine fitted.

The torpedo heads were covered by the deck amidships, and they were launched backwards by a cordite-powered ram with an aluminium cap which surrounded the torpedo head. The torpedoes were fitted with side lugs which rested on rails running the length of the trough, and which extended beyond the stern of the boat to carry the torpedo head clear of the stern on launch. Before launching, the torpedoes were clamped in place by securing arms which pivoted upwards to release the torpedo.

Despite the bravery of their crews, these G5 boats achieved limited success against Axis shipping due to the inherent disadvantages of the stern trough launch system. An additional problem was the fact that, without an auxiliary engine for slow-speed manoeuvring, the boats would not run at less than 18 knots, making slow approaches to the target impossible.

Some seventy-five boats would be lost out of a total production of 300 in the Baltic, Northern and Black Sea fleets. Of the boats transferred to North Korea, three were

destroyed in July 1951 in action with USS *Juneau*, HMS *Jamaica* and HMS *Black Swan* off Chumunjin.

Q-ships

A variant on the CMB launch system was fitted to Q-ships, to allow them to attempt to torpedo an attacking U-boat. The 18in torpedo (K) was carried in a cradle between the supports. Dropping the hatch (P) in the ship's side, and firing the cordite charge in the vessel (I) activated the ram (C). The head of the ram (G) propelled the cradle and the torpedo forward, and ejected the weapon through the hatch. One had to hope the U-boat was not too far off.

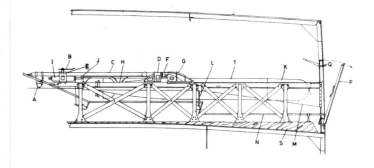

Q-ship launch cradle. (Drawing courtesy of John Lambert)

British Power Boat MTBs (1936)

The first Royal Navy motor torpedo boats to be constructed following the Great War, the 60ft British Power Boat MTBs of 1936 were a curious design. They copied the launch dispositions of the CMBs, with the torpedoes launched tail-first from the stern of the boat, but with the torpedoes carried internally in the engine rooms – a strange arrangement which at least kept them warm and dry.

However, in place of the CMBs' cordite-powered launching ram, which propelled the torpedo at speed into the water behind the boat, the BPB 60-footers had folding launch gantries which extended back over the transom, carrying extensions of the overhead rails from which the torpedoes were suspended in their internal tunnels. In order to launch, it was necessary to point the boat in the required direction, release the torpedo holding catch, leaving the weapon free to move backwards and downwards, then accelerate the boat to make the torpedo slide backwards out of the transom. Naturally, the boat would then execute a rapid turn to port or starboard to avoid her own torpedoes.

Just as with the CMBs, this launch method went contrary to all the precepts of the small, vulnerable wooden torpedo boat, filled with petrol, whose only advantage lay in small size and a silent stalking approach to avoid alerting the target. Crash-starting the engines and throwing up a huge bow wave could be fatal. The boats did their best to combat the Japanese attacking Hong Kong, but their situation was hopeless. The experiment was not repeated by the British.

Loading a torpedo into the engine room of a BPB 60-footer MTB. (From www.hongkongescape.org/CoastalForces)

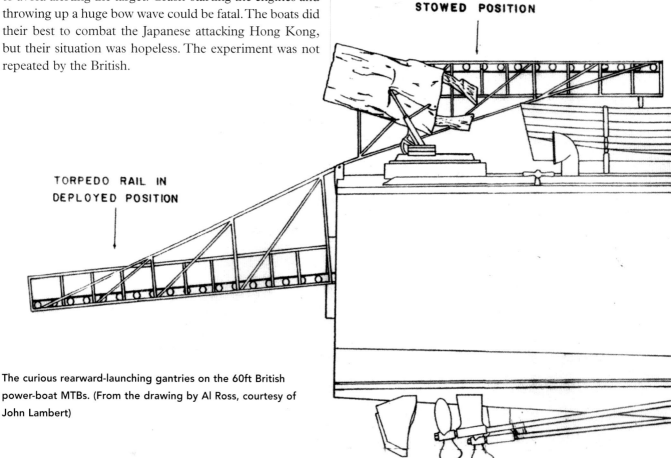

TORPEDO RAIL IN STOWED POSITION

TORPEDO RAIL IN DEPLOYED POSITION

The curious rearward-launching gantries on the 60ft British power-boat MTBs. (From the drawing by Al Ross, courtesy of John Lambert)

Leicht-Schnellboote

A similar arrangement was to be found on the LS-boats ('*Leicht-Schnellboote*', or 'light speedboat') designed to be carried on German auxiliary cruisers. Too small to carry the standard S-boat torpedo tubes and 21in torpedoes, most carried three minelaying tubes, but *LS 4 Esau*, which was hoisted aboard raider *Michel*, was armed with two 450mm (18in) torpedoes carried in internal tubes at the rear of the boat. The LS-boat weighed 12 tons and was capable of speeds up to 42 knots. The lack of the type of rear extension rail as on the 60ft BPB boats suggests that the LS-boats launched their torpedoes by a normal black powder charge or by compressed air, facing sternwards. Launching them backwards at high velocity would cause serious derangement of the control mechanisms, to say nothing of the detonator in the nose, so they would be launched nose-first through the transom hatches, having first pointed the boat at the target. Since most attacks were carried out by *LS 4* at night, stalking unsuspecting merchantmen, sternward launches would cause no problems.

LS 7 in Salonika, summer of 1943. Most LS-boats went to the Aegean. *Michel*'s *LS 4 Esau* was lost with her when she was torpedoed and sunk by USS *Tarpon* (SS-175). Note the torpedo launch hatches in the transom. (Photo from the Jung collection)

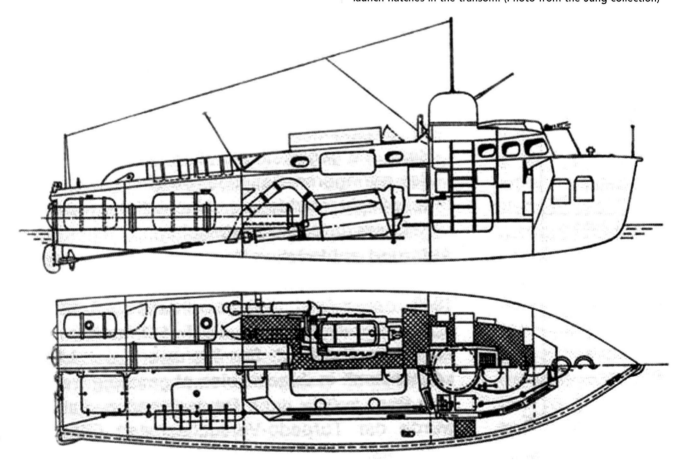

LS-boats showing the internal 18in torpedo tubes and the long 20mm cannon in an aircraft turret (as fitted on, for example, the FW-200 Condor).

CHAPTER 10

Torpedo Boat Carriers

CAPITAL SHIPS

Very early in the story of the Whitehead, the Royal Navy saw the offensive potential of the locomotive torpedo. As well as cutting ports in bulwarks for torpedo launch carriages, they attempted to extend the reach of their torpedoes by carrying onboard small craft capable of attacking an enemy fleet at night or in a defended harbour.

In 1879 HMS *Devastation*, followed by her sister ship HMS *Thunderer* two years later, was supplied with a steam cutter fitted with torpedo dropping gear. In addition, each ship had a port cut in their breastwork armour on each side for torpedo launching carriages. An outfit of twelve Whiteheads was carried by each ship. In 1880 HMS *Sultan* was fitted with four carriages for 14in Whiteheads on her main deck, and two torpedo boats were added, stowed abreast the after mast on crutches. In 1881 HM Ships *Hotspur*, *Ajax* and *Agamemnon* were fitted for torpedo launching and received a 60ft torpedo boat each, as was HMS *Conqueror* five years later. The massive turret ship HMS *Inflexible* in 1881 became the first British ship to be fitted with two submerged torpedo tubes (in the bow), in addition to two above-water launch carriages, a bow torpedo launch skid and a stern launch derrick. She also carried two 60ft second-class torpedo boats, specifically for 'night attacks'. And even as late as 1906 HMS *Dreadnought* stowed in her forward torpedo flat not only the 18in torpedo bodies and warheads for her own underwater tubes, but also 14in torpedoes for her ship's boats.

Ironclads usually had sufficient deck space, and the necessary heavy lifting derricks, to carry small torpedo craft. Smaller vessels such as cruisers could not, so both the British and French attempted to give mobility to the short-range coast-defence torpedo boats by hoisting them aboard special torpedo cruisers.

Interestingly, in 1810 Robert Fulton described a similar plan he had devised six years earlier for the attack on Boulogne. Because the ships of the line at that time did not have the deck space to transport additional craft designed specifically for torpedo attacks, Fulton had asked for four 'ordnance vessels' to be prepared, with large hatchways to carry torpedo boats internally, together with a supply of torpedoes.

HMS *VULCAN*

On 18 June 1888 Portsmouth Royal Dockyard laid the keel of a very special new type of warship, the torpedo-boat carrier (or mother ship) to be named *Vulcan* – a very appropriate name, as the original Vulcan was the Roman god of fire and volcanic eruptions, who forged iron in his workshop under Mount Etna. The modern HMS *Vulcan* also played with fire, carrying a small flotilla of up to nine second-class torpedo boats on her deck and a large number of offensive mines in her holds. She had extensive workshop facilities to maintain her brood of chicks. *Vulcan* was launched less than one year later, on 13 June 1889.

Her original configuration, as a lightly-armed protected cruiser with a fair turn of speed, would have allowed her to carry out trials of an offensive blockade role: carrying her flotilla of torpedo boats to enemy coastal waters, she could lay offensive minefields off the enemy's harbours, and if he emerged to give battle could hoist out her flotilla of torpedo boats and lead them into an attack. If attacked herself, *Vulcan* was speedy and had fair protection; as a last resort she could put up a reasonable defence with her armament of 8 x 4.7in guns, 12 x 3pdrs (47mm) and 16 machine guns. Finally, she carried above-water torpedo tubes of her own, at bow and stern. However, it was unlikely her commanding officer would have risked the kind of jingoistic combat described by a journalist in the *Graphic* of 22 June 1889: 'Her speed being at least as great as that of any large vessel yet afloat, and hardly less than that attained by the quickest torpedo-craft, she will be able to accept or decline an action, while the power and rapid fire of her armament will justify her in engaging any enemy short of a battleship.'

The inclusion of a minelaying capability was far-sighted, although *Vulcan* was never to be used in an offensive minelaying role. In spite of the bravery of their torpedo craft crews, the main Japanese successes against the Russian fleet during their blockade of Port Arthur had come from the minefields they had laid. Mines, however, were a two-edged sword, and the Japanese were to suffer grievous losses themselves in Russian minefields.

As the British and French navies discovered, second-class torpedo boats had very minimal sea-keeping characteristics, and soon were to be countered by torpedo-boat destroyers. Therefore, *Vulcan*'s role quickly evolved to become a general torpedo and mine training ship, and in 1909 she became a depot ship for submarines, the conceptual successors to the second-class torpedo boats.

Her workshop facilities were originally intended to

Vulcan hoisting out a torpedo boat. (© National Maritime Museum, Greenwich, London 59-229)

maintain and repair the flimsy torpedo boats she carried; their highly stressed lightweight machinery was in constant need of care. The workshop could also carry out maintenance and repair of the large number of torpedoes *Vulcan* carried. In it there were five lathes of various sizes, two drilling machines with twist drills and boring bars, machines for planing, shaping and slotting, punching and shearing, and a circular saw bench. The machine tools were driven by belts from overhead shafting powered by a separate steam engine in the workshop. Casting and founding could be carried out in a sandpit and moulding boxes, and crucibles heated by hot air from a high-speed fan were capable of melting down two hundredweight (90kg) of iron or brass at a time. Fitters had the use of workbenches fitted with vices, and naturally a comprehensive set of tools was carried.

FOUDRE

The French navy's response came in the form of the *Foudre* ('lightning'), an appropriate companion to the Royal Navy's god of fire. Laid down on 9 June 1892, she was launched on 20 October 1895. In obvious comparison with HMS *Vulcan*, the French design stood out by virtue of her four large gantry cranes fore and aft. While *Vulcan*'s single goose-neck hydraulic cranes would have had great difficulty in hoisting out a torpedo boat in a seaway, with the boat swinging about on the single hoisting cable, *Foudre* completely eliminated this potential problem by

launching her set of eight second-class torpedo boats by means of overhead gantry cranes, which would not have been out of place in a contemporary railway locomotive construction shop. She even carried midships smaller gantry sets to launch the larger of her ship's boats.

Like *Vulcan*, *Foudre* was a lightly-armed protected cruiser, capable of fight or flight. Built at the end of a period when the designers of French cruisers and battleships seemed to have a complete disregard for added top-weight, piling up superstructures like apartment blocks, topped by cylindrical fighting masts with internal electric ammunition hoists, *Foudre*'s designer appears to have taken the lesson to heart. To counteract her heavy gantry cranes and her deck cargo of torpedo boats, her superstructure, funnels and masting are minimalist to say the least. Her torpedo boats even had hinged funnels to keep down the height of the gantry cranes. She also avoided the second fatal design failure of most contemporary French warships, and lacked the excessive tumblehome sides which caused them to roll like barrels and seriously reduced their margins of stability.

Again, like *Vulcan*, *Foudre* also had extensive workshop facilities. Unlike the Industrial Revolution-era system on *Vulcan*, however, *Foudre*'s workshop had large electric motors powering each machine tool. She also had an elaborate system of overhead transporter rails to move torpedoes around the workshop. This equipment fit stood her in good stead as the mother ship of yet another new invention. She had previously carried an inflatable observation balloon on her after deck, and when she ceased to be a torpedo-boat carrier and her gantry cranes were finally removed, in 1912 *Foudre* was transformed into what may be considered the world's very first specialised aircraft-carrying vessel.

A poor quality image but important, nevertheless, as it is the only known view of *Foudre* hoisting one of her flotilla of second-class torpedo boats. Note the double purchase fore and aft compared to *Vulcan*'s single crane suspension point.

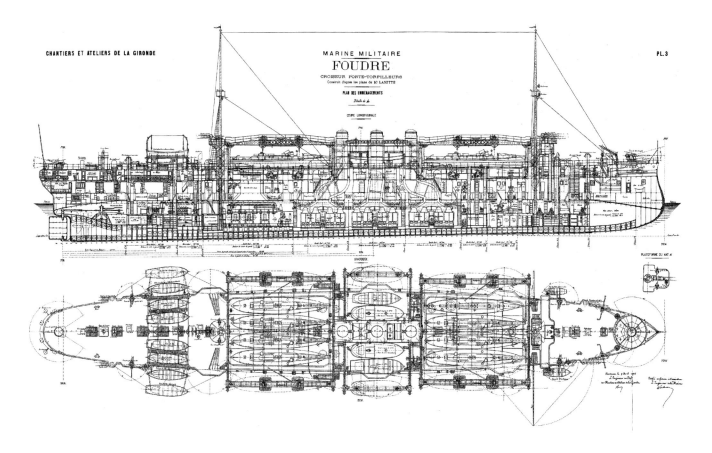

A sectional drawing of *Foudre*, and a deck plan showing her tightly-nested brood of second-class torpedo boats. (Châtellerault Archives, plan no FOUDRE1895C003)

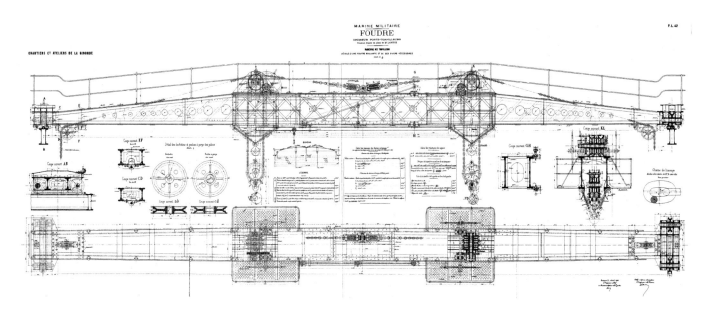

Front and plan view of one of the huge gantry cranes used to hoist the torpedo boats, running out on the girders to left and right, with two sets of hoisting gear in between. (Châtellerault Archives, plan no FOUDRE1895C042).

AUXILIARY CRUISERS

The German raiders *Komet*, *Kormoran* and *Michel* each carried one small LS-boat, numbered respectively *LS 2*, *LS 3* and *LS 4*. Whereas the first two carried only mines, *LS 4 Esau* carried by the 4740-ton raider *Michel* (Ship No 28, HSK No IX) was used in an offensive role, attacking several ships with her two 18in torpedoes, often in stalking attacks after dark.

HMS *Fidelity*

The French cargo ship *Rhin* was sailed by her crew to Britain in 1940 and offered to the Admiralty, bypassing the Free French naval forces. She was commissioned as HMS *Fidelity*, to operate as a clandestine special forces ship, carrying out various missions under different neutral ship disguises. Her commander, Lieutenant Peri, was commissioned into the Royal Navy under the fictitious name of Lt Cdr 'Jack Langlais', RNVR.

In 1942 *Fidelity* was rearmed with four 4in anti-aircraft guns with radar fire control and four 21in torpedo tubes. She also carried two OS2U Kingfisher floatplanes, two landing craft *LCV 752* and *LCV 754*, plus *MTB 105*, one of the experimental MTBs numbered 104–107 built by Thornycroft in 1941. These were 45-footers (9m), displacing just 9 tons.

At the end of December 1942 *Fidelity* joined Convoy ONS154. Her mission was to carry fifty-one Royal Marine commandos for special operations in the Far East. Passing the Azores the convoy came under ferocious attack by U-boats, and the escorts were overwhelmed. No less than fifteen merchant ships, including *Fidelity*, were torpedoed. Her crew and passengers took to life rafts, but in the heavy winter weather not one survived. However, *MTB 105* had been detached from the ship to carry out an anti-submarine patrol, and lost sight of her mother ship. Her crew of eight were rescued by HMCS *Woodstock*, and the crew of one of the Kingfisher aircraft, which had previously crashed on take-off, were picked up by HMCS *St Laurent*. In all 325 officers and men, including all the Marine commandos, perished in the disaster. This was the convoy attack which caused the Admiralty to form the special U-boat hunting groups which were to become so successful under Captain Walker and his successors.

KAITEN CARRIERS

Although not strictly torpedo-boat carriers, these Imperial Japanese navy conversions were designed to fulfil a similar role. Towards the end of the Pacific War, the Japanese began reconstructing surface warships to act as Kaiten carriers and launchers. It is hard to see how these ships could ever have survived to come within launching range of the US fleet, given the Americans' command of the skies. Several destroyers were earmarked for conversion, usually older slower vessels, plus the ex-torpedo cruiser *Kitakami*. It was felt that the hull sponsons fitted for her banks of torpedo tubes could be utilised to carry Kaiten.

The following photos show her test launching Kaiten on 18 February 1945.

IJNS *Kitakami* test-launching Kaiten from her port and starboard stern rails.

CHAPTER 11

Above-water Torpedo Tubes

FIXED TUBES

HMS *Hood*

At the end of the Great War, during a period when battleship designers, particularly those in the United States, were seriously considering omitting torpedo tubes from future dreadnought projects and ultimately removing them from existing ships, the Royal Navy persisted in fitting them to its latest capital ships, the *Hood* class, and subsequently in the *Nelson* and *Rodney* completed in the 1920s.

Hood herself was the only ship of her class to be completed, and she was fitted with two 21in underwater tubes ahead of 'A' turret (see Chapter 12), and four fixed

21in torpedo tubes on her main deck aft, in place of the eight fixed tubes of her original design. From the very start, Sir Eustace Tennyson d'Eyncourt, the director of naval construction (DNC), had expressed his concerns over mounting these above-water tubes. They had been required in order to help her fulfil a basic function of the battlecruisers, pulling out ahead of the main battle line to launch attacks aimed at weakening the enemy battle line, prior to the clash of the battleships.

On 2 September 1918 the DNC warned that if the torpedo tubes were struck by a heavy shell and exploded, *Hood* would probably be cut in half, since the tubes were mounted just over the main strength girders running the

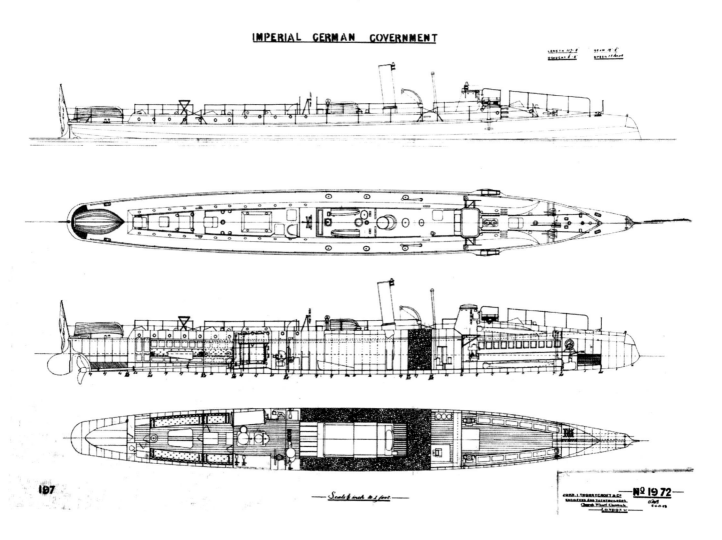

A torpedo boat built for the German navy by Thornycroft in 1884. She appears to be armed with a bow tube and one reload.

Here is a view of the midships starboard side of HMS *Hood* taken in June 1939. The hinged armoured mantlets protecting her aft starboard torpedo tubes are shown abreast the mainmast. The two covers just aft of the second funnel are the 5in armour plates covering the original openings for the forward pair of starboard torpedo tubes that were never fitted.

length of the ship. However, the Admiralty insisted on retaining the aft pairs of tubes, and as a palliative measure the outboard ends of the tubes were surrounded by thin armour boxes of 3in plate, intended to protect the warheads once torpedoes were loaded. The hinged mantlet was the same thickness as the upper belt it pierced, that is to say, 5in.

The positions for the forward two pairs of tubes were left in place, the openings in the upper belt being covered by 5in thick armour plates. It was always intended that in time of war these tubes could be installed and the covering plates converted to hinging mantlets. However, the provisions of the Washington Treaty prohibited this measure, which was never implemented.

When *Hood* sailed to her date with destiny, the tubes and their torpedoes were still on board. During the court of inquiry into her dramatic loss, questions were raised as to whether the explosion of her torpedoes, struck by a shell from *Bismarck* or from *Prinz Eugen*, could have initiated the explosion of the nearby 4in magazines, followed in turn by the aft main 15in magazines. Opinion was divided, with the majority favouring direct penetration of a main magazine by a 15in shell from *Bismarck*, but a minority opinion continued in favour of the torpedo explosion theory. The discovery of the shattered wreck of HMS *Hood* in June 2001 by David Mearns seemed to have laid the torpedo theory to rest. One of the colour photos from the seabed clearly showed the intact torpedo mantlets on *Hood*'s port side, and even one of her torpedoes lying in the debris.

Japanese heavy cruisers

These ships, when first built, featured large torpedo batteries. The lead designs *Kako* and *Furataka* were planned with 24in torpedo tubes mounted on the centre-line as in destroyers, but fears of launching from such a high position with the risk of a torpedo striking the deck edge led to them being armed with fixed pairs of tubes on the main deck, with six tubes on each broadside.

Italian heavy cruisers

Italian heavy cruisers of the *Trento* class had an unusual arrangement: four sets of twin tubes which did not rotate, but were not strictly 'fixed' either. In fact, each twin tube set retracted into the forward and after torpedo rooms. This kept the weight of the torpedoes over the centre-line, and also withdrew the warheads from proximity with the ship's side.

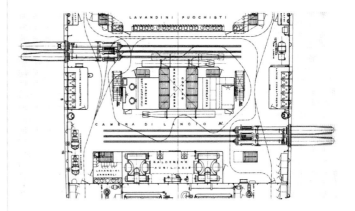

The forward torpedo room on heavy cruiser *Trento*, showing the curious retracting tubes.
(From *Incrociatori Pesanti Classe Trento Parte Prima*)

TRAINABLE SINGLE TUBES

The very first Royal Navy torpedo boat, HMS *Lightning*, which had been designed to carry and launch her torpedoes from two drop collars, was later fitted with a single training bow torpedo tube. To launch a second attack her crew would have to reload one of the pair of Whiteheads she carried on trolleys alongside the engine room casing, not an easy task on such a small vessel in anything but a flat calm.

Thirty-one years after the Thornycroft torpedo boat shown at the beginning of this chapter, the Imperial German navy started construction of a new series of small torpedo boats. Their *A 1* class of 1915 displaced 137 tons on an overall length of 41.6m (136½ft), were armed with two single trainable 17.7in torpedo tubes and two 50mm guns, but on the 1200ihp of their single-screw triple expansion engine were painfully slow, at only 19 knots. No less than five out of the twenty-five were sunk by British destroyers, one succumbed to an air attack, one was mined, and one disappeared without trace, probably another mine casualty.

The succeeding class, numbered from *A 26* to *A 55* and built in 1916 and 1917, were larger, at 227 tons on a length of 50m (164ft), but dropped down to only one trainable tube, in order to mount two 88mm guns. With 3500shp geared turbines they could reach 25.8 knots. This was a fair turn of speed for a small vessel but far below that which contemporary destroyers were reaching. It is a mystery why the Kaiser's navy persevered with these small fragile boats. Since out of this second series of thirty boats only one was lost to a mine, and a second was scuttled in the Adriatic, one must surmise that they did not see much offensive action.

A contemporary model of HMS *Lightning* in the National Maritime Museum collection. (© National Maritime Museum, Greenwich, London, F2451-2)

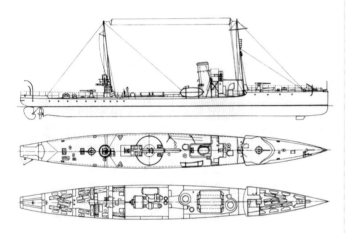

Class A 26 torpedo boat of 1916–17. Note the auxiliary bow rudder. (Drawing from *Z-vor!* by Harald Fock)

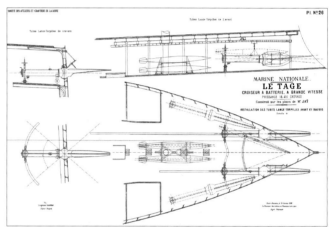

Le Tage bow tubes. (Châtellerault Archives, plan ref LE TAGE 1886CO26)

USS *Oregon*'s training bow tube. Note the torpedoes mounted on the bulkhead, the overhead monorail for loading, and the tube training rack. (Detroit Collection, Library of Congress, photo #LC-D4-20532)

A similar tube in USS *Massachusetts*, training through a ball-joint in the side armour. (Detroit Collection, Library of Congress)

Typical bow arrangement of German destroyers, mounting two single trainable tubes in the well before the bridge, here shown on SMS *V 43* in American hands. Note how the forward tubes can fire virtually straight ahead on either side of the slender bow, by very slight training on either beam – very useful in an attack, but in any sea the well before the bridge threw up a mass of spray, obscuring the vision of the bridge personnel. (Photo courtesy of Tom Tanner of Lothian, Maryland, website www.BB_Ops.tripod.com)

Le Tage was a '*croiseur à batterie, à grande vitesse*' ('broadside battery, high-speed cruiser'), built in 1886. The plans reproduced here show her two single bow torpedo tubes stowed inboard, and also the tubes deployed on either side of the bow. They are transported into position by the same overhead rail system used to load the torpedoes. Note that both can train a few degrees either side of the bow, and they can also elevate and depress. Her broadside tubes shown on the left would be similarly stowed. When rigged in their socket for action they can be trained, but not elevated.

PT-boat torpedo tubes

PT-boats' primary anti-ship armament was either two or four 21in Mark 8 torpedoes, launched from trainable Mark 18 steel torpedo tubes. These were pivoted from the after end to point outwards slightly off the centre-line to port and starboard when readied for firing, so were not strictly 'trainable'.

Single trainable tubes on a French *contre-torpilleur* of the *Claymore* class. Note the raised grating deck on which the crew work, and the reload in its case to port. Torpedo-boat destroyers would later require the space taken up by the tube on the stern to be given over to anti-submarine depth charges. (Originally published in *Le Miroir* of 2 July 1916)

A highly detailed 1/72nd scale model of the famous *PT 109*, built by Fritz Koopman, showing her four training torpedo tubes. At the time of her sinking some sources claim that John F Kennedy and his crew had replaced the after pair of tubes with extra depth charges. The dark olive-green was the same colour as had been used for US torpedo boats over forty years earlier, to camouflage these basically inshore types against the coast. (Photo courtesy of Matt Grzybinski)

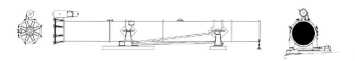

Mark 18 PT-boat tube. (Drawings by John Drain for construction of his scale model, on
http://www.pt-boat.com/torpedotube/torpedotube.html)

TWIN TUBES

By the outbreak of the Great War, twin tubes were the norm in many destroyers, but in the latter half of the conflict larger classes, like the British 'V' and 'W's and the later US 'flush-deckers', began to carry triple mounts. Post-war this escalated to quad mountings, and thereafter the trainable twin mounting found only specialist employment.

In Japanese heavy cruisers, the fixed torpedo batteries were later changed to twin training mounts, without shields, on the upper deck, with adjacent reloads immediately behind the tubes, and further reloads attached one above the other to the superstructure sides inboard of the tubes, for a total of twelve torpedoes per side. These twin mountings were also fitted to the light cruiser *Yahagi* and to the *Kuma* and succeeding classes of 5500-ton cruisers. They were also carried by Japanese destroyers of the 1920s and the torpedo boats of the 1930s.

The twin torpedo tube mounting returned to the Royal Navy on the Type III Hunt-class escort destroyers, ordered under the 1940 building programme. For service in the Mediterranean it was felt they needed to be able to at least threaten torpedo attacks. However, in practical terms the chances of hitting with a broadside of only two torpedoes were slim.

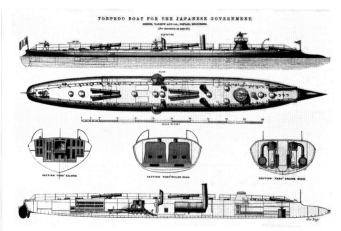

The large torpedo boat (some writers call her the first TBD) *Kotaka*, built for Japan by Yarrow in 1886. (Courtesy of *Grace's Guide to British Industrial History*)

Twin tubes on a *Tatra*-class Austro-Hungarian destroyer, showing the steam-heating elements enclosing the central part of these tubes, which were built by Whitehead Fiume. (Photo courtesy of Erwin Sieche)

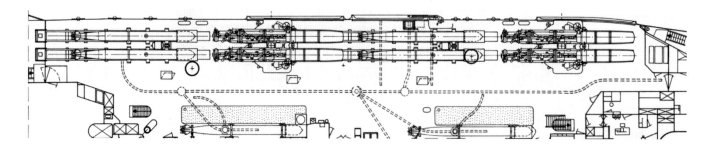

The original twin mountings of the heavy cruiser *Takao*. The dotted lines represent the overhead torpedo transporter rails. (Drawn by Janusz Skulski for his 'Anatomy of the Ship' monograph on the *Takao*)

Russian triple 18in torpedo tube mounting on a *Orfey*-class destroyer.

TRIPLE TUBES

Russian triple tubes

The Russian *Orfey*-class destroyers, of which fourteen were built between 1914 and 1917 as modified versions of the *Novik*, were the first to mount triple torpedo tubes. They carried a total of three triple mounts for 18in torpedoes. Apart from the smaller size of torpedo, these gave the *Orfey*s a larger torpedo broadside than the slightly later US flush-deck destroyers.

RN triple tubes

Later designs of triple torpedo tubes returned to the Royal Navy during the late 1930s, for fitting to 'Town'- and *Dido*-class cruisers. These were arranged as a horizontal group of three.

US Navy triple tubes

With four triple mountings for a total of twelve 21in torpedo tubes, the US 'flush-deckers' of the end of the Great War were the heaviest torpedo-armed destroyers of their day.

Japanese triple tubes

The *Mutsuki* class of first-class destroyers laid down under the 1923 programme introduced the triple tube to Japanese destroyers, in 21in calibre, later changed to 24in. The *Fubuki* class of super-destroyers were built with the 24in torpedo mountings, and increased their broadside from six to nine tubes (three sets of triple mountings).

Loading a greased 21in torpedo into one of the triple tubes of HMS *Vanoc* in 1941. Note that the tubes are lettered 'A', 'B' and 'C' instead of being numbered. The centre tube 'C' is mounted above the outer pair, to save on deck space alongside the mounting.

The business end of a triple tube set on the 'V' and 'W'-class destroyer HMS *Wolverine* in 1944. Note that only the lower tubes 'A' and 'B' are loaded, and also the on-mount torpedo sight manned by the rating second from the left. The rivets running the length of the tubes hold in place the bronze rubbing strakes.

The view looking aft from USS *Little*'s crow's nest during First World War convoy operations, showing her twelve 21in torpedo tubes. (NHHC, photo # NH 51342)

German triple tubes

After the new *Emden* (1925), which carried twin torpedo tubes, all modern German light and heavy cruisers built from the late 1920s onward were designed to carry a heavy torpedo armament of twelve tubes, in four triple mounts. *Admiral Hipper* and *Blücher* each carried ten reloads, and in *Prinz Eugen* the number of reloads was increased to twelve.

In the course of the Second World War, the surviving 'K'-class light cruiser, *Köln*, plus *Leipzig* and *Nürnberg*, were considered of fragile construction and of little front-line combat value, and all landed torpedo mounts. *Leipzig*'s forward mounts were fitted on *Admiral Hipper* in 1941, to replace her starboard mounts which had been wrenched from the deck when HMS *Glowworm* had rammed the *Hipper* off Trondheim.

Scharnhorst and *Gneisenau* had been designed as battlecruisers/fast battleships, initially without torpedo armament, because of the risks involved in carrying them during gunnery duels. However, their initial commerce raids into the Atlantic indicated that they could profitably use torpedoes to despatch merchant ships which refused to sink under shellfire, allowing them to move against other targets in rapidly dispersing convoys. In March 1941 *Leipzig*'s after tube banks were removed and transferred to *Gneisenau*, while *Scharnhorst* received the after mounts which had been removed from *Nürnberg* a year earlier before the latter's transfer to Norwegian waters.

QUADRUPLE TUBES

Japanese quadruple mounts

The torpedo outfit of Japanese heavy cruisers later changed from twin unshielded mountings to shielded quadruples, and the largest such as the *Takao* class had two quadruple mountings and eight reloads per side for a total of thirty-two 24in torpedoes. To cater for the wider quadruple mountings they were sponsoned out from the original ship's sides. Each mount could train through a broadside angle of 105 degrees.

Oi and *Kitakami*

In preparation for the IJN's pre-war battle plan for destroying the US Navy's battle fleet (see Part IV), during 1941 the light cruisers *Oi* and *Kitakami* of the 5500-ton type were drastically modified to carry ten sets of quadruple 24in torpedo mounts, five on each broadside. With the change in tactics to fleet carrier actions, and the devastation caused to the US battle fleet at Pearl Harbor, these two conversions were never employed in their intended torpedo attack role, and they were altered once more. *Kitakami* became a carrier for 14m Daihatsu landing craft, and *Oi* was turned into a carrier and launch vessel for eight Kaiten.

The shielded quadruple Type 92 mount for 24in Type 93 torpedoes was also the classic armament of all the later Japanese super-destroyer classes other than the *Shimakaze*. The torpedoes were launched by compressed air, at a maximum tube pressure of 65psi (4.57kg/cm^2), which would give a tube muzzle velocity of 40ft per second (12m/sec). In an emergency only, because of the resultant flash giving away the launch, 600g (1.3lb) black powder charges could be used instead, giving a similar muzzle velocity. Total weight of the Type 92 mounting, with shield but less torpedoes, was 18 long tons (of which the 0.118in/3mm thick shield accounted for no less than 3 tons). Each torpedo tube was constructed from mild steel plate 0.197in/5mm thick, with steel guides 2in/50.8mm wide running inside the whole length of the tube on each side and along the bottom. The tube doors were made of cast steel and locked by a steel ring rotated by a handwheel and gear rack.

Running depth was set in the torpedo by a spring-loaded plunger. The gyro angle was set by a handwheel, matching pointers on a gyro angle indicator. The setting spindle was inserted by hand but automatically withdrawn

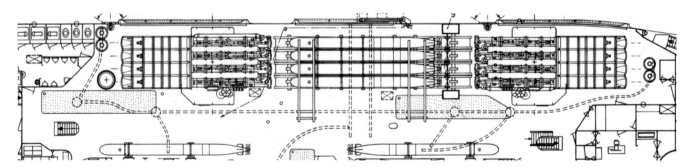

Janusz Skulski's drawing of the later torpedo armament of the heavy cruiser *Takao*, showing the two quadruple shielded mountings, with four reloads between the two mountings and a further two pairs of reloads secured to the superstructure sides one above the other. Also shown are the torpedo overhead transporter rails. (Drawn by Janusz Skulski for his 'Anatomy of the Ship' monograph on the *Takao*)

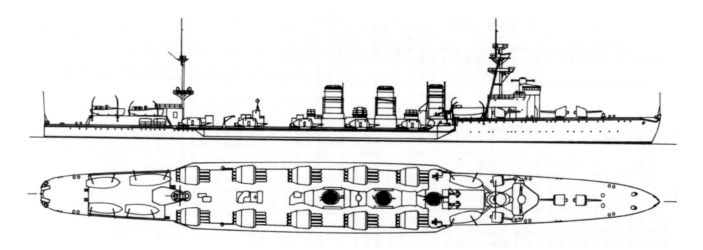

Kitakami as converted to a torpedo cruiser, with ten quadruple 24in torpedo mounts carried on sponsons. (Drawing by Peter Mickel from *Warships of the Imperial Japanese Navy 1869–1945*)

by an air piston arrangement when the torpedo was fired. No speed-changing device was fitted on the tubes. The only method of changing torpedo speed was by removing an access hole cover in the tube and inserting a small hand wrench. However, the torpedo speed was seldom altered as the Japanese favoured using the high-speed setting.

The torpedo was secured in the tube by forward and aft stops at each end of the T-guide on top of the torpedo. When loading the torpedo into the tube, the aft spring-loaded guide was forced up to let the torpedo enter. The forward stop was automatically lifted by an air piston when the torpedo was fired. The mount was normally trained using a 10hp 600rpm motor driven by compressed air at a pressure of 215psi (15kg/cm^2). If necessary, it could be trained manually by two operators turning large handwheels inside the shield.

Normally, torpedoes were fired electrically from the bridge, tripping a lever which indicated on the bridge and at the mounting that the torpedo had been fired. If necessary, in an emergency the torpedoes could be fired manually from the mounting, using the Type 14 torpedo sight mounted on top of the tubes behind the observation port in the shield. The normal crew for a quad mount was nine men.

Reloads

In order to maximise the use of their powerful 24in Type 93 torpedoes, the cruisers and destroyers were fitted with power reloading gear. On the destroyers four reload torpedoes were carried in watertight steel boxes adjacent to the tube mount, four beside the rear funnel for the rear mount and normally split two on either side of the forward funnel for the forward mount. Inside the steel containers the torpedoes were carried on sets of rollers.

The 10hp compressed air mount training motor was connected to a pulley via reduction gears, and loading cables attached to the tail of the torpedo pulled it from its container and into the tube. Speed of loading was almost 8in/20cm per second. The power reloading gear, under ideal training conditions with the destroyer motionless, could reload all four tubes ready to fire in three minutes. Under actual combat conditions, however, tactical considerations could require the destroyer to retire at high speed, often under fire and during a night action, in order to reload. In such circumstances, the average time to reload and return into action was between twenty and thirty minutes.

If the power loading motor was out of action it was possible to load the torpedoes manually, using ten men to haul on a rope wound to a drum. The fastest time to load each torpedo manually was around five minutes.

Torpedo armament vulnerability

Concern was expressed as to the vulnerability to shellfire

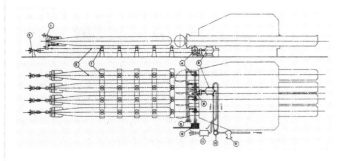

Side and plan view of the Type 92 quad torpedo tube mount reloading gear. (*Japanese Torpedoes and Tubes*, Article 3,' Above-water Tubes', US Naval Technical Mission to Japan, March 1946)

and bomb hits of the large Japanese cruiser and destroyer torpedo batteries. With compressed air-powered torpedoes, the Japanese felt that the effects of splinter damage were survivable, a splinter penetrating an air vessel causing only the escape of the compressed air. One must question this complacency in view of the various incidents detailed in Part V. Oxygen-fuelled Type 93 torpedoes, however, posed increased risks. If a splinter were to penetrate the oxygen vessel, the local heat generated could cause the torpedo to burn. If the fire was adjacent to the warhead this could explode.

To try to minimise at least the effects of shell and bomb splinters, the torpedo tube sides were given 5mm plates of light armour. The undersides and tops were unarmoured, but by training them fore and aft except when actually launching torpedoes, it was hoped to benefit from the protection offered by the ships' superstructures. To protect against the cooking-off of the warheads, water hoses and an emergency water tank were situated near each mounting, and in the event of a fire the damage control parties were trained to play water on the warhead. If necessary, the damaged torpedo would be launched from the tube. These arrangements would work in exercises, but in combat situations too often the damage was uncontrollable, or the damage control parties were knocked out of action, and severe damage and even loss of the ship resulted.

On the night of 11/12 October 1942, during the Battle of Cape Esperance, the heavy cruiser *Furataka* was hit on her torpedo tubes by a shell, which set her on fire. She later sank following a torpedo hit. On 3 April 1943 at Kavieng, the heavy cruiser *Aoba* was hit by bombs from B-17s. Two of her torpedoes exploded, causing serious fires in one of the engine rooms. She was beached to prevent her from sinking. Later salvaged, *Aoba* returned to Kure for repairs, and was out of action until the end of November 1943. During the epic battle of Leyte Gulf on 25 October 1944, explosions of their own torpedoes doomed two Japanese heavy cruisers off Samar. At 0851 the 15,000-ton heavy cruiser *Chōkai* was closing with the escort carriers of 'Taffy 3' when she was taken under fire by the destroyer escort *Roberts* and the single 5in stern guns on escort carriers *Kalinin Bay* and *White Plains*. It is believed that one of the carriers scored a hit on *Chōkai*'s port torpedo tubes, starting a major fire. Eight minutes later the torpedoes exploded, knocking out the cruiser's engines and steering. She sheered out of formation, and was then hit by a 500lb SAP bomb from an Avenger. Left dead in the water, *Chōkai* had to be scuttled by torpedoes from the destroyer *Fujinami*.

A short while later, heavy cruiser *Suzuya* was near-missed by a bomb amidships on her starboard side. Splinters set fire to a torpedo in one of her starboard mounts, which exploded, spreading the fire to the other mounts and reload torpedoes. Ten minutes later these also exploded, damaging the engine rooms and one boiler room. *Suzuya* became unmanageable, and Vice Admiral Shiraishi transferred his flag to *Tone*. At 1150 'abandon ship' was ordered, and just five minutes later *Suzuya*'s remaining torpedoes exploded. She capsized to starboard and sank with more than half her complement of 850 officers and men.

RN quadruple mounts

The Royal Navy fitted quadruple 21in torpedo mounts to most of its interwar cruiser classes, beginning with the heavy Treaty cruisers of the 'County' class. There was some anxiety concerning the launching of a torpedo from the weather deck of such high freeboard ships, but in the event they suffered no undue problems. Certainly HMS *Dorsetshire*'s torpedoes ran faultlessly to strike *Bismarck*.

At the same time, RN destroyers changed over to quadruple tubes, beginning with the leader HMS *Codrington*, laid down on 28 June 1928, and continuing through the following 'A' to 'H' classes, except for *Glowworm* which mounted two quintuple tubes. In addition, the leader *Inglefield*, which was the first to mount quintuple tubes, lost the centre tube of each mounting when converted for Arctic convoy duties. The quadruple tubes were also standard on the ex-Brazilian and ex-Turkish ships purchased for Royal Navy service, and two quadruple mounts were to be the standard outfit of the majority of RN destroyers built during the Second World War.

With four twin 4.7in gun mountings, the RN 'Tribal'-class destroyers maximised gun armament over torpedo armament, in an attempt to counter the Japanese super-destroyers of the *Fubuki* and later classes. So in a period when RN destroyers were starting to mount two quintuple torpedo tubes, the 'Tribals' reverted back to one single

HMS *Devonshire* in 1930, showing just how high above the waterline her quadruple 21in torpedo tubes were mounted. The height of the man standing on the bows of the boat on the left indicates the scale.

quad mount. The need for additional anti-aircraft firepower was the reason why the late war 'Ch'-, 'Co'- and 'Cr'-class ships were designed with only one quad mount.

During the war many destroyers lost one quad mounting to ship one anti-aircraft gun, either a 12pdr HA or a 4in, to give a modicum of HA fire capability.

The sole wartime RN destroyer survivor, HMS *Cavalier*, is well worth a visit in No 2 dry dock in Chatham Historical Dockyard, but she lost her entire torpedo outfit during post-war modernisation.

German quad mounts

During the Great War, German cruisers had aggressively used their torpedoes, notably at Jutland and in attacks on the Norway convoys. Therefore it was no surprise that the three '*Panzerschiffe*' ('armoured ships') *Deutschland*, *Admiral Scheer* and *Graf Spee*, were armed from the outset with two quadruple mounts on their quarterdeck, which would have been useful for commerce raiding. *Deutschland* (later renamed *Lützow*) originally carried 50cm tubes (19.7in) in unshielded mounts, but these were upgraded to 53.3cm (21in) as in her later sisters. Since the tubes were well within the blast area of the after triple 11in turret, these early unshielded mounts on *Deutschland* were quickly fitted with protective shields, and her sisters were built with them fitted.

What was unusual was the siting of the two quad mounts aft on the cut-down quarterdeck, right at the stern of the ship. Admittedly, the design of these ships had prioritised their gun armament, as they were intended to outgun any warship their size and smaller, but with sufficient speed to outrun anything bigger. The only

An aerial view of *Graf Spee* under way, showing the box shields covering her quadruple 21in torpedo tube mounts.

problem was how to escape from the Royal Navy battle-cruisers, which were the only warships capable of running them down and outgunning them.

A clue is given in the armament arrangements of the 'K'-class light cruisers, plus *Leipzig* and *Nürnberg*. Built for a possible employment as commerce-raiders (they were all fitted with cruising diesels to extend their range) each ship presented two-thirds of her armament astern, with a view to escaping from pursuers.

The *Panzerschiffe* copied this arrangement, with eight torpedo tubes available for stern launching. This feature is in complete contrast to the armament arrangement on the two French ships built specifically to hunt them down, the *Dunkerque* and *Strasbourg*. Acting on Royal Navy advice derived from experience with *Nelson* and *Rodney*, the *Dunkerque*s and their successors the *Richelieu*s had all their main armament mounted as chase guns, presenting eight guns forward.

Somewhat surprisingly in view of other navies' removal of torpedo tubes from their capital ships, in 1942 the Kriegsmarine fitted two quadruple 21in torpedo mounts to the *Tirpitz*, presumably for commerce-raiding purposes as with *Scharnhorst* and *Gneisenau*. Siegfried Breyer has suggested that perhaps these mounts were salvaged from the wrecks of German destroyers sunk at Narvik in 1940. Whatever their provenance, these quad above-deck mounts posed a very real risk in the event of a big gun duel, and even a shell from a British cruiser could initiate serious, if not fatal damage, similar to the incidents at Leyte.

But, of course, according to the Germans, the *Tirpitz*'s sister ship *Bismarck* had not been sunk by British shellfire and torpedoes: she had been scuttled by her own crew. The utter devastation caused by the British 16in and 14in shells was revealed only after Dr Ballard's photos of the rediscovered wreck.

US Navy quad tubes

The quadruple torpedo tube became the standard US destroyer outfit when the US Navy commenced new construction, beginning with the *Farragut* class, of which the name ship was laid down on 20 September 1932. The second modern class, the *Porter*s, also carried two quadruple tubes, but in addition shipped eight reload torpedoes around the funnel bases. These reloads were later removed to add increased light AA armament. The *Mahan*s which followed carried twelve tubes in three quadruple mounts, for a broadside of eight tubes.

Copying the precedent set by the flush-deckers of the Great War, in the late 1930s the USN went on to produce twenty-two destroyers in three classes, the *Gridley*s,

DD-389 USS *Mugford* of the *Bagley* class seen after the war being prepared for the Bikini Atoll nuclear tests. As with all the survivors of her class, she has retained her full torpedo armament of sixteen tubes. Note that each set of tubes faces its pair on the broadside; because of the close proximity of the broadside banks, to train one mount requires that the facing mount trains as well. (NHHC, photo # N116832)

*Bagley*s and *Benham*s, with the heaviest torpedo tube armament of any destroyer type (not counting the Japanese reload system). With four banks of quadruple tubes mounted two to port and two to starboard, their torpedo broadside was theoretically halved, but they had the ability to fire salvoes of sixteen torpedoes with gyro angling, in attack or withdrawal. Only Japanese cruisers equalled or surpassed this torpedo armament.

Due to the marginal stability common to these new destroyer classes, caused by Treaty tonnage restrictions, many US destroyers were forced to land torpedo mounts, to be able to carry the increased AA armament shown to be essential by an examination of the combat experience of the Royal Navy in the early part of the Second World War.

QUINTUPLE TUBES
RN quintuple tubes
The Royal Navy introduced the quintuple torpedo mount on the 'G'-class destroyer HMS *Glowworm*, which was the test bed for the new mounting, but the rest of her class received quadruple mounts. The leader HMS *Inglefield* and the following 'I' class were commissioned with two quintuple mounts, but as the extra top-weight affected their stability, in many cases they later landed the centre tube from each set. The 'J', 'K' and 'N' classes all commissioned with the ten-tube armament, although, as with the previous classes, many lost the aft bank of tubes to ship a 4in HA gun. Even when the 'N' class reverted to the full ten-tube torpedo armament, often only nine torpedoes were shipped to save weight. The full torpedo armament was not restored until the 1943 Battle class, none of which would be completed in time to see war service.

HMS *Khartoum* launching a torpedo from her aft quintuple tube mount. This tube mount would be the cause of the loss of *Khartoum* (see Part IV). (Laurence Bagley painting used as the cover illustration for *Model Boats* magazine, July 1968).

US pentad mounts

The pentad mount was introduced to US destroyers with the *Benson* class of 1938, and became the standard outfit for the following *Bristol*, *Fletcher* and *Allen M Sumner* classes.

All the drawings are taken from the Bureau of Ordnance manual on the Mark 14 and Mark 15, 21in above-water torpedo tubes. The Mark 14 was fitted in the forward position on *Fletcher*-class destroyers, and the Mark 15 in the aft position. The two marks were identical, except for the circular blast shield, constructed of two layers of corrugated steel, to protect the torpedo-men from the blast of the nearby 5in gun mount.

The pentad mount weighed 40,970lbs (18.58 tonnes) and the blast shield added a further 1040lbs (472kg). Each barrel was constructed of rolled steel 0.21in (5.33mm) thick, and the inside surface was milled smooth. The guide stud on top of the torpedo body fitted inside a bronze T-guide which was riveted to the top of the tube. The torpedo body was supported on three bronze rollers in the bottom of the tube, for ease of loading and launching. Training was by electric motor driving a hydraulic pump, or in an emergency by handwheels. The torpedo setters sat on top of the tubes, and the mount captain stood on the left, connected by telephone with the torpedo officer at the director on the bridge wing. A simple on-mount sight was available if the torpedo director was out of action.

A retractable crane was used for loading torpedoes into the tubes, but the final effort was by hand, aided by the rollers and a well-greased torpedo. Obviously, this could not be accomplished out at sea or when under fire; in any case, US destroyers did not carry reload torpedoes, and reloading the tubes was always carried out alongside the depot ship or quay. The torpedo would be pushed in until its guide stud engaged with the front stop-latch, after which the rear stop would be lowered, holding the torpedo securely in place. The tripping latch, when set in the 'down' position, would start the torpedo engine on launch.

The depth-setter device set the depth for all five torpedoes at the same setting. The gyro setter could set the gyros for all five torpedoes to the same angle, or it could set the angles for a spread, altering the gyro of each of the left-hand and right-hand pairs to divert at the chosen angle from the line of the centre barrel.

Each black powder impulse charge for launching a torpedo was contained in a case 3in diameter x 13in (76mm x 330mm) long. Mark 14 and 15 tubes required a sodium nitrate black powder charge of 38oz (1kg). The primer inside the cartridge was normally fired electrically, or if necessary by percussion. The gases entered an expansion chamber with a flash eliminator, then passed down into the tube to eject the torpedo. On launching, the tension link holding the front stop in position fractured, the stop swung out of the way, and the trip latch started the torpedo engine. It left the tube at a minimum speed of 50ft per second (15m/sec). Barrels were usually fired in the order: left, right, left-centre, right-centre, centre. This order was fixed to balance the tubes as far as possible when training after having fired one or more torpedoes.

To prevent the tubes and the mount from icing up in cold climates, the mount training circle and the rear part of each individual tube were fitted with heating pipes, fed from the destroyer's auxiliary exhaust steam supply. This enabled the torpedoes to be trained and launched in temperatures as

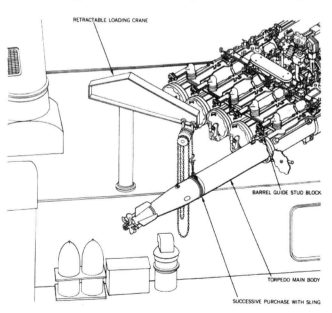

Mark 14 and 15 torpedo loading.

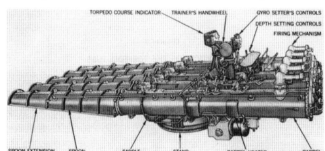

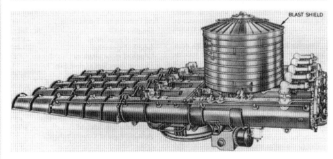

Pentad mounts, Mark 14 above and Mark 15, with blast shield, below.

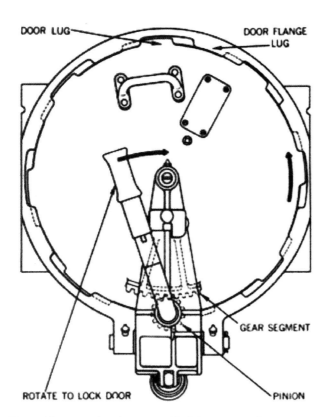

DOOR LUG

DOOR FLANGE LUG

GEAR SEGMENT

ROTATE TO LOCK DOOR

PINION

Above: The rear tube door resembled those on a submarine, with door lugs which engaged in slots in the tube ring, except that on this version, it was the door itself which revolved to close, not the ring, which was fixed.

low as 10°F (-12°C). Overlooked but vital components were the threaded canvas protection covers, which came in a variety of different types, shaped to protect each vital part of the mount exposed to the elements.

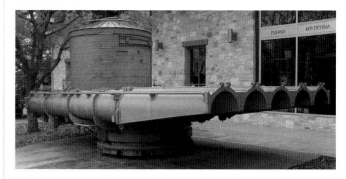

A preserved USN DD pentad torpedo tube mount with blast shield fitted to protect the torpedo-men from the blast of the nearby 5in/38 gun mount. Visible are the rungs to gain access to the interior and the front vision slot; the spoon folding extensions have been removed, and the mount lacks the firing chambers. (Photo courtesy of Robert Elder, National Museum of the Pacific War, Fredericksburg)

Below: Before launching, the on-mount controls set the torpedo speed, depth, gyro angle and spread.

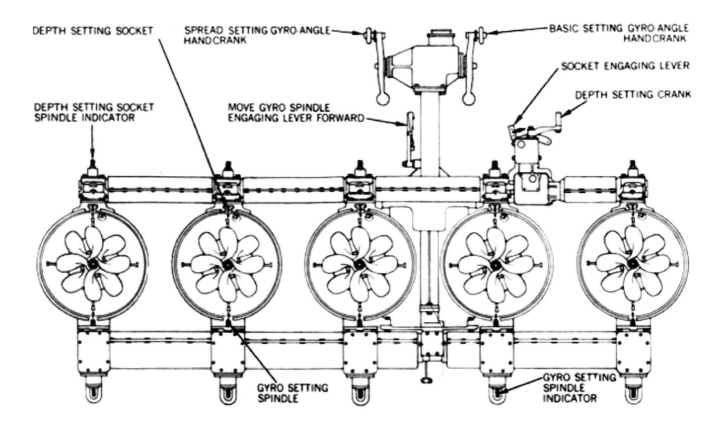

DEPTH SETTING SOCKET

SPREAD SETTING GYRO-ANGLE HAND CRANK

BASIC SETTING GYRO-ANGLE HAND CRANK

SOCKET ENGAGING LEVER

DEPTH SETTING CRANK

DEPTH SETTING SOCKET SPINDLE INDICATOR

MOVE GYRO SPINDLE ENGAGING LEVER FORWARD

GYRO SETTING SPINDLE

GYRO SETTING SPINDLE INDICATOR

Torpedo director

The Mark 14 and Mark 15 above-water torpedo tube mounts were controlled by the Mark 27 torpedo director. One of these was normally mounted on each bridge wing, and served by four men, the torpedo officer who selected the target and the torpedoes to be launched, the director trainer, who used the telescope to sight and keep onto the target vessel, the selector switch operator, who sent the commands to the torpedo tube mounts, and the telephone talker who was in contact with the mount captains.

Japanese quintuple torpedo tube mounts

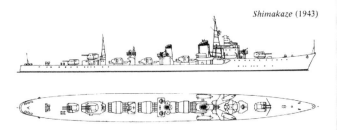

Shimakaze (1943)

IJNS *Shimakaze* ('Island Wind'), prototype Japanese super-destroyer, the only one fitted with quintuple tubes, showing her fifteen-tube broadside of 24in torpedoes. She carried no reloads. (Drawing by Peter Mickel from *Warships of the Imperial Japanese Navy 1869–1945*)

MODERN TORPEDO TUBES

With the need to launch fast-reaction, small anti-submarine torpedoes during the Cold War period, deck-mounted torpedo tubes came back into fashion. The Royal Navy came up with a heavy triple mounting, the STEWS, which in its one-over-two arrangement harked back to their 'V' and 'W' destroyer mounts.

In an effort to save weight, modern torpedo tubes are fabricated from glass fibre. Training twin and even triple mounts, such as the NATO-standard US Mark 32 can be found on many modern warships. They are calibrated to launch the Mark 46 and Mark 54 12.75in (324mm) diameter anti-submarine torpedoes, or the similar Sting Ray and MU-90.

The latest torpedo tube development is the MLS, or magazine launch system, in which the tube and its torpedoes are mounted within the ship's structure, protected from the elements. The torpedo is launched athwart the deck via a hinging flap, and is slowed by its attached parachute before hitting the water.

The Mark 27 as shown in the instruction manual.

The repeater receiver mounted on the tubes and the dials on the receiver with matching pointers.

A Mark 46 practice torpedo being fired from the Mark 32 triple mount on USS *Mustin*. Note the tube muzzle covers attached to the tube sides. (US Navy, photo # 070412-N-9851B-007)

A J+S (Canada) demonstration MLS mounting, complete with a catcher net to trap the practice torpedo.

HMS *Montrose* test-firing a practice Sting Ray torpedo from her MLS. The Sting Ray deploys a parachute to slow its entry into the water. (Photo courtesy of *Navy News*)

CHAPTER 12

Underwater Torpedo Tubes on Surface Ships

Above-water tubes posed a danger in that the torpedo warhead, and in the case of the Whitehead type, the air flask, were vulnerable to counter-fire. Explosion of the air flask could wreak havoc on deck; explosion of the warhead could prove fatal. A case in point is the presumed explosion of a loaded tube under American gunfire on board the Spanish armoured cruiser *Vizcaya* off Santiago on 3 July 1898.

Underwater tubes had the advantage that the torpedo space could be protected by the armoured deck of a protected cruiser. On battleships the mounting was usually positioned well below the waterline and was therefore in theory well-protected from shellfire. Another plus point was that the torpedo was not subject to impact damage on entering the water, and the deep fitting of battleship tubes meant that the effect of surface waves on initial guidance was minimised.

However, submerged tubes did pose several problems, most of which were overcome in the latter part of the nineteenth century. First, there was the problem of watertight integrity. The tube itself would be closed at the sea end either by a hinged flap, or a vertical or horizontal sluice gate. Launching from bow- and stern-mounted underwater tubes was simplified, unless the launching vessel was under tight helm at the moment of firing. This would be unlikely, since aiming was critical. Beam tubes were a different matter. Launching a torpedo broadside-on, or at a slight angle to the keel, exposed the missile to a severe risk of damage or at the very least of diverting it from its planned trajectory because of the motion of the launching ship.

All navies overcame this problem by arranging a support arm, commonly called a spoon ('*cuillère*' in French terminology) or bar, which extended from the launch tube in front of the torpedo and guided the weapon out into the water. A version favoured by Whitehead Fiume was a circular cage which extended to enclose the emerging torpedo. The Armstrong system was similar but comprised an extending slotted tube.

One major problem was, however, never satisfactorily resolved. Bow torpedo tubes tended to weaken the bow structure just where total integrity was required to survive ramming damage or, more usually, grounding incidents. But more serious was the temptation to install spacious underwater torpedo compartments, to be able to keep up a sustained series of launches on either beam. These were

difficult to arm, necessitating the arrangement of torpedo loading passageways through the relevant section of the ship (the German preference seemed to be to load the torpedoes vertically), and offered a large space liable to flooding, either through torpedo or mine damage or by a malfunction of the flap or sluice gate. The Kaiser is said to have personally intervened following the flooding of the forward torpedo compartment on the *Baden* when she was mined in 1917, and demanded the removal of the torpedo tubes.

A further problem was the need to evacuate the seawater entering the tube on each firing. To reload a beam tube, the spoon arm would be withdrawn, the flap or sluice gate closed, and the tube vented to the surface prior to opening. French and Austrian torpedo tubes loaded through a rear door while German and American tubes split lengthwise with pivoting side segments. HMS *Dreadnought* was fitted with a third variant, the first of the 18in Type B, with both a tube splitting lengthwise and a rear 'chopper' door. As Dr Oscar Parkes commented, when describing HMS *Agincourt* in action at Jutland, rapid fire necessitated leaving out the venting sequence, so when the tube was opened for reloading, its water content would spill into the firing compartment. Continuous action could lead to the torpedo-men working in up to 3ft of water.

When the early American dreadnoughts were being reconstructed between the wars, it was deemed prudent to remove their underwater torpedo tubes. Thought was given to repositioning these on deck, but the proposal was turned down because of the risk of exposure to enemy gunfire.

The moment of glory for the underwater tube came on 27 May 1941, during the *Bismarck*'s final action. At 0923 Chief Petty Officer Pollard and his team in the submerged torpedo room of HMS *Rodney* fired the first of two 24.5in torpedoes from her starboard tube. In all, they fired six torpedoes during the ship's run to the south, without scoring any hits. A near-miss by one of *Bismarck*'s 15in shells then damaged the sluice gate and put the starboard tube out of action. *Rodney* was zigzagging, firing gun salvoes alternately to starboard and port, and she fired two torpedoes from her port tube, at a range of three and a half miles, again without hitting. Nearly at the end of the action *Rodney* fired the last two of her complement of ten torpedoes, and claimed one hit. If true, this would have been the only time one battleship had actually torpedoed another.

ROYAL NAVY DESIGNS
HMS *Polyphemus*

The groundwork on designing and operating submerged torpedo tubes in the Royal Navy was carried out by Commander Arthur Knyvet Wilson, in charge of HMS *Vernon* from 1876 to 1881. The future admiral and First Sea Lord would go on to win the Victoria Cross on land at the Battle of El Teb, when the square broke and he fought off the Mahdists with his sword, then with his fists. During his years at *Vernon*, Wilson invented the bar or 'spoon' which enabled underwater broadside tubes to launch without damaging the torpedo.

On 15 June 1881 the Royal Navy launched an extraordinary vessel, the 'torpedo ram' HMS *Polyphemus*: 240ft long (73m) with a displacement of 2640 tons, her cigar-shaped hull was mostly awash when at speed, and her turtle-back was protected by 3in (76mm) armour. A minimal superstructure provided some degree of habitability, and for self-defence she was armed with six 1in Nordenfelt machine guns in circular 'pillbox' turrets, later supplanted by the same number of 3pdr (47mm) QF guns. *Polyphemus* was a fast ship for her day, capable of almost 18 knots, but the most revolutionary aspect was her offensive armament, which comprised five underwater torpedo tubes for 14in Whitehead Mark II torpedoes, of which she carried a total of eighteen. Other innovative features were a drop keel which could be jettisoned in an emergency if the hull was holed, and a pair of large life rafts hung from her boat deck aft of the funnel, which could float free if she sank.

She was built following proposals from Admiral Sir George Rose Sartorius, then in his eighties, who had seen much active service in the Napoleonic wars and later in command of the Portuguese Regent's fleet in the civil war of 1832–33. Sartorius felt that the introduction of the ironclad could only be effectively countered by the introduction of armoured ram ships.

This connection led to various misconceptions of the role intended for HMS *Polyphemus*, and perhaps the choice of her name was intended from the start to mislead.

Classical scholars would have known that the mythological Polyphemus was the one-eyed monster who

Polyphemus in drydock in Malta, showing what was hidden under the surface. Here she looks every bit like a Greek trireme, with her exaggerated ram, the two 'eyes' of her hawse holes, and even the timber supports playing the part of oars. At Malta she was to be rearmed with 47mm QF guns, and by the look of the chalk marks on her bow, to be repainted. (© National Maritime Museum, Greenwich, London 59-806)

HMS *Polyphemus* at high speed, showing how little of her armoured hull she exposed above water. Here she has been rearmed with 3pdr (47mm) QF guns. Abaft her funnel can be seen the two large life rafts carried athwartships under the flying deck. She is carrying the large booms used to extend the early crinoline anti-torpedo nets. (© National Maritime Museum, Greenwich, London 4937)

had tried to capture Odysseus and his companions. The wily king of Ithaca had escaped by driving a sharpened tree trunk into the monster's single eye, blinding him. Just to confuse the issue, of course, HMS *Polyphemus* carried *two* eyes like every ancient Greek or Roman galley, so the pundits would immediately realise that it was she who would be carrying the sharpened instrument, her bow, to the enemy in a ramming attack. To help her in this difficult task, she was equipped with two retractable bow rudders – just visible in the dry-dock photo – to enable her to spin like a top.

But all this was intended to cover her real function, as a fast, armoured torpedo ship, intended to be able to break into a defended harbour such as Cherbourg or Kronstadt, and then spin round inside, firing and reloading her five underwater tubes, creating mayhem among the unprepared enemy ironclads. The ram, once its cast-steel rotating bow cap was closed, would be useful in finishing off any vessel which had not immediately sunk. Taking advantage of the general chaos her action had caused, she would then attempt to escape at high speed. In any case, as with all torpedo boats of the era, even the *Polyphemus* was

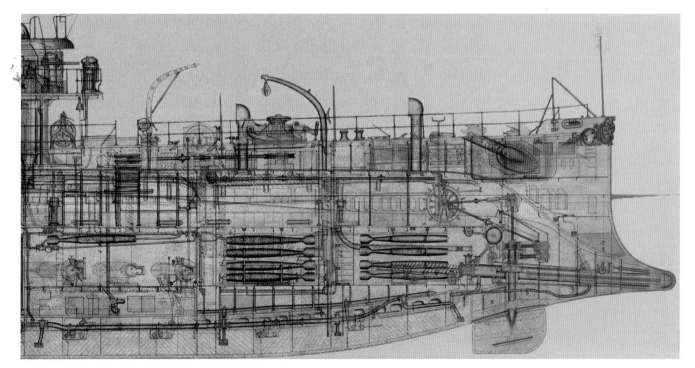

HMS *Polyphemus'* bow in section from the ship's plans. (© National Maritime Museum, Greenwich, London, J8901)

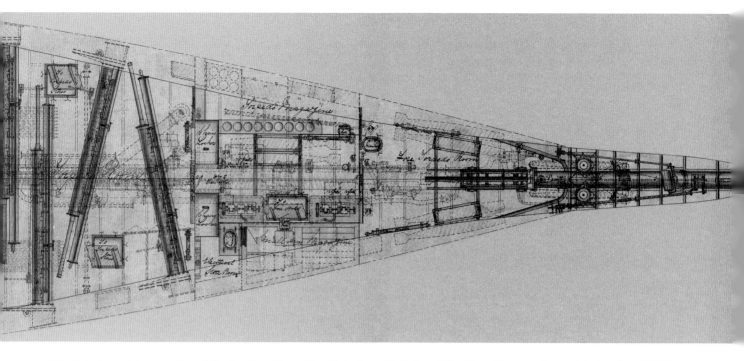

HMS *Polyphemus'* bow section at the hold level from the ship's plans. (© National Maritime Museum, Greenwich, London, J8900)

considered expendable, and her designers had built in lifesaving features to succour her crew. Risking a 2600-ton ship in the hope of crippling the enemy battle fleet was a good trade-off. For *Polyphemus* in action at Berehaven, see Part III.

The sectioned profile shows her retractable twin bow rudders, the shaft for opening the bow torpedo tube cap, the torpedo storage and her broadside submerged torpedo flat. The piping to drain all five torpedo tubes for reloading is included. In addition to the swivelling cast steel cap, the bow torpedo tube was also protected by a sluice gate, in case of damage to the cap during a ramming attack. The bow rudder layout pioneered by *Polyphemus* was to reappear some thirty years later on German torpedo boats and destroyers, although the retracting feature was not copied.

In the plan view it is clear that the broadside tubes split horizontally to open, as there is insufficient space behind the tubes for a rear door, as was fitted on the bow tube. The broadside tubes are sealed against the outside seawater by horizontal sluice gates, while the bow tube is protected by an internal vertical sluice gate. The torpedo warheads are stored in a separate torpedo magazine. Note how, as the beam reduces, the forward torpedo tubes are angled. On the original plan was written the torpedo magazine capacity:

Torpedo Heads War allowance	24
Torpedo Heads Peace allowance	18
Cases for Torpedo Gun Cotton Charges	5
Cases for Damp Gun Cotton	15
Cases for Dry Gun Cotton	9
Cases for 20 Empty Primer Tins	1

Interestingly, although the ship's plan has been amended to show the modifications to *Polyphemus*, and in particular her new 3pdr (47mm) QF guns, the part of the plan detailing the contents of the small arms magazine lists the following:

Nordenfelt Ammunition Boxes	110
Nordenfelt Hopper Boxes Double	4
Nordenfelt Hopper Boxes Single	6
Gardiner Ammunition Boxes	12

In other words, when she originally went to sea, she carried Gardiner machine guns, probably in .45-cal, as well as the 1in Nordenfelts in their pillbow turrets.

As a footnote, it is generally held that HMS *Polyphemus* was the inspiration for H G Wells' HMS *Thunderchild* in his science fiction novel *War of the Worlds*.

HMS *Hood*

Hood had completed with two underwater 21in torpedo tubes, forward of 'A' turret, despite the director of naval construction noting on 10 December 1918 that it would

A photo of *Hood* just prior to launch, her side armour not having been fitted. In the centre of the picture is the outer door for her port underwater torpedo tube.

One of HMS *Hood's* fixed torpedo tubes, with a spare torpedo overhead, and the engine section of a second torpedo on the left. From the limited headroom, it appears that this is one of her underwater tubes photographed prior to 1927.

be difficult to envisage launching the underwater torpedoes at the high speed of which the *Hood* was capable. Nevertheless, the underwater tubes were not removed until 1927, leaving her with the four above-water tubes and mounting points for four more in time of war.

HMS *Rodney*

The plan view shows the fine lines of these battleships up forward, presumably to try to offset their modest engine power imposed by the tonnage limitations of the Washington Treaty.

The torpedo areas were certainly an exposed battle station – the armour belt and the torpedo defence system ended abreast 'A' turret. Between 'A' turret magazines and the torpedo body room with its highly explosive contents, the designers had wisely placed the cold room and its supplies of meat and other perishables.

At least the torpedo-men on *Nelson* enjoyed overhead protection after 3in (76mm) armour plates were worked in above the torpedo body room and the torpedo tube compartment during a refit in 1937–38. *Rodney* never received this extra protection. The torpedo body room where the tubes were loaded was separated by a watertight bulkhead from the actual torpedo tube compartment with the horizontal sluice gate and the launch controls. This was an attempt to limit the possibility of major flooding to a single torpedo flat, as had occurred during the Great War.

From the plan it does not appear the tubes were

HMS *Rodney's* torpedo body room with some of her huge 24.5in torpedoes undergoing maintenance. It is tempting to wonder whether one of these in the photo is the torpedo which the crew claimed struck *Bismarck*. (Imperial War Museum, A820)

A plan view of the platform deck on *Nelson* and *Rodney*. (© National Maritime Museum, Greenwich, London, J8902)

provided with a spoon (or 'bar' in RN terminology), as they were practically bow tubes requiring very little gyro angling for straight ahead launches. The torpedo warheads were stored below the torpedo body room.

When HMS *Nelson* was mined on 4 December 1939, the torpedo spaces were flooded, but were otherwise undamaged. However, when she was in action against Italian aircraft on 27 September 1941 she was hit on the port side forward by an 18in torpedo, and the torpedo body room and ten of the twelve torpedoes she carried were wrecked. Luckily, the captain had ordered the torpedo-men to evacuate the spaces before the torpedo hit.

Torpedo control towers

Obviously, since the crews loading submerged torpedo tubes were out of sight of the enemy they were fighting, some means of directing torpedo launches had to be devised. Just before the start of the Great War, but for different reasons, the old system of individual firing and spotting of the big guns of a battleship's main armament gave way to director-control firing, feeding data from rangefinders and observers into a mechanical computer in the transmitting station.

The same system was applied to controlling torpedo launch. The *Iron Duke*, Jellicoe's flagship at Jutland, had the latest and most elaborate system to control her underwater torpedo tubes. A torpedo control tower with its own 15ft (4.5m) rangefinder in the rotating hood was situated in front of 'X' turret. A repeater indicator from the Forbes log gave the ship's speed. Other instruments in the control tower were used to estimate the enemy's range, course and speed, and the torpedo deflection necessary to hit the enemy where he was likely to be when the torpedo arrived.

This information was transmitted to the secondary torpedo control positions installed near the ship's side, above the underwater tubes port and starboard. Each secondary control position was connected to the torpedo flat beneath it by voice tubes, and by telephone to the ship's main conning tower and the torpedo control tower. The control tower was connected to the gunnery computer in the transmitting station, and if the control tower was put out of action, the Royal Marines manning the transmitting station could take over and transmit the necessary information to the secondary control positions.

Torpedoes from the forward submerged tubes were launched from either the main conning tower or the relevant secondary torpedo-control position. The torpedoes in the aft tubes, however, were launched by the team in the torpedo control tower. The torpedo-men at the tubes received the necessary gyro angles, speed and depth settings, and the order to launch, from Barr & Stroud repeater instruments. For use in night actions, all the instruments in the conning tower, torpedo control tower and the secondary control positions were fitted with shaded lamp holders fixed so as to illuminate the instrument dials.

To control her two underwater tubes as well as her fixed above-water tubes, HMS *Hood* was fitted with three torpedo control towers, one aft overlooking 'X' turret, and one on either side beneath the midships searchlight tower between the funnels.

On *Nelson* and *Rodney*, the last British dreadnoughts to be fitted with underwater torpedo tubes, the torpedo control towers were installed one either side in front of the funnel. These small hooded rangefinders are easily overlooked when studying battleships. It was ironic that this elaborate system produced no confirmed results at

A view of *Rodney* taken in 1928, showing her starboard torpedo control tower just forward of the funnel.

Jutland, where many dreadnoughts on both sides launched a large number of torpedoes without scoring any hits.

FRENCH DESIGNS

Henri IV was a small low-freeboard monitor-type of coast defence battleship, with two novel features: her aft superfiring turret, the first to appear on a warship, and her convex internal anti-torpedo bulkhead. The integrity of the latter was, however, somewhat compromised by the fact that her two underwater torpedo tubes pierced the bulkhead protection.

In the accompanying plan, the bottom cutaway drawing, of the tube in plan view, shows the large curved

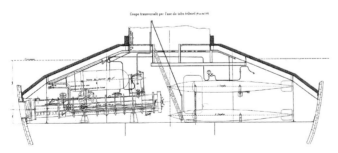

The underwater torpedo tubes on French protected cruiser *D'Entrecasteaux* of 1896, showing how the tube flat is covered by the inclined armour protective deck. *D'Entrecasteaux*'s tubes did not have a 'spoon' but rather the extending inner tube of the Armstrong system. (Châtellerault Archives, plan no D'ENTRE 1896CO32A)

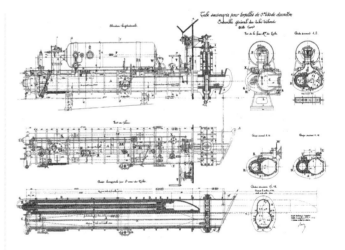

The aft starboard underwater tube on the coast defence battleship *Henri IV*. (Châtellerault Archives, plan ref Henri IV 1899 PL1)

bar or spoon (*cuillère*) which extended out in front of the torpedo to protect it during the launch sequence. Also evident is the substantial vertically-operating sluice gate which closed off the outboard end of the tube. Unlike later German dreadnought designs, there was no outer flap. A slight resistance to water flow from the open port ends was accepted for the sake of simplicity.

Unlike later underwater tubes, these French designs did not split lengthwise to load. The torpedo flat had therefore to be arranged to allow end-loading, which was achieved by simply offsetting the opposing tubes one in front of the other.

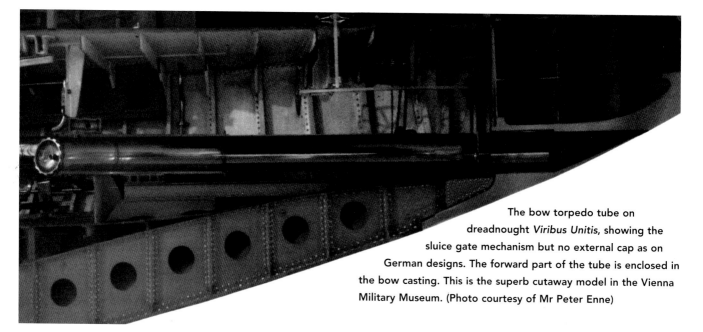

The bow torpedo tube on dreadnought *Viribus Unitis*, showing the sluice gate mechanism but no external cap as on German designs. The forward part of the tube is enclosed in the bow casting. This is the superb cutaway model in the Vienna Military Museum. (Photo courtesy of Mr Peter Enne)

AUSTRIAN DESIGNS

Robert Whitehead had produced the very first underwater torpedo tube in 1866 for the Austrian trials of his new weapon. Subsequently, the Austro-Hungarian navy had adopted underwater tubes in line with all other navies of the period.

US NAVY DESIGNS
USS *Intrepid*

Less extreme than her contemporary, the torpedo ram USS *Alarm*, the *Intrepid* nevertheless exhibited several novel features. Her hull was especially strengthened for ramming, and a torpedo launching tube was inserted in

USS *Intrepid* in dry dock, showing her ram fitted with a torpedo tube, and the curious hull strakes, fitted to strengthen her for ramming. (NHHC, photo # H53251)

USS *Florida* in dry dock, 9 October 1916, showing the spoon, or more correctly here due to its shape, the bar for her forward port underwater tube extended. (US Navy photo, courtesy of Michael Mohr)

An internal view showing USS *Intrepid*'s bow torpedo tube. Note the close frame spacing to add strength for ramming. (Detroit Collection, Library of Congress, photo # LC-D4-20352)

The underwater torpedo room of pre-dreadnought USS *Rhode Island* about 1914, showing the opened pivoting section of tube and how the segment interlocked with the tube top and end to close. A 21in Bliss-Leavitt torpedo hangs from the overhead travelling rail. (NHHC, photo # NH 101087; photograph by Francis Sargeant)

the centre of the ram, obviously inspired by HMS *Polyphemus*. Compared to the latter, however, *Intrepid* was an uninspired design, capable only of a lumbering 10 knots maximum speed – far too slow to catch any ship worth ramming. Plans to strip her of her armour belt and send her to China as a river gunboat came to naught, and she was scrapped in 1892.

For the underwater tubes of US battleships, Bliss-Leavitt designed a special short torpedo, the 21in Mark 3 Mod 1, with a length of 196in (5.4m).

US torpedo battleship design projects

Prior to the Great War, the US Navy Design Bureau of Construction and Repair undertook a series of design studies into alternative forms of dreadnought capital ships. The sketch designs show the barest of details, and if these ships had been constructed, they would have been fitted out with the normal complement of masts and boats. They all did, however, present a minimalist appearance, offering low-profile targets. The design team came up with several interesting alternatives, rather on the lines of a car manufacturer's 'concept' vehicles. Two overriding notions were the desire for high speed, and the reduction of the heavy gun armament in favour of extremely powerful batteries of underwater torpedo tubes.

The heavy torpedo armament proposed in these four concept vessels shows how far torpedo development had progressed, as it was clear that the torpedo was to be the principal armament of at least three of the four. In this respect, the third design was by far the most extreme.

In the event, no battlecruisers would ever be completed for the US Navy, the two giants laid down at the end of the Great War, *Saratoga* and *Lexington*, being converted as the world's largest aircraft carriers. And the 12in-gunned *Alaska*-class ships produced during the Second World War, although having the characteristics of battlecruisers, and being designed as a response to imagined Japanese vessels of this type, were in reality super-heavy cruisers.

GERMAN DESIGNS

Bayern was still undergoing trials when the Battle of Jutland occurred in May–June 1916, but she was available for the next major event, Operation Albion. During this operation she struck a mine that flooded the forward beam torpedo room and she withdrew to a local port, where she was given a poorly constructed cofferdam which failed during her transit back to Germany. Based on inaccurate evaluations of the damage in a brief to the Kaiser, he made the decision to have the forward beam torpedo tubes removed from *Bayern* and her sister.

The early German dreadnought SMS *Ostfriesland* was ceded to the USA at the end of the Great War. Before she was expended in Billy Mitchell's controversial aerial bombing experiments, she was dry-docked in the New York Navy Yard in October 1921 for study of her underwater hull features. At the same time the opportunity was taken to record various features on film, as shown in the following sequence of photos, all kindly provided by Tom Tanner of Lothian, Maryland.

During the Second World War, the underwater torpedo tube once more came into fashion, this time for concealment, on the disguised German auxiliary cruisers. HSK *Kormoran*, sunk in the mutually fatal battle with HMAS *Sydney*, was fitted with a torpedo tube at deck level on each beam, concealed behind a falling flap, but she also had two underwater broadside tubes, one of which was discovered and photographed when her wreck was found.

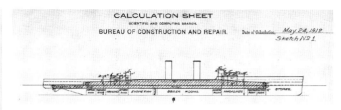

The first torpedo battleship design, dated 24 May 1912. This was to have displaced 30,000 tons, with a top speed of 27 knots, to be armed with six 14in guns in two triple turrets, plus sixteen 6in anti-TB armament, and eight 21in underwater torpedo tubes. With 7½in (190mm) belt armour, they were protected on the scale of the early RN battlecruisers, and would have proved equally vulnerable in the coming conflict.

The second torpedo battleship design study dated 31 May 1915. This kept the displacement at 30,000 tons, the speed at 27 knots, and the secondary armament at sixteen 6in guns, but shed one main armament triple turret in exchange for thicker armour up to 10in (254mm) on the belt, and an increased torpedo armament of twelve 21in underwater torpedo tubes.

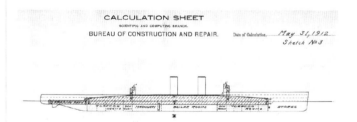

The third torpedo battleship study dated 31 May 1912. Again with a displacement of 30,000 tons, 27 knots and sixteen 6in anti-TB guns, but this one dispensed with the big guns completely, in exchange for belt armour up to 13in (330mm) thick and two underwater torpedo batteries with a total of eighteen 21in tubes.

Fourth torpedo battleship design dated 15 August 1912. The final design study went to different extremes, at 35,000 tons and 30 knots, mounting a single quadruple 14in turret forward, no less than forty 3in anti-TB guns and sixteen 21in torpedo tubes, protected by a belt with a maximum thickness of 14in (356mm).

The substantial reinforcement around the bow torpedo tube, and a close-up view of the mouthpiece from the front. The clumsy fitting cannot have helped hydrodynamic flow. The narrowness of the bow structure would not have permitted any training, so angled launching would have relied on setting the torpedo gyro just as for a broadside launch.

Above: Forward starboard torpedo tube mouthpiece, clapper closed.

Left: The stern torpedo tube door, outlined in white paint for the photographic sequence. The photo hints at another serious disadvantage of these tubes. This one, with its reload torpedoes, is situated between the operating gear for the twin rudders, and any malfunction here could have had disastrous consequences.

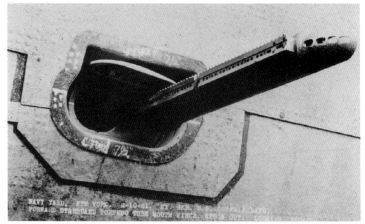

Two views of the forward starboard torpedo tube with clapper open and spoon extended, showing the top rack.

Aft starboard mouthpiece, clapper closed.

One of the underwater torpedo tubes inside the *Ostfriesland*'s broadside torpedo flats.

HSK *Kormoran*'s starboard submerged torpedo tube. (Photo held by the Australian War Memorial)

CHAPTER 13

Submarine Torpedo Launching Gear

From early in the twentieth century, submarines have laid mines; by their very secretive nature they are the perfect minelayers, even though submariners would also suffer cruelly at the hands of enemy mines and, all too often, the mines they themselves were laying. In more modern times, submarines have been converted and built to fire missiles, and today the 'boomers' have taken on the role of the modern capital ship. But for submarines, their most successful weapon is, of course, the torpedo. In fact, it is safe to say that the development of the reliable torpedo made viable the development of the workable submarine, which up till then had lacked a practical weapon. The lethal combination of the torpedo and the submarine came close to winning two world wars for Germany, they made a major contribution to the defeat of Japan, and still today they form a potent combination.

AUSTRIAN SUBMARINE TUBES

During the Great War, Austrian submarines carried three calibres of torpedo, the 53.3cm (21in) Whitehead, the 50cm (19.7in) German Schwartzlose, and the 45cm (17.7in) Whitehead. One Austro-Hungarian submarine was also fitted with trainable torpedo drop collars, but that was because she was the former French submarine *Curie*, lost on 20 December 1914 when she became entangled in the anti-submarine net defending Pola harbour. Raised on 31 January 1915 she was repaired and entered service with the Austro-Hungarian fleet as *U 14*.

RUSSIAN SUBMARINE DROP COLLARS

Early Russian submarines launched their torpedoes from external drop collars invented by Stefan Drzewiecki, a Polish engineer working for the Russian navy (at the time, of course, Poland was still part of the Russian empire). For submarines, the drop collar offered certain advantages. It was much lighter than the bronze torpedo tube, but also, being completely external to the boat, it had no watertight doors front and rear. Therefore there was no hazard of door failure caused by depth-charge attack or diving deep, or of accidental flooding due to faults with, or lack of, door interlocks. Most importantly, when launching submerged it gave away no tell-tale compressed air bubbles, the launch procedure being limited to setting the desired gyro angle, pivoting the collars into the release position, starting the torpedo motor and at the same time releasing the grip of the collars. Finally, as there was no tube to flood and empty, the submarine's trim was affected only by the loss of weight of the launched torpedo itself.

These advantages led the Russians to make extensive use of the drop collar. There were, however, some serious

A fine cutaway model in the Vienna Military Museum of Austro-Hungarian submarine *U 20* of the Havmanden class, with superimposed twin tubes for 18in Whitehead torpedoes. (Photo courtesy of Mr Peter Enne)

A Russian *Bars*-class submarine showing the early low-mounted drop collars, set in recesses in the hull side plating.

The launching gear, unlike a torpedo tube, could not be reloaded when submerged, so many Russian boats carried up to eight torpedoes externally.

From an early stage of submarine development the French, who also used a form of drop collar, well understood the value of hull streamlining to reduce resistance and boost underwater speed. Their drop collars were faired into the casing, or even covered by hinged flaps. The Russians, on the other hand, mounted their drop collars too low, which affected hydrodynamic efficiency on the surface, and cannot have helped the boats when submerged. To remedy this shortcoming, the submarines of the *Bars* class were progressively rebuilt, the collars being moved initially to the curved deck edge of the hull, and finally on to the deck itself. One major problem still dogged the Russian boats: mounting the torpedoes in external drop collars left them exposed to icing up in the severe conditions of the Russian winter.

Volk alongside her depot ship in a wintry scene, showing the final position of the drop collars, moved onto the deck itself. One can imagine that not much routine maintenance was carried out on the external torpedoes in such conditions.

drawbacks: as the torpedo was carried externally, virtually no maintenance could be carried out on it at sea. This question would seem to have been mainly theoretical, since the Royal Navy increased the salvo firepower of its 'T'-class boats during the Second World War by adding external torpedo tubes fore and aft. The US Navy also upped the torpedo salvoes of its submarine cruisers *Narwhal* and *Nautilus* by adding external tubes under the gun deck.

Tygr, launched from the Reval Submarine Yard in April 1916, with the second position of drop collar mounted below the deck edge.

THE FRENCH SIMONOT DEVICE

The French have a penchant for being different. They were attracted to the simplicity of the external drop collar but then turned it into a much more sophisticated version. The result was the 'appareil Simonot', invented by Ingénieur en chef de 1ère classe Jean Ernest Simonot, who was also responsible for designing the carrier submarines. These were armed with conventional fixed torpedo tubes, but also trainable sets of torpedo tubes as on a surface ship. It appears that French had little trust in gyro angling, and went one further in including a version of the drop collar that was also trainable.

The Simonot device held the torpedo in an external cage, suspended from an overhead rail which could pivot out from the line of the hull on a vertical axle at the rear. A compressed air piston released the clamps holding the cage to the hull, and also acted on the swinging arm, starting it on its traversing arc – which relied also on the water pressure from the forward movement of the boat. The forward Simonot devices on the submarine *Diane* could swing through a total arc of 165 degrees, from straight ahead to 75 degrees aft of the beam. When the device was oriented in the desired direction, the torpedo motor was started and it exited the cage. It was to be hoped that the modest forward underwater speed of the boat did not have an influence on the course taken by the torpedo. The French fitted this complicated device to several of their submarines of the Great War period, later removing them from the aft position where they relied instead on traversing torpedo tube mounts, but the forward fittings remained in use until the boats were withdrawn from service in the 1930s. One must assume that, given the effort expended on their conception and manufacture, the French were determined to hang onto them for as long as possible.

BROADSIDE AND TRAVERSING TUBES

Some First World War British submarines, beginning with *E 11*, had broadside torpedo tubes for 18in torpedoes – a curious arrangement, wasteful of space, and difficult to aim compared with bow and stern tubes, requiring the boat to

Here matelots are carrying out maintenance on the training torpedo tube mount on the submarine *Junon*.

slow or stop and fire with gyro settings. The torpedo tubes were of the same split tube pattern as used in the submerged torpedo flats of battleships and cruisers of the era, as there was no space behind the tubes in the narrow confines of the submarine hull to load via a rear door. The tubes also pierced the inner pressure hull, weakening the whole structure, and took up space used by the external ballast tanks. Given the small size of the boats, however, it was one way to drastically increase the torpedo armament.

The steam-powered 'K' class were originally conceived as 'submersible destroyers'. They were provided with a large midships torpedo flat. As well as their four 18in bow tubes, the Ks had four broadside tubes firing two to each beam, plus spare torpedoes hung overhead or stowed between the tubes. In addition, as befitted their high speed surface role of accompanying the battle fleet, the 'K'-class boats were originally designed to carry a training twin-tube mounting on deck, 'for night actions', the submerged tubes being employed for ambushing

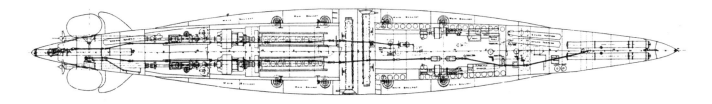

Here in the plan view *E 11*'s two 18in torpedo tubes can be seen mounted amidships, just behind the conning tower.

damaged units of the High Seas Fleet limping home. But the training twin mount had to be removed as it was too exposed to damage in high seas on the low freeboard deck of the 'K' boats.

Some French designs of the Great War era carried internal tubes, external Simonot devices and an external traversing multiple mounting. This must have posed significant tactical problems and was one over-complication too many. French submarines built in the 1930s typically had one eternal training mount aft of the conning tower, and another traversing mount at the rear extremity of the casing.

They were a means of carrying additional tubes, external to the pressure hull, for a larger torpedo armament than normal, while retaining the streamlined lines of the hull. In comparison, British boats of the 'T' class mounted external tubes but as excrescences, which must have detracted from underwater performance and could even have generated additional noise. Naturally, any and all external tubes suffered from the disadvantage of exposing the torpedoes outside the pressure hull, making maintenance difficult, if not impossible, and obviously the tubes could not be reloaded at sea. Finally, some designers felt that having torpedoes carried externally posed an extra

Loading a 600-tonne boat's training tubes. Easy enough in port, it would be impossible at sea.

hazard when under depth-charge attack.

When Ateliers et Chantiers de la Loire built the diminutive boats *Ronis* and *Spidola* for the Latvian navy, they were fitted with six 18in torpedo tubes, two in the bows and four in two twin training mountings, one fore and one aft. The three boats of the *Wilk* class from the same builders, supplied to Poland, had a similar arrangement but with 21in torpedoes.

An additional French speciality was the introduction of a smaller torpedo, of 400mm diameter (15.75in), specifically for sinking merchant ships, leaving the heavier 21in torpedoes for attacks on warships. This was a strange development, as the small 400mm torpedoes might disable a large merchantman, but could not be guaranteed to ensure sinking it quickly. Very few merchant ships, other than tankers, were capable of surviving even a single hit by a 21in torpedo.

The smaller 400mm tubes were incorporated in training mounts, and were even carried in mixed calibre training mounts, with two outside 21in tubes and two inside 400mm tubes. The 400mm torpedoes were reportedly unsuccessful in service. Some submarines operating out of Britain during the Second World War had their mixed calibre (two 21in and two 400mm) tubes rearmed with three 21in tubes instead, but this was probably because of the difficulty of obtaining stocks of the 400mm torpedoes.

Another navy that designed external training tube mounts into its boats was the Royal Netherlands navy. Dutch boats continued to be built with them right up until

Three Dutch boats at Fremantle, Australia. The boat on the right, *O 21*, has her external twin tube mount trained on the broadside. (Photo from the Daily News, Perth)

the outbreak of the Second World War, but it is notable that when the Kriegsmarine took over and completed the unfinished *O 27*, they deleted the training tube mount. Dutch boats normally had covers which enclosed the opening on either side of the hull for the traversing mount, preserving the well-streamlined shape of their boats. In a similar manner to the French yards, when the Dutch built two submarines for Poland, the *Sep* and the *Orzel*, they included the training tubes.

U-BOAT TORPEDO TUBE SYSTEMS
First World War
German U-boats of the Great War did not usually display their torpedo tubes, even when out of water, but a photograph of *U 110* in dry dock provides an opportunity to see the bow tubes. Having been rammed and sunk, then salvaged by the British, *U 110* was undergoing repair with a view to being returned to service in order to examine her characteristics. The quite different upper and lower bow doors are shaped to fit the hull contours. Despite the damage to the bow which was the cause of *U 110* sinking, the torpedo tube section appears intact. The Admiralty plans to study U-boats by re-conditioning *U 110* came to an end with the Armistice, and she was unceremoniously scrapped. Surrendered U-boats in better condition such as the *U 126* and *U 141* were made available to the Royal Navy to dissect and analyse.

Second World War U-boat torpedo tubes
The torpedo tubes used on all the operational U-boats in the Second World War were similar in design to those found in the boats of most other navies, so the description

The business end of a late Second World War German U-boat steel torpedo tube, here a bow tube from a Type XXI. (Photo courtesy of Maciej Florek)

here can be taken as representative of contemporary submarine tubes – apart from two specific German innovations.

The muzzle doors were opened by the rod seen in the photo, and the vertical rod on the right of the door opened the outer hull shutter at the same time. When the boats were submerged, the water pressure pushing against the outer door made it difficult, if not impossible, to open the muzzle door to launch a torpedo, so it was first necessary to flood the tube. This could be done by using water from outside the boat, which would tend to upset the trim, or else by a complicated method of pumping water from an internal tank, which did not have such a marked effect on trim. German U-boats did not have an automatic device for trimming the boat to compensate for the torpedo having been fired, so the retrimming had to be done manually.

U 110 in the Swan Hunter dry dock in late 1918. (Photo courtesy of Tyne & Wear Archives)

The inside of a torpedo tube on *U 995*, a Type VII U-boat transferred to the Norwegian navy, and now on display at Laboe in Germany, showing the guide slots for the launch piston. (Photo courtesy of Maciej Florek)

The tubes were made of bronze, although late-war boats had tubes made of steel because of a shortage of copper, 55.36cm (21.8in) internal diameter and 7.552m (24ft 9in) long. They were built in three sections, bolted together, one section being inside the pressure hull and the other two outside. The tubes had retracting connections which entered the torpedo body and set the depth, speed and gyro angle. One major German innovation was that, from February 1943 onward, an additional device was added, to set the FAT torpedo, which from July 1944 also set the LUT. These connections were automatically withdrawn from the torpedo body when the firing rod was operated. Depth and speed were set manually, but the gyro angle and the settings for the FAT and LUT torpedoes were transmitted by servo motors. The gyro setting control could also be used to set each gyro for firing a spread.

A torpedo was manually loaded into its tube (although the late war Type XXI U-boats had power reloading), and pushed forward until it engaged the front and rear stop bolts. These positioned it correctly in the tube so that the depth and gyro angling connections could be inserted at the correct positions in the torpedo body.

It was too dangerous to start the torpedo engine inside the tube before launching it, because of the hot exhaust gases and the lack of flow of cooling water to the engine. It was started automatically as it was ejected. On activating the firing rod, the torpedo stop bolt was withdrawn and the trigger latch descended into the tube. Compressed air forced the torpedo forward at a speed of 10m/sec (33ft/sec) and the trigger latch started its engine.

This is a view of the launch piston inserted behind the G7e electric torpedo, in a sectioned torpedo tube in *U 505* on display in the Chicago Science Museum. The guide stud for the slot at the 5 o'clock position is clearly visible. Note the buffer on the guide stud. (Photo courtesy of Maciej Florek)

Here the German engineers had added an innovative feature, the launch piston. On launching a torpedo, the compressed air would exit the tube and rise to the surface, threatening to give away the position of the boat. To avoid this, the Germans inserted a piston behind the loaded torpedo. The piston was made of steel, weighed 35kg (77lbs) and was machined to fit closely inside the tube. It had two projecting studs which fitted in guide slots inside the tube. These slots ran for almost the whole length of the tube, ending 90cm (2ft 11in) behind the muzzle door. At this point the outside of the tube was strengthened by external steel ribs, which enabled the bronze tube to stand the shock of the piston reaching the end of its travel.

The system had two operating methods. For submerged launches, the compressed air was injected behind the piston, and did not escape when the torpedo was ejected. The piston was arrested in its forward motion at the end of the guide slots, and the seawater pushed the piston back inside the tube, recompressing the expanded air, which was vented to a holding tank. When the muzzle door had been closed and the tube pumped dry, the piston could be removed ready for reloading the next torpedo.

When launching the torpedo on the surface, it was not necessary to effect this operation, and also the water pressure would be insufficient to push the piston back in place. So the piston was locked in position at the rear of the tube and the compressed air was injected in front of the piston to launch the torpedo.

This system worked well, but the precision sliding fit of the piston caused problems when the tubes were subject to pressure from exploding depth charges or aircraft bombs, and instructions were issued stressing the need to inspect the tubes after each heavy attack.

The breech door was locked shut by a revolving ring on the rear end of the tube. Cut-outs on the ring matched the segments on the hinged door, and when this was closed, the segments on the ring revolved behind those on the door. This was a quick-acting arrangement, but the door could not stand extreme pressures, which posed a threat if the external shutter and muzzle door had been damaged by depth-charge explosions. Also, it meant that torpedoes could not be launched when the boat had gone deep. The Type XXI was redesigned to overcome these problems, but none fired a torpedo in anger before the end of the war.

An interlock prevented opening the breech door if the outer muzzle door was open. Before the breech door could be opened, it was also necessary to recock the firing rod in order to open the breech door-locking ring. This retracted the engine trigger latch, so a new torpedo could be inserted. Another interlock prevented the firing

The four bow tubes on the *U 995*, essentially the same as used on the *U 110* of the Great War. The box with three dials and a handwheel, at top centre, is the gyro and spread angle receiver for the remote control system. The handwheel is for manually setting these if the system fails. The system received its settings from the torpedo data computer. The box at centre with two dials is the LUT control panel. The firing handles and their safety catches can be seen just in front of the breech doors at the 1 o'clock (LH) and 11 o'clock (RH) positions. (Photo courtesy of Maciej Florek)

mechanism from being activated if the muzzle door was closed, and a third device prevented opening of the muzzle door when the tube was being drained.

With the introduction of the electric Type G7e torpedo, it was necessary to preheat the electric storage batteries in the torpedo to 30°C shortly before launch, in order to obtain their maximum rated performance. The cells in the batteries contained thermostatically controlled heater elements, and to activate them an electrical plug had to be inserted through a hole in the torpedo tube to connect with a socket in the top of the torpedo body. This ad hoc arrangement did not lend itself to mechanical interlocks, so none were fitted: the plug had to be manually removed and the hole sealed with its waterproof cover.

The small coastal Type XIII U-boats which entered service towards the end of the Second World War were too small to carry reload torpedoes. They were armed with only two torpedoes, which had to be muzzle-loaded from the outside when in harbour, since the torpedo room was too short to allow the torpedoes to be fully withdrawn rearwards. They could only be partially withdrawn into the torpedo room if it was necessary to carry out repairs or maintenance.

US SUBMARINE TORPEDO TUBES

The earliest Holland-type boats, also used by the Royal Navy, had single bow torpedo tubes, closed at the muzzle end by a vertically hinged bow cap. A single reload torpedo could be carried inside the crew compartment, which severely limited the useable space in these small craft.

As in other navies, the torpedo batteries of US submarines steadily increased until the Fleet boats of the Second World War era reached a total of ten tubes, six forward and four aft. The following description relates to US submarine practice of this period, with all the photos taken from the official manual of 1944.

The late-war tube was designed to take the Mark 14

Late-war torpedo tube lining.

Left, the forward bow tubes on a Fleet submarine of the Second World War era. *Right*, is the gyro setter for all six tubes.

torpedo with the shallow flat guide stud. Earlier torpedoes with the high T-shaped guide stud could be launched after changing their guide stud for the later pattern. The internal view of the tube shows this rectangular guide, and also the recesses in the bottom of the tube for four bronze rollers on which the torpedo sits, to aid in loading. Because of electrolytic corrosion these were changed to nylon rollers later in the Second World War. The various holes in the tube are for the retractable pinions for depth, speed and gyro setting, the stop bolt and engine start latch, the compressed air inlet and the water drain outlet.

The breech end door was machined from solid bronze, slightly concave, with eight studs around its circumference. To lock the door shut, the external ring, which was screwed on to the breech end of the tube, was rotated so its segments turned behind the lugs on the door and locked it. This was the opposite of the system used on US above-water tubes, where it was the door which revolved to lock in a fixed ring. The door was fitted with a pressure gauge, and two reflex water gauges, to check the tube was empty before opening the breech door.

To load a torpedo, the propellers were first locked with the special tool, the starting lever was protected by a safety guard, and a tail piece was inserted in the propeller shaft,

connected to a block and tackle. The block was attached to the eyes on top of the tube breech door ring. Now the torpedo could be eased forward on its runway, ensuring that the guide stud entered the guide slot. When it was part way into the tube, the safety guard was removed from the starting lever, the indexing dials were checked to see they were all properly set, that the torpedo stop valve was open, and that the starting gear was set to run. Finally, the torpedo entered the tube completely, and was brought gently up against the torpedo stop. After the propeller guard had been removed, the door was closed, and the screw pad moved by knurled nut in the centre of the door was brought up into contact with the tail of the torpedo. The tube was now ready to be flooded and the torpedo fired.

If for any reason it was necessary to unload the tube, the same tail piece was inserted in the propeller shaft, the block and tackle was attached at the rear end of the torpedo room, and the torpedo was gently pulled backwards onto the runway, care being taken to ensure that the various setting spindles had been retracted.

Surprisingly, the manual stated that British 21in torpedoes could also be loaded and fired from these tubes, with certain modifications. It was necessary to screw the

Loading a torpedo into a tube.

guide lug to the top of the British torpedo, cut off the tip of the starting lever which otherwise would have fouled the inside wall of the tube on launch, set the various depth, speed and gyro controls before inserting the torpedo in the tube, as the spindle points were different and, amazingly, 'to improvise means, such as a lanyard for starting the torpedo'. Obviously, when one was desperate and replacement torpedoes were a thousand miles away, one could resort to such make-do-and-mend measures.

Another interesting feature was a means of internally venting the compressed air used to launch the torpedo before the weapon completely exited the tube, to avoid excess air bubbles rising to the surface and giving away the position of the boat and the launch.

USN torpedo data computer (TDC) Mark 3

Since the Great War era, major surface warships had their gunnery controlled by the mechanical computer in their transmitting station. Battleship torpedo-firing in British ships was directed from the torpedo control tower, and destroyers of the Second World War had their own torpedo directors.

Submarine commanders faced the same difficulties as their surface counterparts, plus the requirement to act in a vertical plane as well. In addition, their visual tracking means were much more limited and often had to be intermittent, to avoid exposing their periscope head for too long. Otherwise they had to rely on hydrophone bearings. British submariners had experimented with multi-frequency Asdic (sonar) ever since the first hunter-killer set was installed in the experimental submarine cruiser *X 1*, but during the Second World War the Royal Navy only used its submarine Asdic as a listening device, not emitting pulses for fear of alerting the enemy.

The experts could work out the necessary trigonometry in their heads, and even take snap shots at rapidly moving targets. But the variables introduced by launching underwater with limited means of observation meant that far too often, and for far too many crews, the torpedo missed.

To restore the situation the submarine services introduced their own mechanical calculating machines. The model shown here is the US Navy's torpedo data computer Mark 3, which with its predecessors helped the US submarine fleet wreak havoc with the Japanese naval and merchant fleet in the Pacific. (Details of the TDC Mark 3 models 5–8 and 10–12, can be found in the Bureau of Ordnance Pamphlet prepared in June 1944 by the Arma Corporation of Brooklyn, New York.)

The position keeper continually tracked the target ship and updated its actual position at all times in relation to the submarine. In order to do this it automatically received input of the boat's own course from the gyro compass, and of the boat's speed from the pit log. The hand cranks on the face of the TDC allowed for manual input of the target ship's length, estimated speed, and angle on the bow. Sound bearings from the boat's listening sonar were also automatically entered and taken into account in the calculations. Regular visual observations of the target's actual position, speed and bearing could be fed into the machine to correct initial errors. Usually three or four

observations were necessary to have confidence in the results.

The targeting part of the computer continually took the data from the position keeper and used it to work out the torpedo gyro angles to maximise the chances of a hit. As the data changed, so the gyro angles would be automatically updated. The machine was connected to the forward and aft torpedo rooms and input the gyro angles on all ten torpedo tubes by remote control.

The dual functionality of the TDC Mark 3 gave the US submariners a continuous firing solution; it was the only system at that time which both solved the gyro angle equation and also tracked the target in real time, and was thus way in advance of contemporary German and Japanese torpedo computers.

ROYAL NAVY TUBES IN HMS *OCELOT*

By way of comparison with the earlier systems described above, a submarine launch system from the Cold War period is visible inside HMS *Ocelot*, a diesel-powered boat preserved as a museum in Chatham Historic Dockyard. The colour photos are by the author, with the help of Scott Belcher, who kindly provided access. Note the substantial locking arrangements, which allowed these boats to fire their torpedoes from their maximum operating depth. The tube has eight aluminium bronze lands riveted to the inside to act as guides for the torpedo which is a free-floating fit inside the tube. The door is secured primarily by the large rotating ring on the end of the tube, but also by a safety bolt.

There was space forward for twelve torpedoes on three levels, mounted on racks which slid sideways to align with the tubes. With six loaded tubes, *Ocelot* carried a total of eighteen torpedoes. Her two shorter stern tubes had been intended for small anti-submarine torpedoes, but during her time in service the stern tubes were removed and the muzzle orifices plated over.

Ocelot was equipped with a Type 44 TDC, and before pressing his master firing buttons, her commander could call for a readout on the individual torpedo battery charge indicator board. If the electrical systems were out, the torpedoes could be fired manually from a seat squeezed in between the forward tubes.

Two surviving TDC Mark 3 sets are on public display, and the one on board USS *Pamponita* has been restored to working order. Here Terry Lindell, one of her volunteer crewmen, has removed the front cover for cleaning, showing some of the complex internal gearing and electrical connections. (Photo courtesy of Terry Lindell and the San Francisco Maritime National Historical Park)

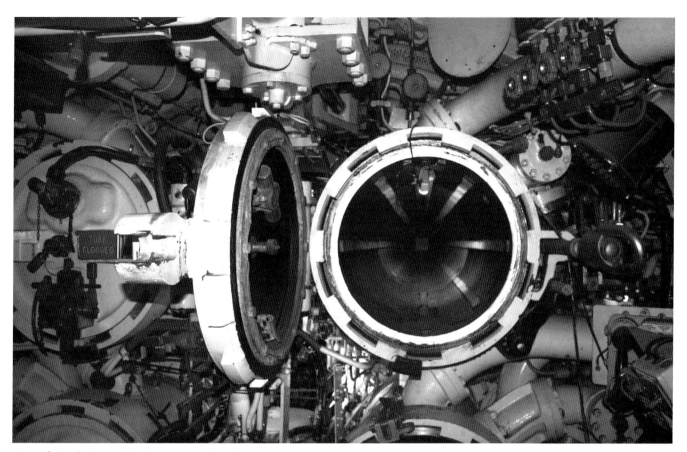

One of *Ocelot*'s six 21in bow torpedo tubes.

Ocelot carried a mix of Mark 24 and the old but reliable Mark 8 torpedoes. Here is a Mark 8 in the upper stowage position.

CHAPTER 14

Torpedo Bombers and Stand-off Weapons

In naval warfare, the gun dominated for centuries, and held onto its leading position, even as newer weapon systems were threatening to dislodge the gun from its position of hegemony. The mine and the torpedo posed major threats to the battleship, and as aircraft developed, they came to add the threat of bombs and aerial torpedoes. While aircraft remained relatively fragile and underpowered, their bombs posed little threat to the largest dreadnoughts, free to manoeuvre in the open sea and capable of offering a powerful anti-aircraft defence. Torpedoes carried by aircraft, however, were to become as potent as any launched by surface and submarine craft.

In the late 1930s a British admiral and a high-ranking RAF officer argued out the respective merits of the torpedo and the bomb, or more specifically the bomb dropped from a dive-bomber. The admiral ended the discussion by noting that, 'Bombs make holes in the tops of ships and let in air; torpedoes make holes in the bottoms of ships and let in water.' This was a slight over-simplification of the question, and many large warships would soon come to be sunk or disabled by bombs alone, but bombs could not on their own have accounted for the huge Japanese super-dreadnoughts *Musashi* and *Yamato*: they were both to be sunk by overwhelming aerial torpedo attacks.

One major problem remained to be solved: the airmen of all the combatants, German, British, Japanese or American, were exposed to suffering crippling losses when going in to attack with torpedoes at low altitude and on a steady approach run. They flew in the face of concentrated anti-aircraft fire, and their slow and heavily loaded torpedo planes often had to run the gauntlet of defending fighters. One suggested solution was to attack at night. But this brought serious problems of its own, as the reduced visibility would lower the chances of target acquisition, and most serious of all, would make the low, slow approach over the water extremely difficult to judge and therefore potentially fatal. The British Swordfish torpedo bombers that attacked Taranto were accompanied by Swordfish dropping flares for that very reason.

Night attack was in fact the preferred tactic of American Admiral Bradley A Fiske, who in 1912 had taken out US Patent No 1032394 dealing with a 'Method of and apparatus for delivering submarine torpedoes from airships'. Three years later he proposed that torpedo bombers should carry out attacks at night, descending in a spiral dive and levelling out just 3–6m (10–20ft) above water level, releasing their torpedo at a range of 1400–1800m (1500–2000yds) from the target vessel. He concluded that if there was enough room the torpedo planes could attack vessels inside their harbours. Truly prophetic ideas.

EARLY TORPEDO BOMBERS

The very first successful torpedo drop from an aircraft was carried out on 28 July 1914, from a Short seaplane based at Calshot. A year later the carrier *Ben-My-Chree* ferried a flight of Short 184 seaplanes to the Dardanelles. Three Turkish ships were sunk by 14in torpedoes, one when the seaplane was waterborne. But the Short 184s were patently underpowered for the task, and a larger, more powerful aircraft, the Short 320, was built to replace it.

The final development of the Great War was the specially-designed Sopwith Cuckoo (so named for the bird which lays its eggs in others' nests), which, however, arrived too late to see active service. It was a single-seater, to allow for the weight of the torpedo. The pilot was thus deprived of the help of an observer, who was useful in judging the height above the water in order to launch at the exact correct altitude to avoid damaging the torpedo. He also lacked a rear gunner to protect his back during the low, slow approach run on a fixed line. This was just acceptable while opposing enemy ships did not carry fighter protection, but since the British had pioneered the use of 'expendable' fighters carried on capital ships and others, and had begun designing viable aircraft carriers, it was obvious that to survive in future the Cuckoo would need close fighter protection. It was supplied with very large span folding wings, useful for aircraft carrier stowage, but also on land in the small hangars of the day. The Cuckoo also had strengthened landing gear, with four pairs of struts, allowing it to carry the torpedo unimpeded beneath the front fuselage.

While the Fleet Air Arm fell under RAF control, and was often seen as the poor relation, the US Navy wisely kept control of its own air arm, which came to be based around the large and powerful converted battlecruisers *Saratoga* and *Lexington*, the largest carriers in the world for many years. It is sobering to reflect that the RN *Hood* and one of her cancelled sisters would have been much better value for money as large aircraft carriers than the converted large cruisers *Courageous*, *Glorious* and *Furious*.

A Devastator releases its Mark 13 torpedo, low and slow, as the weapon does not yet have the nose ring, tail shroud and tail box to protect it.

Its Japanese contemporary, the Nakajima B5N Type 97 carrier attack bomber (Allied codename 'Kate') being loaded with a Type 91 torpedo. This was the plane that torpedoed the battleships at Pearl Harbor (and one high-level Kate bomber sank the *Arizona*).

The Great Lakes and Martin torpedo bombers served the US Navy until the introduction of the Douglas Devastator in around 1938. But because these aircraft were thought incapable of defending themselves, at one point the US Navy considered scrapping the torpedo bomber from its inventory, relying instead on the dive-bomber, in which it led the world at the time. Nazi Germany caught on to the idea of the dive-bomber, which was to result in the Ju-87 Stuka, thanks to a personal import by Ernst Udet of a Curtiss SBC Helldiver.

Luckily, the US Navy persevered, and replaced its vulnerable biplane torpedo bombers with the Douglas Devastator. Although a modern monoplane design with retractable undercarriage, the Devastator was handicapped by the low power (850hp) of its radial engine – good for the 1930s but far outclassed in late 1941/early 1942. It did, however, carry its torpedo semi-recessed within the fuselage, which helped with the streamlining.

HIGH-SPEED, HIGH-ALTITUDE DROPS BY THE JAPANESE

In the early 1920s, retired Lieutenant Commander Frederick Bernard Fowler, RNAS, who pre-war had founded the Eastbourne Aviation Company, led a team of pilot instructors to teach the IJN how, of all things, to operate torpedo bombers and fighters from the deck of their first aircraft carrier, the diminutive *Hosho* (herself designed with the aid of plans of HMS *Argus*). The Japanese learned quickly but retained this traditional launch method up until 1941: basically, the torpedo bomber approached at a low altitude and low speed in order to not damage the torpedo on launch. In any case, the biplane torpedo bombers with fixed undercarriage of this era could not attain high speeds. The torpedo they used was the Type 91, designed in 1931.

All this changed with the introduction of the monoplane Nakajima B5N. The monoplane was difficult to handle at slow speeds and low altitudes, so the Japanese modified the Type 91 with a reinforced lower nose section so that the torpedo could be launched at higher speed from a higher altitude. Then they needed to adapt for attacks in shallow harbours. When training for the attack on Pearl Harbor, the pilots first tried lowering their flaps and landing gear, but it was extremely dangerous and they could easily lose control.

So again the Japanese modified the Type 91, adding wooden stabilising fins to control the glide angle. These broke off when the torpedo entered the water. Captain Sherman on the bridge of USS *Lexington* at the Battle of the Coral Sea noted that the Japanese B5Ns approached at their top speed to launch, and on one plane, shot down while still carrying its torpedo, he saw the box around the rudder. The Americans subsequently introduced a similar modification on their own aerial torpedoes.

The strengthened nose section and tail fins allowed IJN torpedo bomber pilots to drop from as high as 60m (196ft) at a speed of 300kph (160 knots), much higher and faster than contemporary naval air forces. For even faster land-based twin-engine bombers, it was found that the latest strengthened Type 91 torpedo could be dropped from as high as 120m (394ft) and at speeds up to 560 kph (302 knots).

SECOND WORLD WAR TORPEDO BOMBERS

Meanwhile, the cash-strapped British were forced to rely on biplanes such as the RAF Vildebeest intended to defend Singapore, and the Fleet Air Arm's fabric-covered Swordfish, known to its crews as the 'Stringbag'. To comfort themselves, they fondly clung to the belief that for their part, the Japanese had retained their old biplane torpedo bombers, and that these relics were the ones which had destroyed the US Pacific Fleet at Pearl. As the authors of the wartime *Aircraft of the Fighting Powers* so blithely stated: 'The attack on Pearl Harbor … was carried out by a force of Nakajima G-96 biplane torpedo bombers

Torpedo-armed Fairey Swordfish. This obsolescent aircraft scouted the way for *Warspite* in the second Battle of Narvik, decimated the Italian battle fleet at Taranto, crippled the *Bismarck*, and flew anti-U-boat patrols off small escort carriers in all weather in the North Atlantic. They were so slow the *Bismarck*'s anti-aircraft directors had fused shells to burst in front of them. On the other hand, one strike launched from a carrier in the Mediterranean had to be recalled because the retreating Italians would have been safely home in harbour before the Swordfish could have caught up with them. Although this aircraft is carrying a torpedo, the lack of an observer and gunner in the rear cockpit suggests this is a training mission.

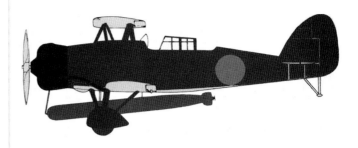

A Nakajima G-96 torpedo bomber. (Based on the drawing in *Aircraft of the Fighting Powers*, volume III, December 1942)

having a performance no better than that of the Swordfish. A few days later … G-96 biplanes carried out a further operation … In cooperation with low-level [*sic*] bombers the G-96 succeeded in sinking HMS *Prince of Wales* and HMS *Repulse*.'

Clearly, there were two elements at work here: first, the need to persuade the public that the Japanese flew obsolescent aircraft, and when the new Allied planes were ready they would obviously sweep them from the skies; and second, to sweeten the pill of the knowledge that in December 1942, a year after the events described, the Fleet Air Arm was still using the Swordfish biplane operationally. The appearance of the twin-engined Mitsubishi G3M and G4M bombers during the devastating attack on Force Z was a very nasty surprise. (For what actually transpired at Pearl and off the coast of Malaya, see Part IV.)

With restricted development funds for new aircraft projects and limited capacity in their carriers, the British favoured multi-role naval aircraft, often compromising all major characteristics to obtain this end. They were also forced for longer than the Japanese and Americans to retain biplane torpedo bombers: the Blackburn Shark, Fairey Swordfish and Fairey Albacore. That the brave Fleet Air Arm crews were able to achieve great successes with these last two obsolete types reflects greatly on their courage and professionalism.

And even when they moved on to an all-metal monoplane in the Fairey Barracuda, the Navy insisted on combining in one aircraft the characteristics of a dive-bomber and torpedo bomber. The enormous combined dive brakes and flaps certainly aided slow-speed deck landings, but their aerodynamic drag limited the range/endurance and climbing ability of these underpowered aircraft. And they were far from vice-free: retracting the dive brakes and applying rudder at the same time could result in an inverted dive, fatal on a low-altitude torpedo run; again the hydraulic system had a nasty habit

A Fairey Barracuda Mark II torpedo/dive-bomber, showing the wooden stabilising fins fitted to its torpedo.

of spraying ether in the pilot's face, quickly rendering him unconscious. The luckier aircrews were glad to convert to the powerful and well-designed Grumman Avenger. The Avenger often carried bombs, but the specific dive-bomber role was taken over by the Curtiss Helldiver. The Avenger would be the torpedo bomber which sank both Japanese 70,000-ton super-battleships, *Musashi* and *Yamato*.

Many Second World War aircraft were fitted to drop torpedoes. German experiments went so far as to fit torpedo gear under a Focke-Wulf Fw-190 and even a Junkers Stuka, but normal Luftwaffe torpedo bombers were the Heinkel He-111 and He-115, and later the Junkers Ju-88. On the Italian side, their most successful torpedo bomber was the three-engined SM.79, which caused severe losses to British warships and transports in the Mediterranean.

RAF Wellington bombers operating out of Malta decimated Italian resupply convoys to North Africa, carrying two torpedoes apiece. And the reason the Avro Lancaster was able to carry such large bomb loads is because originally the bomb bay was intended to carry several torpedoes. The only USAAF twin-engined aircraft to carry a torpedo was the Martin B-26 Marauder, which flew from Midway to attack the Japanese carrier force, but the US Navy's 'Black Cat' crews used Catalina flying boats armed with two torpedoes in night sorties against Japanese shipping.

Perhaps the most successful torpedo bomber concept was the Bristol Beaufighter. Following heavy losses of Bristol Beaufort torpedo bombers in attacks on Axis convoys in the Mediterranean, it was decided to clear the way for them by suppressing the flak defences with Beaufighters, heavily armed with four 20mm cannon, six .303 machine guns, and, later, rockets. The logical development was to add the torpedo under the belly of the Beaufighter itself, which could then carry out its own flak suppression on the attack run. The sturdily built Beaufighter could not only defend itself, but was capable of absorbing quite an amount of battle damage, and its twin air-cooled Hercules engines aided survivability.

A Heinkel He-111 H.6 of KG26, with two practice torpedoes.

Flight deck crews on USS *Wasp* (CV-18) load Grumman Avengers with Mark 13 torpedoes – fitted with plywood nose protectors and tail boxes. (US Navy photo)

Above: A heavily-armed Beaufighter, with cannon and rockets as well as an 18in torpedo, which in 1944 would have been the Mark XVI with 600lbs (270kg) of torpex.

Right: Flak suppression in action.

US NAVY TORPEDO PLANE TACTICS

In 1945 the US Navy produced a training film which described the torpedo as 'the most potent single weapon of destruction against enemy shipping'. Since Grumman Avenger torpedo bombers had just sunk the *Yamato*, they had good reason to be proud of their record. The purpose of the film was to explain the recent launch techniques, described in the film's subtitle *High Speed, High Altitude*. The Americans had learned many lessons at the hands of their opponents in the Pacific, and the new techniques pioneered by Japanese naval pilots were eagerly taken up by the US Navy.

Although successful torpedo drops had been made from as high as 2000ft (610m) and 360 knots, repeated tests had shown that optimum torpedo performance and reliability called for 260 knots at 800ft (243m). Their experience had shown that out of 2000 torpedoes dropped correctly, 92 per cent ran hot, straight and normal, with a higher percentage of hits than any other form of aerial attack against shipping.

Every pilot trained by following the procedures laid down in the torpedo launching guide, in which he could read off combinations of height, speed, glide angle and range to target. The optimum, often stressed, of 260 knots at 800ft involved a torpedo water entry angle of about 28 degrees after a time of fall of 7 seconds, and a horizontal distance of 3000ft (914m) between point of release and water entry. He was advised to add at least 400yds (366m) for water run, meaning he released at a horizontal distance of 1400yds (1280m) from where the enemy ship would be when the torpedo hit.

Pilots executing power dives from high altitude needed to reduce speed and commence a shallow glide, dropping the torpedo at 800ft. Too steep a glide angle and the torpedo risked damaging itself or, in shallow water, even hitting the bottom. Conversely, too shallow a water entry, and the torpedo controls risked not functioning correctly. The comprehensive tables gave allowances to be made for cross-wind, and gave

aim-off points for various ship lengths and speeds.

If a ship manoeuvred to try to avoid an initial attack, following pilots were trained in ship turning characteristics, such as the length of time for the rudder to take full effect, and the loss of speed of different types of ship when turning at full power. From this, with extensive practice they could estimate the correct aiming-off. The most common mistake was to underestimate ranges, as proved by post-combat analysis from the onboard camera. Dropping too far away gave the target time to evade, dropping too close could prevent the torpedo from arming. The Americans possessed a great advantage in that their torpedo bombers were large enough to carry onboard radar sets, and these were used to give slant ranges to target ships.

MODERN MARITIME PATROL AIRCRAFT

These still carry torpedoes, but normally in an anti-submarine role only. The Lockheed P-3 Orion, for example, is fitted to carry the Mk 44, Mk 46, Mk 50, Mk 54 and MU90 torpedoes.

The USA's Cold War Soviet counterparts made good use for decades of the large Tupolev Tu-95, codenamed 'Bear' by NATO, whose four economical turboprops gave it a vast patrol range.

Lockheed P-3 Orion. (US Navy photo)

A VP-16 Squadron Boeing P-8A Poseidon, the replacement for the Orion, test drops a Mark 54 torpedo. (US Navy photo)

FLYING TORPEDOES

This section describes torpedoes which were intended to fly to the vicinity of their target, where they would join their natural environment and make the final part of their one-way journey underwater. The modern term would be a 'stand-off' torpedo.

The Kaiser's navy experimented with radio and cable control during the Great War, producing the successful FL-boats described earlier. The same Siemens designers also came up with an idea for a stand-off glider torpedo to be launched and controlled from a Zeppelin.

The original idea was to resolve two problems facing Zeppelin crews: first, their commanders were unwilling to bring their huge aircraft down to torpedo-launching height because of the ground effect and the difficulty of executing rapid climbs and avoiding action; second, they wanted to keep well out of range of the anti-aircraft guns which were sprouting on the decks of British warships.

Developed from 1916 onward, the 'Torpedogleiter' ('torpedo glider') was designed to be dropped from a Zeppelin from an altitude of 1000–1500m (3300–4900ft). Control by radio was rejected because of the weight of the receiver equipment. Already, to be able to carry a torpedo, the gliders had progressed from monoplane to biplane designs, to reduce the wing loading. Controlled by electrical signals sent from the Zeppelin down a thin wire, the glider was supposed to launch its torpedo between 100 and 200m (110–220yds) from the target, allowing the latter little time to take avoiding action. Tests were carried out with a dummy wooden torpedo weighing 900kg (1984lbs), but difficulties were experienced in controlling the final underwater trajectory of the torpedo once released from the glider. Despite this, trials continued, and a maximum glide range of 7km (4.35 miles) was eventually achieved.

The trials gave encouraging results. But the entire programme was negated by the fact that in late 1918 many British warships were carrying protective fighters such as the Sopwith Camel – to be used in a similar way to the later Camship Hurricanes on the Murmansk route: the pilot would take off *in extremis* when his ship was

Siemens-Schuckert torpedo glider built in 1917–18. (*Scientific Journal of Riga Technical University*)

threatened and would ditch alongside an escort vessel to be picked up. And in addition, early aircraft carriers such as the unsatisfactory HMS *Furious* and the more practical HMS *Argus* were coming into service. Brave would be the crew of a Zeppelin which ventured too close to such a hornets' nest of fighters. But then of course, that left the night attack, preferably by moonlight, to observe the flight of one's own stand-off torpedo.

British 1940s designs – the Z-weapons

In the late 1940s British designers drew up projects for a range of futuristic weapons.

Described as a 'submersible torpedo launcher', the Zannet would have had four retractable biplane wings semi-recessed into the body, two shrouded propellers, one for air travel and the other for underwater propulsion, and a pair of bow doors which opened to release a torpedo once it had plunged beneath the surface. In the photograph it is shown as it would be submerged, with radio mast erected, and the bow torpedo launch doors open.

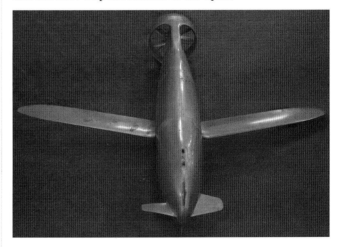

The Zonal model with retractable wings extended. (Photo by the author, courtesy of Explosion, the Museum of Naval Firepower)

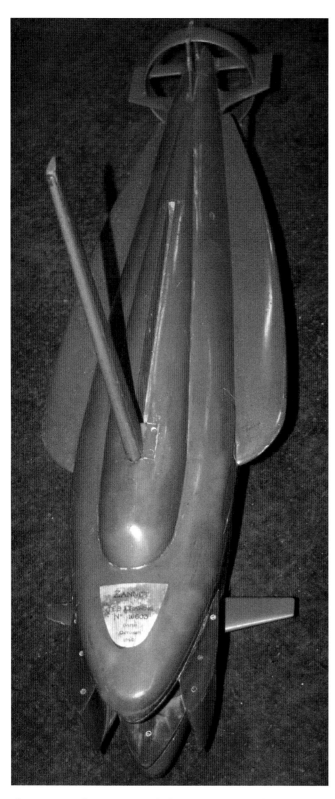

The Zannet, a futuristic torpedo-launching system of the late 1940s. (Photo by the author, courtesy of Explosion, the Museum of Naval Firepower)

A slightly less far-fetched idea was the project for a flying torpedo, this time with only one set of wings retracting into the body; in fact, the 'Z-weapons' were intended to comprise a complete range of winged torpedoes:

> Zonal, a sea-skimmer anti-ship torpedo launched from a tube on the carrier ship. Its three-cylinder, six-piston, hollow-crankshaft engine was to produce 900hp, to propel it in the air at 500 knots at low altitude. Out of range of the target's anti-aircraft guns, the wings would retract and it would enter the water, proceeding to its target at 60 knots, with active homing guidance. The same ducted propeller was to be used in the air and in water, with a change of gearing.
> Zoster, an air-launched anti-ship version of Zonal.
> Zombi, a submarine-launched homing version.
> Zeta, an anti-submarine air-launched weapon.
> Dewlap, a 21in diameter version for launching from MTBs.

A drawing dated 1947 shows one form of Z-weapon with an elliptical body and chisel nose, to cushion the shock of water entry. However, this form of body reduced the internal space for the retracting wings. One must wonder why the designers did not copy the solution adopted by Siemens-Schuckert, to jettison the wings prior to water entry. After all, they were only needed for flight, being initially retracted to be fired from a tube launcher, and they served no purpose once the weapon was submerged.

All these propeller-driven weapons were completely anachronistic in the age of the missile, and despite extensive tank and wind-tunnel model testing, no full-size versions were actually constructed.

It is sobering to think that this was a glorious period when engineers imagined anything would shortly become possible. The author remembers seeing a cutaway colour illustration in the *Eagle*, a popular boys' comic of the early 1950s, depicting a nuclear-powered road truck.

MODERN STAND-OFF WEAPONS

A modern anti-submarine vessel needs to be able to carry out an attack on a submarine at long range, to avoid the danger of herself being attacked by torpedo. In addition, lightweight anti-submarine torpedoes have a strictly limited range compared with 21in torpedoes, typically only 4 nautical miles (7400m) for the Mark 46. Another problem is that with their slow speed, these torpedoes can take over eight minutes to reach their maximum range, after which their fuel is exhausted and they cannot carry out a search pattern. Meanwhile, during the slow approach of a Mark 46, the submarine target can profitably use the time to evade, warned by the initial shipborne sonar signal.

One way to cut down on this reaction time is to use a helicopter to carry the torpedo to the detected position of the submarine. This would require that the helicopter is crewed and armed and ready for immediate takeoff, and its relatively slow speed still allows the target time to evade, and even to counter-attack.

In order to provide ASW defence, the Royal Navy and other Western navies possessing small aircraft carriers converted a number for ASW capability, landing their fixed-wing air contingents and even removing the catapult and arrester gear, and instead shipping a number of ASW helicopters. In place of a rapid-reaction defence, in a war zone they would fly continuous anti-submarine patrols in the same way as their predecessors, the Swordfish and Avengers, had done from 'jeep' carriers in the Second World War.

On smaller escort vessels, helicopters require significant deck space for their rotors. In addition, when not in use they need protection against the elements and rough seas, so that a hangar is required. One reason why the Royal Navy withdrew many of its escort vessels in the 1970s was the sinking of the Indian Type 14 frigate *Khukri* by the Pakistani submarine *Hangor* in December 1971. Escorts too small to operate helicopters were thought to be too vulnerable to attack by modern submarines.

The US Navy took a different route when, at the height of the Cold War, they realised that the Soviet Navy was commissioning new submarines faster than the Americans could build new escort frigates. The US Navy was therefore obliged to upgrade its large fleet of late Second World War destroyers to meet the increased ASW threat. Unable to operate even the small helicopters of the day, these conversions were equipped with a remote-controlled DASH (drone anti-submarine helicopter). The Gyrodyne QH-50 DASH, powered by a 255shp turboshaft engine, which came into service in 1963 was capable of carrying two Mark 44 or 46 torpedoes at up to 80 knots, over a range of 71 nautical miles.

It required two pilots, one to effect take-offs and landings, and the second situated inside the launch ship's CIC to direct the drone to where it would drop its homing torpedoes. On the other hand, it economised in deck space by using two small-diameter axial rotors. Despite reliability problems, it was eventually made to work, and was also adopted by the Japanese self-defence force. However, the US Navy gradually phased out its ASW drones in favour of more flexible and capable manned helicopters, and the Japanese were obliged to follow suit.

However, recently there has been a revival of interest in unmanned aerial vehicles. The latest USN drone is the Northrop Grumman MQ-8 Fire Scout, which in its MQ-8C version can carry a payload of up to 700lbs (318kg). Interestingly, it is also capable of autonomous (i.e., not under human pilot control) landings and take-offs from parent vessels. It has not so far been cleared for ASW operations, this role being reserved to piloted helicopters.

An alternative solution is the stand-off missile. The most significant of these follow.

Malafon

The French Malafon was produced by Groupe Latécoère and entered service in 1966. The torpedo body was enclosed in an unpowered glider, the complete weapon weighing 1330kg (2930lbs). Launched by solid fuel booster rockets at a fixed angle of +15 degrees, it accelerated to 830kph (516mph) when the rockets detached, leaving the Malafon to glide a maximum of 13,000m (8 miles) at a height of 100m (328ft).

Malafon on its launcher onboard the museum ship *Maillé Brézé* at Nantes. (Photo courtesy of Claude Balmefrezol)

A Sting Ray on a Merlin helicopter. (Photo courtesy of BAE Systems)

Teleguided from the launch vessel, when it reached the sonar position of the submarine target the glider was directed to release the torpedo, which on entering the sea commenced a search at 30 knots. The in-flight guidance meant that the Malafon could be directed onto a new sonar bearing, but its relatively slow glide time still allowed the submarine to put in an attack of its own. Malafon was withdrawn from service in 1997.

Ikara

The Australian-built Ikara, named for the Aboriginal word for a 'throwing stick', was a powered stand-off weapon, a winged rocket which carried its anti-submarine torpedo in its belly. Carrying a Mark 44 or Mark 46 homing torpedo, the Ikara accelerated to a cruising speed of 409mph (658kph), and had a maximum range of 10 nautical miles (19,000m) which it reached in around 100 seconds of flight time. Releasing its torpedo by radio guidance, the missile carried on to splash down some distance away from its torpedo in order to not disturb the latter's homing sensors. Ikara was used from the early 1960s by several navies, up until the end of the 1990s.

ASROC

ASROC's initials stand for 'anti-submarine rocket'. It entered US Navy service in 1961, and has since been fitted on over two hundred American warships, as well as on those of many other navies. It consists of a Mark 46 anti-submarine homing torpedo mounted on the nose of a solid fuel rocket with a maximum range of 12 miles (19,000m). On reaching the sonar position of the attacking submarine the torpedo separates from the missile body and parachutes to a sea entry to commence its search.

First launched from an eight-tube mounting, which could also carry other missiles such as the Tomahawk, the ASROC's latest two-stage versions are vertically launched from a deck silo. The vertical launch version went into service in 1993, and from 2004 the torpedo carried is the Mark 54. The new ASROC maximum range has been extended out to 11.8 nautical miles (22,000m). The ASROC's advantage over Malafon and Ikara is that it is much more compact, which allowed the use of multiple launchers and, more recently, the vertical launch cells.

Boeing HAAWC ALA

Since maritime patrol aircraft conduct surveillance from high altitude, to economise on fuel on long missions and to cover a wide search area, to descend from 30,000ft to

An Ikara sold to the Royal Navy as defensive armament for cancelled aircraft carriers, and used instead to rearm eight *Leander*-class frigates. It is currently on display at Explosion in Gosport. (Photo by the author, courtesy of Explosion, the Museum of Naval Firepower)

100ft in order to drop their anti-submarine torpedo would take many minutes, allowing the submarine a chance to evade. The aircraft would then also burn more fuel in climbing back to patrol altitude. Boeing have therefore designed the 'high altitude anti-submarine warfare weapon capability air launch accessory'. This converts the standard lightweight Mark 54 anti-submarine torpedo into a stand-off weapon capable of being released at cruising altitude. After gliding for between seven and ten minutes the torpedo will enter the water when the wings will detach. This attachment allows the P-8A crew to launch from a stand-off distance well outside the cover of shore-based anti-aircraft defences.

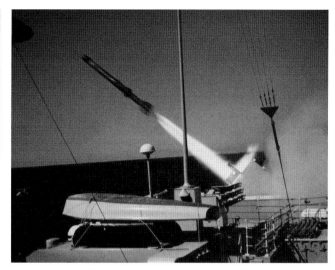

ASROC launched from HMCS *Restigouche* in April 1983. (Photo courtesy of Robert Berbeck)

Boeing HAAWC ALA. (Photo courtesy of Boeing)

CHAPTER 15

Coast Defence

BRENNAN LAUNCH STATIONS

Several Brennan stations were sited around the coast of the British Isles, at Cliffe in the Thames, at Garrison Fort, Sheerness, in Fort Albert on the Isle of White, at Pier Cellars in Plymouth, and at Fort Camden, Cork, Southern Ireland. A further station was planned for Milford Haven but the site was eventually used to house a Zalinski dynamite gun.

Overseas there was a Brennan station at Lye Mun defending Hong Kong, and two at Malta. The first of the Maltese sites was in Fort Tigné and covered the entrance to Marsamxett Harbour and the northern approaches to Grand Harbour, and the second was sited in Fort Ricasoli, on the southern entrance to Grand Harbour, with its torpedoes running inside Grand Harbour itself.

One major drawback to the Brennan system was the fact that the torpedoes on their launch ramp would be in plain sight of the intended target ship, at relatively close range. The launch mechanism itself hardly helped matters, as it consisted of a long overhead girder carrying the winch carriage bracketed out above the launching rails. There was no obvious way to disguise this fitting, although an armoured mantlet was planned to be installed over the launch mechanism at Tigné. However, being sited on the harbour side of the fort, the Ricasoli station was concealed from an enemy vessel entering Grand Harbour, and launched its torpedoes from an ambush position.

In operation, the two wires emerging from the tail of the torpedo were passed through the travelling pulley carriage at the rear of the girder, round the steering pulleys and dynamometer pulleys, and finally were connected to the wire drum on the right in the drawing. The winding engine was then started and the liberating bolt released. The torpedo then began to run down its launch rails, the two propellers turning. When it entered the water, the increased stress on the wires by the propellers being immersed caused the travelling pulley carriage to run out to the left to the end of the overhead girder, powered by

Right: A view of the launch ramp at Fort Ricasoli. The launch rails and their supports have long since vanished, and the opening in the torpedo station building, through which the torpedoes were launched, has been filled in with stonework closely resembling the wall of the building itself. When the station was operational this aperture would have been closed by a sliding armoured door. (Photo courtesy of David Moore)

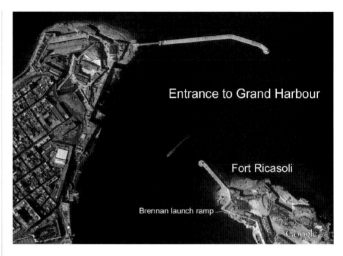

The Brennan defences of Grand Harbour. (Photo from Google Earth annotated by the author)

Another of David Moore's photos, showing the rampart of Fort Ricasoli on the right, with the torpedo launch slot at its base. The launch building is to the immediate right of the photo. On the rampart wall itself can be seen the remains of the support brackets for the launch girder. Above them the wall bears evidence of at least a weatherproof cover, if not an armoured mantlet. The entrance to Grand Harbour is to the right behind the end of the rampart wall.

the drive pulley at the rear of the carriage engaging with the rack on the girder. At the end of the girder the drive pulley disengaged and the pulley carriage would stop. The torpedo continued on to its target, being steered as necessary by moving apart the two steering pulleys.

Although it sounds like a complicated procedure, it actually worked extremely well in practice. The Royal Engineers were tasked with running it, and they were

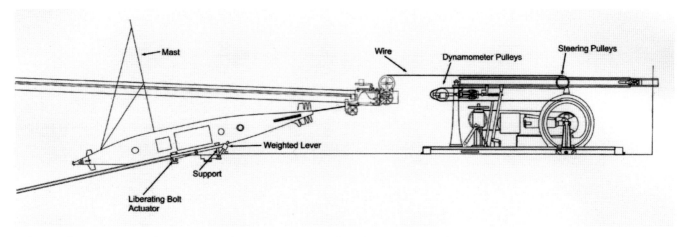

A drawing by David Moore showing one of the weapons on its rails, sighting mast raised into position and held by stays, and ready for launch. (Courtesy of David Moore, based on an original by Alec Beanse, first published in *The Brennan Torpedo* by Alec Beanse)

extremely pleased with all this 'engineering'. However, compared with a simple torpedo tube on a pivoting mount, served if necessary by an air compressor to recharge the torpedo's air flask, the Brennan station was extremely complex and, moreover, prohibitively expensive, considering the need to provide for a boiler, a steam engine, a condenser to avoid giving away the position by allowing steam to vent to the air, a winding and steering engine, and a vulnerable launch girder supporting the pulley carriage. One can see why the number of installations was never increased.

As a footnote, the record of servicemen deaths on Malta notes the funeral of Sapper Gillies, Royal Engineers, held on 8 November 1900. He was endeavouring to recover a torpedo lost outside Grand Harbour. As he was RE instead of RN it must be assumed that this was a Brennan, and from the location it would have been launched from Fort Tigné. The report goes on to state that the depth was extreme but he was a powerful man, and had managed to find the torpedo, signalling that he had done so. By some accident the apparatus sent down to be attached to the torpedo fouled his life line with the result that he became unconscious. He was quickly brought to the surface and taken to the station hospital but he died two hours later.

The type of diving suit used by Sapper Gillies can be seen in the first photo of the Brennan torpedo in the Royal Engineers Museum (see Chapter 5).

SHORE-BASED TORPEDO TUBES
North Kaholmen torpedo battery, Oslo Fjord, Norway
North Kaholmen torpedo battery is part of the Oscarsborg Fortress, the main defensive work protecting the Norwegian capital at the head of Oslo Fjord. The battery was excavated out of the solid rock between 1898 and 1901. Doubtless the Germans planning for the invasion of Norway in 1940 knew of the three old Krupp guns installed in 1898, but the torpedo battery, a closely guarded secret, was invisible and completely unexpected.

Torpedoes arrived at the battery by way of a square stone-built quay, equipped with a small crane. The entrance to the battery was protected by armoured double doors, which were shielded from view from a vessel

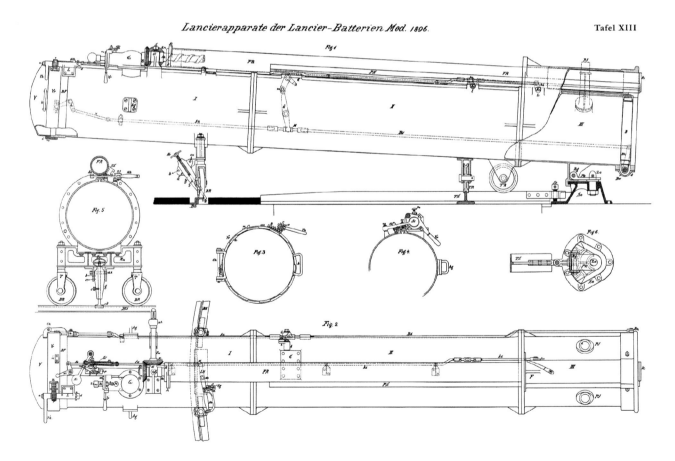

The Whitehead Company in Fiume not only built torpedoes, but also the launch tubes for the Austro-Hungarian navy. Here is a drawing from an official manual, showing a land-based torpedo tube from 1896, installed for coastal defence. (Drawing courtesy of Erwin Sieche)

140 • TORPEDO

The Austro-Hungarian torpedo battery at Mali Brijun, Istria, Croatia. Constructed as part of the outlying defences of the naval base at Pola. The main fort is on the high ground to the left, with heavy gun batteries. (Photo courtesy of Dalibor, brch photography, Croatia)

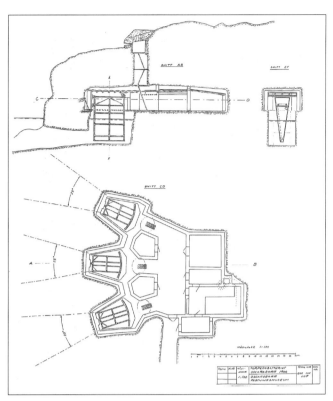

Plan of the North Kaholmen battery, showing the three underwater torpedo launch tunnels and the vertical shafts to the three aiming towers sited 10m (33ft) above the launch bays. In addition to the torpedo body and warhead storerooms, there were a compressor room, a generator room and a torpedo workshop. During the Cold War period a crew accommodation apartment was added. (The interior photos and drawings of the torpedo battery have been provided courtesy of Kjell J Glosli)

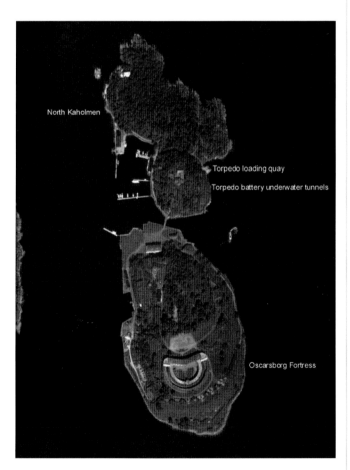

The defences of Oslo Fjord seen on Google Earth (annotated by the author). The main armament of the Oscarsborg Fortress was three 280mm (11in) Krupp breech-loading guns. To the east of the island, on the mainland, were sited two batteries of 6in and 57mm QF guns. The torpedo battery on North Kaholmen is completely invisible.

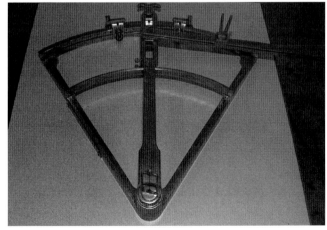

The torpedo leading sight ('Sikketriangel' in Norwegian) from one of the aiming towers. The target's speed and course were calculated and plotted on the bar extending to the right. The V-notch is the forward sight, and when it is aligned on the target the torpedo is launched. The central bar, which trains up to 12½ degrees to left and right, gives the torpedo track.

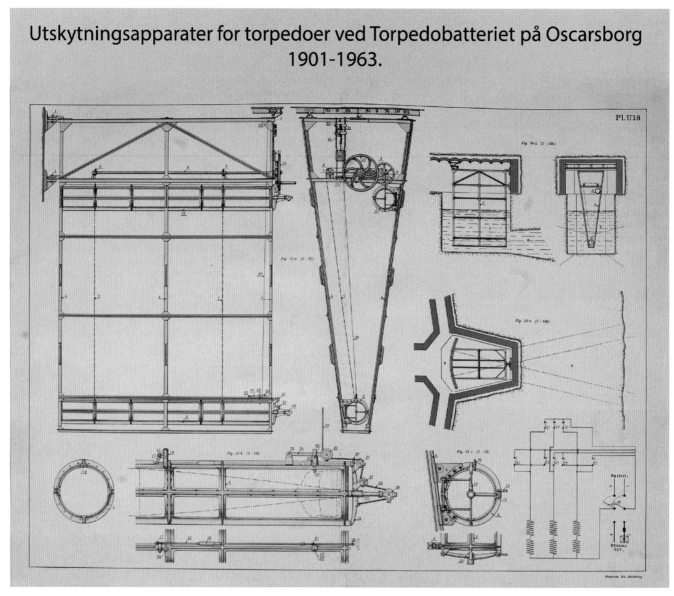

Pl.U18

The torpedo launching gear, comprising a V-shaped steel framework holding two bronze torpedo launch frames side by side at the upper level. The pulleys and chains lower the loaded launch tubes one at a time to the centre of the launch tunnel at a depth of 4m below the water level. The frame pivoted up to 12$^1/_2$ degrees to left and right of the centre-line. There was no need of compressed air: the torpedo engine was started and it swam out of the frame and into the tunnel. This meant there was no escape of compressed air to give away the battery and the launch.

passing up the fjord by a concrete protecting wall. Above the entrance was a plaque bearing the date '1911'.

Today, the battery is a museum forming part of the Oscarsborg Fortress complex. Its torpedo store contains British Mark VIII torpedo bodies, and a separate warhead store has their warheads, practice heads and firing pistols. In April 1940 the battery was armed with nine Whitehead Mk Vd torpedoes.

Along with the rest of the Oscarsborg Fortress, the torpedo battery led a quiet existence for some forty years, punctuated only by the regular summer training exercises.

Since its installation the crews had carried out over two hundred torpedo launches with exercise heads. All that would change dramatically on 9 April 1940 (for details of the action, see Part IV).

The Spinne

'*Spinne*' is German for 'spider', and with the usual German penchant for allocating codenames which contained an element of the device they were intended to conceal – unlike the British attitude of allocating entirely arbitrary codenames – the torpedo controlled by the Spinne coastal

Two torpedo launch tubes at the top of a frame. The door of the right-hand tube is open to receive the Mk 8. The Imperial Japanese Navy's torpedo testing facility at Dainyu had very similar torpedo launch tubes which were lowered below water level.

stations spun a length of wire out behind it as it ran. Building on their Great War experience of the FL-boat and the Siemens-Schuckert glider torpedo, in 1944 the Germans decided to install a large number of coastal stations to house, launch and control the T10 wire-guided torpedo.

The T10, derived from the G7e, was powered by electric batteries, and had a maximum range of 6000yds (5500m) at 30 knots. On this basis it was purely a short-range, close-in defence weapon for ports and smaller harbours, to deny their use to an Allied invasion force. Sites were planned for the French coast, and in Belgium, Denmark, Holland and Norway. The following French ports and harbours were cited in German reports: Brest, Dunkirk, Calais, Boulogne, Fécamp, Le Havre, Port-en-Bessin, Cherbourg, Douarnenez, Audierne, Beg-Meil, Benodet, Larmor-Plage, Turballe, St-Nazaire, Royan, Bandol, Hyères, La Pallice, Marseilles and Toulon; in Belgium, Zeebrugge and Ostend. Although work proceeded on several of these, none ever became operational.

The secret torpedo battery site seen from the fjord. If one knows it is there, it is just possible to make out two aiming towers, but at night they would be impossible to spot.

Launch was to be carried out by trolley, although at La Pallice a report mentioned a lowering device for the battery sited on the mole, so perhaps an underwater cradle was also planned. Again, at Royan a winch and crane were reported destroyed by Allied bombing. Tests refer to satisfactory engine starts at a depth of 0.5m.

The reasons for failure trickle through the progress update reports: lack of resources, Organisation Todt personnel deployed elsewhere, and enemy action. However, at the same time all was not well with the torpedoes themselves. To make their position known to the operator, the T10 could respond to an 'up' command and broach the surface. At night it could be made to flash lights for the same purpose. However, it was found that after this evolution, it was difficult to regain full directional control. The same control relay interfered with the magnetic pistol, which had to be removed.

The final modification cut the torpedo gyro after the first course command received by the torpedo, leaving just the control directional options of full left rudder, rudder central or full right rudder. The torpedo could also be set to circle. This was the definitive production model, but only a tiny handful was ever produced. No record remains of any Spinne war launch.

FUKURYU UNDERWATER INSTALLATIONS

A sketch prepared by USN intelligence officers in January 1946 shows the type of underwater diving chamber planned to be installed at various points around the coast of Japan in readiness for the expected Allied invasion of early 1946. The bases were to be manned by the 'Fukuryu' ('Crouching Dragons') frogmen of the 'Tokkoyai', or Special Offensive Corps, the umbrella unit which organized the kamikaze suicide attacks on the Allied fleet.

The imaginative nature of the proposed installation is worthy of a Jules Verne story. The hidden nature of the underwater base, although at first sight ingenious, suffers from basic problems such as how to man it when the invasion arrives, and how do the occupants actually know where to find the attacking target vessels? They would need at least reliable waterproof underwater telephone lines from a shore-based observer. Again, the depth of water shown in the sketch would tend to negate the suicidal lunges of the Fukuryu armed with their 15kg spar torpedo at the end of a pole just a few metres in length. Finally, it was only to be expected that landing craft would try to steer well clear of underwater obstacles, such as a wreck.

It would appear that the American officers preparing the report had been obliged to interview surviving Fukuryu trainees, and extrapolate information as far as possible from verbal responses, since all documents were burned by the unit's officers on 20 August, five days after the emperor's radio announcement of the Japanese surrender.

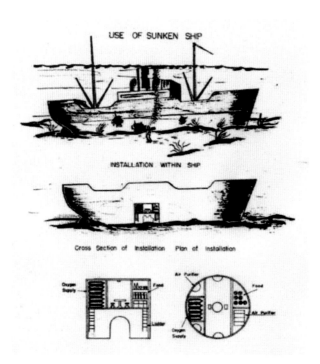

A sketch from the Naval Technical Mission to Japan report, index no S-91(N), *The Fukuryu Special Harbor Defense and Underwater Attack Unit – Tokyo Bay*, dated January 1946.

Part III
Anti-torpedo Defence

Active Defence

Initially, the practical means of defence against a torpedo was to spot its launch vessel, and simply outmanoeuvre the torpedo. In the early days of the Whitehead, the weapon's limited speed and range performance meant that a well-handled armour-clad with an alert crew could, in ideal conditions of sea, visibility and steam availability, evade the attack by torpedo. However, early trials by the French navy indicated that an attack on a single battleship, even if her crew were forewarned, could succeed if at least three torpedo boats attacked simultaneously.

At the time of the introduction into service of the Whitehead, the turret and broadside armament of most modern warships consisted of rifled muzzle-loaded cannon, in the process of being supplanted in some navies by breech-loaders. Accuracy, range and penetrating power were being constantly improved, but these weapons offered scant security against a determined attack by torpedo boats. The guns were too large, too cumbersome to train quickly to follow a rapid target, their rate of loading was abysmally slow, and when they fired the target would be obscured by a thick cloud of propellant smoke.

French sailors on board the armour-clad *Vauban* during the 1890s, firing volleys from their 11mm Kropatschek magazine rifles. At upper left is a 37mm Hotchkiss revolver. (Painting by Paul Jazet, courtesy of the Musée de la Marine, Paris)

MACHINE GUNS

Something more efficient was required. The introduction of mechanical, hand-cranked machine guns was a first step, although the French navy persisted in the hope that 11mm-calibre breech-loading magazine rifles, fired in volleys, could either drive off a torpedo boat or, even more optimistically, explode the warhead of its torpedo. Thus navies everywhere hastily began mounting rifle-calibre machine guns – Gatlings, Nordenfelts and Gardners – followed by upgraded models firing rounds up to one inch in diameter (25.4mm).

The Gatling had a high rate of fire even when hand-cranked, but fatal dispersion at longer range. The faster you turned the handle, so the point of impact varied because the moment of firing in the cycle changed. In the early 1900s the US Navy converted its Gatlings to electric motor drive, to give a rate of fire of up to a thousand rounds a minute. It was this late development, and not some theatrical revival of a Civil War Gatling as has sometimes been cited, which inspired General Electric in the 1960s to produce the Vulcan revolving cannon.

The fighting top underwent a revival, sometimes even castellated as in Tudor warships. Designed as a weapons

Ten-barrelled Gatling on a naval pedestal mount in the Turkish Naval Museum, Istanbul, captured from the Austrians, who manufactured it under licence. (Photo courtesy of Dick Osseman, www.pbase.com/dosseman)

platform to bring fire down on an enemy vessel's deck and exposed gun crews during a close-quarters fight, it was found ideal for mounting the rapid-firing machine guns of the anti-torpedo boat armament. French ships even had electrically operated ammunition lifts inside their fighting masts, which detracted even further from their often tender stability.

A replica Nordenfelt four-barrelled anti-torpedo boat gun mounted on the Victorian sloop HMS *Gannet* in the Historic Dockyard, Chatham. *Gannet* carried eight of these Nordenfelts, four on each beam, in addition to her QF guns. One of *Gannet's* Nordenfelts has been restored to firing condition. (Photo by the author, courtesy of Scott Belcher)

French battleship *Jauréguiberry* at speed, showing her large military masts which, in conjunction with her extreme tumblehome, had a serious effect on stability.

QUICK-FIRING CANNON

All too soon these upgraded rapid-fire machine guns were felt to lack sufficient punch to guarantee disabling or sinking an attacking torpedo boat, so attention switched to small-calibre cannon capable of firing a decent high-explosive shell, or just as useful, a solid armour-piercing shot. To give these weapons the firepower necessary to engage a rapid target, they were made quick-firing, using fixed rounds, with semi-automatic breech blocks which ejected the fired case and closed when a new round was inserted. Free-swinging, pointed by pushing against the shoulder rest, they gave the gunner a reasonable chance of hitting and disabling an opposing torpedo boat.

Because the latter would be unlikely to attack singly, batteries of QF anti-torpedo boat guns sprouted on the broadsides of most warships. Weight considerations restricted them to main- or weather-deck mountings, so to be able to carry anti-torpedo boat armament higher in the ship an interim weapon was introduced, the multi-barrel

A Nordenfelt four-barrelled 1in anti-torpedo boat gun, taken from a contemporary sales brochure – the last thing seen by a reckless torpedo-boat crew, in the mind of the salesman. The gun was fired by pulling back and pushing forward the lever held by the gunner on the left. Each movement of the lever chambered and fired four rounds at a time, thus the gun fired in a continuous series of salvoes. In a separate illustration the gunner on the left is depicted as wearing a cutlass, in the hope of warding off a boarding party, an anachronism in that era of rapid-firing machine guns. The sailor on the right is traversing and elevating the mounting, which would be difficult to accomplish by one man also working the firing lever.

Maxim belt-fed 37mm pom-pom on the training ship USS *Hartford*. The weapon gained its name during the Second Boer War, due to the sound it made when firing. (Naval Historical Foundation)

A US Marine firing a 37mm Hotchkiss revolver on a bulwark mount. Note there is no recoil mechanism, the recoil being absorbed by the bulk of the weapon and transmitted to the mounting. Of necessity, this reduced the powder charge, and therefore the maximum range. (From Chinn, *The Machine Gun*, volume I).

Crews of 6pdr (57mm) Driggs Schroeder guns on the pre-dreadnought USS *Illinois*. Curiously, the gunners stand on platforms which, when not in use, fold away flat against the bulwark. Note that they lack even the protection of a gun shield. (NHHC, photo # NH 79492)

rotary cannon. Patented by Hotchkiss in 1885, the five-barrelled cannon at first sight resembled the earlier Gatling, but its mechanism differed in having only one firing pin for all five barrels, compared to the Gatling's arrangement of a firing pin in each barrel (the Hotchkiss fired each barrel in turn at the 5 o'clock position). Also hand-cranked, the Hotchkiss naval revolver came in 37mm, 47mm and 53mm calibres, firing at up to forty rounds per minute. The ejection port was long enough to eject a complete round if one misfired, thus clearing the gun and avoiding a jam. One unfortunate side effect of this arrangement was that if a round merely hung fire, the live cartridge with its fizzling primer was ejected and landed at the feet of the unfortunate gunner.

A later development was the fully automatic Maxim pom-pom, also in 37mm calibre. Although an impressive weapon, firing at up to two hundred rounds a minute, for the same weight and price the navy could mount the much more destructive 6pdr QF gun. As the torpedo boat developed in size and power, and its weapon added speed and distance, so the range of early single-shot QF guns developed to match: from the 1pdr (Driggs Schroeder), through 3pdr and 6pdr (Nordenfelt, Driggs Schroeder), 37mm, 47mm, 53mm and 57mm Gruson, the French 65mm, and the 3in (or 12pdr) as mounted on HMS *Dreadnought* of 1906. German pre-dreadnoughts carried slightly larger anti-torpedo boat guns of 8.8cm calibre.

47mm (3pdr) on USS *Oregon*. (Detroit Collection, Library of Congress)

A US Marine poses with a 1pdr (37mm) Driggs Schroeder QF gun on USS *Oregon*. (Detroit Collection, Library of Congress)

Sighting practice with 3in (12pdr) guns on armoured cruiser USS *Baltimore* after her modernisation in 1904. (NHHC, photo # 101373).

FIRING TRIALS

Many firing trials were carried out to discover the comparative value of the competing anti-torpedo boat QF guns, including at Portsmouth, St Petersburg, Copenhagen, La Spezia, and on the Gruson range in Germany.

In May 1880 comparative test firings were carried out at Portsmouth, using full-size model torpedo boats as the targets. The weapons tested were the 1in Nordenfelt firing solid shot and the 37mm Hotchkiss revolver, firing shell. The results were publicised in 1884 by Thorsten Nordenfelt in a large marketing brochure describing his weapons. The somewhat unrealistic tests were carried out at distances from 1500yds down to the suicidally close range of 100yds, by which time either the riddled torpedo boat would have sunk, or its torpedoes would have found their mark. The Hotchkiss jammed on the fourth run, much to Nordenfelt's delight, the cause given being 'lack of propellant' in one cartridge case, the primer having forced the shell into the barrel – an embarrassing failure during an important test. Between 600 and 100yds range, the Nordenfelt scored 115 times out of 135 rounds fired, the Hotchkiss 36 times out of 50. Importantly, the mock-up engines in both targets were demolished.

The Gruson firing trials of 22–27 September 1890

Rapid-fire anti-torpedo boat guns of 37mm, 47mm, 53mm, 57mm and 82mm on shipboard mountings on the range at Tangerhütte were tested by the assembled guests, who took turns to aim and fire, mark the target at the butts and take measurements of the muzzle velocities. A special

event was the rapid firing of 2kg (4.4lbs) armour-piercing shot against a mock-up of a torpedo boat bow section, placed 500m (545yds) from the 53mm/L39 gun. The mock-up was constructed with sides and bulkheads of Bessemer 8mm plate, with the 12mm-thick rear plate simulating a boiler. The gun was loaded and fired at a rate of thirty rounds a minute.

Although fired under ideal conditions, in daylight with no pitching or rolling of the static gun platform, against a stationary target at a known range, the results were nevertheless impressive. Given that the foreign and German guests were all experienced artillery officers, all thirteen shots fired in rapid succession were hits. Six shots deformed the hull plating, seven pierced the hull and internal bulkheads, and two pierced the 'boiler' as well. Despite the fact that the firing did not take place under the stress of actual combat, it can be imagined that each firer was under severe peer pressure to do as well as his companions.

The bows, waterline and bulkheads were riddled. A real torpedo boat would most likely have been driven under by the force of incoming water. The two shots which pierced the hull, all the bulkheads and the boiler plate show how vulnerable these frail craft were, and each of these two hits would have led to the loss of a real boat through boiler explosion. Grusonwerke, in their printed report of the trials, commented that this was the result of just one gun firing. In battle the torpedo boat would have come under a hail of fire from an entire battery of quick-firers ranged on the broadside of the target vessel. And Gruson offered two bigger quick-firers to customers who demanded even more.

The mock-up of the torpedo boat bow after the firing trials.

The hits scored on the 'bow' target.

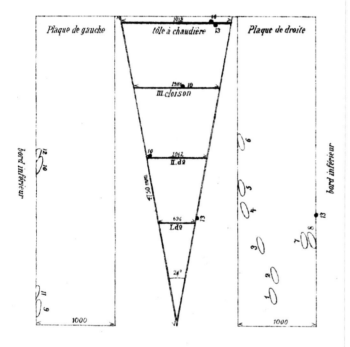

Shoeburyness trials

A large replica of a torpedo boat was built at Shoeburyness and in 1889 and then again in 1894/5 was used as a target for various calibres. The conclusions drawn from these trials were:

> 1pdr shells were found ineffective;
>
> 3pdr shells were ineffective in bows-on shots, often glancing off, or bursting long before they reached a vital area;
>
> 6pdr rounds did better, but only the 12pdr could be relied upon to stop a torpedo boat with one hit.

In 1906 the old destroyer *Skate* was used as a target. With the larger target vessel it was found that at least a 4in gun, with its 25lb shell, was needed to guarantee stopping an attacker.

SEARCHLIGHTS

At night, at anchor, or in poor visibility, the advantage could swing decisively in favour of the determined crew of a torpedo boat. In such circumstances, active lookouts or patrolling picket boats could help warn of the approach of an enemy torpedo boat. Fending it off, however, would remain difficult if not impossible, and the target vessel would be forced to rely on its passive defences. Early torpedo craft were traditionally painted black, for protection at night. Ironically, this paint scheme, under certain conditions of half-light or moonlight, tended to make them stand out more clearly than a vessel painted in grey, and grey paint tended to replace black in most navies during the First World War.

Searchlights were first used in action when the French flotilla repelled an attack by Chinese spar torpedo boats on the night of 23/24 August 1884 off Foochow. The use of searchlights offered possibilities but also severe disadvantages. If the night was very dark, unmasking a searchlight would serve to pinpoint the vessel being stalked by torpedo craft. Not unmasking would rob one's gunners of the ability to riposte accurately. Searchlight discipline was therefore of crucial importance, and was eventually brought to a fine art in the German and Japanese navies: the Imperial Russian navy was sadly lacking in this respect and paid heavily. An accurately aimed searchlight beam could blind the crew of an attacking torpedo boat, but then the attackers could try to shoot out the searchlight with one of their own machine guns.

Ironically, the torpedo boat builders' preoccupation with speed was of less value at night, when a boat coming in at more than 20 knots would betray her presence, if not by her bow wave and the noise of her high-revving engines, then by the huge glow from her funnel(s).

EFFECTIVE ANTI-TORPEDO BOAT GUN CALIBRES

As torpedo boats were supplanted by torpedo boat destroyers, it was felt that a larger gun than the 12pdr was necessary, so the anti-torpedo boat armament of capital ships and cruisers was upped to 4in calibre (105mm in German ships) and to the 5in/51 in USN vessels.

Even this calibre was felt inadequate during the First World War, and super-dreadnoughts of the Royal Navy and German navy opted for the large 6in or 5.9cm guns respectively. This weapon was at the limit of quick-firing by hand loading, and the weight of the gun necessitated mounting them relatively low on the broadside, limiting their effectiveness in anything but calm seas. The French, and the Russian navy who copied the French example, were the first to mount their 5.5in and 6in guns in turrets, but the *Tsesarevich* and the Russian copies of the *Borodino* class carried their 3in anti-torpedo boat guns far too low in the hull.

During the Second World War there was a reversion to smaller quick-firers to deal with the high speed German S-boats (or E-boats as they were known in Britain, standing for 'enemy motor boats') and Italian MAS boats. The much-maligned 2pdr anti-aircraft gun was felt to be ideal for the task, and it was even fitted to single power-operated mountings.

For the British the anti-torpedo boat armament par excellence, however, must have been the twin 6pdr, an army twin mounting for coastal defence, which had wrought such havoc on Decima MAS during their attack on Grand Harbour, Malta. These 57mm guns had a high rate of fire of eighteen rounds per minute apiece, and their high explosive shells were quite adequate for disabling or destroying an S-boat. Several complete army mountings were fitted to old 'V' and 'W'-class escort destroyers and two destroyer leaders, in place of 'A' gun, to counter E-boats in the North Sea and the east coast.

ESCORT VESSELS

The best active defence against the torpedo boat was, of course, a similar vessel but bigger and better-armed than the torpedo boat, to protect the capital ship from its tiny adversary by keeping the latter outside of torpedo-firing range. The first developments of this nature were the 'torpedo boat catchers', basically a diminutive of the cruiser type. When armed with torpedo tubes of their own they were reclassified as 'torpedo gunboats' (or even 'torpedo cruisers'), and they appeared in the early 1890s in several navies. These handy vessels were well armed, with guns up to 4.7in (12cm), but with one exception – the appropriately named HMS *Speedy* built by Thornycroft in 1893 – none managed more than 19 knots. In this the RN boats were misconstrued as needing the speed to *chase* torpedo boats, and were therefore prejudged as failures – whereas, in fact, their extra size and increased freeboard meant they could fulfil their planned role, of keeping the seas in bad weather to blockade French ports which were nests for the French torpedo boats. Most were later converted to minesweepers or depot ships.

Eventually, of course, it was realised that – just as the best gamekeeper is an ex-poacher – the best defence against the torpedo boat was one of its own kind, but larger and even faster. Thus was born the 'torpedo-boat destroyer', which was soon shortened to simply 'destroyer'.

These powerful vessels were multi-tasked, being able to fend off attacking torpedo craft, but also to carry out torpedo attacks of their own on the enemy battle line. Their tasks were later expanded to try to counter the threat of the submarine, although their specialisation as high-speed torpedo attack vessels detracted from their effectiveness in the latter role, which was best left to specialised anti-submarine vessels such as sloops, corvettes and frigates.

The gun deck of the protected cruiser USS *Baltimore* during firing practice with her modernised armament of 6in QF guns, showing the separate cased ammunition which enabled the gunners to fire up to eight rounds a minute: an ejected shell case, still smoking, is in the foreground. (Sargent Collection, Naval Historical Foundation)

Gunnery practice on USS *Utah* with the powerful 5in/51. Note the gun crew are wearing gas masks, which dates this photo to the early 1920s. (NHHC, photo # NH89730)

An army twin 6pdr mounting in place of the 4.7in gun in 'A' position on Admiralty Leader HMS *Mackay*.

HM torpedo gunboat *Dryad*, with all the appearance of a young cruiser.

The equivalent French navy vessel, officially called an *aviso-torpilleur* or 'torpedo-sloop'. *Cassini* of the *D'Iberville* class, built in 1894, here shown with sails for coal economy in distant colonial deployment, is every inch a torpedo gunboat. (Châtellerault Archives, plan ref CASSINI1894CO16)

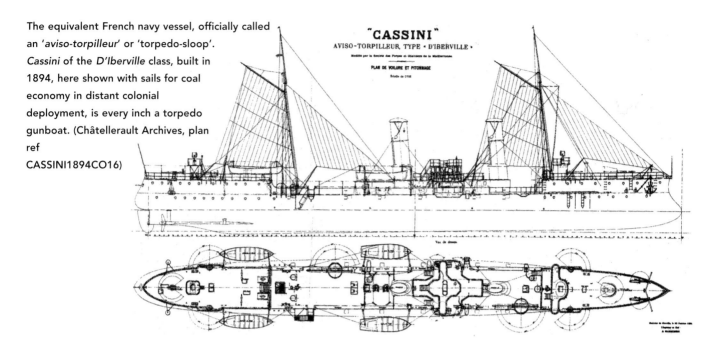

A comparison of size and power: models of HM torpedo boat *TB 17* and torpedo boat destroyer HMS *Tartar* as in 1907. (Photo courtesy of the Science Museum, London)

CHAPTER 17

Passive Defence

The simplest form of passive defence was to prevent the torpedo craft from coming in range of your ship, and then to prevent its torpedo from making contact. This gave rise to various static installations, which varied in their effectiveness.

HARBOUR DEFENCES

Chains stretched across rivers to deter unwanted entry have been known since classical times. In fact the popularity of the traditional London waterfront pub name of 'Cat and Wheel' – often sited one facing the other across the eastern stretches of the Thames in London – has been traced back to the old Roman and medieval 'catanea wheel', the capstan which stretched the chain taut each night: a romantic but vaguely plausible suggestion.

Wider estuaries to be protected in times of war, and especially harbour entrances, were protected by booms, constructed from old ships' spars, chained together. It was long thought that the only way to break through was to send boat parties to hack away at the fastenings or break the boom with gunpowder charges.

This idea was literally dashed to pieces when, during the naval manoeuvres of 1885, the Royal Navy's experimental torpedo ram HMS *Polyphemus* smashed her way through the boom defending the entrance to Berehaven, the Royal Navy's anchorage in southern Ireland. Starting out to sea and building up to her maximum speed of 18 knots, the ram had evaded several torpedo boats sent to intercept her – they can be seen to the right of the small insert view in the engraving – and easily broke through the boom.

Booms were still in vogue up until the Second World War to close the entrance to a harbour, but they were now used to support anti-submarine nets. A far more effective deterrent to surface torpedo-boat attack was the laying of electrically controlled observation minefields, the siting of QF guns, and the provision of defensive torpedo installations such as the Brennan.

Static anti-torpedo nets

These were heavy nets supported by buoys, and were quite effective for protecting individual warships, such as the *Tirpitz*, from torpedo attack, whether from submarines or aircraft. They would not, however, be able to offer protection from attack by underwater stealth craft such as Chariots and midget submarines, whose crews would simply dive beneath the nets, or, if they extended to the seabed, would cut through them.

A detail from an RAF PRU photo showing the battleship *Tirpitz* in Kaa fjord, Norway, protected by anti-torpedo nets. (From *Submarine Warfare Monsters & Midgets* by Richard Compton-Hall)

HMS *Polyphemus* charges the boom at Berehaven.

Bolting the stable door after the horse has fled: USS *Wisconsin* at Pearl Harbor, tied up alongside the hulk of USS *Oklahoma*, 1944, showing the anti-torpedo net protection so sadly lacking on 7 December 1941. (NHHC, photo # h78940)

Ships' anti-torpedo nets

These were originally intended for use not only at anchor, but also when at sea. The early RN 'Bullivant' types consisted of 6.5in (165mm) diameter steel wire rings joined by small steel rings, and weighed only one pound per square foot. They hung down level with the hull

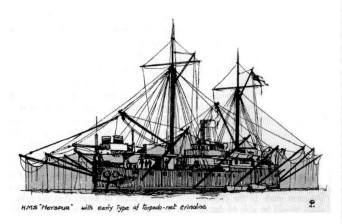

Above: Oscar Parkes' drawing of the first type of net defence, shown deployed by HMS *Hotspur*. (From *British Battleships*)

Right: Battlecruiser HMS *New Zealand* exercising deploying her nets at anchor in 1908. The young officer supervising the operation is Lieutenant Leir, later of the submarine service (from *Submarine Warfare Monsters & Midgets* by Richard Compton-Hall)

bottom, and proved able to stop the original, slow-speed 14in torpedoes.

HMS *Mars* was the first ship to experiment with net booms lowered almost to sea level. She also carried the heavier Gromet net, which weighed 5lbs per square foot. The Bullivant nets introduced in 1906, had much smaller rings only 2.5in (63.5mm) in diameter and interlinked without separate smaller rings. It hung down some 25ft (7.6m). In 1906, the Channel fleet steamed at 6 knots with their nets down.

With the advent of larger, faster and more powerful torpedoes, often with net cutters fastened to their heads, however, the nets became seen in most navies as a mere encumbrance, threatening to entangle propellers if damaged by gunfire. The Royal Navy held onto them for a long time, and the High Seas Fleet for even longer. Significantly, the US Navy never used them.

TORPEDO PROTECTION IN HULL DESIGN

As soon as the effectiveness of the first torpedoes was conclusively demonstrated, ship designers began to attempt to counter the effects of underwater explosions. Surface-running torpedoes, either by design or by faulty depth mechanisms might, with luck, strike not a sensitive part of the hull such as the unprotected bow or stern areas but directly on the massive belt armour. Given the thickness of the early belts, and their backing by flexible wood layers, the chance of the explosive force penetrating the belt and venting inside the ship was limited. However, as Whitehead had correctly surmised, a ship's most vulnerable part was the underwater portion of her hull. Protecting against explosions underwater was a much more difficult problem, never fully solved.

Flotation fillings

The Italian battleships *Italia* and *Lepanto* launched in 1880 had foregone extensive armour protection to concentrate on massive main guns and high speed – probably the most extreme examples of what would later become known as the 'Fisher doctrine' which he applied to RN battlecruisers. To save these Italian battleships from sinking under the effects of concentrated shellfire, the ends of their hulls were closely subdivided in the hope that they would continue to float even when perforated like colanders. Some Victorian ironclads even had whole areas of the hull packed with cork.

Royal Navy designers toyed with the idea of fitting cellulose inside the hulls of battleships, as suggested by the French, in the hope of minimising the effect of a torpedo hit, given that watertight bulkheads often held. The

Torpedo damage to Q-ship USS *Santee*. (NHHC, photo # NH41625)

cellulose was supposed to swell up and help seal the hole. Unfortunately, when this 'protective' system was tested on the old ironclad HMS *Belleisle* on 3 September 1903, the 18in torpedo warhead blew the cellulose filling to bits, and scattered lumps of coal from the bunkers all over the ship. Needless to say, she sank. The results of this trial made designers install armoured screens covering the magazines in the new HMS *Dreadnought*.

The notion of flotation fillings persisted well into the Great War, when Q-ships (armed decoys masquerading as merchant vessels) had their holds packed with timber and empty wooden casks, in the hope that, if the ship's girder structure held, they would stay afloat after a torpedo hit from the U-boat they were planning to lure to the surface. To give one example, USS *Santee* had been transferred from the Royal Navy in November 1917. On 27

December when on exercises for her decoy role, *Santee* was torpedoed off Ireland, probably by *U 109*. The torpedo made a hole 20 x 21ft (6.1 x 6.4m) in the number six hold, at the engine room bulkhead. Her cargo of timber kept her afloat, and in an awash condition *Santee* was towed to Queenstown and repaired. Her long and varied career ended in 1958, when she was scrapped in Hamburg.

Contact explosions on the ship's side

An underwater contact explosion forms an expanding bubble of gas with external walls which move outwards from the point of ignition in all directions faster than the speed of sound in water. The wall of the bubble next to the ship's hull will tear open the outer hull plating. When the force of the expanding gas has expended itself, the bubble collapses inwards towards the centre. As the outer expansion wall next to the ship has encountered the resistance of the ship's hull plating it has expended much of its energy in tearing it open, and therefore does not collapse inwards to the centre of the point of explosion.

The hemispherical outer wall of water on the side away from the ship therefore meets no counter-force coming from the opposite direction. The water wall is directed in a high-speed stream directly into the hole caused by the blast, wrecking internal bulkheads and machinery. This effect is similar to the hollow charge effect of a hit on armour plate in an air environment, but the water is less focused and is moving more slowly than the stream of plasma in the hollow charge. The sheer mass of water, however, is extremely destructive. Venting to the top deck or to the bottom of the ship's outer plating is of no use at all in resisting either the initial gas expansion or the stream of water, as they are moving too fast and cannot be diverted from their path.

No single individual metal bulkhead, whether armoured or not, even when backed by a liquid, will ever be capable on its own of resisting such forces. It will always give way. Accordingly, torpedo defence systems (TDS) aim to slow down the wave of expanding gas and the follow-up stream of water, absorbing energy in layer after layer in the hope of stopping the forces from reaching the inner vitals of the ship.

Explosions beneath the keel

These are even more difficult to counter. Usually non-contact, and initiated by a magnetic influence or proximity fuse, such an underwater explosion acts in the same way as the contact explosion against the ship's side plating. However, the under-keel explosion is aimed at producing a very different effect. The bottom hull plating may be torn open and the keel itself damaged by the initial gas explosion. In addition, the gas bubble acting directly beneath the ship will have the effect of causing the hull to lift in the water. The most serious effects are when this explosion takes place directly amidships.

Since the hull girder is designed to resist the downward weights imposed by the machinery and armament in a displacement condition, it is put under severe strain by the hogging effect. When the gas bubble collapses, the ship will tend to fall downwards into the void created, or suffer a sagging effect, only to be thrust upwards again under the shock of the wall of water beneath the centre of the explosion rushing upwards. Depending on the size of the torpedo warhead, the hull of a small to medium-sized ship, up to a frigate or a Second World War fleet destroyer, will be unable to resist the hogging, sagging and second hogging, and the ship's girder will fail. Typically, the victim will be broken into two sections and will quickly founder.

There is no physical means of fully countering this effect in a smallish ship. It is unlikely to have the same effect on a 100,000-ton-plus nuclear aircraft carrier, although internal damage may be severe. Reinforcing the keel area at the expense of weight taken from elsewhere is a very limited solution. Adding additional double bottoms or even an armoured inner bottom may add resistance but, even so, the shock wave will be transmitted through the structure and may derange machinery and armament. The best remedy is to detect and avoid, or counter, the incoming torpedo.

Underwater armour

In 1884 Sir Edward Reed, the previous chief constructor of the Navy, proposed to the Admiralty his patented design for anti-torpedo defence, comprising a double bottom. The inner bottom was to be composed of armour plate between 2.5 and 4in (63–105mm) thick, with an outer bottom 8ft (2.4m) from the armoured inner bottom,

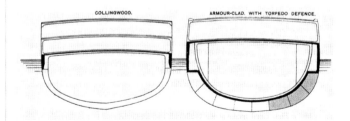

Reed's proposal on the right for an armoured double bottom, compared with a contemporary design conceived against shellfire. Note that the beds for the boilers and engines were accordingly raised, putting their tops above the waterline. (Drawing from Oscar Parkes, *British Battleships*)

the space between to be closely subdivided. The proposals had the twin disadvantage of diverting weight from the main waterline armour belt, resulting in less protection against shellfire, and of raising the boilers and engines above the waterline where they were less well protected against shells. Although not adopted at the time, Reed's plan was, however, the forerunner of internal vertical armoured bulkhead schemes conceived for dreadnoughts.

Torpedo bulkheads as part of a comprehensive torpedo defence system (TDS)

Early anti-torpedo bulkhead systems were limited in their effectiveness. Typically, the designers relied on the coal carried in bunkers on either side of the ship to minimise the effect of a torpedo hit. The inner bulkhead retaining the coal would then become the main holding bulkhead. This posed several problems. Although the coal could act as an energy absorber by being pulverised by the explosion, that held good only as long as the coal bunker was relatively full. When partially or mostly empty, the energy absorption was reduced to nil and, in addition, the presence of coal dust posed the risk of a secondary explosion, as was thought by Ballard to have been the cause of the *Lusitania* sinking so rapidly. Finally, the inner holding bulkhead was of necessity provided with scuttles to access the coal for feeding to the boilers, and even if these scuttles were closed when a torpedo struck it was likely they would be blown open, leading to flooding.

In fact, the realisation that designers' faith in coal as protection was misplaced was as important a factor in deciding to switch from coal-fired to oil-fired boilers as was as the increased thermal efficiency of oil fuel. The fluid nature of the oil in the wing tanks could be used to absorb much of the energy of a torpedo explosion. At first, designers feared that the oil itself could be ignited by a torpedo explosion, but in fact this never actually occurred in action. As the fuel oil was used up, the bunker could be filled with water, thus preserving the energy-absorbing nature of the liquid-filled void.

Such a liquid space could, however, do no more than slow down the destructive force of a torpedo explosion, without stopping it. In fact, it was deemed necessary to back up the oil space with a torpedo bulkhead of thin armour. Following the trials with HMS *Belleisle*, the *Dreadnought* of 1906 was provided with armoured vertical screens covering the magazines. In order to protect her against two torpedo hits, her main bulkheads, unpierced by watertight doors, were carried up to 9ft (2.75m) above the normal waterline, to avoid capsize through flooding of side compartments below the armour deck. For the same reason, she had a large metacentric height, which meant

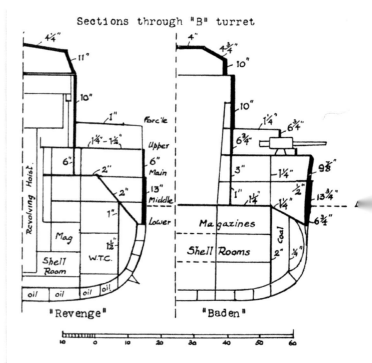

The anti-torpedo protection built into the oil-fired HMS *Revenge* compared with the coal-fired SMS *Baden*. Note how the German designers have placed the magazines and shell rooms much nearer to the external hull than in the British design, even though the Baden was wider in the beam. (Drawing from Oscar Parkes, *British Battleships*)

more rapid rolling and made her a slightly less stable gun platform, but it was considered a worthwhile trade-off.

From HMS *Bellerophon* of 1909, the magazine screens of the type fitted in *Dreadnought* were replaced by internal armoured bulkheads up to 1in (25.4mm) thick, extending from the forward magazines to the aft magazines. This followed reports from the Russo-Japanese War that ships torpedoed or mined had only been lost if their magazines exploded. The armoured anti-torpedo bulkhead was intended to stop plating and torpedo fragments from reaching the magazines. Even so, the shock of a torpedo explosion was likely to send fragments of the torpedo and the ship's outer hull through the oil, and through this inner armoured bulkhead as well. So designers kept adding more and more layers to the side torpedo defence system. Of course, there was a physical limit to this progression, and space was at a premium.

There were two solutions: to increase the beam of the ship, keeping the explosion as far from the vitals as possible; or find more internal space by replacing boilers and machinery with more compact modern versions. The latter solution explains why, when the Royal Navy was rebuilding its *Queen Elizabeth*-class battleships in the late

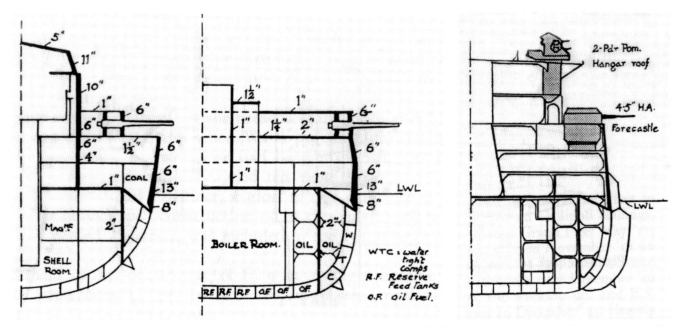

The original 1915 protective system in the *Queen Elizabeth* class compared to the rebuilt *Valiant*. (Drawings from Oscar Parkes, *British Battleships*)

1930s, instead of going for more powerful power plants, as the Japanese were doing, they opted instead for more compact machinery.

The best TDS turned out to be the American 1915 design built into the *Tennessee*-class super-dreadnoughts. They benefited from multiple layers of vertical bulkheads, voids and liquid-loaded spaces in the following order:

- outermost, a void, which carried the risk of asymmetrical flooding if pierced, but which could easily be rectified by counter-flooding the voids on the opposite side of the ship;
- next, a plain bulkhead;
- then a liquid-loaded layer;
- bounded by a first elastic armoured bulkhead;
- a second liquid-loaded layer;
- bounded by a second elastic armoured bulkhead;
- a third liquid-loaded layer;
- a third elastic armoured bulkhead;
- an inner void;
- an unarmoured holding bulkhead.

Each armoured bulkhead was sufficiently spaced from the next inboard to avoid touching the latter under the expanding force of the explosion. This system worked exactly as planned when USS *California* was twice torpedoed at Pearl Harbor. Her inner holding bulkhead was not perforated. She still sank, however, because of a lack of preparedness which compromised her watertight integrity.

In ships where it was desirable to increase the distance between the outer plating and the vitals, a simple remedy was to graft an external bulge or blister onto the outside of the hull. Bulges were first applied to coast-bombardment monitors before their general application to capital ships. In the RN *Renown* class, *Courageous*, *Glorious* and *Furious*,

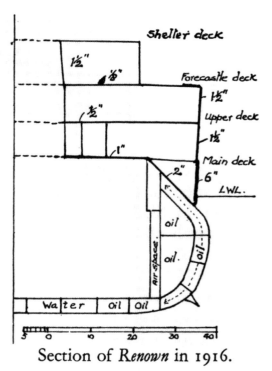

Section of *Renown* in 1916.

Renown TDS as designed. (Drawing from Oscar Parkes, *British Battleships*)

and later HMS *Hood*, this bulge was made an integral part of the hull design.

As an example of a TDS which was modernised and extended, illustrated here is the scheme as originally built into the USS *Arizona* in 1915, and her modernised protection as reconstructed in 1929–31. Note in the hold plans that the multiple layer bulkhead protection was at its widest abreast the boiler rooms. If the ships had been refitted with the more compact but heavier turbo-electric drive as suggested, they would have saved sufficient internal space to have extended this system to abreast the engine rooms.

Examples of ineffective TDS were many and varied. HMS *Hood*'s bulges were filled with sealed hollow steel tubes, designed to absorb the effects of a torpedo explosion by being crushed. A similar arrangement was fitted inside the bulges added to the 'R'-class battleships. They appear to have been completely ineffective. Possibly the worst TDS system of all was that conceived by Italian designer Pugliese, and fitted to the *Littorio* class as well as the rebuilt *Cavour* and *Andrea Doria* classes. Pugliese placed his faith in a large horizontal cylinder running the length of the TDS. Inside the cylinder were the ineffective sealed steel tubes. The main disadvantage of this system was that the explosive force, finding its way around the sealed tubes, met up with the inner holding bulkhead which, because of the large cylinder outboard of it, was concave in design, in other words the very opposite of what was required to resist the explosion. The results were plain to see at Taranto.

Skegs

The TDS did nothing to protect the narrower ends of the ship. A torpedo hit on the unprotected bow area could reduce her speed and seaworthiness. A hit on the stern could damage or even destroy the rudders and propellers. One feature which American designers favoured was the skeg, an extension of the hull structure to surround and protect the propeller shaft, fitted in place of the more usual external struts. These could have a serious effect on handling, but if correctly designed could, as a minimum, reduce the risk of damage to the inner shafts. A side effect of the use of skegs was the ability to increase the width of the stern area, thus providing increased protection to the aft magazines.

Hull subdivision

Here, once again, size did matter. The more complete the watertight integrity of individual compartments, the better were the chances of a ship struck by a torpedo surviving. Late British designs such as HMS *Vanguard* largely did away with horizontal openings in lateral bulkheads, many compartments being accessed only from above.

Providing a longitudinal bulkhead down the centre-line of the boiler and engine rooms seemed initially to guarantee against losing all power to a torpedo hit on one side. Many examples of loss through capsize were needed before this dangerous arrangement was superseded. On the other hand, dividing compartments by means of lateral bulkheads running across the ship from one side to the other posed the risk of the free water effect seriously reducing the ship's stability, also leading to capsize. Combining the two into multiple compartments was the best solution.

Too many ships had to be abandoned or scuttled after they lost power to lighting and pumps. Organising the machinery on the unit basis, where instead of boilers and engines being grouped together in two large compartments, the propulsive machinery was divided up into separate units of boiler/engine combinations, reduce the risk of losing all power to a single torpedo hit. Similarly, shock effect from explosions led to the need to cushion machinery from its effects, again to ensure power to lighting and pumps, to aid maximum survivability.

DEFENSIVE ASDIC

Asdic (the British designation for sonar) was originally designed for offensive purposes, to hunt down and destroy enemy submarines, and was extensively fitted to destroyers, frigates, sloops and smaller anti-submarine vessels. In the late 1930s the Royal Navy gave thought to providing its larger ships with Asdic sets, to be used not for attacking U-boats, but for listening out for the approach of a torpedo. In order to give sufficient time for avoiding action to be taken, a torpedo had to be detected at a range of at least 2000yds (1800m).

The prototype Type 132 set was tested in the cruiser HMS *Southampton* in May 1938, in a large retractable dome. It could also be used for echo-sounding. On the successful completion of trials, the Type 132 and its wartime successor the Type 149 were fitted to many cruisers and even several battleships and aircraft carriers. A final development was the introduction, beginning in 1943, of the simplified Type 136 defensive Asdic, intended for medium-sized merchant ships capable of a maximum speed of 15–18 knots.

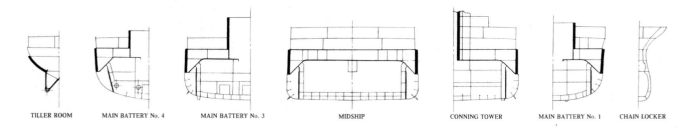

| TILLER ROOM | MAIN BATTERY No. 4 | MAIN BATTERY No. 3 | MIDSHIP | CONNING TOWER | MAIN BATTERY No. 1 | CHAIN LOCKER |

Arizona sections of the TDS as built 1915. All the *Arizona* drawings by Alan B Chesley appear in *Ship's Data #3* on the ship by Leeward Publications.

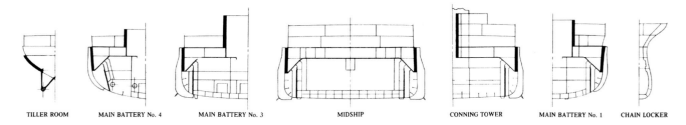

| TILLER ROOM | MAIN BATTERY No. 4 | MAIN BATTERY No. 3 | MIDSHIP | CONNING TOWER | MAIN BATTERY No. 1 | CHAIN LOCKER |

Arizona sections of the TDS as modernised and widened during *Arizona's* rebuilding in 1929–31

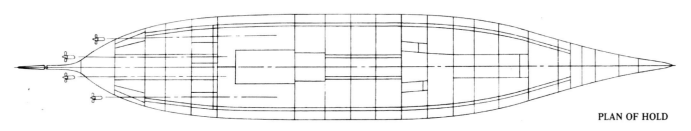

PLAN OF HOLD

Plan of HOLD *showing compartmentation, torpedo defense system, and shafting for the* **BB** 38 *and* **BB** 39 *class battleships as originally built.*

Arizona plan view of the TDS as built 1915. Note there is no protection at all for the large bow area.

Plan of HOLD *showing compartmentation, torpedo defense system, and shafting for the* **BB** 38 *and* **BB** 39 *class battleships as modernized 1929-1931*

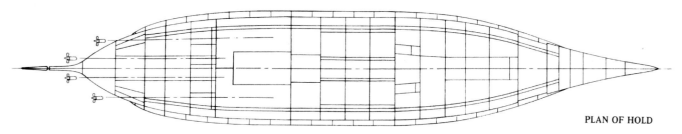

PLAN OF HOLD

Arizona plan view of the TDS as modernised and widened. Still no protection for the bow area. The TDS abreast the boiler rooms has been widened to encompass four voids and fluid-loaded spaces. But the engine rooms have to make do with only three spaces each side.

CHAPTER 18

Modern Developments

Active and passive anti-torpedo measures today fall into the two classifications of 'hard-kill', meaning an incoming torpedo is counter-attacked and destroyed, either by direct impact or by proximity fuse, and 'soft-kill', meaning that the torpedo is lured away from the target ship and pursues the decoy until it runs out of fuel at the end of its run.

SOFT-KILL MEASURES

U-boats commenced the countermeasures battle when they began launching BOLD pellets in early 1943. These were small metal canisters some 4in (100mm) in diameter containing calcium hydride. A U-boat commander under attack would order the release of these canisters using a '*Pillenwerfer*' ejector (literally, a 'pill thrower'). On contact with seawater the chemical produced hydrogen bubbles which created a false Asdic target, allowing the U-boat to escape. The Royal Navy referred to them as SBTs (submarine bubble targets), and an experienced Asdic operator could recognise them by the fact that they were designed to remain stationary at a set depth, which a U-boat under attack was unlikely to do. A modified device known as '*Sieglinde*' was meant to overcome this problem, by being able to move at up to 6 knots.

During the Second World War, the introduction of GNAT homing torpedoes by U-boats was a serious development, especially as they began by targeting the escort vessels which had been so successful in driving

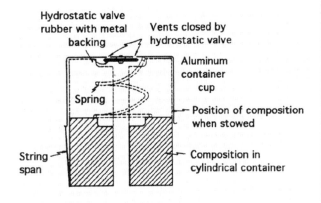

Individual Bold Pellet

An Allied drawing of an SBT pellet, the very first type of submarine countermeasure used in combat. (From *Battle of the Atlantic, vol IV: Technical Intelligence from Allied Communications Intelligence*)

them away from the convoys. The first time they were deployed, against convoys ONS18 and ON22, three escorts were sunk with heavy loss of life. Captain Walker's escort group had on more than one occasion resorted to the desperate anti-torpedo hard-kill measure of dropping a shallow pattern of depth charges astern of their ships, as a defence against homing torpedoes. But doing this at slow speed, even if it succeeded in detonating the approaching torpedo, posed the very real risk of blowing the stern off one's own ship, if not inflicting considerable damage to her hull and systems.

A soft-kill rapid response to the GNAT was needed, and it arrived in the shape of the Foxer, a noise-making device towed behind the escort vessel, with the aim of attracting the GNAT to attack the device and not the towing ship. Foxer was constructed of two lengths of piping, with holes cut in them, chained together, the whole assembly weighing some 3000lbs (1360kg). When towed through the water 200yds (180m) behind the ship they made a noise estimated by U-boat hydrophone operators as ten to a hundred times louder than that from a ship's propellers. They referred to it as the '*Kreissäge*' ('circular saw') or '*Rattalelboje*' ('rattle buoy'). Foxer was usually deployed as a pair, streamed astern of the ship and kept around 100yds (91m) apart by means of paravanes. It was cumbersome to stream and recover, could not be towed at more than 15 knots, and wore out quickly. One problem was that in some cases the Foxer interfered with the escort's own Asdic (sonar), but experienced operators could compensate. A more serious drawback was that it could also be picked up on hydrophones from a great distance away, revealing the convoy's position.

The Canadian version, the PNM or 'pipe noise maker' (codenamed 'Cat'), was a much simpler device consisting of two lengths of metal fastened to a frame, which was towed sideways through the water. One of the two bars was free to move and bang against the other and the frame. Cat could be deployed by one man throwing it overboard, it could be wound in by a simple hand winch, it allowed for speeds of up to 18 knots, and it lasted several times longer than Foxer. Cat was the device chosen for employment by the US Navy.

After the Second World War the US Navy introduced Fanfare, a towed acoustic device which mimicked the sounds made by the towing ship's propellers. Modern towed devices include the Nixie. When launched and

Ocean Systems countermeasures devices come in a variety of shapes and sizes. (Ocean Systems brochure)

The tail of Camrose/Bootleg in store in Gosport, showing the rocket nozzle and the electrical starter cable. (Photo by the author, courtesy of Explosion Museum of Naval Firepower)

towed behind the ship its signal generator acts as a decoy to homing torpedoes using passive sonar. They can also receive an incoming active sonar emission from the torpedo and send it back at an intensified level, making the torpedo think it is coming from a large target such as a ship's hull.

Modern countermeasures devices launched from a submarine or surface ship under torpedo attack work in the same way as the original Pillenwerfer/SBT, creating gas bubbles which mimic a propeller to an acoustic homer and a large target to an active sonar homer. Its launching from a surface ship or a submarine depends on being able to detect an incoming torpedo in time to activate the countermeasure, as it is not a continuous decoy like the Foxer and Fanfare. Today, many firms offer expendable countermeasure devices in diameters from 75mm up to 200mm, such as American Ultra Electronics Ocean Systems, who claim to have sold ten thousand devices since 1986.

HARD-KILL SYSTEMS

The modern alternative to this 'soft-kill' approach is to react with a 'hard-kill' weapon, which will destroy the incoming torpedo.

The Royal Navy spent a great deal of time and money in developing the Camrose 18in anti-torpedo rocket torpedo, which merged with the Bootleg design. Test runs had produced an underwater speed of 65 knots, and the homing circuitry was proving workable. However, it was feared that frigates would not be capable of carrying sufficient Camrose/Bootleg missiles for a protracted

defence in hostile waters, so the project was cancelled. One prototype is preserved in storage at Explosion, the Museum of Naval Firepower at Gosport.

Shkval supercavitating rocket torpedo

The Russian Shkval has been discussed in Part I. It is mentioned here again because, in order to avoid torpedo attack from another submarine, the Shkval can be used to put in a first strike attack itself. As discussed, its ability to block an incoming torpedo is strictly limited unless the Shkval is armed with a nuclear warhead.

Paket

This is a smaller-diameter rapid-reaction anti-torpedo hard-kill weapon, marketed by the Russian Tactical Missile Corporation. Paket is 324mm in diameter, the standard 12.75in ASW torpedo size, 3.108m (10ft 2^1/2in) long, and weighs 400kg (882lbs) with an 80kg (176lbs) warhead. It can be fired in all weather conditions up to sea state 5, wind speed not exceeding 20m/sec and a launching vessel speed of up to 20 knots. Temperature is not a serious consideration, as Paket can operate in -40°C to +40°C. Minimum depth of water is 40m (130ft), so it might not be effective in inshore waters where seabed reflections could confuse its homing signals.

After launch it attains a cruising speed of 25m/sec (56mph/64.5 knots) with a maximum range of 1400m (1530yds). Its active and passive homing sensors are effective up to 400m (437yds).

Paket nose view.

Torbuster in action.

Torbuster

An illustration from Raphael Industries' brochure showing the Torbuster anti-torpedo torpedo interceding between its launch submarine and an incoming threat. Described as a fourth-generation hard-kill countermeasure, the Israeli-produced Torbuster homes on the incoming torpedo and then detonates to destroy it.

CAT countermeasure system/SSTD

This modern development, aimed at protecting aircraft carriers from submarine torpedo attack, is based around the new US Navy's hard-kill ATT (anti-torpedo torpedo) with a diameter of 6.75in (171mm), 105in (2.7m) long, weighing 200lbs (441kg). The ATT relies on a sophisticated detection and warning system, which gives the target the option of an automated defensive launch. The ATT is particularly useful against wake follower torpedoes, and the 'surface ship torpedo defense' will be fantail-mounted on all US aircraft carriers, following tests on the USS *George HW Bush* in 2013.

THE HUNTER-KILLER

All the above modern systems are basically last-ditch defences. They rely on being able first, to detect the presence of a submarine threat, then second, to detect an incoming torpedo fired from it. The speed of modern torpedoes leaves precious little time to react.

Just as with the threat of the torpedo boat, when the best gamekeeper was an ex-poacher, the best defence against a submarine threat is your own hunter-killer submarine, which can shadow a hostile boat and detect when it is preparing to launch against one's own side. At that point, the speed of your own torpedo becomes an advantage in taking out the hostiles before they themselves can obtain a firing solution and launch. The encounter off the Falklands proved this point, even though the target was a surface vessel: the moment *General Belgrano* appeared as a credible threat to the British Task Force, the nuclear hunter-killer submarine that had been shadowing the cruiser took her out with a well-aimed salvo of torpedoes.

Part IV
Notable Torpedo Actions
and Incidents

CHAPTER 19

Torpedo Attack Tactics

The original plans by Fulton were for stealth attacks by very small units, each one incapable of standing up to the target in a firefight. Attacking by night, using pilots clothed in black – these were his watchwords for success. Because of the lack of a suitable means of motive power, his stealth weapons relied on wind, tide and manpower to place them in position. His submarine attack boat also fitted in with this stealth approach, but once again lacked a suitable power source to be really effective. Spar torpedo attacks also offered the prospect of most success when carried out by stealthy approach under the cover of night. The introduction of the reliable steam engine dramatically changed torpedo attack tactics, although even the revolutionary torpedo ram HMS *Polyphemus* ended up painted grey – in an era of colourful Victorian liveries – to aid her in carrying out stealth attacks.

The Germans handled their torpedo boats with as much daring as any other major naval power. Here a torpedo boat from the *S 7* to *S 57* series practises the breakthrough of the line, darting out from behind a pre-dreadnought of the *Brandenburg* class and a sister-ship whose masts are just visible in the funnel smoke. Note the leading ship's two above-water bow tubes visible abaft her hawse holes. (Photo from *The Ships of the German Fleets 1845–1945* by Hans Jürgen Hansen).

During the Spanish-American War, the torpedo boat *Porter* breaks the line of the armoured cruisers off Cuba. The nearest ship is the USS *New York*, followed by the *Brooklyn*. During a night action, the same boat narrowly missed *New York* with a torpedo, thinking she was Spanish. (Pen-and-ink drawing from *Harper's Pictorial History of the War with Spain*, volume II).

The French navy of Napoleon III tried to counter British supremacy in capital ship design by building large numbers of small torpedo boats. This gave them the ability to plan for mass attacks, to overwhelm each individual target vessel with a swarm of attacking torpedo boats. As a result of extensive exercises, the French calculated that, if an ironclad was attacked by at least three torpedo boats simultaneously, the attackers stood a good chance of hitting her. But small torpedo boats meant limited range and poor sea-keeping, so they underwent rapid growth in size and power. For their part, at the turn of the nineteenth century the Imperial Japanese navy preferred to carry out night torpedo attacks, usually of a first-strike nature.

When submarines became workable, they reverted naturally to the stealth attack from submerged against an armed opponent, but when faced with a helpless merchant vessel they would revert to the surface warship role, using their deck gun to economise on torpedoes. The German U-boats of the Second World War might hunt in packs, but when they took on a located convoy it was by stealth that they attacked, either from submerged or by acting as surface torpedo boats by night.

By the time of Jutland, fleet commanders on both sides were riveted by the dangers and the opportunities of the massed torpedo attack by their escorting destroyers. Jellicoe was criticised for turning the Grand Fleet away from Scheer's desperate torpedo attack, but that was the laid-down tactical doctrine of every dreadnought fleet worldwide, and as Jellicoe was well aware, he was, in Churchill's phrase, the only man who could lose the war in a single afternoon.

It was of course the *threat* of a torpedo attack that could be almost as useful as an actual mass torpedo launch. In the Second World War, the Royal Navy used the same tactic to fight off the vastly superior Italian force attacking a Malta-bound convoy in the Second Battle of Sirte in March 1942, and to protect Convoy JW51B from attack by the *Hipper* and *Lützow* in the German debacle of the Battle of the Barents Sea on the last day of 1942, which so enraged Hitler. After the 1940 Battle of Narvik, Royal Navy flotilla attacks were carried out against single opponents: the *Bismarck*, *Scharnhorst* and, finally, the *Haguro*.

AMERICAN DESTROYER ATTACKS

Using their extremely potent destroyer torpedo armament, US Navy torpedo doctrine laid down a large range of attack options, which as in every fleet were practised to perfection, but which in their case would never be put to use in a major fleet action – unless one counts the series of torpedo attacks carried out in the Surigao Strait against the *Fuso* and *Yamashiro*.

The very comprehensive *Destroyer Torpedo Attack Instructions (Tentative)*, issued by Commander Destroyers Pacific Fleet, as *Destroyer Tactical Bulletin No 4-43*, described how to carry out a wide range of torpedo actions, and gave prominence to the 'threat'.

PART I

Objects of Torpedo Attacks

A strike is a torpedo attack to destroy or damage the physical objective.

A threat is a torpedo attack to influence the enemy's tactics.

A strike may be ordered for:
1. A primary blow against the enemy.
2. As an initial blow against the enemy to be followed by destruction by other weapons.
3. As a secondary blow to complete the destruction of vessels damaged by other weapons.

A threat, if accepted by the enemy, may become a strike, but its original purpose remains unchanged. It is employed to:
1. Prevent the enemy from closing the range.
2. Force the enemy to open the range.
3. Dislodge the enemy from a position which is advantageous to him.
4. Force the enemy to break off the action and enable his own forces to retire.

In a threat, complete concealment is not generally wanted, although advantage may be taken of concealment during the approach to reduce the effectiveness of enemy gunfire and thus reach a more effective firing position. Torpedoes may be expended more sparingly than in a strike, and torpedo fire may be withheld altogether if the enemy maneuvers as we desire.

A melee is a close range encounter in which the combatants form a confused mass. Our objective in provoking a melee will be to create such a situation for the destroyer torpedo attack possibilities which it offers, while the enemy is temporarily disorganised and unable to take coordinated action to repel or evade the attack. In a melee, the advantage often lies with the inferior force, and in all cases to the force which is on the offensive.

These instructions might have been written twenty-seven years earlier, for the Battle of Jutland, and they described the type of fleet actions which would never again occur.

JAPANESE MAIN BATTLE PLAN
The IJN's pre-war plan for engaging the numerically superior US Pacific Fleet involved three succeeding phases, in which the powerful 24in Type 93 'Long Lance' torpedoes were to play a major role:

1. First, attrition by submarines and surface forces.

2. Then a night attack by fast battleships of the *Kongo* class, Type 'A' heavy cruisers, and Special Type destroyers. This force was to launch a long-range salvo of 130 torpedoes from 20,000m (22,000yds). The *Kongo*s, heavy cruisers and destroyers would then break through the American screen and bring their remaining ready torpedoes and those of the special torpedo cruisers *Oi* and *Kitakami* to bear at ranges down to 2000m (2200yds). After fighting their way clear, the night attack force was to reload torpedo tubes and prepare for further attacks. If the officer in tactical command judged it appropriate, the main battle line could be committed to the night attack if that effort was going better than expected.

3. Finally, a daylight battle line engagement at dawn following the night attack. This would begin with a long range salvo of 280 torpedoes, and when the Japanese battleships opened fire on the American line, light cruisers and destroyers would close and launch their remaining torpedoes.

Based on over-optimistic forecasts of a hit ratio of at least 15 per cent of all torpedoes expended, both the night and dawn torpedo attacks were predicted to cause the loss of up to six American capital ships.

The Japanese appear to have misjudged the potential of their Type 93 torpedoes, overemphasising their extremely long range instead of their high speed. At the Battle of the Java Sea the Japanese heavy cruisers and destroyers launched a total of some 164 torpedoes. They did sink the Dutch cruisers *Java* and *De Ruyter*, and the destroyer *Piet Hien*, but this represented only three hits or 1.8 per cent of expenditure, far below the hoped-for hit ratio necessary to decimate the full American battle line. The Japanese came closer to their required hit ratio when they sank HMAS *Perth* and USS *Houston* in Sunda Strait, with five hits from a total of thirty-seven torpedoes expended. But when opposing lines were free to manoeuvre, it was highly unlikely that the Japanese battle strategy would have worked.

In any case, Admiral Yamamoto decided that to reduce the Americans' overwhelming superiority in numbers, the Japanese were going to have to sink them in their base at Pearl Harbor.

CO-ORDINATED TORPEDO BOMBER ATTACKS

Towards the end of the Second World War the sheer size and power of the Japanese super-dreadnoughts *Musashi* and *Yamato* required mass torpedo attacks, co-ordinated with dive-bombing, to overwhelm and sink them. In its training film entitled *Aerial Torpedo Attack: High Speed, High Altitude* produced in 1945, the US Navy stressed the vital need for co-ordinating torpedo attacks with other types of attack, dive-bombers, strafing runs and rocket attacks by fighters. With the massive anti-aircraft batteries mounted on Japanese capital ships – the *Yamato* class super-battleships even adding their 18.1in guns to the AA barrage by firing *San-Shiki* incendiary shrapnel shells – torpedo plane pilots were formally forbidden to attack well-defended ships unless they had support.

Back in 1942, the low, slow American torpedo planes from their carriers had suffered crippling casualties at the Battle of Midway, because they had bravely gone into the attack with very few fighter escorts, and the dive-bombers which caused the fatal damage to the Japanese carriers did not arrive until most of the torpedo planes had been shot down.

The timing of joint attacks was therefore critical. Torpedo plane pilots were advised to time their runs to come into range at the same moment as dive-bombers' bombs were actually hitting. This would mean that part of the target ship's AA batteries should be knocked out, and also that the ship might suffer loss of control or propulsion, making her an easier target. If only strafing fighters and rocket-firing aircraft were available to support the torpedo pilots, the latter were warned not to hesitate, as the speed of the fighters meant they pressed in their attack much quicker. Finally, all forms of supporting attack would aid the torpedo planes in safely retiring from the scene.

NOTABLE WARTIME TORPEDO ACCIDENTS

'*You know, that looks remarkably like one of ours!*'

Used correctly, the torpedo can be a devastating weapon. Sadly, there are numerous accounts of torpedo launches causing unintended damage to their own side and even sinking their own vessel. The most notorious was the Battle of Sunda Strait, but each incident was a tragedy for the side involved. Early doubters, including the future Admiral Fisher, regularly expressed fears of the effects of launching a Whitehead in the midst of a general melee as at Lissa. As the then Commander Fisher reported on Whitehead's weapon to the Admiralty in 1869, 'it must be remembered that, once started, his Torpedo is beyond control and will blow up anyone it comes across.'

Modern torpedoes fired in error can be left unarmed, and even be made to self-destruct before they strike their launch vessel. With early torpedoes there was no such opportunity. Two French destroyers, a British cruiser and at least two US submarines managed to torpedo themselves. The destroyers and the submarines sank, and the cruiser was so crippled she later succumbed to air attack.

Circular runs could occur when a torpedo's gyro was upset or failed, or when a wave or shell-burst caused the torpedo to roll. In the latter case the horizontal planes would operate to try to control the torpedo's depth, but would instead act as the vertical rudders, turning it in a circle. Receiving no response, the depth-keeping mechanism would stubbornly continue to try to correct the depth, and the torpedo would continue to circle.

The incidents of torpedo explosion on board caused by enemy fire are noted in the following chapters, but there was also the self-inflicted injury, from the explosion of an air flask. Often serious, in one case it led directly to the loss of a large modern fleet destroyer.

The air flask of a torpedo is a highly stressed component, and when charged at full pressure it poses a significant risk if somehow the flask is ruptured. Even a flask which has undergone the most rigorous construction and testing can fail: repeated cycles of charging and releasing the pressure can set up fatal metal fatigue; to this must be added the risks of the corrosion always present in a sea-going environment; and, lastly, the factor of handling. When a ship at sea rolls and pitches, moving and loading a torpedo can cause minor blows which, in time, could lead to flask failure. In more than one case, the failure was suspected to have been caused by over-pressure as a result of the ambient temperature.

Sadly, torpedo incidents have continued into the post-war period, and while the Germans experienced no naval losses with HTP fuel, the Japanese had several spectacular explosions during laboratory testing, but none at sea. The Americans have been careful, or perhaps fortunate, in their use of navol, but it was left to the Royal Navy to suffer the first deadly explosion, and it is feared that the *Kursk* disaster must also be laid at the door of this extremely volatile fuel.

CHAPTER 20

Early Torpedo Actions

The armament manufacturer's dream is to sell to both sides in a major conflict. And then to sell further units to replace those lost in that conflict, creating an upwardly spiralling arms race. Such was the situation in Latin America in the last quarter of the nineteenth century and the early years of the twentieth, culminating in Brazil's order for the *Rio de Janeiro*, the longest dreadnought in the world with the greatest number of big guns (which became the *Sultan Osman I* and eventually HMS *Agincourt*), and Chile's contract to purchase two super-dreadnoughts (which became HMS *Canada* and the aircraft carrier *Eagle*).

Conflicts there were, between the Pacific Coast nations but also between government and rebel factions in these young republics. One of these internecine squabbles resulted in the launch of the first ever Whitehead used in combat, and a later rebellion led to the first documented sinking of an ironclad by a locomotive torpedo.

THE BATTLE OF PACHOCA

The background to the encounter was that on 6 May 1877 Peruvian rebels in their civil war against the elected President Prado seized the small ironclad turret ship *Huáscar* at Callao. *Huáscar*'s captain, Germán Astete, needed fuel and supplies, which he proceeded to take from passing merchant ships, four of which happened to be British-registered. On 23 May *Huáscar*'s crew were in the process of plundering the port of Pisagua, to the north of

The Fred Mitchell lithograph of the *Shah–Huáscar* action. (From *Ships of the Victorian Navy*, reproduced by courtesy of the Society for Nautical Research)

Iquique, when a loyalist squadron appeared and tried in vain to capture her. A few days later Admiral Algernon de Horsey, commander of the British Pacific Fleet, arrived with the large unarmoured iron frigate HMS *Shah*, and the smaller wooden corvette HMS *Amethyst*. Horsey's orders were to seek reparations for the plundering of British ships, and his command cornered the *Huáscar* in Pachoca Bay on 29 May 1877.

Refusing de Horsey's demand that he surrender his ship, Captain Astete cleared for action, and battle commenced. The *Shah* was armed with two 9in and six 7in rifles, plus two 14in Whitehead torpedoes. *Amethyst* carried 64pdr smoothbores, and two torpedoes. *Huáscar* was armed with two 10in guns in a single Coles-type turret, plus several smaller weapons.

While *Huáscar* manoeuvred in shallow water where the British ships could not follow, and three times lined up to ram, the British fired off no less than 427 Palliser shells and solid shot at her, hitting *Huascar* fifty times but penetrating her armour only once. Seeing the lack of effect of his guns, de Horsey decided at last to resort to that most ungentlemanly of weapons, the new Whitehead. *Shah* launched one of her torpedoes … and missed. As night was falling, the inconclusive action was called off.

However, since *Huáscar* had fired off most of her ammunition, Astete put into Iquique for a parley with the government forces. As a result they took back the ship, and the rebels departed under safe conduct. De Horsey was severely criticised in Parliament for failing to capture the *Huáscar*, until it was pointed out that she was, after all, a British export, and therefore proof of Britain's supremacy in naval matters.

The first circular run

To continue the story of the renegade ironclad, the *Huáscar* led a charmed life, and survived many naval actions to become the famous Chilean navy museum ship of today. But her career could have been cut short in the hands of her original Peruvian owners due to an incident with one of Lay's enormous dirigible torpedoes.

On 27 August 1879, Peruvian Contra Almirante Don Miguel Grau embarked two Lay torpedoes and an operator, and set out in *Huáscar* to search for Chilean warships. He found the Chilean corvette *Abtauo* anhored off Antofagasta and attacked. Instead of coming in to ram, as *Huáscar* had done when sinking the Chilean corvette

Tailpiece: after an adventurous career, the turret ship *Huáscar* lives out her peaceful retirement as a Chilean navy museum ship, here seen moored in Talcahuano harbour in 2005. (Photo courtesy of Usuario Valo)

Esmeralda in an earlier encounter, Grau slewed her broadside on and launched one of his 23ft long (7m) Lay torpedoes. The monster headed for the enemy corvette, to the cheers of the Peruvian onlookers, but before reaching her it turned back and headed directly towards *Huáscar*, despite all the efforts of the operator to regain control. Luckily a young officer, Teniente Diez Causeco, dived into the water and managed to push the Lay off course so it missed. The errant torpedo was duly recovered and returned in disgrace to Iquique where both were landed.

No doubt this near-fatal malfunction, plus a later failure on 3 January 1881, when the Peruvians had attacked the *Huáscar*, now in the hands of the Chileans, with another Lay torpedo, was due to the primitive state of electrical technology of the period.

MAKAROV

In the meantime, far away from Latin America, another long-running conflict flared up in the Black Sea, between Imperial Russia and her old enemy the Ottoman Empire, and this time it involved torpedoes. The major Russian player was Captain, later Admiral, Makarov.

On 24 April 1877 Russia declared war on Turkey, claiming the need to protect Christian populations in the Balkans. Captain Makarov arrived at the head of a flotilla at the mouth of the Danube, at the time controlled by the Turks. His ships were armed with towed torpedoes designed by a German, Captain Menzing, with spar torpedoes, and with several Whiteheads. Attacks with Menzing's towed torpedoes were carried out in May, June

and August, and although several torpedoes reached their targets, the electrical firing contacts failed to detonate them. The levers on the Harvey would have not suffered the same problem.

Spar torpedoes were used on three occasions. On the night of 25/26 May 1877, two spar torpedo launches attacked and sank the Turkish monitor *Seifi*. But following attacks in June failed completely, and in the second attack, on the corvette *Idjilalie*, Lieutenant Rozhestvensky was lucky to escape with his life. On 27 December 1877 Makarov tried again, this time bringing into action two Whiteheads, one launched from a tube fixed on a raft lashed alongside the *Sinope*, while the second was secured by ropes beneath the keel of the *Tchesma*. These strange methods of launching a Whitehead failed to work, one torpedo exploding astern of the target and the second stranding on a beach. Finally, on 25 January 1878 both launch vessels penetrated Batoum harbour and at the short range of 80yds (73m) successfully launched their Whiteheads at the revenue steamer *Intikbah*, which sank in less than two minutes, taking twenty-three of her crew down with her. The Whitehead had struck its first blow in wartime.

Captain Makarov went on to take part in polar research expeditions, and at the outbreak of the Russo-Japanese war he was thought of as the most competent Russian naval commander. His death in March 1904 when his flagship *Petropavlovsk* blew up on a Japanese mine was to plunge the Russian Far East fleet into a deep despair from which it would never recover. Lieutenant Rozhestvensky, for his part, rose to command the Second Baltic Squadron which set off on its journey halfway round the world, to meet its fate at the battle of Tsushima in May 1905.

There was a curious sequel to Makarov's first attempt with Whiteheads.

WOODS PASHA

The following photograph appears on page 52 of Edwyn Gray's book, *The Devil's Device*, and he describes it as perhaps the earliest photo of Robert Whitehead with his lost 1866 prototype torpedo. Closer inspection will reveal that this is a Whitehead torpedo dating from after the introduction of the contra-rotating propellers, and consequent suppression of the stabilising fins top and bottom, which took place from 1874. The man on the right is too young to be Robert Whitehead in 1877, the most likely date for the photo.

The author suspects that this is in fact a photo of Woods Pasha, the young British officer seconded to the Turkish navy, examining the battered 15in Russian

An extremely battered Whitehead (discovered by Edwyn Grayin the archives at Explosion at Priddy's Hard)

Whitehead launched by Makarov's men at the Turkish flotilla at Bakoum on 27 December 1877, being the example which ran up on a beach and was captured relatively intact. It was numbered, according to a report in *The Times* (doubtless written by Woods Pasha himself), either No 250 50 or 255 50. These were part of a batch of Whiteheads supplied to Russia in February 1877. The Turkish flotilla at Bakoum was coincidentally commanded by another Englishman, Hobart Pasha.

In his autobiography *Spunyarn*, Woods Pasha describes how he opened up the captured Whitehead and examined its mechanism, including the 'Secret'. He then engaged in negotiations with the Fiume factory, requiring them first to repair the errant torpedo (plus the second example which had lost its warhead); and also to offer a batch of Whiteheads for sale to the Turkish government at a discounted price – all in return for his silence as regards what he had discovered.

Apparently, the battered torpedo was 'repaired' – probably by dismantling the internals and mounting them in a new shell with replacement propellers – and was returned to Turkey. There is an entry of such a delivery noted in the factory register in 1878 but with no serial number marked alongside, an omission which occurs nowhere else in the Fiume records. Presumably, it had already appeared in the register under the batch delivered to Russia, and it would have been 'indiscreet' to show the Russians' torpedo redelivered to their enemies the Turks. It seems that the torpedo which had lost its warhead, presumably due to a low-order explosion, was deemed irreparable; probably its air flask had been damaged when the warhead exploded.

For his part, Woods Pasha rose to be in charge of the Turkish navy's torpedo school, and retired with the rank of admiral.

SPAR TORPEDO SUCCESSES IN THE SINO-FRENCH WAR

In 1884 France and China were disputing control of Tonkin, which would later become French Indochina. Admiral Courbet's fleet attacked the Fujian fleet at Foochow on 23 August. In the action, which resulted in the complete destruction of the Chinese fleet, electrically detonated spar torpedoes were used with success. Torpedo boat *No 46* sank the Chinese cruiser *Yang Wu*, the enemy flagship, while torpedo boat *No 45* crippled the sloop *Fu Sing*, which was later sunk by a spar torpedo carried by an armed pinnace from the French flagship. An attempted Chinese riposte with their own spar torpedoes was driven off in confusion when the French unmasked their searchlights, the first time these projectors had been used in naval warfare.

While on land the outnumbered French columns fought desperate hand-to-hand battles with overwhelming numbers of Chinese and Black Flag troops, at sea the French struck again at Shaipoo on 14 February 1885. Two torpedo boats armed with spar torpedoes sank the Chinese cruiser *Yu Yen* and the despatch boat *Chien Chiang*.

The French squadron had been helped by diplomatic approaches which persuaded the German shipyards to delay delivery of two powerful ironclads under construction for China, and by the fatal rivalry between the northern and southern Chinese fleets, which meant that the French could concentrate on destroying the southern fleet without fear of intervention by the northern forces.

French torpedo boat No 143, showing the torpedo spar equipment at left. Note the commander's face peering through the top vision port in the conning tower. (Photo from *Development of a Modern Navy*)

SINKING OF THE *BLANCO ENCALADA*

To return to the naval hotbed of Latin America, we can with certainty attribute the first sinking of a warship by a locomotive torpedo to the loyalist naval forces of the government of Chile. The victim was the 3560-ton central battery ironclad *Blanco Encalada*. Built by Earl's Shipbuilding Company of Hull to the design of Edward Reed, *Blanco Encalada* was completed in 1875 as an armoured frigate. Four years later, she crossed swords with the notorious ironclad *Huáscar*, which she overwhelmed and captured at the Battle of Angamos on 8 October 1879.

During the Chilean civil war of 1891, between the presidential forces and those of the Congress party, *Blanco Encalada*'s crew joined the latter. On 23 April 1891 she was anchored at the port of Caldera, when she was attacked by the 713-ton torpedo gunboats *Almirante Lynch* and *Almirante Condell* which fired a total of six Whiteheads at the old ironclad. Just one from *Almirante Lynch* struck her, but it was enough to send her to the bottom in minutes, with the loss of eleven officers, 171 men and several rebel civilians. Her anti-torpedo nets had been left in harbour, and doors in her watertight bulkheads had been left open. One Junta member, Ramón Barros Luco, who could not swim, gained a certain notoriety when he saved himself by clinging to the neck of a cow which had formed part of the cargo of provisions for the rebels. For his part, the captain, Don Luis Goñi, who had been blown bodily up a ventilation shaft and into the water, gained the shore by clinging to the neck of a pet llama. It was evident that in Victorian times even officers did not learn to swim.

The age of the locomotive torpedo had well and truly dawned, for 'El Blanco' was the very first warship to be authenticated as being sunk in action by one. Her wreck lay in 18m (60ft) of water in Caldera Bay until 1954, when it was dynamited to make way for a new bridge, with not a thought for the fact that it was a war grave. Perhaps as rebels her lost crewmen were thought to deserve less consideration.

AQUIDABÃ

The next torpedo victim was also a breakaway ironclad, this time one taking part in the Brazilian civil war of 1893–94, on the side of the rebels led by Rear Admiral Custódio José de Mello. Built by Samuda Brothers and launched in January 1885, the *Aquidabã* (normally rendered in English as *Aquidaban*), was a turret ironclad armed with twin 9.2in guns in each of two turrets, placed *en echelon* fore and aft. She displaced 4950 tons and could reach a top speed of 18.8 knots.

Her crew had joined an earlier rebellion started by de Mello in November 1891, and in 1893, after visiting New

The torpedoing of *Blanco Encalada*.

York for the Colombian Exhibition fleet review, her crew once more joined de Mello when he started a second rebellion. In the early morning of 16 April 1894, *Aquidabã* was anchored off the coast at Santa Catarina, when she was attacked and torpedoed by the loyalist torpedo gunboat *Gustavo Sampaio*. She was hit in the bows by two Whiteheads, the surprised officer of the watch being thrown overboard by the shock of the explosions. As she did not immediately sink, the engines were started and she was grounded in 22ft (7m) of water. The crew were able to reach shore and nobody was lost in the sinking.

This disaster was the start of the collapse of the rebellion. Fortunately – or perhaps unfortunately in light of her eventual fate – *Aquidabã* was able to be salvaged by government forces in the following June. Sent to Germany and England, she was fully repaired and modernised.

To complete her story, in 1906 *Aquidabã* hosted no less than three admirals and navy officials who were accompanying the navy minister on board the cruiser *Barroso*, on an official visit to select the site for a new naval base. In Jacuacanga Bay on 21 January, her magazines suddenly exploded and she sank in less than three minutes, killing a total of 212 officers and men, including all three admirals.

JAPAN

As a young man, the future Admiral Togo had helped carry the stone cannonballs for the ancient cannons firing back at the British fleet under Admiral Kuper, which was in the process of destroying the city of Kagoshima in 1863. He learnt at first hand the need to rapidly acquire the technology to be able to defend his country against foreign invaders. The Japanese nation as a whole quickly adopted modern technologies: railways, steelworks, telegraph, electricity, shipbuilding, and warships.

By the time of the Sino-Japanese War in 1894, the IJN was ready to go head to head with the Chinese northern fleet. But torpedoes did not feature greatly in the conflict. Indeed, in chasing down and sinking a fugitive from the Battle of the Yalu, the Japanese resorted to the spar torpedo to destroy the

Aquidabã, acting the part of a small battleship.

Yang Wei the day after the Chinese retreat from the debacle. The Chinese did have a few Whiteheads, and went into battle with the tubes loaded and pistols in place, with spare torpedoes ready on trolleys close by. But when Japanese shells started landing aboard, the Chinese launched all their ready torpedoes, even though the Japanese ships were well out of range, and took the warheads off the spare torpedoes and stored them in the magazines. Whiteheads that ended up on a neighbouring beach were sold back to the Chinese navy by enterprising fishermen. It was believed that the loss of the Chinese ship *Chih Yuen* was caused by the explosion of one of her own torpedoes. Navies everywhere took note, and the general move to place torpedo launching tubes underwater began to gain momentum.

The Japanese did not expend torpedoes during their capture of Port Arthur, nor during the blockade of Weihaiwei. A decade was to pass before the Japanese torpedo force went into serious action.

The Triple Intervention of 1895 had stolen from Japan the fruits of the war, and the Chinese had promptly leased Port Arthur to the Russians for use as an ice-free naval base for their Far Eastern fleet. The national humiliation served to accelerate the forging of the powerful Imperial Japanese navy, and in nine years the Japanese felt able to act. And they were no longer isolated internationally, since the signing of the Anglo-Japanese Alliance in 1902.

On 8 February 1904 the viceroy's chief of staff in Port Arthur was comforted to read in a telegram received at 2300 from St Petersburg that, since negotiations with the Japanese were progressing well, 'any fear of armed conflict is mere fancy'. In the harbour a group of officers had decided to invite some ladies back to their ship, fully illuminated like all the Russian warships, but on the way their boat was nearly run down by a slow-moving destroyer. Someone in the boat jokingly said that it was the Japanese monkeys come to attack them. Suddenly, three torpedoes exploded on the hulls of Russian ships, and firing broke out on all sides. The Japanese had put in a surprise torpedo attack with ten destroyers.

They had fitted the heads of their Whiteheads with scissor-type cutters as the Russians were known to protect their ships with nets. Even so, only three of the torpedoes hit their targets, and many others could be seen caught in the nets, their propellers whipping the water into foam. The French-built battleship *Tsesarevich* was torpedoed amidships, the American-built *Retvizan* was hit in the stern, and the protected cruiser *Pallada* also was hit, on the port side amidships. She suffered a fire in a coal bunker, but was not seriously damaged. The three ships were soon repaired and returned to service.

The results of the attack were militarily disappointing, and many observers felt the torpedo to be an overrated weapon, of potential for the future but not for the present. The failure of net cutters to overcome these obstacles was deceptively encouraging. The battleship *Sevastopol* was subsequently moored in the outer reaches of the harbour surrounded by double nets, and survived repeated torpedo attacks. The resistance of *Pallada*, protected by her coal bunker, led designers to put too much reliance on this method of anti-torpedo protection, instead of conducting meaningful tests of the growing explosive power of modern torpedoes, and paying more attention to proper internal subdivision.

Subsequent losses during the siege of Port Arthur were caused by the mine, both sides suffering grievously, up until the survivors of the blockaded Russian fleet were sunk by Japanese army howitzers.

The lessons to be drawn from the Battle of Tsushima, when the Russian Baltic squadron under Zinovy Petrovich Rozhestvensky was annihilated by Togo's ships, were carefully examined by naval officers and designers worldwide. It was generally agreed that the Japanese destroyers and torpedo boats, although participating in the final sinking of the *Kniaz Suvorov* and other cripples, had failed to live up to the promise expected of them. Two comments seemed pertinent: first, the Japanese had launched from too great a range, because they needed to husband their resources, lost destroyers not being easily replaced; and second, launching at long range and therefore slow speed meant that too many torpedoes missed their targets.

A dramatic Japanese print showing their torpedo boats attacking Port Arthur. The battleship hit by a torpedo is the American-built *Retvizan*.

CHAPTER 21

The Great War

U-BOAT SUCCESSES EARLY IN THE FIRST WORLD WAR

Käpitanleutnant Otto Eduard Weddigen was a competent and daring submarine commander, every bit the equal of his Royal Navy counterparts. Unlike them, he was offered far more targets by the large Royal Navy, but he was also aided by the disparaging attitude of British naval commanders towards the potential of the submarine. When in October 1900 the British Admiralty had reluctantly ordered the first five submarine boats – the *Holland*s – Rear Admiral Wilson, Third Sea Lord and Controller of the Navy, who had won his VC on land during the Sudan campaign, famously declared the submarine a 'damned un-English weapon'. Wilson was no Luddite – indeed he was one of the Navy's leading torpedo experts and went on to support the development of the British submarine – but at the time he was expressing a reservation felt by many naval officers, and not just in the Royal Navy.

Despite this unpromising start, in March 1904 the five early Royal Navy *Holland* boats, assigned to the defence of Portsmouth in the naval manoeuvres, had 'torpedoed' four battleships of the Channel Fleet, including the flagship. Unfortunately, this theoretical success was marred in succeeding years by the loss of the larger *A 1* through collision with SS *Berwick Castle*, the swamping of *A 4* by a passing ship, a fatal explosion on *A 5* and the loss of *A 7* in heavy seas in January 1914. Such disasters helped confirm the Admiralty in the belief that the submarine did not pose a significant threat to their command of the sea.

The German submarine service was even slower off the mark, having to overcome Tirpitz's aversion to such craft – the first U-boat was not launched until 1906 – but once at war these primitive warships were quick to prove their worth. This occurred in dramatic manner. One month into the Great War, on 6 September 1914 off St Abbs Head, Käpitanleutnant Hersing in the diesel-powered *U 21* sighted the light cruiser HMS *Pathfinder* cruising slowly at some 5 knots to economise on her limited reserves of coal. Hersing fired one torpedo, which was spotted by a lookout on *Pathfinder*. Her captain ordered evasive action but to no avail: the torpedo struck under the bridge and caused the explosion of the forward magazine. Divers report that all the ship forward of the first funnel vanished in the explosion. *Pathfinder* sank in less than five minutes, with the loss of 250 men, just eighteen surviving. *Pathfinder* was the very first ship to be

sunk by a locomotive torpedo fired from a submarine. We will meet with Käpitanleutnant Hersing and *U 21* again in the next section.

It was not just the British who were blind to the potential of the submarine. Three days after the loss of the *Pathfinder*, the German light cruiser *Hela* was torpedoed by the British *E 9*.

Much worse was to follow a fortnight later. On 22 September, Otto Weddigen was in command of *U 9*, one of the older submarines, commissioned in April 1910 and powered by unreliable Körting paraffin engines which emitted vast clouds of white exhaust smoke when running on the surface. He was patrolling the Broad Fourteens, in the southern North Sea, when his first officer, Spiess, spotted the masts of a ship and smoke. Weddigen ordered *U 9* to dive. His targets, which he first took to be four-funnelled light cruisers of the *Birmingham* class, turned out to be three obsolescent armoured cruisers of the *Cressy* class, the name-ship and her two sisters *Aboukir* and *Hogue*. Built at the turn of the century, they displaced 12,000 tons, and carried a crew of 760 men at a top speed, when new, of up to 21 knots. By September 1914 they were well past their best, and the fact that they were manned largely by raw reservists led them to be referred to as the 'Live Bait Squadron'.

Although the Royal Navy was large, it still needed to press into service every available ship, and these old and vulnerable vessels were performing an important function, screening transports carrying vital troop reinforcements to France. On paper, their heavy armament of two 9.2in and twelve 6in guns, protected by an armour belt up to 6in thick, should have stood them in good stead in a surface action against anything less potent than a battleship. They were, however, left fatally exposed with no destroyer screen, which had withdrawn because of bad weather.

In the absence of his admiral, Captain Drummond in *Aboukir* was left in charge. He was leading the other cruisers on a straight course at around 10 knots, not zigzagging as his standing orders required him to do. Weddigen manoeuvred *U 9* into position for a submerged torpedo attack on *Aboukir* and at 0625 fired the first torpedo, which struck his victim on the port side. Rapidly flooding, *Aboukir* began to sink. Captain Drummond initially believed his ship had struck a mine, and he called the other two in to rescue his crew. *Hogue*'s Captain Nicholson stopped to lower boats, but as *Aboukir* rolled over and sank thirty minutes after being hit, Weddigen hit HMS *Hogue* with two torpedoes, sinking her in less than ten minutes. To compound the tragedy, Captain Johnson of *Cressy* had also stopped to lower boats, but began to take avoiding action when his crew spotted *U 9*'s periscope. It did not save his ship. The first torpedo launched by Weddigen missed, but the second struck home, and she sank in fifteen minutes.

In the Second World War, many cruisers of similar size survived torpedo hits, even from the powerful Japanese 24in Type 93 torpedo. What is clear is that these armoured cruisers shared the Achilles' heel of all the major warships designed by Sir William White: the large boiler and engine room spaces divided by a longitudinal bulkhead. A torpedo hit opening up one of these large spaces was virtually certain to cause the ship to capsize, especially since there were no compensating voids on the opposite side to counter-flood.

From the three crews, 837 men were rescued, but a total of 1459 died, including many sea cadets aged fifteen, who should never have been aboard. The death toll exceeded that of all of Nelson's ships engaged in the Battle of Trafalgar. Weddigen and his crew returned to Wilhelmshaven and a hero's welcome.

Just three weeks later, Weddigen added to his laurels by sinking the old protected cruiser HMS *Hawke*, in the North Sea. Once again, a German torpedo exploded a magazine, and she sank in less than five minutes. The British press commented that the loss of so old a ship (*Hawke* had been launched in 1891) was of little consequence, but they lamented the loss of her captain, twenty-six officers and 497 men out of her crew of 594.

Otto Weddigen went on to command the diesel boat *U 29*, but on 18 March 1915 his luck ran out. In the Pentland Firth he had launched a torpedo at the battleship HMS *Neptune* but *U 29* broached surface after firing. The battleship HMS *Dreadnought* spotted the U-boat and came in to ram at full speed, cutting her in half and causing the deaths of Weddigen and his entire crew – ironically, the only time when the battleship, which had given her name to an entire new breed of fighting ship, had actually come into action with the enemy.

THE MYSTERIOUS LOSS OF SMS *KARLSRUHE*

The *Karlsruhe* was a fast light cruiser of the Imperial German navy, commissioned on 15 January 1914. The outbreak of war found her in the Caribbean, and her commander, Fregattenkapitän Erich Kohler, commenced a short but successful campaign of commerce-raiding. En route to attack Barbados and Fort de France, on the night of 4 November 1914 the *Karlsruhe* suddenly suffered an internal explosion which blew the ship in two. The bow section quickly sank, together with Kohler and most of his crew. The stern remained afloat long enough for 140 survivors to transfer to one of *Karlsruhe*'s accompanying colliers.

The reason for her loss has never been explained. Several navies suffered losses from spontaneous

Obverse and reverse of a commemorative medal struck by H Ziegler. (© National Maritime Museum, Greenwich, London)

combustion and explosion of their gun propellant. The French, British and Japanese suffered the most, but the Italians, Russians and even the Americans also lost ships. But not one single other German warship. German discipline in storage and handling of propellant was obviously superior to that of the other navies, or was her propellant much more stable, especially in hot climates, than that of the others?

The examination of the loss of HMS *Khartoum* in July 1940 in the Red Sea begs the question of whether it is possible that the loss of *Karlsruhe* was caused by the rupture of a torpedo air vessel, always a risk in the heat of the Caribbean. Her torpedo room and torpedo magazine were sited just forward of her bridge, as proved by the vertical torpedo loading shaft placed there. Just forward of the torpedo flat was the forward magazine for her 10.5cm guns.

A torpedo explosion, more plausible than an ammunition explosion, would have led to a fire and detonation of the stored torpedo warheads, in turn setting off the forward magazine. In any case, explosion of the torpedo warheads in the submerged flat would have sufficed to blow the ship in half, killing her commander and his officers on the bridge above.

NASMITH AND THE 'BRENNAN'

Edwyn Gray, in his book *A Damned Un-English Weapon*, describes how Martin Nasmith, stalking the Bosporus in *E 11*, fired two torpedoes at a large Turkish transport, the *Stamboul*, moored beside the Arsenal. The port torpedo ran wild, breaking surface and then sinking. While Nasmith successfully fired his starboard torpedo, which made a direct hit, he was startled to see what he took to be a Brennan controlled torpedo head from the shore towards *E 11*. Nasmith avoided it by swinging to starboard and diving deep. Only later he reflected that the 'Brennan' must have been their own port torpedo coming back at them.

Given the density of traffic in the Bosporus it is probable that a wave from a passing ship had rolled the Whitehead. Some years later an agent named Slade reported the eventual activities of the rogue torpedo. He claimed he had seen it execute several manoeuvres, before hitting a merchant ship tied up at a wharf.

THE DARDANELLES: GRAVE OF THE PRE-DREADNOUGHTS

The first old pre-dreadnought to be sunk by torpedo was the ancient ironclad frigate *Messudiyeh*, 9250 tons, built by Thames Iron Works, and launched in 1874. Rebuilt to a 'modern' appearance in Genoa in 1903, her main 9.2in guns were never fitted, being replaced by wooden dummies. Anchored at Sari Sigla Bay as a guard ship, she was torpedoed and sunk on 1 December 1914 by the British submarine *B 11*.

The second torpedo victim was the *Canopus*-class HMS *Goliath*, 13,150 tons, four 12in, launched 1898. Anchored off Cape Helles, she provided close gunfire support for troops ashore. On the night of 12/13 May 1915 she was torpedoed by the Turkish torpedo boat *Muavenet* and sank with a loss of 500 lives.

Third down was HMS *Triumph*, 12,175 tons, a light battleship with four 10in and fourteen 7.5in guns, built for Chile but taken over by the Royal Navy, launched in 1903. Anchored off Gaba Tepe with her nets deployed, on 25 May 1915 she was torpedoed by Hersing in *U 21*. She quickly capsized with a loss of seventy men.

Just two days later on 27 May, Hersing returned to the same area to torpedo HMS *Majestic*, 14,580 tons, four 12in, launched in 1895. Once again the battleship had her nets out, and she was surrounded by smaller vessels as protection. Hit by two torpedoes, *Majestic* capsized and sank in seven minutes, with the loss of forty men, many being trapped in her nets.

The final torpedo loss was *Haireddin Barbarossa*, the ex-German *Kurfürst Friedrich Wilhelm*, 10,727 tons, six 11in, launched 1891 and purchased 1910. Torpedoed by Nasmith in *E 11* off Bulair on 8 August 1915, she capsized and sank in seven minutes with the loss of twenty-one officers and 237 men.

All of the pre-dreadnought battleships designed by Sir William White, director of naval construction from 1886 to 1903, were ill-equipped to resist even one torpedo hit amidships. In order to give priority to gunnery, White had deliberately provided his designs with low metacentric heights (for example only 3.4ft in the *Majestic* class). This made them steady gun platforms, but reduced their reserve of stability. Another feature of White's ships, shared, it must be said, by many foreign contemporaries, was the longitudinal watertight bulkhead in the large spaces amidships, the boiler and engine rooms. It was feared that dividing these spaces laterally would leave too large a space across the ship from one side to the other. An ingress of water could quickly form a free surface situation and lead to rapid capsize.

Unfortunately, the longitudinal bulkheads posed the same risk. Since there were no voids at the sides of the ships which could be rapidly counter-flooded to offset damage to the opposite side, the large spaces such as the boiler room, once penetrated by a torpedo or mine

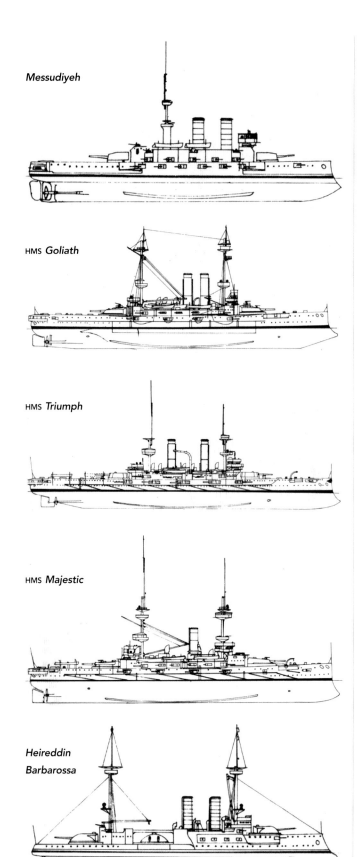

Messudiyeh

HMS *Goliath*

HMS *Triumph*

HMS *Majestic*

Heireddin Barbarossa

(Line drawings from *Battleships of World War I* by Anthony Preston)

explosion, coupled with the low metacentric height, would almost certainly end in capsize. It was a question of size, the pre-dreadnoughts, and even the earliest dreadnoughts, being too narrow in beam to allow for a meaningful TDS in depth. Accordingly, when *Goliath*, *Triumph* and *Majestic* were torpedoed, they all capsized, the first with heavy loss of life.

Kapitänlieutenant Hersing of *U 21* was the submariner who had torpedoed HMS *Pathfinder* in 1914. For his exploits in the Mediterranean he was known by his fellow officers as '*Zerstörer der Schlachtschiffe*' – 'destroyer of battleships'.

JUTLAND

Although the outcome of the Battle of Jutland, which took place on 31 May and 1 June 1916, would appear to have hinged on the effects of heavy shells against armour plate, the torpedo was the weapon which simultaneously robbed the Grand Fleet of the conclusive victory which was within its grasp, and allowed the German High Seas Fleet to escape and claim a tactical victory.

Royal Navy destroyers put in three mass torpedo attacks on German ships; German destroyers put in four mass torpedo attacks on British ships. The fourth German torpedo attack, which started at 1917, was the decisive moment in the battle. Jellicoe ordered his ships to turn away from the threat, and Scheer escaped the trap the Grand Fleet had laid for him. In between these mass attacks there were several individual encounters when torpedoes were launched, with mixed results.

The first major clash between opposing destroyer flotillas occurred after 1630, during the 'run to the south', when Beatty's battlecruisers pursued their German opposite numbers, not suspecting that they were being led onto the main body of the High Seas Fleet. The destroyers and light cruisers attached to the opposing battlecruiser squadrons clashed between the firing lines, each side attempting to break through and torpedo the enemy battlecruisers. Success went to the British: at 1657 the destroyer HMS *Petard* hit the German battlecruiser *Seydlitz* with a torpedo, and shortly after torpedoed and sank the German destroyer *V 29*. All other torpedoes launched by both sides were avoided.

At 1756 the German light cruiser *Wiesbaden* was disabled by shell hits from HMS *Invincible* of Admiral Hood's 3rd Battlecruiser Squadron and was left between the opposing lines, seemingly dead in the water. Despite attracting the attention and fire of several passing capital ships, *Wiesbaden*'s crew continued to load and launch torpedoes at passing targets of opportunity for almost an hour. At the same time German destroyers put in a mass attack on Hood's 3rd BCS, but his battlecruisers avoided all the torpedoes. Simultaneously, British destroyers launched their second assault on the German battlecruisers, again without result. At 1810 the destroyer HMS *Moresby* launched a torpedo at the battleship *Markgraf*, but missed.

When at 1830 the leading German ships came within sight of the Grand Fleet's dreadnoughts crossing their 'T', Admiral Scheer realised he was sailing into certain death, and ordered all ships to execute a battle about-turn to starboard, turning through 180 degrees, and managed to disengage temporarily. Wary of running onto torpedoes, Jellicoe continued to head south. During their battle turn the German ships had, in fact, launched torpedoes, and by 1840 battleships at the rear of the British line reported having to take avoiding action. Fourteen minutes later, the battleship HMS *Marlborough* was hit in the diesel room by a single torpedo. Her crew had not seen from where it had been launched, and they suspected a U-boat. In fact, it is likely that the torpedo had come from the stationary *Wiesbaden*, which continued to take torpedo shots of opportunity.

When Scheer once more found himself heading into the teeth of the firing line of the Grand Fleet at 1917, he ordered a second battle turn-away, calling on his four remaining battlecruisers and all his destroyers to cover his retreat – the famous 'death ride' of the battlecruisers. In all, thirty-one German torpedoes were launched at the British battleships, some coming very close, but all missed, and the British anti-torpedo boat gunners sank the destroyer *S 35*.

The two battle fleets lost contact, and during the hours of darkness several confused actions took place at the rear of the British line. Although Jellicoe and his officers did not realise it, these were the High Seas Fleet fighting its way to safety through the rear of the British formation. Both sides incurred losses, the light cruiser *Southampton* torpedoing and sinking the light cruiser *Frauenlob* at 2223, the German ship going down with all hands. Between 2330 and 0215 British destroyer flotillas put in torpedo attacks on units of the German fleet, sinking the cruiser *Rostock*. At 0210 the pre-dreadnought *Pommern* was torpedoed and also lost with all hands. The final German loss was the destroyer *V 4*, which had her bows blown off. It was believed she had struck a mine, but it is more likely a British torpedo had found her. The final torpedo attack

In the kind of manoeuvre they carried out at Jutland, black-painted torpedo boat destroyers (with *V 183* nearest the camera) break through a line of *Nassau*-class dreadnoughts at high speed. (Photo from *The Ships of the German Fleets 1845–1945* by Hans Jürgen Hansen)

A painting by Claus Bergen of *Pommern* and her sisters under fire at Jutland. They were known as the 'five-minute ships' – the length of time they were expected to survive in a duel with dreadnoughts.

was made at 0237, when the destroyer HMS *Moresby* attacked the battlecruiser *Von de Tann* with a single torpedo, which missed.

The experience of the crew of HMS *Marlborough*, as the sole British dreadnought to be hit by a torpedo, is instructive. The following narrative was taken from the report of her commanding officer, Captain George P Ross, and her gunnery officer, Lt Cdr G C C Royle. The latter's report begins:

6.10pm Sighted British battle cruisers engaging enemy's ships.

6.12 Red 7, cruiser, four funnels, one mast (disappeared in smoke and mist before fire could be opened).

6.15 After deploying to port. Battleship, two funnels widely separated, two masts (probably *Kaiser* class) estimated range 10,000yds, rangefinders could not get a range.

6.17 Opened fire. Seven salvoes were fired in 4 minutes; 5th and 7th were clearly seen to hit. In the 5th salvo a deep red flame could be seen and salvo struck, in the 7th salvo a large volume of grey smoke appeared.

6.21 Ceased firing, as enemy was hidden by cruiser on fire (*Roon* class).

6.24 Green 98, a cruiser, 3 funnels (*Roon*, one funnel gone). Range by rangefinder 10,500yds.

6.25 Opened fire. 5 Salvoes were fired. Hits could not be distinguished for certain, as two or three ships were firing at same object.

6.27 6-inch guns opened fire at same object. It was during this firing that right gun of 'A' turret was severely damaged and put out of action, cause not known for certain, but probably due to premature.

6.29 Checked fire. There was a pause of ten minutes, during which the ship was altering course, and enemy was hidden by smoke.

6.39 Object a battleship of *Kaiser* class. Range 13,000yds; one salvo was fired, and enemy turned away and disappeared.

6.42–6.54 Ship was altering course, and enemy's movements were very difficult to follow.

6.54 *Marlborough* was hit by a torpedo or mine in Diesel Engine Room. The shock was sufficient to shake off switches on lever power board, and some fuses in telephone circuits. These were very quickly replaced, and all control instruments were found to be in step.

The captain's narrative takes up the story:

At 6.54 p.m. on the 31st May, the ship was **struck by a torpedo** in the Diesel Engine Room. At the same time a periscope was observed by witnesses about 1,000 yards on the starboard beam. No track of this torpedo was observed, though looked for by several observers immediately after the explosion.

The explosion caused a list to starboard of seven degrees, and flooded the Diesel Engine Room, Hydraulic Engine Room, and water was reported to be entering 'A' boiler room, the biggest leak being between the framing of the watertight door to the lower bunker 100-111, and the bulkhead to which it is secured, which had parted. I then telephoned orders to draw fires in 'A' boiler room. Speed was now reduced to 17 knots.

Marlborough continued in the line, and at 7.0 p.m. **three torpedoes were reported** on the starboard beam and bow. Course was immediately altered to starboard and then to port; two torpedoes passed ahead and one astern of the ship.

The T.B.D. *Acasta*, lying disabled, was then passed one cable on the port beam. At 7.0 p.m. fire was reopened on a disabled enemy ship, range 9,800 yards, four salvoes were fired, and the third and fourth were observed to hit. Ceased fire at 7.07 p.m.

At 7.10 p.m. fired a torpedo at a disabled German ship with three funnels. This may have been the same ship. At 7.12 p.m. opened fire on battleship of *Markgraf* class, one point before the starboard beam, distant 10,200 yards, steering south. Fourteen salvoes in six minutes were fired at this ship, and the sixth, twelfth, thirteenth, and fourteenth were observed to hit. The speed was now 15 knots. Ceased firing at 7.18 p.m.

At 7.19 a T.B.D. flotilla was sighted attacking on the starboard bow, opened fire at them with range 11,000 yards. Course was altered away two points to S.S.E., and at 7.22 the flotilla scattered in a dense cloud of funnel smoke, two boats being hit. At 7.24, altered course to S.E. by S., and fired a torpedo at a battleship of the *Markgraf* class. At 7.33 **three torpedoes were observed** on starboard beam and bow, course was immediately altered to starboard and then to port, one passed ahead, one astern, and the other very close astern or under the ship.

Ship was steadied on course S. by W., and at 7.52 to

S.S.W. At 8.0 p.m. course was altered to West and speed to 17 knots, a report also was made to the Commander-in-Chief that *Marlborough*'s maximum speed was reduced to 17 knots.

At 8.20, altered course to S.W., 9.0 to S. 4 E., and 9.15 to S. 7 W. At 10.5 p.m. there was gunfire on the starboard beam and again at 10.40, abaft the starboard beam, distant about 8 miles.

At 11.44 p.m. gunfire heavy on starboard quarter, and again at 00.10 a.m. about 7 points abaft starboard beam. A very heavy explosion was observed, evidently a ship blowing up.

At about 2 a.m. 1st June, Commander Currey reported to me that the water was gaining, and that he and Engineer Commander Toop considered that it was dangerous for the ship to steam any longer at a speed of 17 knots, so with great regret I immediately informed you that speed must be reduced.

Speed was then reduced to 15 knots, and *Marlborough* hauled out of line, the *Revenge*, *Hercules*, and *Agincourt* proceeding at 17 knots.

At 2.15 a.m. speed was reduced to 13 knots and *Fearless* ordered alongside port side. Engines were stopped at 2.30 a.m. *Fearless* came alongside, embarking you and your staff.

At 3.0 a.m. I proceeded N. 4 E., and later on the *Fearless* joined as escort. A Zeppelin was sighted at 4.0 a.m. passing astern and steering to the Eastward. Two common and two A.P. shells from 13.5-inch guns and twelve H.E. shell from H.A. gun were fired, and the Zeppelin was observed to dip suddenly, but proceeded on its course.

Orders were now received from the Commander-in-Chief to proceed to Tyne or Rosyth via M channel, so at 4.30 a.m. course was altered to S. 38 W., 14 knots. Owing to the deep draught of the ship I decided to proceed to Rosyth.

At 9.30 a.m. two submarines were observed, bearing west about 8 miles off and steering towards *Marlborough* with conning towers showing. Five minutes later they dived, so course was altered away from them, course being resumed at 10.50 a.m. to S. 56 W. At 10.52 a.m. an oily patch was observed about

2 miles astern, and **the track of a torpedo overhauling the ship**, the torpedo passed along the port side, two cables off. At 11.10 a.m. course was altered to westward, and at 1.45 p.m. Commodore (T) with Harwich Flotillas was sighted bearing S.E. T.B.D.s *Lark*, *Lance*, *Lysander*, and *Lassoo*, and shortly afterwards *Laforey*, *Lookout*, *Lawford* and *Laverock* joined as escort. At 4.0 p.m. T.B.D.s *Ness* and *Albatross* joined.

At 8.0 p.m. the wind was freshening from the S.W., force 5, and by 10.0 p.m. W.S.W., force 6, with a rising sea.

About 10.0 p.m. the water was rising in 'A' boiler room through the suction of the ash expeller pump and submersible pump continually choking and the canvas hose of the ejector bursting. At midnight the water was still gaining, and was now about 4 feet below the grating around the top of the boilers. Commander Currey reported that matters were serious below, and asked that a salvage tug might be signalled for. I then altered course to S.W. by W. reduced, to 10 knots, and steered for the lee of Flamborough Head, which was distant about 50 miles, stationed the *Fearless* one and a half cables to windward of the fore bridge as the sea was breaking over the starboard side of the upper deck. At the same time I informed the Commander-in-Chief of the state of affairs, and asked the S.N.O., Tyne, to send tugs to meet me off Flamborough Head. I also warned destroyers to be prepared to come alongside lee side.

The *Laforey* and *Lookout* then asked if they could be of use in laying an oil track ahead of *Marlborough*. At 2 a.m. *Lance*'s division was ordered to lay oil track ahead, and to windward of *Marlborough*. This proved most successful, and I was very grateful to the destroyers for the suggestion. My wireless messages were intercepted by the Admiralty and a signal was received from the Admiralty to proceed to the Humber. In the meantime in 'A' boiler room, Stoker Petty Officer Ackerman was sent down in a diving dress and cleared the suctions of the pumps, and at 1 a.m. the water was stopped from rising. Speed was increased to 12 knots at 3 a.m.

At about 4.30 a.m. the steam ejector was repaired and the boiler room was cleared of water well below the floor plates at about 5.15 a.m. As the land was closed the weather improved, and at 5.30 a.m. the destroyers stopped making oil track.

Marlborough passed Spurn Light Vessel at 7.35 a.m., and secured to No. 3 buoy off Immingham at 10 a.m.

When the ship was torpedoed, Stoker William Rustage, Official Number K. 20,877, and Stoker Edgar G. Monk, Official Number K. 4,266, who were on duty in the Diesel Room, were instantly killed.

Marlborough's crew saw no less than seven torpedoes fired at them, which they avoided. They never saw the eighth which hit!

Controversy over the battle raged for decades and, even today, opinions are divided over whether Jellicoe should have turned away in the face of the mass torpedo attack at 0717, or whether he should have taken the risk of torpedo hits in order to ensure the complete destruction of the enemy fleet. Hindsight is always 20/20. One has to realise that with the rapid growth in the performance and lethality of the torpedo in the early twentieth century, the standard procedure for all fleet commanders, British or otherwise, was always to turn away.

In fact, on that very point, Jellicoe had gone out of his way to lay down such a principle in a letter to the Admiralty in October 1914, and Their Lordships had approved his strategy. Of course, it is easier to be wise after the event, and it is perhaps sobering to read in the new Fleet Standing Orders issued after Jutland that, if the fleet was instructed to take evasive action against torpedoes, 'Commanders were given discretion that if their part of the fleet was not under immediate attack, that they should continue engaging the enemy rather than turning away with the rest of the fleet.' Good in theory, and naturally leading to the breakup of a cohesive formation. The orders went on to insist that 'All ships, not just the destroyers armed principally with torpedoes but also battleships, were reminded that they carried torpedoes intended to be used whenever an opportunity arose.'

It seems that not all the battleships' torpedo-men were as eager to get to grips with the enemy as were those of HMS *Marlborough*. At least one other battleship, and there would have been many more, certainly fired off as many torpedoes as possible: Oscar Parkes comments that the torpedo flat team of HMS *Agincourt* were deep in water at the end of the action, not from flooding through shell hits, but by their own zeal in opening the underwater tubes to reload without bothering to wait until the water inside had been pumped topside.

UNRESTRICTED U-BOAT WARFARE

When the Imperial German navy attempted to impose a blockade of the merchant fleets of her opponents, she had long lost the means to carry out the classic *guerre de course* using surface ships. Her regular warships had been swept from the seas, and her handful of disguised raiders could make barely a dent in the vast numbers of British and French merchant ships, which were busily bringing the Allies all they needed for the pursuit of the war: food, armaments, munitions medicines and fuel. The High Seas Fleet was certainly not ready in 1915 to challenge the Royal Navy for command of the North Sea, let alone the wide-open spaces of the Atlantic trade routes. There was only one arm which could take up the struggle, and that was the U-boat.

The long-established rules of a *guerre de course* demanded that the corsair vessel intercepting a belligerent ship other than a warship should allow the crew to take to the safety of their boats before destroying the ship. Vessels flying the flag of neutral states should stop and allow inspection of their cargo manifests, to prove they were not carrying 'contraband' goods on behalf of the enemy. Early in the Great War, submariners on both sides had attempted to apply these gentlemanly rules, but the rapid onset of total war had cast aside such niceties. And there were other pitfalls for the submarine crews. Their craft were small and relatively slow. If a merchantman attempted to make off at speed, it could often escape the U-boat. Then there were the aggressive captains who took every opportunity to ram the much smaller submarines. And, finally, the British began to mount guns on their merchant ships, intending that they should not go down without a fight.

A final restraint was the availability of adequate torpedoes. They were bulky and expensive. For a U-boat on an extended cruise, the expenditure of the last torpedo meant a return to base. As commanders such as Nasmith had discovered in the Sea of Marmora, a deck gun, on the other hand, was a much cheaper weapon, which could be furnished with a decent supply of ammunition without taking up excessive room aboard the submarine. So U-boat crews attacking merchant ships began to use their 8.8cm and 10.5cm guns to stop and, if necessary, attack merchant ships. A shot across the bow might suffice to bring the captain to his senses, and if he tried to make a run for it or radio a warning, then the gun could be aimed at his bridge and radio room.

Then the British introduced decoys, better known under their designation of Q-ship – an innocent-looking vessel designed to lure an unsuspecting U-boat captain into surfacing and using his deck gun. At which point the White Ensign would – or should – be raised as the prelude to opening deadly fire with a concealed battery of quick-firers. Unfortunately, not all U-boats so lured were sunk, and those that escaped the trap soon gave the alarm.

Weighing up all the pros and cons, it appeared unavoidable that the U-boats' *guerre de course* would henceforth take a sinister turn. On 4 February 1915 the German navy declared that:

1. The waters around Great Britain and Ireland, including the whole of the English Channel, are herewith declared a War Zone. From 18 February onward, every merchant ship met within this War Zone will be destroyed, nor will it always be possible to obviate the danger with which the crews and passengers are thereby threatened.

2. Neutral ships, too, will run a risk in the War Zone, for in view of the misuse of neutral flags ordered by the British Government on 31 January and owing to the hazards of naval warfare, it may not always be possible to prevent the attacks on hostile ships being directed against neutral ships.

The mention of the use of neutral flags arose because in January 1915 Captain Turner of the *Lusitania* had flown American flags to show he was carrying a large number of American passengers. There were also confidential instructions issued to U-boat commanders, to the effect that, since the safety of the boat was paramount, rising to the surface to examine a ship was to be avoided. In other words, 'Shoot first and ask questions later'.

Following this declaration there were to be many sinkings deemed to be outrageous by the Allies, and which tended to inflame public opinion, especially in the United States. But the most infamous attack was the torpedoing of the 30,396-ton Cunard liner *Lusitania* on 7 May 1915 by the *U 20* commanded by Walter Schweiger. To be fair to Schweiger, he identified the *Lusitania* as a Royal Naval auxiliary as noted in the 1908 edition of *Brassey's Naval Annual*, Cunard having received government subsidies to prepare the vessel to receive an armament of 6in guns as an armed merchant cruiser.

The fact that this huge vessel should sink so quickly – in just eighteen minutes – after having been hit by only one torpedo, helped on her way by a large secondary explosion which Schweiger and everyone else ascribed to the detonation of a cargo of munitions, only served to justify the action.

Following Dr Ballard's dives on the wreck of the *Lusitania*, it was generally thought that the secondary explosion incurred in an almost empty coal bunker, when the torpedo ignited coal dust. However, in November 2012 the Supplementary Manifest of the cargo *Lusitania* carried was obtained from the Franklin D Roosevelt Presidential Archive. FDR had requested sight of it in January 1940 and had then locked it away. This revealing document details tens of thousands of .303in rifle cartridges, not in themselves a high explosive risk, but the 1248 cases labelled 'shrapnel', intended to give the impression they contained the lead balls used in shrapnel shells, were in fact a consignment of 4992 live 13pdr shrapnel shells, with their cases filled with cordite. In addition, a 90-ton consignment labelled as 'butter and cheese' was not kept in the ship's refrigerators, and was consigned to a Royal Navy Weapons Testing establishment in Essex. It is probable that the 'butter and cheese' was a cover for gun-cotton, used for many years in torpedo warheads.

Worst of all, the high explosives were stowed in the forward cargo hold, in approximately the position Schweiger's torpedo hit. He had aimed to strike *Lusitania* amidships, but overestimated her speed, so his G7 torpedo struck just behind the foremast, in the area of the hold.

Despite this highly illegal transport of high explosive munitions, to the British and the Americans, the slaughter of 1198 passengers, including ninety-four children and 128 American citizens, was outrageous. Former President Theodore Roosevelt described it as piracy on a new, vast scale. To rub salt in the wound, the patriotic German artist Karl Goetz designed and issued a commemorative bronze medal of the event. Goetz depicted the *Lusitania* with a warship's ram bow, and represented her foredeck as carrying artillery pieces and aircraft. To make matters

worse, if that were possible, Goetz embellished the reverse with an imaginary New York scene, showing passengers queuing to buy their tickets on the *Lusitania* from a skeleton at the Cunard ticket office, representing death. In the crowd, a businessman points to a newspaper warning of the likely fate of the passengers.

The medallion was in very bad taste, but what shocked even more was the fact that Goetz had accidentally dated it 5 May 1915, or two days before the sinking, as if it had been planned in advance. He soon reissued the medal, restruck with the correct date of 7 May, but the damage had been done.

In an extraordinary move, copies of Goetz's medal were produced in Britain in cast iron, packed in a presentation cardboard box complete with a certificate detailing the facts of the sinking. The date on the British version, although an indistinct strike, is more akin to a 5 than a 7, but this was a minor point compared to the ghastly caricature which the Goetz original represented. The copy was the inspiration of Captain Reginald Hall, RN, director of naval intelligence, and much of the cost of producing the 300,000 or so copies was borne by Mr Gordon Selfridge, the department store owner. Proceeds from the sale of the copy went to St Dunstan's Blinded Soldiers and Sailors Hostel.

Many scholars argue over whether the *Lusitania* sinking was instrumental in bringing the United States into the Great War on the side of the Allies. Others feel that the more immediate *casus belli* was the infamous Zimmermann telegram to the Mexicans offering them German aid to reconquer the territories lost to them in Santa Anna's war.

Obverse and reverse of the British propaganda copies of the Goetz medal, from the author's collection.

Whatever the political outfall, it is certain that the explosion of *U 20*'s single torpedo that fateful day ignited the powder trail which would, on 11 November 1918, blow Imperial Germany's ambitions sky-high.

THE SINKING OF THE *SZENT ISTVÁN*

Szent István (St Stephen) was a *Tegetthoff*-class battleship, the first, and only, Hungarian-built dreadnought. Launched in 1914 she displaced 21,343 tons at full load on a length of 152.18m (499ft) and beam of 28m (99ft). She was armed with twelve 12in guns in triple turrets, and her two turbines drove her at up to 20 knots. She carried a crew of thirty-eight officers and 1056 men.

Szent István was built with twin shaft machinery, large skegs supporting the propeller shafts, compared with the normal four-shaft arrangements of her sisters with shaft brackets (supports). An alarming incident occurred during *Szent István*'s machinery trials held at the end of November 1915. When steaming at full speed the helm was put over 35 degrees and the ship took on a list of 19 degrees as she turned. This caused water to enter through the secondary armament casemates which had not yet had their hatches installed. Investigations carried out by the director of construction revealed that the metacentric height was much lower than that planned for the ship, but it was felt that the real reason for the ship heeling so much was the massive skegs of her twin propellers.

During the Great War the *Szent István* spent most of her time swinging at anchor in the Austro-Hungarian naval base of Pola. On the one occasion she sortied with the fleet, on her way to try to break the Otranto Barrage on 8 June 1918, she was intercepted off the island of Premuda by the tiny Italian *MAS 15* under the command of Luigi Rizzo.

MAS 15 was built by the Societa Veneziana Automobili Navali (SVAN). She weighed 12 tons, was 16m (52ft 6in) long with a beam of 3.2m (10ft 6in). She

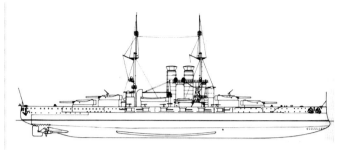

Szent István in 1918. (Drawing courtesy of Erwin F Sieche)

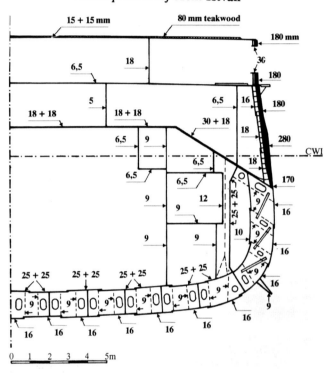

Midship section of Szent István

The torpedo protection was designed following underwater explosion tests carried out in August and November 1906 using the old hulk *Kaiser Max*. Based on inconclusive results, General-Schiffbauingenieur Siegfried Popper designed what he called a 'Minenpanzer' or 'armoured bottom'. This comprised a double bottom with the reinforced internal skin of 25mm + 25mm of steel (0.98in + 0.98in) spaced 1.22m (4ft) from the outer layer. German trials had concluded that the double bottom skins should be separated by at least 2m (6ft 6in), and that the internal torpedo bulkhead, preferably not vertical but inclined inwards at the bottom, should be placed at least 4m to 4.5m (13ft 1in to 14ft 9in) from the outer hull plating to have any effect. The vertical torpedo bulkhead on *Szent István* was placed only 2.5m (8ft 2?in) from the outer plating. (Drawing courtesy of Erwin F Sieche)

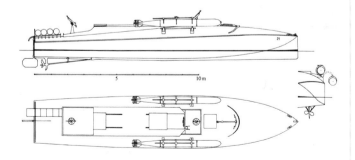

MAS 21, similar to *MAS 15*. (Drawing by Aldebaran, Trieste, courtesy of Erwin F Sieche)

Rizzo making good his escape (from a period postcard).

was armed with two 45.5cm (18in) torpedoes, four to six depth charges and two 8mm Colt machine guns, and carried a crew of eight. Her twin 225bhp Isotta-Fraschini petrol engines drove her at up to 24 knots, and she also had two 5ehp electric motors for creeping at 4 knots.

On the evening of 9 June 1918, *MAS 15* and *MAS 21* left Ancona under the command of Luigi Rizzo on board *MAS 15*, towed by two steam torpedo boats to save fuel. Their mission was to search out valuable torpedo targets of opportunity in Dalmatian inshore waters. After finding none, Rizzo led the two boats back to their rendezvous point with the torpedo boats, but at 0315 he spotted smoke, which turned out to be the Austro-Hungarian battleships and their escorts. Avoiding the escort screen, he launched his two torpedoes at 0325 at some 800m (875yds) range. Both hit the *Szent István* amidships at the point where a bulkhead divided off her forward and aft boiler rooms. *MAS 21* launched at *Tegetthoff* but missed. While the stricken dreadnought came to a stop and began to list, Rizzo accelerated, and escaped the pursuing torpedo boat *No 76* by dropping depth charges.

On board *Szent István* the crew attempted to rig collision mats over the torpedo holes, and began to counter-flood to reduce the list. Gradually, however, the forward boiler room flooded, and she lost power to her pumps. The list inexorably increased and at 0605 she capsized. 1005 men were saved by escorts, but 89 were drowned.

A film crew was on board the *Tegetthoff* to record the intended successful sortie, and together with Linienschiffsleutnant Josef Meusberger, who was a film enthusiast, they shot two movie films of the disaster. Spliced together, it was later sold in the USA. Along with the newsreel of HMS *Barham* capsizing, it forms a rare record of the sinking of a dreadnought. Both the *Szent István* and the *Barham* movies are often misused in documentaries to represent some other dreadnought disaster.

MAS 15 is still in existence today, preserved as a

monument in the Museo del Risorgimento beneath the Victor Emmanuel monument in Rome. By a twist of fate, the two torpedoes used by Rizzo to sink *Szent István* had been made in 1906 in the Whitehead factory in Fiume just a few kilometres away from the Gantz & Co Danubius shipyard where *Szent István* was launched eight years later. The two torpedoes had been exported to Italy, and their individual torpedo record sheets included with Rizzo's action report, preserved in the Ufficio Storico della Marina Militare in Rome under Dossier Ref 1211, give the following details:

No 1, Batch Number A.90/450 x 4,83m = 150kg = Production Number 9235.
Produced by Whitehead Fiume in 1906. Last check in March 1917 and regulated for 1200m run at a depth of 2m.

No 2, Batch Number A.90/450 x 4,83m = 150kg = Production Number 9252.
Produced by Whitehead Fiume in 1906. Last check in March 1917 and regulated for 1200m run at a depth of 2m.

[Where '450' is the calibre in mm, '4,83m' the length, and '150' the explosive payload. Details thanks to Erwin F Sieche.]

Two clips from the combined cine films of the capsize.

CHAPTER 22

The Second World War – The North Sea, Mediterranean and Atlantic

BALEARES: A REHEARSAL

The tragic Spanish Civil War was used by the Germans, Italians and Russians as a proving ground for the weapons systems they would use in the coming world war. Compared with the ferocious land and aerial combats, naval engagements were few and far between, due to the small size of the Nationalist fleet. The Nationalists did, however, hold two ace cards, in the heavy cruisers *Canarias* and *Baleares*.

Designed as a modified version of the Royal Navy's 'County'-class heavy cruisers by Sir Philip Watts, the *Canarias* class displaced 13,280 tons at full load, were armed with eight 8in and eight 4.7in guns, and were originally designed to carry twelve 21in torpedo tubes. Their 90,000shp turbines drove them at 33 knots.

In an action which in some ways was a rehearsal for the Second World War, *Baleares* was sunk during the Battle of Cape Palos on 6 March 1938. In a night-time action in company with *Canarias*, she intercepted a Republican force comprising the cruisers *Libertad*, *Méndez Núñez* and five destroyers. Unfortunately, Admiral Vierna on *Baleares* made the error of firing star-shell which gave away the position of his ship. Republican destroyers launched torpedoes, and at least two, and possibly three, from the *Lepanto* struck *Baleares* abreast the forward turrets.

Her forward magazines exploded, *Baleares* went dead in the water, enveloped in flames from bow to stern, and then sank with the loss of some seven hundred of her crew. Survivors were rescued by two British destroyers on neutrality patrol. The sinking of *Baleares* foreshadowed the losses the US Navy would experience when their heavy cruisers went up against Japanese destroyers during the Guadalcanal night encounters.

HMS OXLEY: BLUE-ON-BLUE

When snap decisions were taken where the shooter was unable to verify the target's identity, this would always represent a certain risk. RN submariners relied on staying within their designated patrol area. Any boat then seen was virtually certain to be enemy. But sometimes the system would break down…

On 10 September 1939, just a week after Great Britain declared war on Nazi Germany, the 'O'-class submarine HMS *Oxley* (commanded by Lt Cdr Harold Godfrey Bowerman, RN) was torpedoed in error by submarine HMS *Triton* (Lt Cdr H P De C Steele, RN) some 28 nautical miles south-southwest of Stavanger. Just two survivors from her crew of fifty-five were picked up by *Triton*. At the subsequent Board of Enquiry, Lieutenant Commander Steele gave the following testimony:

I surfaced at about 5 minutes to eight on the evening of 10th September and fixed the position of the ship

Baleares, showing the two boiler uptakes trunked into one, which together with her streamlined tower bridge gave her a much more modern appearance than the three separate funnels and platform bridgework of the British County-class ships.

HMS *Oxley* seen pre-war. She became the first Royal Navy warship to be lost in the Second World War.

Obrestad Light 067°, Kvassiem Light 110°. That position put me slightly west and south of my patrol billet which was No. 5. My intention for the night was to patrol to the southward on a mean course of 190° and in order to get on that line I steered 170° zigzagging 30°, 15° each side of the mean course at about three to four knots, slow on one engine, charging on the other. The submarine was trimmed down. [....]

Shortly before nine o'clock I was in the control room and there was a message from the bridge: Captain on the bridge immediately. I went straight up. The night was dark and there was a slight drizzle and I could see nothing except the shore lights. The Officer of the Watch informed me that there was a submarine fine on the port bow which for the moment I could not see. The ship was swinging to starboard and the officer of the watch was in charge. The signalman was sent for. In fact I am not certain whether he followed me up. I then made out through binoculars an object very fine on the port bow and I gave orders for the bow external tubes to stand by – Nos. 7 and 8 tubes.

At the same time the crew went to diving stations. I broke the charge and got on the main motors at once and it was at this moment that I recognized the object as a submarine. I took the ship and kept *Triton* bows on. From what I could see I appeared to be on a broad track, I should say about 120 degrees, and the object was steering in a north-westerly direction. It occurred to me that it might be *Oxley* and I dismissed the thought almost as soon as it crossed my mind because earlier in the day I had been in communication with *Oxley* and I had given her my position accurately, which was two miles south of my billet, No. 5, and *Oxley* had acknowledged this, and I had also given him my course which was at the time 154°. By this time the signalman was on the bridge and I gave him the bearing of the object or the submarine. I told him not to make any challenge until he got direct orders from me. He knew the challenge and the reply. I then ordered the challenge to be made as soon as my sights were on and I knew the armament was ready, and the signalman made it slowly. No reply was received. After about 20 seconds I ordered the challenge to be made again. During this time I had been studying the submarine very closely indeed. She was trimmed down very low and I could see nothing of her bow or shape and the conning tower did not look like *Oxley*'s, and I could not see any outstanding points of identification such as periscope standards, etc.

Accordingly, I ordered the second challenge to be made. Receiving no reply to the second challenge, I made a third challenge again after a short interval. Receiving no reply to the third challenge I fired a grenade which burst correctly. I did not see the grenade actually burst although I knew it had burst because of the light as I had my eyes fixed on the submarine. By this time I was completely convinced that this was an enemy submarine. I counted fifteen to myself like this: and-one, and-two, and-three … When I had counted fifteen to myself I gave the order to fire; No. 7 and No. 8 tubes were fired at three-second intervals. About half a minute after firing, indeterminate flashing was seen from the submarine. This was unreadable and stopped in a few seconds. The Officer of the Watch also saw this. It gave me the impression that somebody was looking for something with a torch – it was certainly not Morse code. Very shortly afterwards, a matter of a few seconds after the flashing had stopped, one of my torpedoes hit. I told the Officer of the Watch, Lieutenant H A Stacey, to fix the ship, and he fixed the ship as follows: Obrestad Light 035° Egero Light 105°. This fix placed the ship 6.8 miles 189° from No. 5 position, which put me 4 miles inside my sector. I took the bearing of the explosion and proceeded towards the spot at once. The sea state was about 3 and 2. Very soon we heard cries for help and as we came closer we actually heard the word 'Help'. There were three men swimming. I manoeuvred the ship to the best of my ability to close the men and kept Aldis lights on. Lieutenant Stacey and Lieutenant Watkins attached lines to themselves and dived in the sea which was covered in oil and succeeded in bringing Lieutenant Commander Bowerman and Able Seaman Gukes to safety. The third man who afterwards transpired to be Lieutenant Manley, RNR, was seen swimming strongly in the light of an Aldis when he suddenly disappeared and was seen no more.

Evidence to explain the lack of response from *Oxley* was given by Lieutenant Commander Bowerman. He stated he was called to the bridge following the sighting of *Triton*'s signal grenade, but when he tried to answer, his grenade malfunctioned. The OOW, Lieutenant Manley, claimed to have answered *Triton*'s challenge, but Bowerman was not sure this had been done properly. Before he could put things right, however, *Oxley* was struck by *Triton*'s torpedo and he was thrown into the sea.

No blame was apportioned to the crew of *Triton*. *Oxley* was found to have been out of position and her watchkeeping had been at fault. All the blame fell on her officer of the watch, Lieutenant Manley, RNR. Viewed from an astern position it would have been difficult to pick out the distinctive gun mounting of the 'O'-class boats.

DID THEY NEVER LEARN? THE
COURAGEOUS AND *ROYAL OAK* DISASTERS

Naval and military complacency in the face of determined enemies can lead to disaster. Also, forgetting past lessons can be costly.

Early in the Great War, German U-boat commanders had boldly brought the fight to the British, with the sinking of several cruisers, causing great loss of life. It was only to be expected that their successors would seek to capitalise on this reputation, and strike before the Royal Navy could put itself into top gear to fight yet another 'total war'.

In the Western Approaches, misplaced confidence in the abilities of British Asdic to detect U-boats led to the organisation of four hunter-killer groups, each based around an aircraft carrier. Common sense would have dictated that such valuable vessels be kept well away from any reported U-boat sightings. The carriers could in fact be considered the Second World War equivalents of the 'live bait' armoured cruiser squadron sent to patrol the Broad Fourteens at the start of the Great War.

In the Orkneys, despite repeated warnings from Admiral French that the eastern approaches to the great British naval anchorage of Scapa Flow were passable with care, nothing was done. He was later to be made a scapegoat for the loss of the *Royal Oak*. Retribution was not long in coming.

On 14 September the new aircraft carrier *Ark Royal* and her escorts received a distress call from a merchant ship under attack from the *U 30*. As she launched Skuas and Swordfish, *Ark Royal* came under attack from *U 39*, which launched three torpedoes at her. All three torpedoes exploded prematurely and brought down her escorting destroyers, which depth-charged *U 39* to the surface and took off her crew as she sank. The attempted rescue of the merchantman turned to tragic farce when two Skuas attempted to bomb the *U 30* but crashed, the observers being drowned. *U 30* was able to escape with the captured pilots after having torpedoed the freighter.

Three days later it was the turn of the hunter-killer group formed around the old carrier HMS *Courageous* to respond to a message from a merchantman that she was under attack. The carrier detached two of her destroyers to search for the U-boat and, in turning into the wind to launch aircraft, headed directly across the bows of *U 29*, whose captain Otto Schuhart had been stalking her for

ninety minutes, having first seen a Swordfish aircraft flying so far from land that he was convinced a carrier was near. Two of the three torpedoes he launched at 1940 from just 3000yds (2740m) struck the old ship on her port side, knocking out her electrical power. She capsized and sank less than fifteen minutes later, with the loss of 519 of her crew of 1,260 officers and men. Captain Makeig-Jones went down with his ship.

Following the near-miss on *Ark Royal* and the disaster which had overtaken *Courageous*, the remaining hunter-killer groups were dissolved and henceforth aircraft carriers were forbidden to enter the U-boat-infested waters of the Western Approaches.

At the beginning of October 1939 the Scapa Flow anchorage had been overflown by a Luftwaffe reconnaissance aircraft, leading Admiral Forbes to order the dispersal of the majority of the warships, in the expectation of a major air attack. Several ships, however, including the brand-new heavy cruiser HMS *Belfast*, were left behind. The muddled thinking behind the decision to leave the old 'R'-class battleship HMS *Royal Oak* was that her eight 4in anti-aircraft guns could add to the meagre AA defences of Scapa. In fairness, it must be said that in September 1939, the battleship still ruled supreme in British naval thinking. Few could predict the vulnerability of these behemoths to lesser adversaries such as aircraft and submarines. And, of course, *Royal Oak* was one of the first ships to receive anti-torpedo bulges, which were expected to make her highly resistant to underwater damage.

On the night of 13/14 October 1939, having conned *U 47* into the main anchorage on the surface via the channel between Lambs Holm and the mainland, Günther Prien lined up his four bow tubes at the *Royal Oak*, and launched three torpedoes at 0058, one tube having malfunctioned. Of the three torpedoes, two missed, but one struck *Royal Oak* right forward in the bows.

The shock and noise of the explosion woke the crew, but it was thought the problem was in the inflammable store right forward. A submarine attack was not suspected. One must ask why not, and presumably the mindset of the ships' officers was turned towards the air threat, thinking that the blockships and boom defence would prevent entry of a submarine. Prien turned and launched one torpedo from his stern tube, but that also missed. Reloading the three empty bow tubes, he came round and at 0113 fired a salvo at *Royal Oak*, and this time all three torpedoes exploded against the starboard side of her hull.

The cordite in a 6in magazine ignited, and a ball of fire quickly engulfed the open spaces of the ship, while she took on a serious list to starboard. At 15 degrees, water

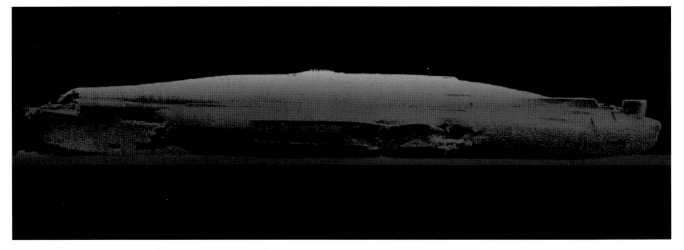

A sonar image of the wreck of HMS *Royal Oak* taken by adusDEEPOCEAN in 2006, in order to facilitate starting to remove some of the fuel oil escaping from her bunkers. The damage to her bow from Prien's first salvo and the massive disruption caused to her starboard side by Prien's second salvo of three torpedoes can clearly be seen. (Image courtesy of adusDEEPOCEAN and SalMO)

entered through her open portholes, she continued to roll over and capsized, just minutes after being hit. The death toll in the freezing water was extremely high: of *Royal Oak*'s crew of almost 1250 officers and men, no less than 833 were killed, including Rear Admiral Blagrove. More than a hundred of the victims were boy seamen less than eighteen years of age, mirroring the tragedy of the boy seamen lost in Weddigen's attack on the 'live bait' squadron at the start of the Great War.

In a typically belated move to bolt the stable door, the eastern entrances to Scapa Flow were eventually blocked by the 'Churchill barriers', concrete causeways built mainly by Italian PoWs, and which replaced the inefficient blockship and boom defences of 1939.

NORWAY, TREACHERY AND RETRIBUTION I: OSLOFJORD

Operation Weserübung was the German codename for the invasion of neutral Norway. Hitler was concerned that the Allies were about to attempt to cut Germany off from its vital source of iron ore in Sweden, carried by rail to the port of Narvik and from there by ship through neutral Norwegian waters to Germany. In fact, the British had determined to carry out a 'peaceful' occupation of Norway to do just that, and also in order to come to the aid of the beleaguered Finns under attack by Russia.

The British and French started out first, but the Germans had a shorter distance to cover, and arrived first. The Norwegians had been warned of German intentions when the Polish submarine *Orzel* torpedoed and sank the German transport *Rio de Janeiro*. Norwegian ships picking up survivors were shocked to learn that most were in fact armed German soldiers on their way to invade their country. Still the Norwegian government prevaricated. But time was running out.

In the night of 8/9 April 1940, German Group V under Admiral Kummetz entered Oslofjord with orders to proceed to the Norwegian capital, and land troops to seize the Royal Family and members of the Parliament. Kummetz's flagship was the new heavy cruiser *Blücher*, followed by the 'pocket battleship' *Lützow* and the light cruiser *Emden*, plus three torpedo boats and smaller vessels. In addition to her normal crew, *Blücher* was transporting over eight hundred soldiers for the occupation of the capital, plus a group of Gestapo agents whose role would be to seize the Royal Family.

After sinking a small Norwegian patrol vessel, the whaler *Pol III* at 2300 on the 8th, Group V landed troops

Two Whitehead Mark V torpedoes streak towards the heavy cruiser *Blücher* in Mark Postlethwaite's painting of the dramatic scene. (www.posart.com)

to seize the Norwegian forts defending the entrance to the fjord and swept on to the north. At 0420 Colonel Eriksen, the commander of the Oscarsborg Fortress, observed the *Blücher* passing in front of his guns. Correctly estimating the range at 1200m (1310yds), one minute later he gave the order to open fire with the only two 28cm guns which the few men at his disposal could man.

Both high-explosive shells struck the *Blücher*, the first at the base of the bridge superstructure, severing the controls to the steering and knocking her secondary armament fire control out of action. The second hit the aircraft hangar, loaded with petrol and bombs, and started a major fire. At that moment, from the opposite side of the fjord, the three 15cm guns of the Kopås Battery and the three 57mm guns at Husviktangen opened fire at the German flagship, scoring forty-three hits between them.

With his ship badly damaged by shells, on fire and out of control, Captain Heymann attempted to steer by throwing her starboard engines into reverse to avoid the island of Kaholmen. At that moment *Blücher* crossed the sights of Captain Andreas Anderssen, commander of the Kaholmen torpedo battery. Of the nine Whitehead Mk Vd torpedoes with 120kg (264lbs) warheads at his disposal, he ordered six to be loaded into the firing frames, having decided to fire two at each of the three larger German warships.

The first torpedo aimed at *Blücher* was fired from the southern No 1 shaft, and the second from the middle No 2 shaft. With their 40-knot speed, at a range of 500m (545yds) he could hardly miss. The first torpedo hit the forward part of the ship, and the second hit amidships. *Blücher* lost all steam and electric power, her torpedoes were launched to avoid them exploding, and the anchors were let go. When the fires reached a 10.5cm magazine and it exploded, blowing out a large part of the hull, the doomed ship capsized and sank by the bow. Heavy casualties were suffered by her passengers and crew, and it is rumoured the entire Gestapo contingent drowned.

Lützow and *Emden* briefly duelled with the shore batteries but their commanders, believing the flagship to have run into a minefield, retreated back down the fjord. Oslo was not captured until later in the day, allowing the Royal Family and the government to evacuate to safety, not before having finally sent out general mobilisation orders – by post!

The wreck of *Blücher* still lies where she sank in Oslofjord, fully loaded with ammunition, and threatening to pose an environmental hazard from leakage of her fuel oil. The torpedo battery, rearmed during the Cold War with British Mark VIII torpedoes, was demilitarised in 1993, and is now part of the Oscarsborg Museum complex.

NORWAY, TREACHERY AND RETRIBUTION II: NARVIK

Group I of the German force for the invasion of Norway consisted of ten large destroyers under the command of Commodore Friedrich Bonte, which were transporting General Dietl and two thousand mountain troops, for the seizure of the iron ore port of Narvik.

At 0515 on the morning of 9 April 1940, Bonte's force was sighted and challenged by the Norwegian coast defence ship *Eidsvold*, a 4000-ton armoured vessel built in 1900, armed with two 8.2in, 6 x 5.9in and 2 x 76mm guns, plus 20mm, 12.7mm and 7.92mm AA weapons. She and her sister *Norge* were old – in fact the admiral commanding the Norwegian navy had always referred to them as his 'old bathtubs' – but their powerful armament could cause serious damage to the German flotilla.

Eidsvold fired a warning shot across the bows of the German flotilla leader, *Wilhelm Heidkamp*. Bonte hove to, and sent a boat with Lt Cdr Gerlach, to parley with the Norwegians under a white flag. *Eidsvold*'s commander, Lt Cdr Willoch, refused Gerlach's demand that he surrender, and kept Commander Askim, on *Eidsvold*'s sister ship *Norge* inside Narvik harbour, informed of the negotiations by radio.

Gerlach headed back to his own ship, but when halfway he fired a red flare, the signal that negotiations had failed, and took his boat out of the line of fire, still flying the white flag. On the *Heidkamp*, Commodore Bonte turned to General Dietl and asked if the action they were committed to was absolutely necessary. Dietl reminded Bonte of Raeder's orders to carry out the operation with

Ross Watton's painting of *Norge* and *Eidsvold* at gunnery practice in Narvik Fjord. (Courtesy of Ross Watton at navalarte-heryn.demon.co.uk)

complete ruthlessness, and Bonte gave the order to fire torpedoes. Two hit *Eidsvold* amidships, she broke in two and immediately sank with heavy loss of life.

Her sister ship *Norge* now opened fire on the German destroyers, and manoeuvred to avoid the first five torpedoes launched from *Berndt von Arnim*, but the sixth and seventh torpedoes found their mark and she went down. In all, 276 Norwegian officers and men were killed on the two coast defence ships.

Nemesis for the German duplicity was not long in arriving. While the German destroyers were slowly refuelling from the one small tanker available, one other having failed to arrive, Captain Warburton-Lee of the Royal Navy was leading a flotilla of five British destroyers up Narvik Fjord to attack the German forces reported in control of the town. He had under his command the *Hardy*, *Hunter*, *Havock*, *Hotspur* and *Hostile*, armed with eight 21in torpedo tubes apiece.

At 0430 on 8 April 1940 Warburton-Lee's ships launched torpedoes and opened fire on the German destroyers and iron ore ships at Narvik. The first torpedo to hit exploded *Heidkamp*'s aft magazine and destroyed the ship, causing heavy casualties, including Commodore Bonte himself. Then the *Anton Schmitt* was hit by two torpedoes, broke in half and sank. Other torpedoes found their mark among the anchored iron ore ships. After a fierce gunnery duel, the British destroyers turned to withdraw, seeing several German torpedoes pass directly beneath their ships without exploding. As they withdrew down the fjord, they were pursued by three German destroyers, and then a further two appeared, cutting off their retreat. The flotilla leader, HMS *Hardy*, was badly hit and driven ashore, with Warburton-Lee mortally wounded. HMS *Havock* astern of her managed to avoid a salvo of German torpedoes seen to be running on the surface. Then two of the British ships collided, and *Hunter* was sunk. The three survivors fought their way out to sea and safety.

Although the eight remaining German destroyers had fought off their attackers, they had suffered badly in the engagement, and several had shot off most of their ammunition. One of the retiring British destroyers had sunk their ammunition supply ship making her way up the fjord to Narvik. The officer next in command, Captain Erich Bey, hesitated fatally, holding back his undamaged ships which could well have escaped from the coming British retribution.

On the night of 10 April a patrolling U-boat, the *U 25*, fired a salvo of torpedoes at British destroyers sighted off Ofotfjord. Two torpedoes detonated prematurely, because of failure of the magnetic pistols in the northern latitudes.

While Bey still hesitated, British Admiral Whitworth led the battleship HMS *Warspite* and nine destroyers up Narvik Fjord to attack on the morning of 13 April. In a fierce exchange of gunfire, all eight German destroyers were sunk, but not before they had inflicted damage on two of the Tribals, *Punjabi* and *Cossack*. A third sister-ship, *Eskimo*, pursued the *Hans Lüdemann* and *Georg Thiele* into the dead-end Rombaks Fjord. Before her captain ran her onto the rocks, *Lüdemann* fired her remaining three torpedoes at *Eskimo*. They missed, but running on down the narrow entrance to the Fjord they headed for the two following British destroyers, *Forester* and *Hero*. With no room to turn, both destroyers went full astern and managed to outrun the German torpedoes. *Eskimo*, meanwhile, failed to avoid one of the last four torpedoes launched by *Thiele*, and had her bows blown off.

All damaged British ships were eventually recovered to safety, but their action had resulted in the loss of the entire

Narvik after the first British attack. Torpedoed iron ore ships litter the harbour, and the German destroyer at the right of the jetty may be the immobilised *Diether von Roeder*.

German flotilla of ten large destroyers. This loss, together with the cruisers sunk by submarines and dive-bombers, so crippled the Kriegsmarine's offensive power that it was clearly a major factor in Hitler's failure to launch Operation Seelöwe later the same year, the planned invasion of Great Britain.

MAILLÉ BRÉZÉ AND LA RAILLEUSE

Two rare examples of mishaps involved French warships which literally torpedoed themselves.

Maillé Brézé pre-war.

Maillé Brézé was a large destroyer (or '*contre-torpilleur*' in French nomenclature) of the *Vauquelin* class, ordered in the 1928/1929 programme. Laid down in 1930 at Penhöet in St-Nazaire, she was launched on 9 November 1931 and was commissioned in 1932. Displacing 2441 tons (3140 tons full load), length 129.3m (424ft 2in), beam 11.84m (39ft), she could reach 35 knots. Her armament comprised five 138mm (5.5in) LA guns, four 37mm and four 13mm AA weapons, plus seven 550mm (21in) torpedo tubes, a triple aft of the fourth funnel and two pairs between the second and third funnels. After escorting convoy FS2, *Maillé Brézé* returned to the Clyde on 27 April 1940, and anchored off Greenock. Three days later, in the early afternoon, the crew carried out a simulated torpedo firing practice, using the remote launching controls on the bridge. At the end of the exercise the starboard twin tube mounting was realigned fore and aft, and a leading seaman began greasing the tubes, not suspecting that the powder launching charge was still in place in the No 1 tube. For some reason this fired, and the torpedo was launched into the rear of the forecastle.

The air chamber burst, causing serious damage to the superstructure and the forward boiler room. The warhead then exploded, starting a fire which quickly engulfed the forward part of the destroyer. The *Maillé Brézé* began to list to starboard, and despite assistance from nearby British vessels, the fire spread out of control. Due to the risk of magazine explosion, the ship was abandoned at 1515. At around 1900 the fire was finally extinguished by firemen from Greenock, but an hour later the *Maillé Brézé* foundered in 12m (40ft) of water, leaving just the top of her bridge, the mast and three of the four funnels above the surface. The disaster had cost the lives of twenty-seven men, many trapped in the burning forecastle by a buckled hatch, and a further forty-seven were injured. *Maillé Brézé* was not raised until August 1954, when she was scrapped at Greenock.

A similar accident had occurred just five weeks earlier in the port of Casablanca, when the 1500-tonne destroyer

Maillé Brézé on fire and listing. (Photo courtesy of Terry Dickens ,'astraltrader')

La Railleuse was also lost. The commission of enquiry into the two accidents reported that:

- the extremely complex firing arrangements had made it impossible to determine the exact causes of the accidents;
- there were, in fact, two separate firing systems activated from the bridge, the main one relying on compressed air, fitted with a safety interlock, and the backup system, using a powder charge, with no safety;
- it appeared the air chambers had never been tested to full designed pressure, and in fact in the case of accidental over-pressure they represented a severe risk;
- the torpedo warheads were not fitted with a safety delay on firing – they went live the moment they left the tube.

HMS KHARTOUM

On 23 June 1940, near Perim in the southern entrance to the Red Sea, the Royal Navy destroyer HMS *Khartoum* suffered an explosion in her aft quintuple torpedo mount. This caused a serious fire, which led to the explosion of the aft magazine and sank the ship in shallow water in Perim Harbour, where her wreck still lies today.

Crew members who testified at the subsequent enquiry stated that the air flask of the Mark IX⋆⋆ torpedo loaded in the starboard wing tube of the aft-facing rear mount had exploded. The tube was burst open, the engine of the torpedo was blown bodily overboard, and the aft part with the propellers was lodged in the rear of the tube with several propeller blades puncturing the tube rear door.

The torpedo warhead flew aft, through the galley where friction set fire to the paint. It then smashed the

The wreck of HMS *Khartoum* off the port of Perim, where she still lies.

support for 'X' gun mounting on the deckhouse overhead, severing hydraulic oil pipes to the mounting, which added to the flames. The warhead did not explode, but ended up lodged against the minesweeping gear on the quarterdeck, where it burst open. The fire in the aft deckhouse could not be mastered as the water mains were severed. The aft magazine flooding panel was also smashed, and the magazine could not therefore be flooded. The ready-use 4.7in rounds on 'X' mounting began to burst, the explosive content of the torpedo warhead began to burn, and the fire threatened not only the aft magazine but also the depth charges.

The crew performed admirably, fighting the fire with the limited means available, small hand extinguishers. One man climbed onto the mounting to ditch overboard as many cordite charges as he could reach, while another jettisoned those depth charges not already surrounded by the flames. Meanwhile *Khartoum*'s captain, Commander Donald Thorn Dowler, RN, ordered the forward torpedoes to be jettisoned to lighten ship, as he knew that if the aft magazine exploded there was a serious risk she would capsize in deep water. In order to save his crew and to facilitate possible salvage he headed for the harbour at Perim at all available speed.

Unfortunately, an order to evacuate all extra hands from the engine room was misinterpreted as 'all hands', and steam power was lost. A crew member returned to the engine room just in time to restore enough steam to carry the ship into Perim, where Commander Dowler dropped anchor and gave the order to abandon ship. Shortly after, a large explosion took place aft, then a second more violent explosion. The ship settled by the stern and heeled to port. One boy seaman was killed by a piece of wreckage as he was swimming ashore, and several other men were injured or burned. The destroyer was a total loss.

The subsequent inquiry into the sinking addressed several points:

1. It was considered possible that a shell or shell fragment fired by the Italian submarine *Torricelli*, which HMS *Khartoum* had engaged in company with sister ships *Kingston* and *Kandahar*, plus the sloop HMS *Shoreham*, earlier that day could have struck the torpedo tube mounting, damaging the air vessel which subsequently failed.

This hypothesis was discarded, as Commander Dowler stated that at no time had any shell fired from *Torricelli* fallen nearer than 6 cables length (more than 1200yds or 1100m) from *Khartoum*. Also, the *Torricelli* had been sunk at 0524 local time;

the air flask had exploded at 1150, or more than five and a half hours later.

2. Sixteen Italian survivors from *Torricelli* had been taken briefly on board *Khartoum*, and it was considered whether one of them had carried out an act of sabotage on the torpedo mount. All crew members questioned stated categorically that, although the Italians had passed the starboard wing torpedo tube which exploded, they had at all times been under guard. Again, the lapse of time made this hypothesis extremely unlikely.

3. The question of sabotage by local workmen was discussed, and quickly ruled out.

4. That left the final question: was the explosion caused by a defect in the air flask, or was it caused by the pitting that had been noted by the torpedo crew and previously reported to the dockyard? Mark IX★★ torpedoes on *Kingston* and *Kandahar* were examined and traces of deep external pitting were discovered on all. This was held to be the cause of the explosion and fire, which inevitably led to the loss of the ship.

HMS *CLYDE*, ANOTHER BLUE-ON-BLUE

The fleet submarine HMS *Clyde* was busy in the summer of 1940. On 21 July she sighted the battlecruiser *Gneisenau* and the heavy cruiser *Admiral Hipper* en route to attack the Atlantic shipping lanes. *Clyde* cut short their expedition by putting a torpedo into the bows of *Gneisenau*, which had to return to Trondheim for repairs.

A day later, to the west of Bergen, at 2355 Commander D C Ingram in *Clyde* fired six torpedoes at what he took to be a German U-boat. Luckily all torpedoes missed, as the target was the 'T'-class boat HMS *Truant*, which had been supposed to have vacated this area earlier that day but was delayed. *Clyde*'s CO was therefore justified in carrying out an attack in an area where enemy submarines were expected.

MUTUAL DESTRUCTION IN THE MEDITERRANEAN

Following the alienation of the majority of the French fleet, through Churchill's direct orders to Admiral James Somerville to open fire on their ships at Mers el-Kébir in July 1940, the over-stretched Royal Navy was left to bear the brunt of the battle for the Mediterranean, at least up

A still from the well-known film by Gaumont-British cameraman John Turner, showing HMS *Barham* capsizing after being hit by three torpedoes from von Tiesenhausen's *U 331*. Seconds after this shot, as the battleship lay on her beam ends, the aft magazines detonated, tearing the ship apart and causing the deaths of 861 of her crew

until the arrival of US Navy reinforcements in late 1942. In three years of fighting the British and Italians lost dozens of warships sunk, and dozens more knocked out of action by serious damage that took many months to repair. The British could count on the vast resources of the US dockyards, but damaged Italian ships were often never repaired for lack of time or resources.

The two sides sparred continually over resupply convoys: the British trying to cut the lifelines to the Italo-German forces in North Africa, and the Axis forces attempting to isolate and capture the strategic island of Malta. The losses on both sides were severe, and the majority of these losses were caused by the torpedo, whether launched by submarine, destroyer, aircraft or torpedo boat. So devastating were the Royal Navy's depredations on the convoys to North Africa that a repeat class of Italian escort vessels, the *Ariete*s, were rearmed with no less than six 18in torpedo tubes to try to counter their heavy opponents.

Torpedo hit on HMS *Arethusa*

In addition to the ships sunk, many Royal Navy warships suffered serious damage from torpedo hits.

Arethusa was lead ship of a class of 6650-ton light cruisers. In November 1942 she left Alexandria as part of

Arethusa down by the bow after torpedo hit.

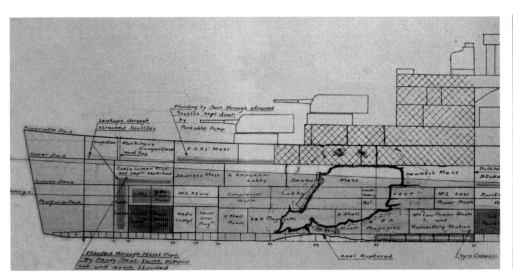

The Admiralty Damage Report drawing shows the extensive damage to *Arethusa* from the 18in Italian torpedo. The cross-hatched area on the plan was severely damaged by fire. (The National Archives, Kew)

The torpedo hole seen in dry dock in Alexandria. (The National Archives, Kew).

the escort for a Malta convoy codenamed 'Stonage'. As one of the four ships of the 15th Cruiser Squadron, *Arethusa* was the last ship in a diamond formation. On 18 November at sunset the cruisers and the fleet destroyers moved to the north of the convoy to guard against attack. An hour later they were attacked by torpedo bombers. One was heard, then seen coming in from the starboard bow. The ship went to starboard to avoid its torpedo, but a second aircraft came in from the port side and dropped a torpedo at close range, which could not be avoided.

The torpedo hit on the port side abreast 'B' turret, blowing a hole 53ft (16m) long and 35ft (11m) high in the ship's side. Oil from her bunkers was thrown up inside the bridge structure and sprayed over the outside of the ship. When this caught fire the entire bridge was engulfed and her captain suffered burns. One officer and 155 men were killed in the explosion or died during the following night. By daybreak the survivors had brought the fire under control and stabilised the initial 15-degree list to port. The ship, however, was down by the head, and all possible loose gear, including spare torpedoes, was piled on the starboard quarterdeck to try to level the ship.

During the night *Arethusa* had made good a speed of 12 knots back towards her base in Alexandria, some 450 miles away, escorted by the destroyer *Petard*, and fighting off several air attacks. On the 20th *Petard* took her in tow going stern first, and that is how she finally arrived off Alexandria. As the tow was being transferred to two tugs, *Arethusa* drifted into a British minefield, and threatened to go ashore. When finally she was towed in and surveyed, the dockyard staff declared they did not know how she had stayed afloat. After temporary repairs, she sailed for Charleston Naval Yard where the damage was made good.

HMS *Indomitable*

Aircraft carriers were priority targets for air and submarine attack. The 29,730-ton (full load) aircraft carrier HMS *Indomitable* was providing air cover for Operation Husky, the invasion of Sicily, in July 1943. On 16 July, just after midnight, her crew detected the sound of an approaching aircraft. From its engine note and its approach towards the stern of the carrier they took it to be one of their own Albacore torpedo bombers returning to the ship in difficulty. However, the aircraft then dropped something into the sea about 300yds off the port beam, opened up and flew directly across the flight deck just in front of the bridge. The object dropped was seen to be a torpedo, running on the surface, and the order was given to go full ahead and come hard to port to comb its track. When it was 50yds from the ship, it dived, and hit her on the port side amidships, where the port side hull had been

The damage to *Indomitable* from an 18in aircraft torpedo, showing the armour plates displaced. (The National Archives, Kew)

widened asymmetrically to offset the weight of the island to starboard. Observers confirmed that the aircraft which had carried out the daring attack had been Italian.

Unlike the earlier *Ark Royal*, sunk by just one torpedo hit, *Indomitable* was able to return to Grand Harbour, Malta, at 11 knots, for temporary repairs. Fully repaired and refitted in the USA, she joined the Pacific Fleet a year later.

In the Mediterranean the Royal Navy lost to torpedo attack: two aircraft carriers, the new *Ark Royal* and the old *Eagle*; one battleship, the *Barham*; eight cruisers; twenty-two destroyers and a destroyer depot ship; one fast minelayer and two submarines – a total of thirty-seven vessels which would have in themselves constituted a sizeable fleet, and which would be sorely missed in the Far East for the defence of Singapore and Malaya.

In addition to the aircraft carrier *Indomitable*, and the *Arethusa* noted above, ten cruisers (*Liverpool* twice), and five destroyers were badly damaged by torpedo strikes and were out of action for lengthy periods.

Added to these losses by conventional torpedo attack, the rebuilt battleships *Queen Elizabeth* and *Valiant* plus the destroyer *Jervis* were damaged by Decima MAS SLC attacks, the two battleships, in fact, settling on the shallow bottom of Alexandria harbour; the heavy cruiser *York* was crippled by an MT-boat attack in Suda Bay, while the AA cruiser *Delhi* was seriously damaged by the blast from an exploding Linse motorboat in Split in early 1945.

In retrospect, it is true to say that, in return for these extremely heavy losses – added to the ships lost to bombs and mines – the Royal Navy not only saved Malta but made a major contribution to the ultimate defeat of Rommel's attempt to capture Egypt and the Suez Canal. Nor would the invasions of Sicily and mainland Italy have been possible if the British had lost control of the Mediterranean.

Italian losses to the torpedo

The Regia Marina, for its part, was decimated by torpedo attacks, many carried out by the small 'U'-class submarines of the Royal Navy. In all, the victims of torpedo attack comprised: one rebuilt battleship, the *Conte di Cavour*, sunk and never repaired; a second rebuilt battleship, *Caio Duilio*, beached and repaired; one brand-new battleship the *Littorio*, sunk but repaired; three heavy cruisers and five light cruisers; eighteen destroyers and torpedo boats; and no less than thirteen submarines fell

Light cruiser *Muzio Attendolo* showing the substantial damage caused to her bow by a torpedo from HM Submarine *Unbroken* on 13 August 1942. She lost her entire bow forward of 'A' turret. The damage looked worse than it actually was, with the shattered bow plating folded back along the ship's side. She remained afloat to be towed to Messina and Naples, where she was fully repaired in three months.

The rebuilt dreadnought *Conte di Cavour*, sunk at Taranto in the Fleet Air Arm Swordfish attack of 11/12 November 1940. In this daring action, obsolescent Swordfish biplanes launched eleven torpedoes in the shallow water of Taranto harbour, torpedoing three Italian capital ships. *Conte di Cavour*, rebuilt at vast expense from a Great War dreadnought, put on an impressive show with her much higher top speed, thanks to new engines. But her armour protection remained far too weak, as was the case with her Pugliese anti-torpedo system which failed completely.

victim too. In addition, one light cruiser, *Ulpio Traiano*, was sunk by a Chariot/Maiale joint team. Ships damaged by torpedoes were two battleships, the *Vittorio Veneto* and the repaired *Littorio*, the heavy cruiser *Bolzano* which was later sunk in another torpedo attack, three light cruisers and two destroyers.

Greece

The tiny Royal Hellenic navy suffered its first casualties, to an Italian submarine's torpedo, two months before the Italians formally declared war on their Mediterranean neighbours. In a deliberate act designed to provoke the Greeks, the old, small Greek protected cruiser *Helle* was sunk by the submarine *Delfino* off the island of Tinos on 15 August 1940, while the crew were celebrating a saint's day. Nine petty officers and sailors were killed, and twenty-four injured. Parts of the torpedo were recovered and markings proved their Italian origin, but Greece was unprepared for war.

One of the set of victory commemorative stamps issued by Greece in 1946 showed the torpedoing of the cruiser. And at the same time the Italian navy transferred the light cruiser *Eugenio di Savoia* to Greece as compensation for the loss of the *Helle*.

OPERATION RHEINÜBUNG

Bismarck had escaped from Admiral Holland's trap in the Denmark Strait, having sunk HMS *Hood* and driven off the new battleship *Prince of Wales*. Her consort *Prinz Eugen* had been successfully detached, and now the giant battleship was running for safety in occupied France, to lick her wounds. Nine rookie Swordfish crews from the new aircraft carrier HMS *Victorious* launched a torpedo attack on *Bismarck* in bad weather, scoring one hit under her bridge, but the battleship's TDS shrugged off the torpedo damage and her speed was unaffected. Twice she slipped the British net, and twice she was found. But it seemed she would be within range of Luftwaffe air cover before the British could bring her to battle.

Force H was coming up from Gibraltar; Admiral Somerville's lightweight battlecruiser *Renown*, no match for the *Bismarck*, was ordered to stand clear and not risk an engagement. But his cruiser *Sheffield* took over shadowing *Bismarck*, and his aircraft carrier HMS *Ark Royal* was ordered to send her Swordfish crews to try to slow down the escaping German. The first Swordfish strike force mistook the shadowing *Sheffield* for *Bismarck*, and put in attacks on her. Luckily their torpedoes' magnetic influence detonators malfunctioned and exploded prematurely. Recognising their own cruiser at last, the final crews broke off the attack.

The second strike went in with fifteen Swordfish carrying torpedoes fitted with traditional impact fuses. A low cloud base and *Bismarck*'s fierce anti-aircraft fire and manoeuvring at speed disrupted any notion of a co-ordinated attack from both sides, and each Swordfish pilot had to press an individual attack as best he could, so the planes came in singly from every direction. At their loaded airspeed of only some 90 knots, they completely threw out the *Bismarck*'s anti-aircraft gunnery controls, the Germans being unwilling to believe their attackers would be approaching so slowly. Accordingly, they fused their AA shells to burst too short, at the range where a more modern torpedo plane would have reached. They missed the Swordfish but the planes still had to fly through the enormous waterspouts thrown up by the exploding shells. Pilot John Moffat remembered his observer hanging over the side of the rear cockpit calling out instructions, to ensure that their torpedo would drop into the trough of a wave and not porpoise by striking a wave crest. No planes were lost, and this time the *Bismarck* was hit with three 18in torpedoes. Two of the hits were amidships and again did little to stop or even slow the giant battleship. But one torpedo coming from *Bismarck*'s starboard quarter had hit at her most vulnerable spot, the rudders.

When a warship is manoeuvring at speed to evade a torpedo attack, the last order should always be to put the rudder amidships. Then if a torpedo puts the steering gear out of action, at least the inline rudder has no adverse effect on the ship's handling, and her commander can proceed to manoeuvre her using the propellers alone.

At the moment the torpedo hit, *Bismarck* was under port helm – Lieutenant Burkard von Müllenheim-Rechburg in *Bismarck*'s after fire control position reported having looked at the rudder indicator and seen that it read 'left 12 degrees'. The explosion not only disabled the steering gear but jammed both rudders to port. Previous trials in the Baltic of trying to steer *Bismarck* by using the propellers alone had been far from successful. Hampered by jammed rudders, the ship now became unmanageable.

Attempts to free the rudders were unsuccessful. The sea surging in through the torpedo hole prevented any divers from entering the steering compartment. In desperation, it was proposed to blow the damaged rudders off the ship using explosive charges, but this was rejected because of the risk of damaging the propellers. It should be noted that the stern areas of Kriegsmarine warships proved weak on more than one occasion: *Lützow* had almost lost her stern on her return from Norway in 1940, the torpedo from HMS *Spearfish* blowing off both her propellers. *Prinz Eugen* was to suffer similar damage on 23

February 1942 to a torpedo hit from HMS *Trident*, and when Dr Ballard's team first found the wreck of *Bismarck* they were surprised to find the hull basically intact, but with the complete stern section detached.

Throughout the night of 26/27 May *Bismarck* had been kept under the threat of torpedo attack by the ships of the 4th Destroyer Division, HMS *Cossack, Maori, Zulu* and *Sikh*, plus the Polish *Piorun*, which had pressed home their assaults in atrocious weather conditions and in the teeth of *Bismarck*'s impressive secondary armament of 5.9in (15cm) turret guns. The destroyers scored no known torpedo hits, but they did ensure that *Bismarck*'s crew had no respite during the whole of the night before their final battle.

At dawn on 27 May Admiral Tovey drove his battleships *King George V* and *Rodney* directly at *Bismarck*, closing the range as rapidly as possible. *Bismarck*'s gunnery officer Adalbert Schneider knew that *Rodney* was the more dangerous opponent and concentrated his fire on her, but to no avail. HMS *Rodney* opened fire with her 16in guns at 0847. Just twenty-three minutes later, all of *Bismarck*'s guns were silent, and although turrets 'Caesar' and 'Dora' managed to fire a few sporadic rounds after that time, by 0931 both these turrets had been destroyed. *Rodney* and *KGV* had each scored forty main armament hits. To these eighty heavy shells were added between two and three hundred shells from 5.25in, 6in and 8in guns. Plus the 24.5in torpedo hit claimed by Chief Petty Officer Pollard and his team.

At this stage the British heavy ships were all running critically low on fuel, but Churchill was determined that the *Bismarck* be sunk, to avenge HMS *Hood*. He radioed to Admiral Tovey that he should continue the action until the bitter end, even if it meant towing home the *King George V*. As this would have guaranteed her loss to U-boat and Luftwaffe attacks, Tovey wisely ignored the order, sent a general signal to the warships in company, 'Any ship with torpedoes to close *Bismarck* and torpedo her', and turned his heavy ships for home. Even then, it was a close-run affair: Luftwaffe bombers sent to succour *Bismarck* found one of *Rodney*'s escort destroyers, HMS *Mashona*, and sank her.

Only *Dorsetshire* still had torpedoes – three 21in Mark IXs – and she deliberately fired two at *Bismarck*'s starboard side, which both hit, and then went around the wreck to

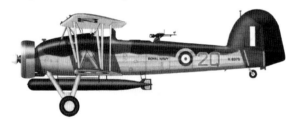

The 50,000-ton Bismarck, down by the bows and short of fuel after two shell hits from HMS *Prince of Wales*, shown with her minuscule nemesis, Swordfish K8375 Code 2Q from *Ark Royal*, the plane which delivered the fatal torpedo. Strange as it may seem, these two apparently ill-matched opponents were both military anachronisms, the *Bismarck* being little more than an updated, enlarged version of the old SMS *Baden* dreadnought design of 1915, with the same outmoded armament, armour scheme and control systems layout. The Swordfish, a slow but manoeuvrable multi-role biplane would not have appeared out of place in the skies over the Western Front in 1918. (Swordfish profile by Pierre-Andre Tilley)

fire a third at *Bismarck*'s port beam, which also hit. By that time, *Bismarck*'s main deck was awash, and her shattered hull was flooding with thousands of tons of water, so that one of the torpedoes was seen to strike *Bismarck*'s catapult deck, normally high above the waterline. Down below, scuttling charges were exploded, but these merely hastened her end, and she sank at 1040. Very few survivors were picked up by British and German vessels, and more than two thousand of her crew were lost.

Dr Ballard's team, which rediscovered the wreck of *Bismarck* in June 1989, were only able to photograph her from above. The second expedition which explored her in July 2001 sent remote cameras down to photograph the underwater hull. The outer plating had been torn away over considerable lengths of the hull, which seemed to indicate that *Dorsetshire*'s torpedoes had inflicted the fatal damage which sank *Bismarck*. However, the team estimated that the plating had been ripped away when *Bismarck* hit the seabed and slid down the slope of an undersea mountain. They examined the inner torpedo bulkheads and claimed that the parts they saw were undamaged. That is not the same as saying that they had not been pierced by shell, torpedo or plating fragments, or been displaced from their attachment points, causing widespread leakage into the ship's vitals, or that the sections not visible to the team had not been disrupted. Thus the argument over what finally caused *Bismarck* to sink so quickly – the shell and torpedo damage or the scuttling charges – has not been resolved, and it may never be.

SHOOTING WAR IN THE ATLANTIC

The US Navy was actively involved in the Battle of the Atlantic long before the official entry of the USA into the Second World War. Prior to 7 December 1941 and the attack on Pearl Harbor, Roosevelt had done everything in his power to help the Allies, short of declaring war on Germany. Notably, in March 1941 the Lend-Lease Act was passed into law, meaning that Britain could receive arms and other urgent supplies without the need for immediate payment. The US Navy would be tasked with seeing that these American products reached their destinations. In April FDR extended the Pan-American Security Zone almost as far east as Iceland. American warships would escort convoys as far as the Mid-Ocean Meeting Point, and several clashes with German U-boats took place.

On 10 April destroyer USS *Nilblack*, rescuing survivors from a torpedoed Dutch ship, the *Saleier*, detected a sonar echo and dropped three depth charges on the assumed position of a U-boat, without result. On 27 May FDR proclaimed the existence of a state of unlimited emergency, in June US forces landed in Iceland, relieving occupying British troops, and between 9 and 12 August FDR and Churchill met in Ship Harbour, Newfoundland, and drafted the Atlantic Charter.

On 4 September the destroyer USS *Greer*, carrying mail for the Iceland garrison, was attacked by *U 652*, whose commander took her to be one of the fifty old flush-deckers being transferred to the Royal Navy. The *Greer* dropped two depth charges, *U 562* fired two torpedoes, but both vessels escaped unscathed. In his next 'Fireside Chat' FDR claimed the U-boat had deliberately targeted the US destroyer.

On 16 October the USS *Kearny* (DD-432), a 1630-ton destroyer of the *Livermore* class, was one of four US destroyers called to help defend a convoy under attack by a German wolf pack, and she dropped several depth charges during the night. The next day *U 568* retaliated by firing a torpedo which struck *Kearny* in the forward boiler room, killing eleven of her crew and injuring another twenty-two. Able to steam at slow speed, *Kearny* made for her base at Reykjavik, Iceland, where temporary repairs were carried out by the base ship USS *Vulcan*, using a cofferdam of yellow pine positioned by hogging lines and held against

The torpedo damage to *Kearny*. These longitudinally-framed US destroyers were tough.

the destroyer's hull by water pressure. *Kearny* later sailed to Boston, Massachusetts, for permanent repairs.

Her survival provided proof of the advantages of arranging the machinery on the unit system. By this, her boilers and engines were arranged so that one shaft was powered by the forward boiler and turbine set, while the opposite shaft was powered by the rear boiler and turbine set, each set being separated longitudinally. The forward boiler room (fire room in USN parlance) was damaged but the rear unit was able to continue operating.

Ten days after the attack on *Kearny*, in a radio broadcast on Navy Day, FDR used this provocation to launch a rhetorical attack on Hitler and the Nazis. He reiterated that American goods would continue to be sent to help the Allies, and he reminded Americans of his order to the navy to 'shoot on sight'. On 31 October the old destroyer USS *Reuben James*, escorting convoy HX156, was torpedoed and sunk by *U 552*: 115 sailors, including all her officers, were lost and only forty-four survived. In memory of those lost, folk singer Woody Guthrie composed his ballad, 'The Sinking of the *Reuben James*'.

HMS *TRINIDAD*

A *Fiji*-class light cruiser displacing 10,450 tons, HMS *Trinidad* was laid down at Devonport in 1938, launched on 21 March 1940 and completed on 14 October 1941. She was armed with twelve 6in guns, eight 4in AA, two quadruple 2pdrs and two banks of triple 21in torpedo tubes. Her top speed was 32.25 knots.

On 23 March 1942 she sailed as part of the escort for convoy PQ13 bound for Murmansk, commanded by Captain Leslie Saunders, and flying the flag of Rear Admiral Bonham-Carter. At 0943 on the morning of 28 March, *Trinidad*'s radar picked up the approach of three large German destroyers, the *Z 24*, *Z 25* and *Z 26* which had sortied from their base in Norway to intercept the convoy. *Trinidad* turned to engage the enemy in poor visibility, and when *Z 26* emerged from a snow squall the cruiser opened fire at the close range of under 4000yds (3660m), scoring several hits. She switched target to *Z 24* which launched a spread of torpedoes, but *Trinidad* successfully avoided them all. She once more targeted the retreating *Z 26*, hitting her with several shells which knocked out the destroyer's armament and set her on fire.

Trinidad now moved in to finish off her crippled opponent with a spread of three torpedoes from her port tubes. But two torpedoes failed to leave the iced-up tubes, and the third torpedo which did launch circled back on *Trinidad* and struck her on the port side below the bridge, blowing a hole 60ft by 20ft (18m x 6m) in the hull. The

Trinidad crippled and burning, before being abandoned and scuttled.

force of the explosion travelled across then ship and blew a second hole, 20ft by 10ft (6m x 3m), in the starboard side of the Marines' mess deck. The forward boiler rooms were flooded, fuel oil caught fire, *Trinidad* temporarily lost power and for a while had to be taken in tow; thirty-two members of her crew were killed, including seventeen Marines in the transmitting station who were engulfed in a flood of oil. Captain Saunders is reported to have leant over the bridge wing as the torpedo raced towards *Trinidad* and said, 'You know, that looks remarkably like one of ours!'

She limped into Murmansk on 30 March escorted by the destroyers *Fury* and *Oribi*. In April *Trinidad* was taken in hand at Murmansk for temporary repairs to allow her return home. The steel plates for the repairs were brought by the cruiser *Edinburgh*. On her return voyage, with her speed limited to 20 knots, she was caught by Luftwaffe aircraft on 14 May. While avoiding torpedoes, she was mortally damaged by four bombs dropped from a Ju-88, and was scuttled after her survivors had been taken off by escorts.

THE *IOWA* INCIDENT, 14 NOVEMBER 1943

A potentially catastrophic blue-on-blue was the launch of a live torpedo by the US Navy destroyer *Willam D Porter* aimed directly at the battleship USS *Iowa*, carrying US President Franklin D Roosevelt, Secretary of State Cordell Hull, and high-ranking military and naval personnel including Admiral King, Chief of Naval Operations. They were en route to meet Churchill at Cairo and then Stalin at the Teheran Conference.

Early on 14 November 1943 the *Iowa* and her destroyers were east of Bermuda, and it was decided to show the president how *Iowa* could defend herself against an air attack. Several weather balloons were launched to serve as targets, and more than a hundred AA guns opened fire. One of *Iowa*'s escorts was the new *Fletcher*-class destroyer USS *William D Porter*. In her brief career *Porter* had already begun to acquire a certain reputation for misadventure. Going astern from her moorings to begin the mission she had brushed the side of a sister-ship, carrying away the other's boats and tackle. While en route to Bermuda the *Porter* had accidentally loosed a depth charge, causing general alarm. Now the jinxed ship was ready for the big one.

As her commander, Captain Walker, called his crew to action stations and gave the order to join in the firing at the aerial targets, her torpedo officer decided it would be a good opportunity to carry out a torpedo-firing exercise. Training the pentad mounts to port, he lined up the bulk of *Iowa* in his torpedo director sights. The battleship was just 6000yds away when he began to go through his ritual to space out the shots of a spread. He pressed the firing button on the bridge to simulate launching the torpedo from tube No 1. Calmly reciting the required phrase, 'If I wasn't a torpedo officer, I wouldn't be here,' he pressed the firing button for tube No 2. 'If I wasn't a torpedo officer, I wouldn't be here,' and he pressed the button for tube No 3. His ritual was interrupted by the unmistakable sound of a live torpedo being launched from the tube.

Up on the bridge Lieutenant Lewis turned to his captain and innocently asked if he had given the order to fire a torpedo. General panic broke out as the torpedo headed for the president's ship. *Porter*'s signalman flashed out a warning by signal lamp, but inadvertently warned that the torpedo was heading in the opposite direction. He then sent a correction, but used the code sequence indicating that *Porter* herself was going full speed in reverse.

Finally, the captain authorised breaking radio silence

USS *Iowa* as she would have appeared in the torpedo director sights on the bridge of USS *William D Porter*. (NHHS, photo # K-15631, reversed)

and *Porter*'s radioman sent the message 'Lion [the codename for *Iowa*], Lion, come right'. The *Iowa*'s radio operator was concerned at the breaking of radio silence and demanded the sender identify himself. Eventually, the message got through, and *Iowa* put on speed and turned to port, to comb the track of the fast-approaching torpedo. The increased wash of her propellers luckily caused the torpedo to explode harmlessly astern of her.

In the meantime, President Roosevelt, who had heard the announcement of an approaching torpedo, moved his wheelchair over to the bridge wing to observe what was happening. It is reported that his Secret Service bodyguard actually drew his pistol, ready to shoot at the warhead of the offending torpedo – shades of the French navy of the 1880s shooting at torpedoes with their repeater rifles.

When *Iowa* enquired who had launched the torpedo, Captain Walker weakly replied, 'We did it.' The *Iowa* accordingly trained her guns on the unfortunate *Porter*, which was suspected of being the instigator of an assassination attempt. The *Porter* was ordered to Bermuda, where the ship was surrounded by armed Marines while the official enquiry was conducted behind closed doors. This uncovered the fact that Lawton Dawson, the torpedo-man responsible for inserting the torpedo launching charges for action, and then removing them before a practice launch, had inadvertently left in place the charge for tube No 3. To try to cover up his mistake he had even thrown the fired case overboard, to no avail.

Torpedo-man Dawson eventually confessed, and was sentenced to fourteen years' hard labour. His sentence was later commuted by President Roosevelt who asked that no punishment be handed out for what was clearly an accident. Someone had to carry the blame, however, so Captain Walker and several of his crew were drafted to mundane shore assignments.

It is interesting to note that an earlier torpedo boat named *Porter* (TB-6) had fired a torpedo at the armoured cruiser *New York* during a night engagement off Cuba in 1898, also luckily missing.

BITER BITTEN

The escort carrier HMS *Biter* was with the 5th and 7th Escort Groups in mid Atlantic in November 1943, covering several convoys, when on 16 November one of her own Swordfish aircraft carrying a homing torpedo crashed just astern of the carrier when coming in for a landing. The torpedo was released by the impact, its engine started, and it homed on *Biter*. The torpedo hit her rudder, but with only a low-order detonation. The bottom

Escort carrier HMS *Biter* preparing to recover aircraft.

aft corner of the rudder was blown off, and hull plating below the waterline suffered mild damage, but still sufficient to require a month's dockyard attention on her return to the UK.

NORTH CAPE 1943: FIFTY-FIVE TORPEDOES RUNNING

KM *Scharnhorst* was designated a 'battlecruiser' because of her light main armament guns – chosen for political reasons at the time the ships were designed, and capable of eventual upgrading to 15in – and for her extremely high speed: 165,000shp turbines propelled her at a designed top speed of 32 knots. Her later 'Atlantik' bow enabled her to maintain high speed in sea conditions where other large warships fell behind.

But in every respect except her 11in triple turrets she was a 'fast battleship', displacing 38,900 tons at full load, with an armour belt up to 350mm (13.8in) thick and with 100mm (3.9in) total deck armour, although the latter was arranged on the old Great War style of 'multiple thin decks' (in *Scharnhorst*'s case 2 x 50mm/2 x 1.97in) – a defect she shared with the *Bismarck* class – instead of one single, very thick deck as had been introduced in the RN *Nelson* class. Her inner armoured torpedo bulkhead was 45mm thick (1.77in) and her TDS extended inward for a total distance of 5m (16.4ft).

The *Scharnhorst* had led an eventful career, and appeared to have a charmed life; indeed, she was known in Germany as the 'lucky *Scharnhorst*'. With her sister the *Gneisenau*, *Scharnhorst* had sunk the AMC *Rawalpindi* on 23 November 1939, and escaped from forces sent to intercept them. In the early stages of the Norwegian campaign, the two sisters had been chased by the

battlecruiser HMS *Renown*, nominally outclassed by *Scharnhorst* and *Gneisenau* together, but armed with 15in guns. The two *Scharnhorst*s had run away in high seas, accepting damage – flooding of their forward turrets – in order to escape possible destruction under the heavy guns of *Renown*. If and when they were upgunned it would be a different matter.

In the British withdrawal from Norway, on 8 June 1940 she and her sister ship had surprised and sunk the old aircraft carrier *Glorious* and her two destroyer escorts, but before sinking, HMS *Acasta* had launched her eight 21in torpedoes at *Scharnhorst* and scored one hit abreast turret Caesar. The torpedo made a hole 14m long by 6m high (46ft x 20ft), flooded thirty watertight compartments and let some 2500 tons of water enter her hull. Two of *Scharnhorst*'s three shafts were temporarily stopped, and two officers and forty-six men were killed in the explosion or drowned in the influx of water. This hit by *Acasta* saved a troop convoy not far away over the horizon.

During the Atlantic sortie in early 1941, *Scharnhorst* was spotted on two occasions by British battleships escorting convoys, HMS *Ramillies*, then HMS *Malaya*, but on each occasion the Germans withdrew without offering combat, eventually making port in occupied France. At Brest *Scharnhorst* was undergoing repairs to her boilers, so she missed the first and last sortie by *Bismarck*. Then at La Pallice she was hit by five bombs, of which three were 1000lb (454kg) armour-piercing weapons. These, however, passed completely through the ship without exploding.

During Operation Cerberus, the 'Channel Dash', *Scharnhorst* detonated two mines but arrived safely home in Wilhelmshaven. Cerberus was a tactical victory but a strategic failure, as it meant the ships were no longer based in French ports and capable of operating against the transatlantic convoy routes. It was following this operation that the two sister ships were to be permanently separated. *Gneisenau* in port had not been de-ammunitioned, and a British heavy bomb struck her and burned out the complete forecastle. Although this was taken as the opportunity to lengthen her bow and rearm her with 15in guns, the project was never started, and *Gneisenau* remained a hulk until the end of the war. Separated from her sister, 'lucky *Scharnhorst*' was moved to Norway to threaten the convoys to Russia.

Finally, on 26 December 1943 her luck ran out, off the North Cape of Norway, in the last big-gun encounter between battleships in European waters. Ordered by Dönitz to attack Russian-bound convoys to aid the struggling German war effort in Russia, *Scharnhorst* sortied from her Norwegian lair under the command of

Konteradmiral Erich Bey, whom we last met at Narvik, when through his prevarication he doomed the entire German destroyer flotilla to destruction. He was to display far more elan during the action off North Cape.

Admiral Bruce Fraser set a trap for *Scharnhorst*, using the conjunction of outward Convoy JW55B of nineteen merchantmen and inbound Convoy JW55A with twenty-two. Their escorts included a total of eighteen destroyers. Immediate support was to be provided by Admiral Burnett's Force 1 consisting of the cruisers *Belfast*, *Sheffield* and *Norfolk*. Distant support was provided by Force 2, comprising Fraser's flagship the *King George V-*class battleship *Duke of York*, with cruiser *Trinidad* and four destroyers in company.

In the first of two engagements with Force 1, *Scharnhorst*'s forward radar was destroyed by an 8in shell from *Norfolk*. Bey, thinking he had made contact with a battleship, withdrew at high speed, and sent his five destroyers to search for the convoy, thus losing his own close escort and scouting screen. Trying to circumvent the cruiser force and fall on the convoy, *Scharnhorst* was illuminated by star-shells fired from the shadowing *Belfast*, and surprised by *Duke of York*, the German battlecruiser's turrets clearly seen aligned fore and aft. Under heavy fire from *Duke of York*'s 14in guns, Bey turned for home at high speed, which again the British ships could not match.

As the range opened, so the descending angle of *Duke of York*'s 14in shells became steeper. The inevitable happened at 1800 when a shell hit *Scharnhorst* and penetrated her armour, bursting in No 1 boiler room. Her speed was reduced, which allowed pursuing British destroyers to finally close with her.

Over the next hour, the destroyers and *Trinidad* and *Belfast* launched a total of fifty-five torpedoes at *Scharnhorst*. The Norwegian destroyer *Stord* actually closed to only 1500yds (1370m) to launch her full salvo of eight torpedoes, firing her 4.7in guns at the same time. No single battleship could hope to survive such an onslaught. Admiral Fraser, with so many torpedoes running, withdrew *Duke of York* to a safe distance. Hit by at least eleven torpedoes, *Scharnhorst* came to a stop, capsized and sank. *Rawalpindi*, *Glorious*, *Acasta* and *Achates* had been avenged. When *Scharnhorst* sank, Admiral Bey, Captain Hintze and 1966 of her crew were lost with her. Only thirty-six survivors were picked up by the British ships.

Her wreck was rediscovered by a Norwegian team in September 2000, and they reported that *Scharnhorst* lies inverted in 300m (984ft) of water. Her stern has detached and lies upright, but a large part of the bow section has detached and lies at an angle from the main part of the hull. It appears that *Scharnhorst* suffered a forward main magazine explosion, either on the surface or when sinking, blowing the ship in two.

TORPEDO EXPLOSION DESTROYS FORT

A strange incident involving torpedoes took place in September 1944 at Mercy, to the east of the city of Metz in northeast France. Following the German takeover of unoccupied France in 1942, the infantry fort of Mercy was being used by the Kriegsmarine to store two thousand torpedo warheads they had seized from the French naval arsenal in Toulon. The very day the Normandy landings took place, the Germans began to shift this huge store of explosives into Germany, with the aim of using the warhead explosives in their V-2 rocket construction programme.

By 19 September, they had moved some thousand warheads to the nearby railway station, and two trucks loaded with six torpedo warheads apiece were in the courtyard outside the entrance to the fort, ready for their next delivery run. At around 1745, the pilot of an American P-47 fighter-bomber flew over the fort. Spying the two loaded trucks he dived and strafed them with his eight .50cal machine guns. The trucks caught fire, the pilot zoomed upwards, banked over the fort and came back for a second run. At that moment the burning trucks exploded, the blast travelled inside the entrance, set off the stored torpedo warheads, and the entire fort erupted in a huge explosion.

The P-47's engine cut out, but the pilot had just enough time to restart it and managed to return to his base near Nancy. Behind him, the entire fort had disappeared, along with eleven German naval personnel, and seventy Waffen SS troops returned from the Normandy front, who had bivouacked their vehicles loaded with booty in the woods around the fort. Huge blocks of concrete rained down all around, some even landing in the city of Metz. The blast travelled along the underground tunnel connecting the fort to a smaller fortification in Jury, and blew out a casemate end wall. All that is left of the infantry fort of Mercy today is a small lake which marks the crater left by the explosion, and three large crosses erected by the Germans with the names of those killed in the disaster.

CHAPTER 23

The Second World War – The Pacific

PEARL HARBOR

The Americans should never have been taken by surprise by what happened at Pearl Harbor on 7 December 1941, if they had studied their likely antagonists in the Pacific. War between Japan and China, which became known as the First Sino-Japanese War, was formally declared on 1 August 1884. However, the first combat had taken place six days earlier, at Pungdo, when Japanese warships attacked and drove ashore the Chinese gunboat *Kwang-yi*, captured a second gunboat, the *Tsao-kiang*, and sank a British steamer, the *Kow-shing*, which was carrying 1200 Chinese troops to Korea. Some nine hundred of the troops died in the incident.

On 8 February 1904 Japan had issued a declaration of war against Russia. However, three hours before the declaration was received, Admiral Togo had launched what would now be termed a pre-emptive strike against the Russian fleet at anchor in Port Arthur. The tsar's government, taken by surprise, did not declare war on Japan until eight days later. When the Russians complained at the Japanese action, the latter referred to the Russians' own attack on Sweden in 1809 without a declaration of war. The Japanese action was mirrored by Churchill during the Great War, when on 3 November 1914 he ordered the Mediterranean Fleet to bombard the Turkish forts at the mouth of the Dardanelles, again without a formal declaration of war.

In 1941 the Japanese combined fleet was numerically inferior to that of the Americans, and to even the odds it was always possible the Japanese would resort to a pre-emptive strike. Despite warnings signalled by the destroyer *Ward*, which had fired on one of the five Japanese midget submarines trying to enter Pearl Harbor, and reports from their new radar station, the Americans were taken completely by surprise as Commander Mitsuo Fuchida ordered his radio operator to send the famous signal '*Tora! Tora! Tora!*'

The Americans had assumed that their ships in Pearl Harbor were safe from torpedo attack as the water was too shallow. They had failed to appreciate the lessons of Taranto, which were not lost on the Japanese. As noted in Chapter 8, they had made special provisions for shallow torpedo drops, and had trained extensively for such an operation.

Their main targets were the battleships anchored in Battleship Row, unprotected by anti-torpedo nets. The *Nevada* (launched 1916, modernised 1929, 34,000 tons, ten 14in guns) was moored to dolphins on her own at the rear of the line. Next came the *Arizona* (launched 1916, modernised 1931, 36,500 tons, twelve 14in guns), with the repair ship *Vestal* moored outside her. Then came *Tennessee* (launched 1920, 35,190 tons, twelve 14in guns) with *West Virginia* (launched 1923, 33,590 tons, eight 16in guns) moored outboard, and lastly *Maryland* (launched 1921, 33,590 tons, eight 16in guns), with *Oklahoma* (launched 1916, modernised 1929, 34,000 tons, ten 14in guns) moored outboard. At the head of the line was the oiler *Neosho*, and moored ahead of her, some distance away, was the *California* (launched 1921, 35,190 tons, twelve 14in guns). The fleet flagship *Pennsylvania*, sister ship to the *Arizona*, was in dry dock and safe from torpedo attack, as were the three battleships moored inboard in Battleship Row.

A series of photos taken from Japanese aircraft show how the torpedo attacks developed.

Looking east, Ford Island is in the centre. The plume of water in Battleship Row comes from the explosion of a torpedo hit on *Oklahoma* or *West Virginia*. Both are already listing from previous torpedo hits. A Japanese B5N torpedo bomber can be seen right of centre, pulling out of its torpedo run, and a second Japanese plane can be seen at top right. In the line of ships on the north of Ford Island, the second ship from the left, the light cruiser USS *Raleigh*, has been torpedoed, as has the training ship *Utah* behind her. Both are beginning to list. *Utah*, an old battleship partially disarmed and converted to a gunnery training ship, was mistaken by Japanese torpedo plane pilots for an active dreadnought. (NHHC, photo # NH50930)

Overflight of Battleship Row. *Nevada* on the left, obscured by smoke, has been torpedoed and is losing oil. Despite this her captain would decide to try to make a run for the open sea. Ahead of her *Arizona* has taken one bomb hit. *West Virginia* and *Oklahoma* have lost a large amount of oil, and are listing. *Oklahoma*'s port deck edge is level with the water and she is about to capsize. (NHHC, photo # NH50472)

Battleship Row. *Nevada* is the first battleship, followed by *Arizona* with *Vestal* outboard. *West Virginia* ahead of her, and *Oklahoma* next in line outboard, have both been torpedoed and begin to list to port, and the ripples caused by the torpedo explosions can still be seen. Oil is spreading from *West Virginia*. On the right, *California* has also been torpedoed, and is losing oil. The white smoke in top centre comes from Hickam Field, and the grey smoke to its left from the torpedoed light cruiser *Helena* moored at 1010 Dock. (NHHC, photo # NH50931)

Ford Island looking south. The white plumes on the left are two more torpedo hits on *West Virginia*, and the wider, greyish plume on the right is a torpedo hit on *Oklahoma*. The much larger volume of water thrown up may indicate this to have been a hit from an 18in Type 97 oxygen-fuelled torpedo. Recent evidence suggests that this was fired by the A-Type midget submarine *I-16tou*. (NHHC, photo # NH50929)

Second overflight of Battleship Row. *Nevada* has not yet cast off her moorings. *Arizona* has blown up and sunk from a bomb hit, *Vestal* is burning from bomb damage, *West Virginia* is settling on the bottom, and *Oklahoma* has capsized. (NHHC, photo # NH50932)

Of the most serious casualties, *Oklahoma* was hit by a total of nine torpedoes. Of these, at least eight were the 18in Type 91 aircraft torpedoes. It is just possible that the third torpedo hit was by an 18in Type 97 from the Type-A midget submarine *I-16tou*. Although all watertight doors had been left open for a captain's inspection that fateful morning, the sheer number of torpedo hits on the port side had not allowed the ship time to flood progressively and settle upright on the bottom. No amount of counter-flooding could have affected the situation. Ironically, the Japanese pilots had expended a large number of their torpedoes on what was probably the least combat-effective battleship at Pearl.

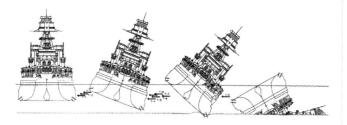

Oklahoma: the sequence of capsizing and finishing upside-down in the harbour mud. (Detail from NHHC, photo # 013719a)

Oklahoma's salvage was a difficult and lengthy job, and by the time she was recovered, she was of little use to the fleet. In addition to the severe damage, *Oklahoma* was handicapped by being one of the last US dreadnoughts to have reciprocating steam engines instead of turbines.

After being hit by just one torpedo, *Nevada* was attacked by bombers which tried to sink her in the entrance channel. She was hit by five bombs, and was beached, slowly filled and sank. After salvage she was brought into dry dock No 2 on 18 February 1942. Although bulged, *Nevada*'s bulkhead had held with only slight leaks. The watertight integrity of the ship was preserved, and no significant damage inboard of the TDS was noted. So not only was *Nevada* the first dreadnought with 'all or nothing' armour protection against shellfire, but in her modernised state she also had an effective TDS.

Nevada's torpedo damage, seen from the dry-dock floor. A large section of the torpedo bulge had been blown away. The hole measured 16ft long by 27ft high (4.9m x 8.2m). (USS *Nevada* Torpedo and Bomb Damage report)

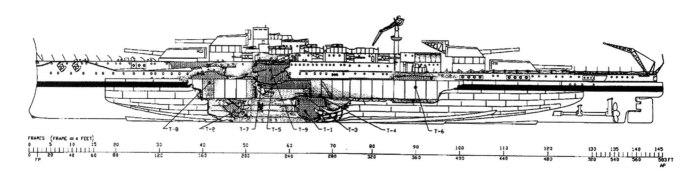

Drawing of *Oklahoma*'s torpedo damage. This shows the scope of damage discovered when she was in dry dock. Large areas of the bulge have been blown away, several armour plates are missing. and the lower curve of the hull was also crumpled in the capsize and the subsequent operation to roll her upright. (Detail from NHHC, photo # 013719a)

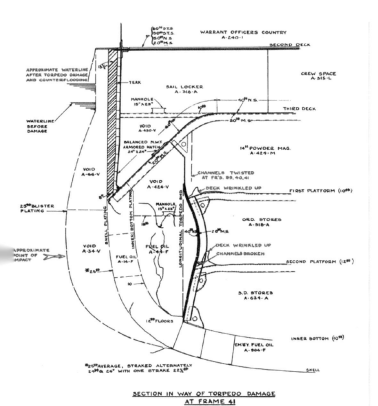

West Virginia refloated, entering dry dock on 9 June 1942. (NHHC, photo # NH64491)

A cross-section of the torpedo damage on *Nevada*. The TDS was composed of the bulge, which was left void, then two internal spaces filled with oil, then the torpedo bulkhead which had been doubled with 40lb (2.8kg/cm^2) nickel steel plate at the time *Nevada* was modernised. Total width of the TDS was 14ft (4.27m). (USS *Nevada* Torpedo and Bomb Damage report)

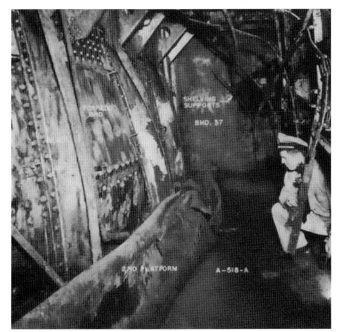

A rare internal view of the torpedo bulkhead of the TDS at the point of torpedo impact. (USS *Nevada* Torpedo and Bomb Damage report)

Removal of the cofferdam in progress, showing part of the extensive damage to *West Virginia's* hull from the multiple torpedo hits, and the armour belt bent inwards. (NHHC, photo # NH 83058)

West Virginia's port side had been struck by an estimated five torpedoes, and a sixth had hit and blown off her rudder. Salvage work required the construction of a large cofferdam bolted to the ship's side. Even when she had been refloated, *West Virginia* was in a 'tender' state and liable to capsize if any leaks had developed. A detailed stability analysis was carried out, and special contingency plans were made for countering any ingress of water, for example from further air attacks. Eventually, however, she was placed in dry dock No 1, where it was found necessary to lower the docking blocks to get her inside.

A curious find was the air vessel of a Japanese Type 91 torpedo found lying on one of *West Virginia*'s lower decks. The saddest task for the salvage team was the removal of sixty-six bodies of her crew which were found in various areas of the ship. One group of three bodies was discovered in a storeroom, with evidence that they had been still alive on 23 December, when they had died through exhaustion of the oxygen in the air bubble where they were trapped.

The *California* also required the construction of a large cofferdam and many pumps to refloat her.

The Japanese congratulated themselves on sinking five battleships (*Arizona*, *Oklahoma*, *West Virginia*, *California* and *Nevada*) plus the demilitarised *Utah*, damaging two more (*Tennessee* and *Maryland*), badly damaging two cruisers (*Helena* and *Raleigh*) and demolishing three destroyers (*Shaw*, *Cassin* and *Downes*), all for the price of twenty-nine aircraft shot down, and five midget subs lost. However, Nagumo's refusal to launch a follow-up strike left untouched the US Navy's dry-dock repair facilities which were to accomplish such herculean salvage work. *West Virginia*, *California* and *Nevada* would all be salvaged

Torpedo hit on *California*, showing her thick armour belt virtually undamaged. (NHHC, photo # 80-G-32917)

and repaired to fight again. The Japanese also missed the opportunity to destroy Pearl's oil fuel tanks, some of which can be seen in the Japanese aerial photos.

The Americans were left to ponder on what might have happened to their fleet if they had been caught out at sea. It is likely that many more ships would have been sunk, in deep water, with extremely heavy loss of life. Finally, of course, the elimination of virtually all of the American battleships in the Pacific theatre forced the US Navy to rely on their aircraft carriers, luckily absent on 7 December, which would ultimately bring about the utter defeat of the Imperial Japanese navy.

THE HUNTING OF FORCE Z

A somewhat dramatised Japanese wartime postcard depicting the attack on Force Z by torpedo-armed Mitsubishi G3M 'Nell' bombers. *Prince of Wales* appears to be firing her main 14in guns, which she never used during the Japanese attacks. (Courtesy of pacificwrecks.com)

The *Bismarck* action in May 1941 had highlighted the danger of torpedo hits on the vulnerable stern area of even the most heavily protected of ships. This drawback had been noted on Britain's very first ironclad battleship, HMS *Warrior*, back in 1860. Commentators had noted the beautiful lines of the new ship, while severely criticising her fine clipper bow as adding useless weight but nothing to her fighting abilities, but more importantly, her traditional frigate stern, which left the single propeller and steering gear with no protection at all. These flaws were to come home to roost with a vengeance in Britain's last class of battleship, the *King George V* class of 1940.

Much has been written on the wisdom or otherwise of Churchill's despatch of the new battleship HMS *Prince of Wales*, already blooded in the *Bismarck* encounter, to the Far East, supported only by the unmodernised battlecruiser HMS *Repulse* and a handful of destroyers. The new aircraft carrier, the *Indomitable*, which was allocated to the small squadron, had run aground in the West Indies, and although not seriously damaged, was never to join up with Force Z under Admiral Tom Phillips at Singapore. As none of the destroyers had a high-angle anti-aircraft gun capability, the ships' only effective defence against air attack came from the sixteen 5.25in DP guns on *Prince of Wales*.

Despite warnings from General Chennault, who had been sent to command the Chinese air force in its struggle with Japan, the Western democracies ignored completely the dramatic increase in combat potential of the latest Japanese army and navy aircraft, such as the Mitsubishi A6M 'Zero' fighter. According to aviation pundits, Japan's air forces consisted of underpowered copies of outdated Western designs. Moreover, her bomber force was handicapped by the 'natural' short-sightedness of the bomb-aimers, typically portrayed as wearing thick pebble-glass spectacles (see also Part II, Chapter 14*)*.

Churchill's underestimation of the fighting capacity of the Japanese, which paralleled his dismissal of the Turks in the lead-up to the Gallipoli campaign a quarter of a century earlier, was matched by Phillips's over-confidence in his force's ability to fight off sea and air attacks, without the need for air cover. Significantly, at the same time as he despatched Force Z to its fate, Churchill sent two hundred brand-new cannon-armed Hurricane fighters to the Soviet Union, leaving the defence of Singapore and Force Z to a handful of squadrons flying the underpowered Brewster B-339 Buffalo fighter.

The scene was set for high drama and a disastrous engagement, which simultaneously rang the death-knell of the battleship, and also began the train of events which would ultimately bring about the fall of the British Empire in the Far East.

In order to fulfil its intended role as a deterrent, it was important that the appointment of Admiral Phillips and the despatch of Force Z was fully reported in the press. The Japanese therefore had adequate time to prepare a warm reception for them. In particular, the 22nd Air Flotilla was moved to the airfields the Japanese had seized from the Vichy French in Indochina, within striking distance of Singapore. The Genzan and Kanoya groups, flying Mitsubishi G3M twin-engined bombers, were well-practised in attacks on warships. To support them, Admiral Yamamoto also despatched the new G4M bombers of the Kanoya group.

When news arrived of the Japanese attack on Pearl Harbor, Admiral Phillips sortied Force Z to intercept a Japanese invasion force reported to be en route for Malaya. He was spotted by a patrolling submarine, the transports were ordered to scatter to the north in the Gulf of Siam, two *Kongo*-class fast battleships plus a force of cruisers were detailed to intercept Force Z, and the 22nd Air Flotilla Groups at Saigon and Thŭ Dâu Môt with their total of eighty-six bombers were alerted.

On the morning of 10 December 1941, when Force Z was returning to Singapore, having failed to find any invasion forces, they were set upon by the highly trained Japanese aviators not far off the Malayan coast. At 1113 first blood went to G3M high level bombers, which closely straddled *Repulse* with 250kg (550lbs) bombs and scored one hit amidships.

Then at 1141 nine Mitsubishi G3M torpedo bombers commenced an attack on the port side of *Prince of Wales*, but one aircraft turned away and attacked *Repulse*. Approaching at 150 to 180 knots, the eight remaining planes descended to 30–35m (100–115ft) and at ranges from 1500m down to as close at 600m (1640–650yds) dropped their 18in torpedoes, set to run at a depth of 4–6m (13–20ft). This kind of attack was not what *Prince of Wales*' anti-aircraft gunners had experienced from single Italian torpedo planes in their brief sortie into the Mediterranean.

Moving at maximum speed, the flagship turned to port to comb the torpedo tracks. But there is a fatal period of time before the helm of a large ship moving at speed takes effect, and at the same time her speed is reduced. Nevertheless, moving at 24 knots *Prince of Wales* avoided

A Mitsubishi G3M2 twin-engined bomber codenamed 'Nell' by the Allies. This drawing represents one of the Nells from the Genzan Kokutai based at Saigon, which took part in the attacks on Force Z.

A drawing representing a typical Mitsubishi G4M codenamed 'Betty' by the Allies. (Drawings from *Flying Colours*, by permission of the artist John Weal)

the first seven torpedoes. But the last torpedo struck the ship far aft on her port side, just above the outer port propeller shaft, at about 1144, and set in motion a train of events which would lead inexorably to her loss.

The explosion tore a large rent in the hull, but it also damaged the shaft supports for the outer port propeller shaft. With the shaft revolving at high speed, the supports fractured and the propeller began to turn out of centre. This led to the watertight glands in the bulkheads, through which the long shaft passed, coming adrift from their bulkheads, allowing water to flood into the ship through the shaft alley. The port outer engine was initially shut down, but the water flow continued to free rotate the propeller. When the turbine was restarted, the rear section of shafting, 17.7in (45cm) in diameter, came apart at an internal coupling. At this point, the rear part of the shaft, with the broken brackets and the stern tube broke away from the hull, destroying many already compromised internal bulkheads. In its passage the shaft damaged the port inner propeller, which led to its turbine also being shut down.

The ship had lost propulsion from its port propellers, reducing speed to just 15 knots. The serious flooding caused a list to port, which was increased to 11.5 degrees when the handling crews in the port aft 5.25in shell and cartridge rooms, believing from the noise of the break-up of the shafting that the ship had received a second torpedo hit in their vicinity, flooded the magazines.

The torpedo hit had also caused widespread damage in other areas, the shock damage knocking out the electrical system. This cut out the power supply to the aft 5.25in turrets and the clumsy eight-barrelled pom-poms, to the pumps, the ventilation and the lighting system. The steering gear also failed, and despite the helm remaining set at 20 degrees to starboard *Prince of Wales* began a slow turn to port under the impulse of her remaining starboard propellers. The list to port meant that the heavy 5.25in turrets could not be trained, so Captain Leach ordered the counter-flooding of the external and internal voids of the TDS on the starboard side forward. The list to port was reduced to 9 degrees, but the move risked compromising the effectiveness of the triple-layer TDS on the starboard side.

While the flooding was progressing throughout the stern of *Prince of Wales*, at 1219 another twenty-six torpedo planes arrived and commenced a mass attack on the two ships. Seven planes headed for the starboard side of *Prince of Wales*, but three veered off to attack *Repulse*. From the remaining four aircraft, three torpedoes struck the starboard side of the sluggish *Prince of Wales*, which was unable to manoeuvre to avoid them. To make matters worse, the forward starboard 5.25in turrets could not depress adequately to engage the torpedo planes, due to the ship's list to port.

The first torpedo tore a hole 7m (23ft) in diameter straight through the bow from starboard to port. The second struck abreast 'B' turret, on the compromised TFD, and caused major damage. Shock wrecked equipment in the 14in cordite and shell-handling rooms of 'B' turret, and in the transmitting station. Surprisingly, diver surveys carried out in 2007 and 2008 found no damage to the internal TDS, and it is surmised that the force of the explosion may have vented upwards. Certainly, a degaussing generator was flung bodily through an upper deck, creating a large hole.

The third and last torpedo hit far aft, above the starboard outer propeller, and the effects were devastating. The starboard outer propeller shaft was bent downwards, leaving the propeller wedged in the hull. This caused the starboard outer turbine to come to an abrupt stop. With only the starboard inner shaft turning speed dropped to just 8 knots. A hole 11m long x 4m high (36ft x 13ft) was torn in the hull. The starboard hits had the effect of righting the ship, until her list reduced to only 3 degrees to port. But the additional flooding aft doomed the *Prince of Wales*.

The final attack was carried out at 1244 by eight high-level bombers with 500kg (1100lbs) bombs, and with the target barely moving, they managed to score one hit and six near-misses, which caved in the hull sides. All power was lost, and the *Prince of Wales* came to a halt, slowly sinking. The destroyer *Express* came alongside to evacuate survivors, but at 1324, the flagship lurched to port and capsized, sinking a few minutes later. HMS *Express* was almost caught and rolled over by *Prince of Wales'* bilge keel and only just managed to avoid being capsized in her turn. Of her complement of over 1500, almost 1200 were rescued, but 327 officers and men died, including the admiral and Captain Leach.

When the flagship had hoisted the signal that she was not under control, Captain Tennant of the *Repulse* had closed *Prince of Wales* to offer assistance. At that point torpedo planes had put in an attack on the *Repulse*, coming in from port and starboard at the same time. Captain Tennant managed to avoid nineteen torpedoes in all, but *Repulse* was struck by one torpedo on the starboard side and by at least three, and possibly four, on the port side. Captain Tennant knew his old ship could not survive such punishment, and he gave the order to abandon ship. *Repulse* capsized and sank at 1233, taking 508 men down with her. Captain Tennant and nearly seven hundred of his officers and men survived.

Just three Japanese aircraft were shot down, all by the pom-pom gunners on *Repulse*. Standard procedure was to fire on a torpedo plane only up to the point where it released its torpedo, then to switch fire to the next attacker. However, *Repulse*'s gunners saw to their dismay that the Japanese were dropping their torpedoes outside the maximum range at which their 2pdr shells were self-destroying. Therefore they ignored standing orders and continued to fire on those torpedo bombers overflying their ship after dropping their torpedo.

As the destroyers were rescuing survivors struggling in the water, RAF Flight Lieutenant Vigors, who was responding to the only call for air cover, sent by Captain Tennant, flew over the scene in his Brewster Buffalo. The Buffalo fighter was to be later criticised for its lack of performance compared with contemporary Japanese aircraft. However, the actual combat performances of RAF, New Zealand and Dutch pilots flying the Brewster give the lie to this condemnation. It is now thought that the Buffalo was damned in order to explain away the shortcomings of the Allies' preparations for a war with Japan. If the air cover had been requested before the Japanese attackers had arrived over the ships, it is obvious that things might have turned out very differently. The .50cal heavy machine guns of the Buffalo would have caused serious damage to the lightly armed and unarmoured Japanese bombers, which had no self-sealing fuel tanks, the G4M 'Betty' in particular being nicknamed the 'flying cigar' for its propensity to catch fire under attack.

In the Fleet Air Arm attack on Taranto, and the Japanese attack on Pearl Harbor, the targets had been lying immobile in harbour. The destruction of Force Z proved that even capital ships, fully prepared for action and free to manoeuvre in the open sea, were liable to destruction by aircraft when not provided with effective fighter cover. The day of the battleship as the predominant capital ship was over, and its place would be taken by the new capital ship, the aircraft carrier.

BATTLE OF THE JAVA SEA

The Netherlands East Indies traced their origins to the first Dutch ships which arrived at the end of the sixteenth century searching for spices. To protect their commercial interests the Dutch incorporated the Dutch East Indies Company (VOC), which was nationalised by the State in 1800. Colonial expansion by military conquest continued into the twentieth century. They provided many valuable products such as quinine, but the most desirable were rubber and oil, both considered vital to the Japanese war effort.

To defend their rich colonial possessions the Dutch had established a local army, the KNIL and airforce, and major units of the Dutch navy were stationed in the East

A pre-war shot of *Java*'s sister-ship HMNS *Sumatra* at speed, showing the German design features – looking like a cross between the *Hindenburg* and a Panzerschiffe – and the fine hull lines of this class of light cruiser.

Indies. In early 1942, the Dutch naval forces available for the defence of the Netherlands East Indies comprised three light cruisers (*De Ruyter*, *Java* and *Tromp*), seven modern destroyers, and sixteen submarines. When the Japanese invaded, these forces were bolstered by a number of British, American and Australian ships, to form a unified command, ABDA, under Dutch Admiral Helfrich. From the outset, Allied efforts were hamstrung by the severe losses inflicted on them everywhere throughout the Pacific theatre, at Pearl, in the Philippines, and off Malaya.

On 9 February 1942 Vice Admiral Ozawa set sail with the Japanese Southern Expeditionary Force, to conquer the Netherlands East Indies. In a series of sorties, the ABDA command was whittled down, with several ships and submarines lost or damaged, until the final battle on 27 February in the Java Sea. Admiral Karl Doorman in *De Ruyter* headed the line, followed by HMS *Exeter* of River Plate fame, heavy cruiser USS *Houston* (with her rear turret out of action following Japanese bombing), HMAS *Perth* whose crew had seen action at Matapan, and light cruiser *Java*. They were screened by British destroyers *Electra*, *Encounter* and *Jupiter*, by the veteran American flush-deckers *John D Edwards*, *Paul Jones*, *John D Ford* and *Alden*, and by Dutch destroyers *Evertsen*, *Witte de With* and *Kortenaer*.

Facing them were the Japanese covering force for the forty-one invasion transports, comprising light cruiser *Naka* and ten destroyers, *Jintsu* leading four more destroyers, and their eastern covering group, the heavy cruisers *Nachi* and *Haguro*.

On paper the two opposing sides appeared relatively evenly matched: two Allied heavy cruisers against two Japanese, three Allied light cruisers against two Japanese, and ten destroyers against fourteen Japanese. However, each Japanese heavy cruiser carried ten 8in guns, to which *Exeter* and the damaged *Houston* could only oppose six apiece, the *Java* and *De Ruyter* were a close match for light cruisers *Naka* and *Jintsu*, and *Perth* carried a heavier broadside than them all, but apart from the RN *Jupiter*, the Allied destroyers were smaller and far less powerful than their modern Japanese opponents. And the Japanese were armed with large batteries of the long-range 24in Type 93 'Long Lance' torpedoes.

When battle was joined at 1616, the Japanese ships were about to cross the 'T' of the Allied line. *Nachi* and *Haguro* opened fire with their twenty 8in guns, at a range where the 6in Allied cruisers could not reply. Only the forward turrets of *Exeter* and *Perth* could open fire. The Japanese cruisers were using their floatplanes to spot the fall of shot. It was not until 1629 that Doorman brought his light cruisers into extreme gun range. Some six

minutes later, the *Naka* led seven destroyers into a torpedo attack, and at 16,000yds range (14,600m) they launched forty-three torpedoes. Several exploded before reaching the Allied line, possibly through collision, but which caused confusion in the minds of the Allied crews, and the remainder all missed.

Just after 1700 Jintsu led her destroyers in for a second torpedo attack, this time closing in to just 7000yds (6400m) to launch their sixty-four torpedoes at the Allied line. At that very moment the *Exeter* was hit by an 8in shell which penetrated her No 1 boiler room and exploded on entering the boiler. The ship immediately lost speed, electrical power to her armament was knocked out, and Captain Gordon realised he could not remain in the line of battle. He ordered a rapid turn to port. Following astern, the *Houston* turned inside *Exeter* to avoid her, and *Perth* and *Java*, last in line, followed suit. To the Japanese it appeared that the Allied cruisers were executing the standard turn away to comb the torpedoes. All torpedoes missed, except for one which struck the Dutch destroyer *Kortenaer* at 1715 and broke her in two.

At 1806 the four US flush-deckers were ordered to counter-attack, and Commander Binford led them into a torpedo attack on *Nachi* and *Haguro*. By 1822 they were in position and at the long range of 10,000yds (9100m) launched all their twenty-four starboard torpedoes at the Japanese, before executing a 180-degree turn and launching their twenty-four port torpedoes. All missed.

Separated from their remaining destroyers, the four Allied cruisers (*Exeter* having withdrawn from the battle) zigzagged to the north in search of the invasion transports. They were reacquired by *Nachi* and *Haguro* at 2322 and both cruisers launched Type 93 torpedoes, eight from *Nachi* and four from *Haguro* at a range of just 8000yds (7300m). The first struck home on *De Ruyter* some eight minutes later, followed by a second hit on the *Java*. The results in both cases were devastating. *Java* pointed her bows skywards and sank, and the blazing *De Ruyter* followed soon after. The surviving Allied cruisers *Perth* and *Houston* retired from the scene, and the disastrous Battle of the Java Sea was over. The end of these two cruisers will be described shortly.

The lesson which can be drawn from the torpedo actions is that the Japanese Type 93 was less effective at its extreme long range. It was deadly when at normal torpedo ranges, due to its high speed and the effects of its large warhead, one hit being sufficient to cripple or even sink a pre-war light cruiser. This was a lesson the Allies would come to learn over and over again in the months to follow.

BATTLE OF THE SUNDA STRAIT

Probably the most dramatic blue-on-blue torpedo incident occurred on 27 February 1942 in the Dutch East Indies. The heavy cruiser USS *Houston* and light cruiser HMAS *Perth* were attempting to escape to Ceylon following the disastrous Battle of the Java Sea. Heading for the Sunda Strait, at 2215 they ran straight into the Japanese western force landing troops at Banten Bay. Over thirty transports were unloading close to shore, covered by only three Japanese destroyers, the *Harukaze*, *Hatakaze* and *Fubuki*. Without hesitating the two Allied cruisers attacked the transports and began to score hits. *Fubuki* radioed the alarm and counter-attacked with a spread of nine 24in torpedoes.

At 2300 light cruiser *Natori* led her ten destroyers into the fray, followed by heavy cruisers *Mogami* and *Mikuma*. At 2327 *Mogami* launched a spread of six 'Long Lance' torpedoes at the *Houston*, but they all missed and passed into Banten Bay. Eight minutes later, torpedoes struck and sank Japanese minesweeper *W 2* (826 tons) and four transports, the *Sakura Maru*, *Horai Maru*, *Tatsuno Maru* and the *Shinshu Maru*. The last vessel was in fact a 12,000-ton Japanese army special landing ship, carrying the commander of the 16th Army, Lt Gen Hitoshi Imamura. He jumped overboard as *Shinshu Maru* settled in shallow water and was picked up by a small boat.

Of the eighty-seven torpedoes launched by the Japanese ships during the engagement, four hit the *Perth* and six the *Houston*. The torpedoes which struck the transports and the minesweeper are believed to have been launched by *Mogami* but it is possible some may have come from *Fubuki*. Both Allied cruisers sank with heavy loss of life. The *Shinshu Maru* was salvaged and repaired,

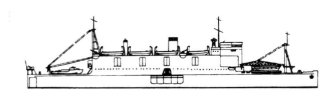

Japanese army landing ship *Shinshu Maru* (also known by the codenames 'Ryujo Maru' and 'Fuso Maru').

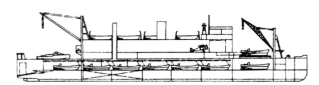

The internal layout of this specialised vessel, showing the aircraft hangar and the landing craft in the through hold, which could be discharged through two stern doors or by the crane forward.

only to be damaged by submarine torpedo on 3 January 1944 and sunk by aircraft two days later.

The Imperial Japanese Navy was obliged to apologise to the army for sinking their landing ship. Honour thus being satisfied, the army then amended their records to record that the *Shinshu Maru* had been sunk by a 'Dutch torpedo boat'.

USS *PORTER*

A different type of blue-on-blue torpedo launch involved the large destroyer USS *Porter* (DD-356) on 26 October 1942, during the Battle of Santa Cruz. The *Porter* was assigned to Task Force 16, as part of the escort for the carrier USS *Enterprise*. After helping the carrier fight off attacking Japanese planes, *Porter*'s crew observed a Grumman Avenger torpedo bomber returning from a strike on the Japanese carriers. Low on fuel, the plane ditched near *Porter* and Lt Cdr Roberts conned his ship to pick up the crew.

Unfortunately, on hitting the water the Avenger's torpedo left the aircraft and its engine was activated. It was obviously damaged in the crash, as it apparently made two circular runs, the crew believing they had spotted two torpedoes, fired from a Japanese submarine. On the second circular run it hit *Porter* in the forward engine room, killing eleven men and wounding nine others, of whom four more died later from their injuries. Another destroyer, USS *Shaw*, arrived to offer assistance but broke away to hunt a suspected submarine contact. Finding none, she returned to pick up *Porter*'s survivors.

After the end of the war, Japanese records were searched for information on the submarine which could have fired the fatal torpedo, but no such entry was found. The US Navy was therefore left with the probability that the *Porter* had been sunk by the Avenger's torpedo.

IRONBOTTOM SOUND AND THE TOKYO EXPRESS

In the desperate night-time combats for control of Guadalcanal and the surrounding islands, which lasted from August 1942 until February 1943, the torpedo was to be the dominant weapon, responsible for most of the nearly fifty wrecks littering the seabed that became known to the Americans as 'Iron Bottom Sound'.

The US Navy had withdrawn the torpedo tubes from its cruisers in the 1930s, because of the potential fire and explosion risks during surface and air attacks, and to concentrate on gun action. The Japanese were well aware of the hazards, but because they felt they had a winning weapon in the oxygen-fuelled 24in Type 93 torpedo, their cruisers retained their tubes.

The Americans relied on overwhelming firepower from their cruisers' turret guns, unaware of the potential of the Japanese torpedoes, which in addition to their high speed, were wakeless. And they were launched by compressed air, giving no warning powder flash at night, as did American destroyer torpedo tubes. Despite possessing radar, in their early encounters the Americans failed to make full use of this crucial asset, and too often the Japanese captains hugged nearby islands, giving false radar returns. For their part the Japanese, lacking radar at the time, had trained extensively in night-attack tactics. Their lookouts were supplied with excellent night optical aids, and they practised the use of flares dropped by their cruisers' floatplanes. The scene was set for some dramatic confrontations.

The Battle of Savo Island
Just two days after the Americans landed on Guadalcanal, the Allied warships were soundly defeated in the first of four major naval confrontations. On the night of 8/9 August, Japanese Admiral Mikawa passed down the 'Slot' with five heavy cruisers, two light cruisers and one destroyer.

His forces fell upon the unprepared and divided Allied cruisers and destroyers guarding the invasion transports. They illuminated the southern force, disabling HMAS *Canberra* with gunfire – she was later scuttled – and hitting USS *Chicago* with two torpedoes. The second failed to explode, but the hit on the bows caused a whiplash through the ship's structure that put her main fire control director out of action.

The Japanese swept on and came upon the northern force. On board the US cruisers, their captains were all asleep. At 0144 Mikawa's ships fired a salvo of Type 93 torpedoes, illuminated the US cruisers and opened heavy gunfire. *Quincy* was hit by two torpedoes from *Tenryu*, and was badly damaged. Then she was hit by a torpedo from *Aoba*, and sank by the bow at 0238. Meanwhile, at 0155 two torpedoes from *Chōkai* struck USS *Vincennes*. She sank at 0250. Since he did not know that Admiral Halsey had pulled his carriers away from close air support, Mikawa turned to withdraw, to clear the area before his ships could come under air attack at dawn. En route to their base the heavy cruiser *Kako* was torpedoed and sunk by the submarine *S 44*, small consolation for the Allies who had lost so many heavy cruisers.

Second Battle of Savo Island
Also known as the Battle of Cape Esperance, this encounter took place took place on the night of 11/12 October. A Japanese bombardment force under Rear Admiral Gotō consisting of three heavy cruisers and two destroyers was covering a reinforcement run by two seaplane carriers, which were to unload artillery and other heavy supplies for the Japanese troops attempting to retake Guadalcanal. In a confused action, thanks to American use of radar the Japanese cruiser force was surprised by the four cruisers and five destroyers of Rear Admiral Scott. At 2349 the heavy cruiser *Furataka* was hit on her torpedo tubes by an American shell, which set her on fire, and nine minutes later a torpedo launched from American destroyer *Buchanan* hit her in the forward engine room. At 0006, two torpedoes narrowly missed the heavy cruiser USS *Boise*. The crippled *Furataka* eventually sank at 0228.

The Japanese had lost their admiral, mortally wounded on the bridge of *Aoba*, and his chief of staff ordered the bombardment force to break off action and retreat northwards. Although this part of their mission had failed, while the battle was raging the Japanese seaplane carriers had successfully unloaded their cargo.

The encounter reinforced the Americans' confidence in their own ships' heavy firepower, while lulling them into a false sense of security regarding the Japanese Type 93 torpedoes, which would feature prominently in the following action, as well as the overwhelming Japanese superiority in close-quarters night-fighting.

Third Battle of Savo Island
This took place over the period 12 to 15 November 1942. The encounter on the first night is also known as the first part of the Naval Battle of Guadalcanal, described by a participant as a 'bar room brawl after the lights had been shot out'. On the night of 12/13 November, a Japanese bombardment force, centred around the fast battleships *Hiei* and *Kirishima*, planned to repeat the successful bombardment of Henderson Field one month earlier, and at the same time cover a resupply convoy. The Japanese ran into an American force of cruisers and destroyers, and a confused close-range battle began at 0148 when *Hiei* and a destroyer illuminated the leading American light cruiser *Atlanta* at a range of only 3000yds (2700m).

Atlanta was hit by a Type 93 torpedo and was crippled. *Hiei* was hit by one, or perhaps two, American torpedoes, and had to be scuttled by her crew. The destroyer *Laffey* took a torpedo hit amidships which broke her back. She caught fire, blew up and sank. The heavy cruiser *Portland* was hit in the stern by a torpedo and forced into a turn, her steering damaged. She completed a full circle then managed to withdraw. The destroyer *Barton* was torpedoed twice by *Amatsukaze* and sank, then *Amatsukaze* torpedoed and badly damaged the light cruiser *Juneau*.

USS *New Orleans* after Tassafaronga. She was lucky to survive the explosion of her forward magazines and the loss of No 1 turret. The crews of both forward turrets and the handling rooms were killed in the explosion. (NHHC, photo # NH 0403229)

Two American destroyers hit the destroyer *Yudachi* with torpedoes and her crew abandoned ship.

On the following morning, *Atlanta* finally sank, and on her withdrawal for repairs, *Juneau* was torpedoed by the submarine *I 26* leading to the loss of almost all her crew, including the five Sullivan brothers later commemorated by naming a destroyer USS *The Sullivans*.

The following night the Japanese returned with their surviving battleship *Kirishima* to once more attempt the bombardment of Henderson field and cover the transports, in the action known as the second part of the Naval Battle of Guadalcanal. Unknown to them the Americans had sent in two modern battleships, *Washington* and *South Dakota*.

First blood went to the Japanese at around 2230, when their Type 93 torpedoes sank the destroyers *Wake* and *Preston*, and crippled *Benham* and *Gwin*. The US battleships had lost their screen, and during the fire-fight which ensued, *South Dakota* lost electrical power and suffered damage to her bridge area, but *Washington* so damaged *Kirishima* in return that she capsized and sank. The bombardment mission had failed, and the transports

that had beached themselves were destroyed before much of their cargo could be unloaded.

Battle of Tassafaronga

Also known as the Fourth Battle of Savo Island, this took place on the night of 30 November 1942, and resulted in heavy American losses. Eight Japanese destroyers under Rear Admiral Tanaka were conducting a regular nightly supply run down the 'Slot' to the troops on Guadalcanal in the type of operation which became known as the 'Tokyo Express'.

At 2312 the Japanese sighted the American force of five cruisers and four destroyers, and in turn they were tracked on American radar just two minutes later. The captain of USS *Fletcher* requested permission to launch his torpedoes, but Admiral Wright hesitated, losing precious minutes. When he gave the go-ahead, the optimum launch position had been passed, and all twenty American torpedoes launched, missed.

In response Japanese destroyers launched a total of forty-four Type 93 torpedoes, and the American cruisers, which maintained their original course, crossed their tracks. At 2327, Wright's flagship *Minneapolis* was hit by

USS *Minneapolis* with a temporary reinforcement of coconut logs. (US Navy photo)

one torpedo which blew off her bows as far back as turret No 1, and a second torpedo hit amidships and put out of action three of the four boiler rooms. Less than a minute later, a Type 93 hit *New Orleans* abreast No 1 turret, and her forward magazines exploded, blowing off 125ft of the hull forward of No 2 turret.

Next to be hit was *Pensacola*, which was struck by a torpedo abreast the mainmast, causing serious damage and casualties, and leaving her crippled. *Honolulu*'s captain conned his ship to avoid the torpedoes, but the last in line, *Northampton*, ran across the tracks of two, and was hit in the aft engine room, which flooded. She was left with only one of her four shafts still turning, caught fire and took up a 10-degree list to port. The fire spread out of control, she was abandoned, and sank at 0130.

The three other heavily damaged cruisers managed to make temporary repairs, and were eventually to be permanently repaired and returned to service. However, after this encounter the US Navy was left with only four heavy and nine light cruisers in the entire Pacific theatre.

Battle of Rennell Island, 29/30 January 1943

In the course of a heavy air presence to cover their planned troop withdrawal from Guadalcanal, the Japanese launched torpedo bomber attacks on a group of six US heavy cruisers. USS *Chicago* was hit by two torpedoes and crippled. As she was being towed from the area a further two groups of Bettys arrived, and put a further four torpedoes into *Chicago*, which sank twenty minutes later.

Battle of Kula Gulf

This encounter took place when an American task group intercepted a resupply run by the ten destroyers of the Tokyo Express to land troops on the island of Kolombangara, on 6 July 1943. When the American ships opened radar-controlled gunfire, two of the Japanese destroyers launched their Type 93 torpedoes. USS *Helena*, a survivor of the Pearl Harbor attack, had used up all her flashless powder and was forced to revert to normal smokeless, which made her the prime target. Hit by three torpedoes, she jack-knifed and sank.

Battle of Kolombangara

Also known as the Second Battle of Kula Gulf, it took place on the night of 12/13 July 1943, when an Allied force of cruisers and destroyers intercepted a run by the Tokyo Express to land troops at Vila on Kolombangara. The Japanese destroyers were aware of the Allied force and were able to launch their Type 93 torpedoes. HMNZS *Leander* was struck in a boiler room and badly damaged, the American cruisers *St Louis* and *Honolulu* were also hit and damaged, and destroyer USS *Gwin* was hit amidships and had to be abandoned.

HMNZS *Leander* was a 9144-ton (full load) light cruiser manned by the Royal New Zealand Navy. At 0124 a torpedo track was seen approaching 100yds away, running on the surface at slow speed. *Leander* turned, but the Japanese torpedo struck her on the port side amidships, some 10ft below the waterline. The contact pistol detonated the warhead on the Type 93 24in torpedo, blowing a hole 40ft long and 20ft deep. 'A' boiler room was immediately flooded, and the ship was temporarily

USS *Honolulu*'s damaged bow after the battle of Kolombangara. (NHHC, photo # 80-G-259422)

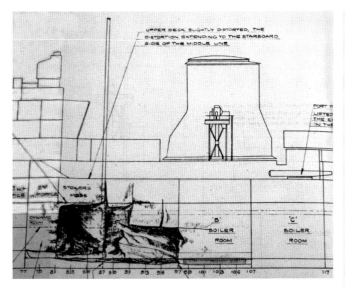

The Damage Report drawing of the torpedo hit on *Leander*. (The National Archives, Kew)

immobilised. After temporary repairs she continued at 12 knots, but her main armament and anti-aircraft fire control positions were out of action. Power was restored to 'X' and 'Y' turrets, but 'A' and 'B' turrets were worked in hand control, as were her twin 4in AA guns. The torpedo fire control was knocked out, and the port quad torpedo tubes

Damage to one of her water-tube boilers. *Leander* received temporary repairs in Auckland, then sailed for Boston, Massachusetts, for permanent repairs. The extensive damage took so long to repair that she took no further part in the war. (Photo from '*Leander*', by S D Waters in *Episodes & Studies*, vol II, War History Branch, Department of Internal Affairs, Wellington, 1950)

were actually wrenched off their pivot by the shock of the explosion and deposited upside down on the deck a short distance astern. The talk-between-ships set was smashed, as was the radar, and the gyro repeaters failed. Her casualties were seven killed, twenty-one injured, and twenty-one missing.

USS *Selfridge*

On the night of 7/8 October 1943 USS *Selfridge*, a 1850-ton destroyer of the *Porter* class, was engaged in intercepting Japanese destroyers carrying out a typical Tokyo Express mission, attempting to evacuate troops from Vella Lavella Island. At 2300 *Selfridge* engaged a group of Japanese destroyers and turned to comb torpedo tracks seen approaching from starboard. At 2306 she was hit simultaneously by two 24in Japanese torpedoes, one coming from starboard and the other from port. The entire bow of the ship was severed, and floated away down the starboard side. Her engines were undamaged, and were put full astern until she could be brought to a stop. The bulkheads aft of the extensive damage held, and *Selfridge* proceeded at 10 knots to Purvis Bay, some 120 miles away.

Here the damaged sections were cleaned up by a repair ship, and after it was determined that her stability remained adequate, she was despatched to Noumea, where a temporary bow was welded on in a floating dock, from where she proceeded to Mare Island for full repairs.

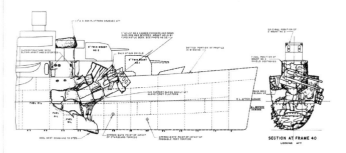

Drawing showing *Selfridge*'s completely severed bow. Her No 1 mount had disappeared, and the No 2 mount hung down over the wreckage.

HOLOCAUST IN THE PACIFIC

Once their torpedo problems had been resolved, the growing fleet of long-range modern US Navy submarines, backed by small numbers of Royal Navy and Dutch boats, began a wholesale slaughter of Japanese maritime shipping. It is estimated that by the time Japan surrendered, she had lost over 4 million tons of merchant ships and tankers.

The well-known photo taken through the periscope of the cruiser submarine USS *Nautilus*, showing the last moments of the destroyer *Yamakaze*, torpedoed and sunk by *Nautilus*, with the loss of all hands. (NHHC, photo # DP262487)

The IJN was targeted by aircraft, carrier- and land-based, when they attacked and when they holed up in their ports and bases, and by surface warships in actions in narrow waters. On the open seas, on a day-to-day basis, it was the submarines which inflicted crippling losses, and their weapon was the torpedo. Between 7 December 1941 and 15 August 1945, when the emperor broadcast his surrender speech, the IJN, as a fighting force, had virtually ceased to exist. It had taken the span of just one generation to take Japan from a backwater to dominance in the Pacific, and then back to zero, truly a 'Morning Glory' as author Stephen Howarth so aptly described it.

Submarine torpedo attacks had sunk no less than 300 Japanese warships: 1 fast battleship (*Kongo*), 4 fleet carriers (including the giant *Shinano* and the armoured-deck *Taiho*), 4 escort carriers, 8 seaplane carriers and tenders, 5 heavy cruisers and 11 light cruisers, plus 4 armed merchant cruisers (and a German raider, *Michel*). No less than 47 destroyers, 3 torpedo boats, 37 escorts, 9 sub-chasers and 3 gunboats had followed them to the bottom, most when vainly attempting to protect their convoys against American submarine attack; 18 submarines and 3 submarine depot ships had gone down to torpedo attack by their Allied opposite numbers; 19 minelayers, 15 netlayers and 24 minesweepers had been sunk by submarine torpedo, many when pressed into the role of escorts; 2 landing ships, 2 specialised fast attack transports and 2 aircraft transports were lost, plus the special turret transporter ship for the *Yamato* class.

Finally, and most significantly, 71 naval oilers and 8 naval colliers had gone to the bottom. Without fuel a fleet cannot operate, and these devastating losses effectively strangled the remaining warships. When the *Yamato* sailed on her final sacrificial mission, she carried only sufficient fuel for a one-way trip.

USS *Tautog* (SS-199)

US submarine *Tautog*'s Second World War battle flag. *Tautog* herself sank two Japanese destroyers, *Shirakumo* and *Isonami*, plus the submarine *I 28*. (NHHC, photo # 98808-KN)

Tautog's crew were extremely lucky to bring their battle flag home, because of a circular run incident. If a submerged submarine was the firer of a circular runner and time permitted, she could dive deeper to try to avoid her own torpedo, as was the case with USS *Tautog*. During her second combat patrol, to the Marshall Islands in May 1942, *Tautog* fired two Mark 14 torpedoes at *Goya Maru*. One torpedo hit, forcing the merchantman to beach herself, but the other came back in a circular run, and *Tautog* had to go deep to avoid it. She survived the war.

No such good fortune attended the two US submarines definitely known to have been sunk by their own torpedo.

USS *Tullibee* (SS-284)

On 26 March 1944, the USS *Tullibee* was accidentally sunk by a circular run of one of her own torpedoes off the Palau Islands. Of her crew seventy-nine died, and one crewman survived to report what had happened.

Tullibee departed Pearl on 5 March 1944 on her fourth war patrol. Nine days later, she called at Midway Island to top off her fuel and then proceeded to her patrol area in the Palau Islands where she was to support air strikes. On the night of 26 March she made radar contact with a small Japanese convoy of a large transport vessel, two smaller freighters and three escorts. *Tullibee* made several surface attack runs on the large transport but kept losing her in

USS *Tullibee* off Mare Island Naval Yard, 2 April 1942. (NHHC, photo # NH 98409)

rain squalls. Eventually, she got a good contact at just 3000yds (2700m) and fired two torpedoes from her bow tubes.

Two minutes later one of her own torpedoes, which had run a circular course, struck the submarine. Gunner's Mate C W Kuykendall, who had been on the bridge at the time, was knocked unconscious by the blast and thrown overboard. When he came to, the *Tullibee* had already sunk. He recalled hearing voices in the water in the dark, but after ten minutes they stopped and he was left alone. The following day he was picked up by a Japanese escort vessel and spent the rest of the war as a prisoner of war (PoW).

USS *Tang* (SS-306)

On 25 October 1944, USS *Tang* was accidentally sunk by one of her own torpedoes in the Formosa Strait. This time seventy-eight crewmen died, but nine survived to become PoWs.

For her fifth war patrol, the USS *Tang*, under the command of Richard O'Kane, left Pearl on 24 September 1944 en route to the Formosa Strait. *Tang* had an eventful patrol in the course of which she sank several ships, including an exciting encounter with two enemy vessels which came in to ram, but only succeeded in colliding with each other.

On the evening of 24 October *Tang* surfaced off Turnabout Island and commenced a surface attack on a large convoy including tankers and merchant ships

transporting aircraft as deck cargo. *Tang* fired two torpedoes from her bow tubes at each of three targets, then fired her two stern tubes at another two ships. Having reloaded two bow tubes with his last remaining torpedoes, at 0230 Commander O'Kane closed to finish off a damaged transport. The first torpedo ran straight and true, but the last torpedo broached the surface, turned left and headed back towards the submarine. *Tang* fishtailed to avoid it, but 20 seconds after firing it, the torpedo struck the boat abreast the after torpedo room.

As she sank by the stern, the nine officers and men on the bridge were left swimming, but only three were left alive by daybreak. The three were joined by an officer who had escaped from the conning tower as *Tang* sank. The survivors trapped in the sunken submarine burned confidential papers, then tried to escape to the surface. Of the thirteen men who made the attempt, only nine reached the surface, and of these only five were still alive at dawn. The final total of nine survivors, including Commander O'Kane, were picked up by a Japanese escort vessel. She had already saved many burned and injured men from *Tang*'s victims of the previous night, who vented their anger by clubbing and kicking the Americans. Fortunately, all survived as PoWs to relate their escape.

Detail from the painting of Commander Richard O'Kane on the bridge of *Tang*, by Albert K Murray. (NHHC, photo # NH 97859)

DEATH OF GIANTS I: LEYTE GULF

The fleet encounters collectively known as the Battle of Leyte Gulf – which encompassed the sinking of the *Musashi*, one of the two largest battleships ever built – included the very last surface encounter between dreadnoughts in history, and brought home the dangers of the large torpedo batteries on Japanese warships, demonstrated how a torpedo threat could be as useful as an actual attack.

American torpedoes began the action when Admiral Kurita's flagship *Atago* was torpedoed out from under him by US submarine *Darter*. He was picked up out of the sea and transferred to *Yamato*. Then USS *Dace* sank another heavy cruiser, the *Maya*, and finally *Darter* put two torpedoes into *Takao* that sent her back to Brunei. Three heavy cruisers down and more to come.

Then in the Sibuyan Sea, on 24 October 1944 US carrier air groups concentrated their attacks on the 70,000-ton *Musashi*. Despite her anti-aircraft armament of twelve 12.7cm guns and a total of no less than 130 x 25mm Hotchkiss cannons, she was unable to fight off the concentrated and co-ordinated attacks by hundreds of dive- and torpedo-bombers. For the loss of five Avenger torpedo bombers and five Helldiver dive-bombers, the *Musashi* was progressively hit by nineteen armour-piercing bombs and, more damagingly, a total of seventeen torpedoes. Counter-flooding helped reduce her list, but she trimmed seriously by the bows due to multiple torpedo hits forward of No 1 turret. Abandoned by the rest of Kurita's force, her captain tried to beach her, but with her forward turret already awash it was hopeless. He gave the order to abandon ship, in time for 1376 members of her crew of 2399 men to be rescued. From the very first torpedo hit amidships, *Musashi* had begun to take in a large amount of water and to list significantly, indicating failures in her TDS.

The next act of the drama took place in the Surigao Strait, on the night of 24/25 October 1944, where Admiral Nishimura's battleships *Fuso* and *Yamashiro*, the heavy cruiser *Mogami* and three destroyers were heading for the southern entrance to Leyte Gulf. They were ambushed by PT-boats and destroyers. *Fuso* took two torpedo hits from the destroyer salvo amidships on her starboard side, slowed and hauled out of line. She then reversed course, evidently fighting internal fires started by the torpedo explosions, as she headed away from the coming battle at slow speed.

Some time later secondary magazines started exploding, as heard by shadowing PT-boat crews, and at 0345 *Fuso* blew up in a brilliant fireball and apparently broke into two halves, which continued to drift for a considerable time, blazing furiously. Following Japanese ships identified the two halves as *Fuso* and *Yamashiro*, thinking both had been destroyed. Shortly after, more US destroyer torpedoes reached the Japanese line, sank one destroyer, left a second crippled, and blew the bow off a third, leaving Nishimura with only one undamaged destroyer.

Meanwhile, Nishimura's flagship *Yamashiro* had taken two separate torpedo hits from destroyers, one in the port quarter and one in the starboard bow. She initially slowed after each hit, but each time regained speed and carried on to her hopeless battle with the large force of battleships, cruisers and destroyers awaiting her at the mouth of the strait. After taking a third torpedo hit in her starboard engine room, and a fourth soon after in the same area, *Yamashiro* began to list, and capsized at 0419, confirmed by the fact that at that moment her blip disappeared from US radar screens.

Finally, it remains to describe the torpedo actions in the main battle, which took place when Kurita's centre force bore through the San Bernardino Strait to fall upon the invasion transports. The only surface forces in his way were the light escort carriers (CVEs) off Samar, used for air combat patrol, ground attack and anti-submarine patrols. In addition, their screen consisted of just three destroyers and four destroyer escorts. Without hesitation the captains of the destroyers *Johnston*, *Heerman* and *Hoel*, together with the DE *Samuel D Roberts*, engaged the immensely powerful Japanese force, consisting of battleships, heavy and light cruisers, and fleet destroyers. When their own torpedoes were expended, they continued to make torpedo attack feints, while all the time engaging the Japanese with rapid 5in gunfire.

The escort carrier USS *Kalinin Bay* engaged in a fire-fight with Japanese heavy cruisers, replying to their 8in salvoes with rapid fire from her single 5in stern gun. After the cruisers turned away she duelled with the large destroyers of Destroyer Squadron 10. Kept at bay by the counter-attacks of USS *Johnston*, at 0915 the Japanese destroyers launched a torpedo attack from the long range of 10,500yds (5¼ miles). As the torpedoes approached *Kalinin Bay*, they were seen to be slowing. A Grumman Avenger from CVE *St Lo* strafed and exploded two torpedoes in *Kalinin Bay*'s wake, and her own 5in gun crew deflected a third which missed astern.

A turning point came when Kurita's flagship *Yamato*, turning north to comb the tracks of six torpedoes, found them running alongside at the same speed, so she was unable to turn and come back into the battle for almost ten minutes. This loss of control added to the confusion in the mind of Kurita. The vulnerability of the Japanese cruisers' torpedo armament has already been mentioned in Part I. The damage his ships were taking from the desperate air attacks from the small escort carriers, hidden behind smoke screens, convinced him that he was facing a full-blown carrier group, and he threw in the towel, ordering his ships to break off the pursuit. The battle, to all intents and purposes, was over. And once again, the torpedo had proved itself the decisive weapon.

During their withdrawal, the Japanese were to lose one more dreadnought to torpedo attack. On the night of 21 November 1944, the *Kongo* was accompanying *Yamato* returning to Japan, when the flagship detected radar emissions from a surfaced submarine. The fleet took evasive action, but *Kongo* was struck by one torpedo from a spread launched by USS *Sealion II*, commanded by Captain Eli T Reich. *Kongo*'s commander Rear Admiral Shimazaki Toshio kept her under way to escape further submarine attack, but one by one her bulkheads gave way under the pressure of inrushing water. Inexorably she flooded, listing more and more to port. Her exhausted damage control officer committed suicide, despairing of saving his ship. The news of this personal tragedy convinced *Kongo*'s CO to stop the vessel and give the order to abandon ship. But suddenly, when her list reached 60 degrees, the forward 14in magazines erupted in a series of giant explosions, and *Kongo* plunged to the bottom with heavy loss of life.

DEATH OF GIANTS II: *SHINANO*

On the evening of 28 November 1944 the giant aircraft carrier *Shinano*, planned as the third of the *Yamato*-class super-battleships, but converted after Midway to an armoured deck support carrier for battle groups, left Yokosuka on her maiden voyage to Kure to complete fitting-out. The largest carrier built during the Second World War, she would also have the shortest life.

During her initial voyage *Shinano*'s crew became aware that they were being shadowed by an American submarine, as they picked up her radar emissions. The carrier and her escorts were capable of a much higher speed than a surfaced submarine so they continued on their way unconcerned. The submarine was USS *Archerfish*, under the command of Joseph P Enright, who doggedly pursued his prey through the night, until her continual zigzags, and a reduction in speed caused by a hot propeller shaft bearing, enabled him to get within torpedo range. Having dived, Commander Enright set his torpedoes to run at 10ft (3m), and launched six at *Shinano*.

Four hit on the starboard side, causing serious flooding. *Shinano* had sailed with many watertight doors lacking their waterproof rubber gaskets, which were to be installed at Kure. In addition, the watertight integrity of her compartmentalisation had not been able to be checked using air pressure. Piping and wires passing through bulkheads had not been backed with stuffing materials to

render them watertight, the ship's pumping arrangements were still incomplete and she was supposed to rely on portable pumps. Despite all these drawbacks, Captain Abe evidently had confidence in his massive 70,000-ton ship to absorb even four torpedo hits, as her half-sister *Musashi* had survived many more before finally sinking.

He therefore kept running at *Shinano*'s best speed, thereby causing the entry of thousands of tons of water. Attempts to control her list by counter-flooding did not work, and eventually she heeled so far that the water inlet valves on the port side were above water level and ineffective. In a last desperate bid to save the ship, Abe ordered the flooding of the port engine rooms, and called for two of his escort destroyers to tow the ship to shore. To expect two 2000-ton destroyers to move a waterlogged 70,000-ton deadweight was patently impossible, and the cables parted immediately.

When the list reached 30 degrees Abe ordered abandon ship, and when she capsized shortly afterwards, she took 1435 officers, men and civilian contractors down with her. As with her half-sister, *Shinano* had suffered severe internal disruptions from the initial torpedo explosions, meaning that like *Musashi*, the design of her TDS was inadequate.

DEATH OF GIANTS III: *YAMATO*

When in April 1945 *Musashi*'s sister ship *Yamato* was sent on her one-way mission to Okinawa, to beach herself as an artillery battery, it was inevitable that the Americans would concentrate massive air attacks to sink her. And in three concerted attacks, lasting just over an hour, this is precisely

Yamato under heavy air attack during the last sortie. (US Navy photo)

what they proceeded to do, for the loss of a handful of planes. It is estimated that it took at least six bomb and eleven torpedo hits to sink *Yamato*. As she capsized, *Yamato*'s magazines erupted in a huge mushroom cloud that was seen as far away as Kyushu. She took down with her 3055 officers and men.

The last of the super-battleships, the largest the world would ever see, and built to resist one-ton armour-piercing shells, had succumbed to the aerial torpedo hitting in her most vulnerable region, her underwater hull.

LAST OF THE HEAVYWEIGHTS: *TAIHO, HAGURO* AND *INDIANAPOLIS*

Taiho

Taiho was to be the first of a new breed of Japanese aircraft carrier. After the disastrous Battle of Midway, when four carriers had been sunk by dive-bombers, she copied the Royal Navy's philosophy when faced with superior air power, in adopting an armoured flight deck. This was 3in (76mm) thick, and the hangar deck itself was again armoured to 4.9in (125mm). She displaced 37,270 tons at full load, could accommodate up to seventy-five aircraft, and had a top speed of 33.33 knots.

Having solved, as they thought, the principal problem with their aircraft carriers, the Japanese fell foul of a more widespread problem, the lack of adequate anti-submarine escorts. So it was that the virtually brand-new *Taiho* sailed to participate in the Battle of the Philippine Sea, with high hopes. Unfortunately, at 0745 on 19 June 1944 the submarine USS *Albacore* launched six torpedoes at her. One of her pilots, Warrant Officer Sakio Komatsu, who had just taken off to participate in the second wave of attacks on the American carrier force, spotted the torpedo wakes and selflessly dived his plane onto one, which caused it to detonate. Of the remaining five torpedoes, four missed, but one hit the carrier on the starboard side just forward of the island.

The shockwave jammed her forward elevator in mid-rise, and fractured her aviation fuel tanks. She carried on operating aircraft, her crew even planking over the forward elevator with benches and tables taken from a mess deck

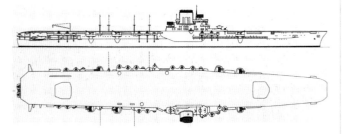

Taiho. (From Warships of the Imperial Japanese Navy 1863–1945)

to let planes pass over it, but all the time petrol fumes were invading the ship. Her damage control parties were completely inexperienced, and when finally, six and a half hours after the torpedo hit, the ventilator fans were turned on to clear the ship of the vapour, an electrical circuit caused a devastating explosion. *Taiho* lingered for almost two hours before a second huge explosion sent her to the bottom, together with 1650 officers and men. After this disaster, the giant carrier *Shinano*, also fitted with an armoured flight deck, had her aviation fuel tanks encased in a layer of concrete.

Haguro

Haguro was one of the large Japanese heavy cruisers responsible for the sinking of *De Ruyter, Java* and *Exeter* in the Battle of the Java Sea and its aftermath. She survived the debacle of Leyte Gulf, and returned to Malayan waters. On 16 May 1945 she was on a supply run to the Japanese garrison at Port Blair in the Andaman Islands in the company of the destroyer *Kamikaze* when she was intercepted just after midnight by British destroyers southwest of Penang.

Reports that two destroyer formations had been sighted in the area caused Vice Admiral Hashimoto to order the two ships to return to Singapore, but they were not to escape. In an action codenamed Operation Dukedom, the five destroyers, *Saumarez, Verulam, Venus, Vigilant* and *Virago*, of the 26th Destroyer Flotilla under the command of Captain Manley Laurence Power, tracked down the *Haguro* on radar and prepared for a flotilla torpedo attack, at a closing speed of some 60 knots. Power's torpedo officer on the bridge of *Saumarez*, Lieutenant Douglas Scobie, was drenched as one of *Haguro*'s 8in shells exploded alongside, but he wiped his eyes dry and launched all eight of *Saumarez*'s torpedoes. An 8in shell from *Haguro* passed straight through the forecastle without exploding, a second took off the top of the funnel, and a third killed two men and injured three more in her boiler room. Splinters cut away her radio aerials.

The ferocious gunnery duel between the 13,300-ton cruiser and the destroyers abruptly ended at 0115 when *Haguro* was hit by three torpedoes from *Saumarez* and *Verulam*. A British officer was heard to remark that the three gold-coloured towers of water resembled the Prince of Wales' feathers – a very appropriate comment as the wreck of HMS *Prince of Wales* lay not far off. *Venus* hit *Haguro* with one torpedo ten minutes later, and at 0127 she took two more torpedo hits from *Virago*, and went dead in the water. The destroyers were not finished, however, for *Vigilant* hit her with one torpedo

Haguro in 1945. (From *Warships of the Imperial Japanese Navy 1863–1945*)

and *Venus* a final two. *Haguro* sank at 0209, taking down with her over nine hundred officers and men, including Vice Admiral Hashimoto and Rear Admiral Sugiura.

Apart from *Saumarez*, none of the other British destroyers received any damage. For her part, *Kamikaze* was slightly damaged but escaped, returning the next day to pick up 320 survivors from *Haguro*. When *Haguro* sank, the French battleship *Richelieu* was steaming at full speed to join in the destroyer attack, but arrived just too late. The sinking of *Haguro* proved to be the last major action between surface ships in the Second World War, and likely the last ever destroyer flotilla torpedo attack.

USS *Indianapolis*

USS *Indianapolis* was one of the third class of US 'Treaty' heavy cruisers, displacing 12,775 tons full load, and capable of a top speed of 32.5 knots. After the repair of damage to her propeller shafts caused by a kamikaze off Okinawa, *Indianapolis* sailed for Tinian carrying components for the first atomic bombs. She then sailed for Leyte via Guam. Her commander, Captain Charles B McVay had asked for a destroyer as escort, since his ship had neither sonar nor hydrophones, but his request was denied. Meanwhile, the Japanese submarine *I 58* commanded by Lt Cdr Hashimoto had departed Hirao on her seventh Kaiten-launching mission. Fleet Radio Unit Pacific intercepted and decoded a Japanese Sixth Fleet radio transmission detailing the composition and patrol areas of the Tamon group of Kaiten carriers, and alerted CINCPAC. Because the intercept was classified as falling under the ULTRA programme, it was not passed on to American units in the area.

By 27 July 1945 Hashimoto had reached his patrol area on the shipping route between Guam and Leyte. On 29 July, *Indianapolis* was 250 miles north of Palau, zigzagging at 17 knots in decreasing visibility. At 2305 *I 58* surfaced and sighted *Indianapolis*, which Lt Cdr Hashimoto identified as an *Idaho*-class battleship. She was proceeding at 12 knots, and was no longer zigzagging. It took him twenty minutes to reach a suitable firing position for a conventional submerged torpedo attack, but in case he missed he put two of his four remaining Kaiten pilots on alert.

There was no need, for after firing six Type 95 torpedoes at a range of 1650yds (1500m), at 2335 he observed three hits on the cruiser's starboard side, closely grouped abreast the two forward turrets. *Indianapolis* came to a stop and began to list to starboard. Hashimoto dived to reload two forward tubes, but when he resurfaced thirty minutes later, *Indianapolis* had already capsized and sunk. He departed at high speed on the surface, later reporting that he had sunk an *Idaho*-class battleship. His radio report was also intercepted by the Americans and decoded, but because no US battleships were due in the area, his report was ignored.

Indianapolis's crew were unable to send out a Mayday because she had lost power. Of her crew of 1196, many were killed by the torpedo explosions or went down with the ship, but some nine hundred men were left in the water. Because Lt Cdr Hashimoto's report had been disregarded, it was 84 hours before *Indianapolis* was reported overdue, and a search was begun to find survivors. By the time help arrived, there were only 316 men, including her captain, still left alive. Many of those who died had succumbed to shark attack.

USS *Indianapolis* in July 1945. (Photo courtesy of Floating Drydock)

CHAPTER 24

Post-Second World War

HMS *KEMPENFELT*

The *Sydney Morning Herald* of 30 November 1945 reported an incident which had occurred the day previously. A torpedo air flask exploded on the destroyer HMS *Kempenfelt*, the 'W'-class leader, while she was moored alongside depot ship HMS *Tyne* at Kirribilli Point, Sydney. The torpedo body was driven into the radar room and penetrated the funnel. The warhead exited overboard, carrying away an aerial on HMS *Wager* and debris fell on HMS *Whirlwind*. A fire sprang up and spread to the awnings, but it was quickly extinguished. Only slight damage was caused to the *Kempenfelt* but one rating, named in the newspaper report as Able Seaman D J Pullin, was seriously injured, and several others suffered from shock and slight burns.

A photo retrieved from the *Sydney Morning Herald*, bearing the caption: 'A view showing portion of the torpedo which exploded and punctured four bulkheads, the radar room and the funnel, on board the destroyer HMS *Kempenfelt* in Sydney harbour yesterday.' (Courtesy of Scotia Ashley of the National Library of Australia)

LAST OF THE DAM BUSTERS

The Hwachon Dam in South Korea is a concrete hydroelectric dam built by the Japanese on the North Han River. The Han River Hydroelectric Company began construction in July 1939 and the dam was completed in October 1944. A gravity dam 435m (1427ft) long, with a hydraulic head of 74.5m (244ft), fed from a catchment reservoir with a surface area of almost 39 square kilometres (15 square miles), its turbines are rated at 108MW.

During the Korean War, control of the dam and its associated power station were key objectives for both sides. The United Nations forces were concerned that the North Koreans would make tactical use of the dam, disrupting military operations downstream by the simple expedient of releasing spillwater through the dam's sixteen sluice gates, leading to major flooding. Alternatively, the Chinese could try to cut the flow of water completely, enabling their troops to more easily ford the river and attack the UN forces. It was therefore felt vital to either capture the dam or damage its sluice gates. Destroying the dam itself was not considered an option, since this would, in fact, cause the flooding on a vast scale which the UN forces wished to avoid.

Already, at midnight on 8 April 1951, the Chinese Communist forces had opened crest spillways and released large quantities of water. The level of the Han River was raised by 4ft (1.22m), sweeping away one UN military bridge and forcing the dismantling of a second bridge to avoid its destruction. Accordingly, on 9 April the 7th Cavalry and the 4th Ranger Company were tasked with taking the dam and its environments. The 7th Cavalry advanced to within half a mile of the dam by 10 April, but were halted by two dug-in companies of Chinese troops. The next day they renewed the attack, while the Rangers and other troops tried to cross the reservoir in an amphibious assault. This latter effort made slow progress, not surprisingly, since only nine assault boats arrived, and only four of these had motors. As only one 155mm howitzer could actually range the dam, the attack was called off.

The onus for neutralising the spill gates shifted to American aviators. B-29 bombers tried to hit the dam but failed. Navy Skyraiders attacked with 2000lb (900kg) bombs and 11.5in Tiny Tim rockets, but again they failed. The steel sluice gates were 20ft tall by 40ft wide (6.1m x 12.2m), situated on the top of the dam beneath reinforced concrete frames. They were a small target which was difficult to hit.

Searching around for a solution, Skyraider pilots flying from the carrier USS *Princeton* (CV-37) wondered if they could torpedo the sluice gates. After all, the *officially-stated* aim of the Japanese aircraft carrier submarines of the *I 400* class and their Aichi Seiran attack aircraft had been to block the Panama Canal by torpedoing the lock gates. It was recalled that *Princeton* carried several Mark 13 aerial torpedoes of the type used in the Pacific War, but there was no one on board who had ever tried to attach one to an aircraft. Digging through instruction manuals, the ordnance handlers were surprised to discover that the Douglas AS-4 Skyraider, nicknamed the 'flying dump truck' (many years before it earned its better-known nickname of 'SPAD' in Vietnam) actually had the connections to both carry and launch the Mark 13.

A Mark 13 torpedo slung from a Skyraider on the *Princeton*, showing the plywood nose protector and the plywood box around the tail rudders and propeller. (US Navy photo)

Luckily, three of the pilots aboard *Princeton* had actually practised dropping torpedoes years earlier, and they set to initiating five more pilots from Attack Squadron VA-195 in the special techniques involved. The attack by the eight torpedo planes, escorted by twelve Corsair fighters for AA suppression, was launched on 1 May 1951. Their aim was to destroy at least two of the sluice gates, blowing holes in the top of the dam which would allow a steady flow of water to pass.

A torpedo-armed Skyraider en route to the dam. The impressive bulk of the Skyraider makes the Mark 13 appear quite small. (US Navy photo)

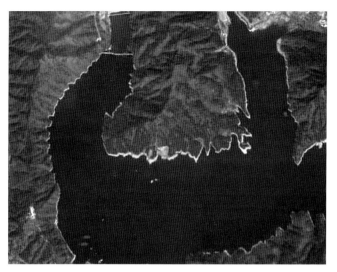

Hwachon Dam at top left, showing the tight turns the Skyraider pilots had to make to line up on the dam. Several of the mountain peaks surrounding the reservoir reached up as high as 4000ft (1200m). (From Google Earth)

Arriving over the target area, the Skyraiders broke into two-plane sections and began their runs. They intended to drop their torpedoes at a speed of 160 knots just 100ft (30m) above the surface of the reservoir. Six of the eight torpedoes struck on or near sluice gates. One of these was destroyed and a second one damaged. The dam was breached at both extremities, and the mission was deemed a success. Attack Squadron VA-195 took on the official title of 'The Dam Busters'. The dam, which was later captured by UN Forces, remains in use today.

'The Last of the Dam Busters', the attack on the Hwachon Dam, Korea. (Painting courtesy of Marc Stewart)

HM SUBMARINE *SIDON*

The explosion of an air flask, or even the open-air explosion of a warhead on deck, can cause serious damage, but is unlikely to lead directly to the loss of a large vessel such as a cruiser – unless an uncontrollable fire results. On the other hand, submarines are vulnerable to explosion of a torpedo mechanism inside a loaded tube, especially when the torpedo fuel is highly volatile hydrogen peroxide.

HMS *Sidon* was an 'S'-class submarine displacing 990 tons submerged, commissioned in November 1944. On 16 June 1955 *Sidon* was alongside her depot ship HMS *Maidstone* in Portland. Her crew were preparing to test fire two 21in Mark 12 torpedoes, codenamed 'Fancy', for testing. Design of the Mark 12's power plant was based on Second World War German technology, using high test hydrogen peroxide (HTP) as fuel. At 1825, the Mark 12 loaded in *Sidon*'s No 3 tube suffered a violent explosion, which ruptured the torpedo body, burst the tube and disrupted the two forward watertight bulkheads. *Sidon* listed to starboard and began to sink by the bows.

Twelve crewmen were killed in the explosion and seven seriously injured, but Lt Cdr Verry ordered the evacuation of the remainder of her crew via the aft and engine room escape hatches. Unfortunately, the medical officer on HMS *Maidstone*, Temporary Surgeon Lieutenant Rhodes, who had descended into the sinking submarine wearing a breathing apparatus he had not been trained to use, was overcome by the toxic fumes and also died.

The investigation determined that the engine of the Mark 12 had run hot, having accidentally started while still in the tube. Out of its water environment, it had over-speeded, creating high pressure in its fuel system. The HTP fuel line burst, spraying peroxide onto internal copper fittings, which caused it to decompose into oxygen and steam. The warhead itself had not exploded, but the

expanding gases trapped in the torpedo body had burst it, sinking the submarine.

HMS *Sidon* was salvaged and towed to Chesil Beach, where the bodies of the victims were recovered. Never returned to service, two years after the accident she was scuttled to serve as a target for Asdic. Her wreck lies 34m (111ft) below the surface in Lyme Bay.

USS *LIBERTY*

On 8 June 1967, during the Seven Day War between Israel and her Arab neighbours, the USS *Liberty* was attacked by Israeli jet fighters then struck by a torpedo. *Liberty* (AGTR-5) was a wartime 'Victory' type standard ship converted to an auxiliary technical research ship for the US Navy, and began deployment in this role in 1965. Her duties included electronic eavesdropping of radio and radar signals.

Before the war started, the USS *Liberty* was ordered to the north coast of Sinai to collect signal intelligence. When fighting broke out on 5 June 1967, a signal was sent to the *Liberty* ordering her to stay well clear of both the Egyptian and Israeli coasts, but due to lengthy message routing, the ship did not receive the warning in time. On 8 June *Liberty*, flying a large American flag, and with her hull marking GTR-5 clearly visible, was over-flown by several Israeli aircraft, ostensibly on anti-submarine patrols.

At 1124 Israeli High Command received a report that Arish was being shelled from the sea, and three torpedo boats were despatched to the area. Their commanding officer radioed that he was tracking an unidentified ship 14 miles off the coast, and that her speed was calculated at between 28 and 30 knots. Despite the fact that the *Liberty* was moving at around 5 knots at the time, and carried no armament larger than .50cal machine guns, she was identified as the attacking vessel.

Based on this, two Israeli Mirage fighters carried out an attack on the *Liberty* with 30mm cannon and rockets. The unprepared vessel was badly damaged, eight crewmen were killed and seventy-five wounded, including her captain. She radioed for help, and the aircraft carrier USS *America* launched eight aircraft. Because a strategic exercise had been underway, they were still armed with nuclear weapons, and as Vice Admiral Martin feared the attackers might be Russian, he recalled the aircraft in order to avoid a possible nuclear conflict.

Meanwhile, the three torpedo boats closed with the *Liberty*, still unsure of her identity. Crewmen manning two of her .50cal machine guns briefly opened fire and bracketed one of the torpedo boats, which returned the fire with cannon and machine guns, and launched five

A photo of *Sidon* being raised a week after the disaster. This was one of a series of shots of the lifting operation taken with a tiny pocket Brownie camera, hence the indistinct nature of the photo. (Courtesy of the Dorset Branch of the Submariners Association)

torpedoes. *Liberty* managed to avoid four but the fifth hit the ship on the starboard side just forward of the bridge, blowing a 40ft wide (12m) hole in the cargo hold which had been converted as the main intelligence-gathering station; twenty-five crewmen were killed and many wounded, but the ship remained afloat.

The Israeli boats continued to strafe the *Liberty*, until a life raft thrown overboard from the stricken ship was seen to bear US Navy markings. At this point the torpedo boats ceased fire. Eight aircraft launched from the USS *Saratoga* were recalled, and the Israelis offered help to the survivors, which was refused. The *Liberty* managed to leave the area under her own power and, escorted by several warships, she made for Malta, where temporary repairs enabled her to return to the United States. The cost of repairs to the old ship was considered prohibitive, and she was never repaired, being scrapped in 1973.

The Israeli government apologised to the United States for what it claimed was a case of mistaken identity. The USA conducted several inquiries into the attack, the final one in 1981. Despite the contrary findings of all the inquiries, conspiracy theories have long dogged the episode. In 2012 the matter flared up again, following the

allegations made by a crew member of the US submarine *Amberjack* that it was his submarine which had fired the torpedo which struck the *Liberty*. Although at first sight a surprising allegation, it becomes possible when we now know that all US intelligence-gathering ships were accompanied by a submerged submarine. The submarine commander's orders were that if it looked likely the intelligence-gathering equipment on board was in danger of being seized, then he was to torpedo and sink the ship. This theory, however, then raises the question of why a similar solution was not applied during the *Pueblo* incident the following year – perhaps because of the secret high-level outcry over the *Liberty* torpedoing.

INS *KHUKRI*

Although not a major naval battle, the encounter between the Pakistani navy submarine *Hangor* and the INS frigate *Khukri* was highly significant. It was the first time since the end of the Second World War that a submarine had torpedoed and sunk an enemy ship. Moreover, the small modern diesel-electric boat had taken on two specialised anti-submarine frigates and torpedoed one before either of the Indian vessels knew she was in the vicinity.

INS *Khukri* (F45) was one of three Type 14 anti-submarine frigates of the Royal Navy *Blackwood* class bought by the Indian navy. Laid down in 1955, she was commissioned in 1958. The *Khukri* was 310ft (94m) long and displaced 1200 tons. Her single-shaft geared steam turbine propelled her at up to 28 knots. The RN *Blackwood* class was an experiment to see if a ship half the size of a modern frigate, and suitable for mass production in time of war, could still be an efficient escort vessel. Because of their small size they were specialised, indeed over-specialised, in the anti-submarine role. Their only surface armament was three single 40mm Bofors. They did, however, carry a full sonar outfit and two Limbo anti-submarine mortars. The PNS *Hangor* ('shark') was a French-built diesel-electric submarine of the *Daphné* class. Launched in 1968, she commissioned in 1970. She was 57.75m long (189ft 6in), displaced 1038 tons submerged,

The torpedo damage to *Liberty*'s hull, seen in dry dock in Malta where she was towed for emergency repairs. (NSA photo)

A Type 14 AS frigate in service with the Royal Navy. INS *Khukri* was identical apart from her pennant number, F45.

A French-built *Daphné*-class diesel-electric submarine of the same type as PNS *Hangor*. (Painting courtesy of Captain (retd) Tim Johnson of the South African Navy)

could reach 15 knots underwater, and was armed with twelve 21in torpedo tubes (eight bow, four external stern).

During the Indo-Pakistani War of 1971, the two vessels would come into fatal contact. On the night of 2/3 December 1971 the *Hangor* radioed in a report of an Indian squadron off Bombay. The Indian navy intercepted the message, and despatched two anti-submarine frigates, *Khukri* and *Kirpan*, to search the area for the suspected submarine. On 9 December *Hangor* made sonar contact with the two frigates, and began stalking them. The *Khukri* and *Kirpan* remained unaware of the presence of the submarine, and carried out a slow-speed sonar search on a steady course. *Hangor* revealed her presence by firing her first torpedo at the *Kirpan*, but it was detected on the ship's sonar and she evaded it at full speed. Her sister-ship then came in for an attack on the *Hangor*, but the submarine scored first, hitting *Khukri*, which sank in two minutes with heavy loss of life. *Hangor* avoided a depth-charge counter-attack by *Kirpan*, whose Limbo mortars had malfunctioned, and fired a third torpedo at the frigate. *Kirpan* again detected the approaching torpedo and exited the scene at full speed.

Hangor was decommissioned in 2006 and today serves as a museum ship. *Khukri*'s crew are remembered on a monument at Diu, which consists of a large model of the lost ship inside a glass case, on a hill overlooking the sea.

Navies everywhere studied this incident, and came to the conclusion that the only sure way to conduct anti-submarine operations in future was for surface vessels to work in conjunction with aircraft, or by using a hunter-killer submarine. Subsequently, the Royal Navy shed all of its smaller escort vessels, which were incapable of handling an A/S helicopter.

GENERAL BELGRANO

On 2 May 1982 the British nuclear attack submarine HMS *Conqueror* launched three torpedoes at the Argentinian cruiser ARA *General Belgrano*. The cruiser was a survivor of the Japanese attack on Pearl Harbor. Undamaged during the torpedo and bombing attacks, she had been ordered to sortie to hunt for the Japanese carrier force. Twice lucky, she was soon recalled.

On 7 December 1941 cruiser USS *Phoenix* passes the blazing wrecks of Battleship Row. (NHHC, photo # NH 50766)

Belgrano had been launched in 1935 as the USS *Phoenix*, a *Brooklyn*-class cruiser, designed to counter the Japanese *Mogami* class which originally carried fifteen 6in guns. The same armament, in five triple turrets, was built into the *Brooklyn*s. *Phoenix*, completed in 1938, displaced 12,207 tons at full load, was protected by an armour belt up to $5^5/_8$in (133mm) thick, and could reach a top speed, when new, of $32^1/_2$ knots. In April 1951 she was sold to Argentina and renamed the *17 de Octubre* after a significant date in the rise of President Peron. After Peron's fall, in 1956 she was again renamed, this time as *General Belgrano*, after the liberator of Argentina.

At the time of the Argentine invasion of the Falkland Islands in 1982, the 42-year-old cruiser was on patrol to the south of the Falklands, accompanied by two destroyers, the *Hippolite Bouchard* and *Piedrabuena*. The destroyers were armed with Exocet anti-ship missiles. The British thought the *Belgrano* carried them as well, but in

2000 Captain Nestor Cenci, who at the time had been the cruiser's supply officer, revealed that the ship's carpenters had fabricated fake Exocet launchers out of wood to fool the British. This subterfuge backfired in a tragic way.

When Margaret Thatcher's government received the news from the shadowing HMS *Conqueror* that the *Belgrano*'s battle group were manoeuvring not far from the British-declared exclusion zone around the islands, they feared that at any moment they could turn north and attack the British Task Force engaged in the reconquest of the Falklands. The Exocet missiles they thought the *Belgrano* carried, in addition to her heavy armament of fifteen 6in guns, would be a devastating weapon against the transports and aircraft carriers.

Accordingly, on the afternoon of 2 May the *Conqueror*'s commanding officer, Commander Chris Wreford-Brown, received permission to attack and sink the *Belgrano*. *Conqueror* was armed with the wire-guided Mark 24 Tigerfish torpedoes which had entered service just two years earlier, but as he had little confidence in them, Wreford-Brown decided to launch three of the older, unguided Mark VIII★★ torpedoes. The Mark VIII had originally been designed way back in 1925, and the Mark VIII★★ was the principal torpedo used by the Submarine Service in the Second World War. The latest Mod 4 versions carried an 805lb (365kg) charge of torpex over 7000yds (6400m) at up to 41 knots.

Launched at 1557, the first torpedo struck the cruiser to port aft, exploding in an engine room. The blast vented upwards through two mess areas and a recreation area, killing more than two hundred crew members. The second torpedo arrived soon afterwards and blew off the bows, but the remaining forward watertight bulkhead held. The *Belgrano* lost all power and drifted to a stop. Her electrical systems were knocked out so no distress signal could be sent. With no power to the pumps the influx of water could not be countered, and the ship took on a list to port.

A dramatic photo taken by one of the survivors aboard his life raft.

After twenty minutes, when the list reached 30 degrees, Captain Bonzo ordered 'abandon ship', and the survivors, many burned or injured by the aft torpedo hit, scrambled into life rafts in a rising sea.

Meanwhile, the *Belgrano*'s two destroyers, unaware of her sinking, carried on their way. The crew of ARA *Hippolite Bouchard* felt an impact on the hull, which was suspected to be a torpedo that failed to explode. Later, in dry dock, it was found she had four 5in-long (127mm) cracks in her hull, and it was thought the third torpedo had actually exploded, but at some distance from the hull. By this time it was dark, and in the storm conditions the *Belgrano*'s survivors were not noticed.

For her part, HMS *Conqueror* went deep, and her crew thought they were being depth-charged, as they heard muffled underwater explosions. The commander of *Hippolite Bouchard*, Captain Washington Barcena, confirmed in 2000 that in fact they had dropped no depth charges, and that the noises heard by *Conqueror*'s crew were probably the *Belgrano*'s boilers exploding. *Conqueror* spent the next several days avoiding the Argentinian Air Force's attempts to find her.

Out of the 1093 crew aboard the *Belgrano* at the time she was torpedoed, it is thought that 275 died in the initial explosion aft. Of the survivors, another forty-eight men died either in the life rafts or of their wounds after being rescued. They had been left adrift for 36 hours after the sinking, and in the freezing conditions those on the overcrowded life rafts had survived only because of huddling together; rafts with only a handful of survivors were found with the occupants frozen to death.

Belgrano would probably have survived losing her bow, as had many other US Navy cruisers during the Pacific War. The hit aft was crucial, denying her electrical power for pumps and lighting, the classic prelude to a breakdown of effective damage control measures. That the veteran vessel had remained afloat for so long was commendable, and led to many of her crew surviving.

The Argentinian response was immediate and dramatic. A naval Super Etendard launched an attack on the British destroyer HMS *Sheffield* with an Exocet missile. The ship's computer detected the incoming missile but recognised it as 'friendly', which gave insufficient time for the crew to react. The resulting missile impact killed twenty men and disabled the ship, which later sank under tow.

KURSK

K-141 *Kursk* was a Project 949A nuclear attack submarine given the NATO codename of 'Oscar II'. Displacing some 16,000 tons, she was 154m long (505ft), and her two

A US Navy photo of an 'Oscar'-class submarine, showing the bulge in the top of the fin which is believed to house an escape capsule.

nuclear reactors gave her a submerged top speed of 32 knots. Her outer hull of stainless steel 8.5mm (0.33in) thick was distanced 2m (6ft 7in) from the inner pressure hull, which was 50.8mm (2in) thick. *Kursk* was armed with Granit missiles, and had four 21in and two 26in torpedo tubes, all mounted in the bow. Commissioned in December 1994, she joined the Russian navy's northern fleet. At the beginning of August 2000, *Kursk* sortied to join three other attack submarines, the flagship *Pyotr Velikiy* and several smaller ships, as part of a summer exercise, in which she was scheduled to fire practice torpedoes at *Pyotr Velikiy*.

At 1128 on 12 August 2000, an explosion occurred on board *Kursk*, which seismographic detectors recorded as 2.2 on the Richter scale, estimated as a blast equivalent to up to 250kg (550lbs) of TNT. Just over two minutes later, a second explosion was detected, measuring between 3.5 and 4.4 on the Richter scale, the equivalent of up to 7 tons

A painting by Dennis Andrews showing Dutch salvors examining the wreck.

of TNT. The *Kursk* sank to the bottom, 135km off Severomorsk, at a depth of 108m (354ft).

Alerted by the seismographic readings, British and Norwegian rescue teams offered their assistance, which the Russians declined. The Russian Admiralty assumed that the powerful explosions had killed the entire crew of 118 officers and men. When the wreck of the *Kursk* was recovered by Dutch salvors Mammoet and Smit International, the harrowing discovery was made of notes written by one of twenty-three survivors of the explosions, who had remained alive in the furthest aft compartment 9, for some time after the sinking.

The investigation in 2002 concluded that the disaster had been caused by the explosion of a HTP-fuelled Type 65-76 Kit torpedo, which had caused a major fire in the torpedo compartment, leading to the explosion of up to an additional seven torpedoes.

ROK *CHEONAN*

The heavily armed 1200-ton corvette *Cheonan* of the Republic of Korea's navy sank on 26 March 2010 in waters disputed by both North and South Korea. Ever since the armistice which ended the fighting on the Korean Peninsula on 27 July 1953, technically the two Koreas have remained at war, as no peace agreement has ever been signed between the two. Although on land the two sides are rigidly separated by the Demilitarised Zone, no such division operates at sea. In particular the North claims certain rich fishing grounds to the south of the dividing line.

There have been several naval confrontations, collectively known as the 'crab wars', including the First Battle of Yeonpyeong on 15 June 1999, when the corvette *Cheonan* was slightly damaged and a North Korean MTB was sunk, and the Second Battle of Yeonpyeong a fortnight later, when a North Korean patrol boat was badly shot up but towed away, and a South Korean patrol boat was sunk.

On 26 March 2010 the *Cheonan* was on patrol about one nautical mile off the southwest coast of Baengnyeong Island in the Yellow Sea. The vessel was well within the waters South Korea claims as its own, a claim disputed by the North. At around 2120 an explosion occurred near the stern of the ship, which broke in two. The severed stern part sank within five minutes and the bow some time later. From the crew of 104 officers and men, fifty-eight were rescued by South Korean ships.

South Korea called in foreign experts to help them establish the cause of the sinking, including representatives from Canada, Britain, Sweden and Australia. Just one day after the salvage of the bow section, South Korea's defence

The stern of the ship had sunk and come to rest on its port side in 45m (150ft) of water. The upturned bow section came to rest in 20m (66ft) of water some distance away, with part of the hull visible above water. Twenty days after the sinking, the stern section was lifted by a floating crane and placed on a barge to be transported to Pyongtaek naval base. Nine days later the bow section was also recovered by the same method.

South Korean and American naval officers inspecting the sections of the *Cheonan* at Pyeongtaek on 19 September 2013.

minister announced that the most likely cause of the sinking was a torpedo explosion. On 20 May an international commission presented its findings, stating that the *Cheonan* had been sunk by a North Korean CHT-02D torpedo, parts of which were claimed to have been dredged up at the scene of the sinking. A final report concluded that the *Cheonan* was struck by a torpedo with a warhead equivalent to 250kg (550lbs) of TNT which exploded 3m (9.8ft) to port of the centre of the gas turbine room at a depth of between 6 and 9m (20–30ft).

The North Korean government at all stages continued to deny involvement. In particular, its Central News Agency asserted among other points that it was unbelievable that a part of a torpedo doing so much

Parts of a North Korean torpedo claimed to have been discovered at the wreck site.

damage to a ship would survive. They had obviously not read the Royal Navy divers' report on their findings at the wreck of HMS *Royal Oak* in 1939, when a part of one of the German G7e torpedoes was recovered.

CONCLUSION

In accepting the commission to compile this encyclopedia, I thought I had a reasonable knowledge of the torpedo. As my research progressed, I discovered that previously I had only scratched the surface of this multi-faceted weapon system. On consideration, I would suggest that the story of the torpedo can be summed up in three separate phases.

Firstly, there was the Mechanical Age of the Torpedo, when assorted inventors and engineers thought of an idea and pursued it tirelessly, to conceive, modify and finally bring the torpedo to a state of mechanical perfection. It then entered its second phase, the Age of Torpedo Warfare, when the weapon rose to threaten domination of naval operations, a threat which remains valid in the twenty-first century. The third phase began during the Second World War, and is still with us today, namely the Electronic Age of the Torpedo.

Possibly more development effort and money are today being expended on the torpedo and on anti-torpedo defence than at any other time in its history. The very real threat to all surface ships, and the free movement of goods and supplies – to say nothing of the deployment of armed forces – all around the world, requires that every effort is made to defend against the modern torpedo. Luckily, to date no major conflict has erupted where the powers of defence have been realistically tested against the powers of offence. But the ease with which a supposed North Korean torpedo blew in half and sank a modern anti-submarine corvette involved in an ASW exercise, points to the fact that attacker will always hold the advantage over the defender in this deadly game of cat and mouse.

Bibliography

Admiralty Reports of World War II, 'HMS *Khartoum* – Loss due to defective torpedo air vessel, 23rd June 1940', transcribed by Don Kindell, <http://www.naval-history.net/xDKWDa-KhartoumLoss.htm>

————, 'The Admiralty's appreciation of the German U-Boat force, June 1944' <www.uboatarchive.net/BritishReports.htm>

Alden, John D, *American Steel Navy* (Naval Institute Press, 1972)

Arndt, Rob, 'Ladungsschnellboot Linse (Lentil) 1944', <http://strangevehicles.greyfalcon.us/Ladungsschnellboot%20Linse.htm>

Bagnasco, Erminio, *Submarines of World War Two* (Arms & Armour Press, 1977)

Ballard, Robert D, *The Discovery of the Bismarck* (Hodder and Stoughton, 1990)

————, *The Lost Ships of Guadalcanal* (Weidenfeld & Nicolson, 1993)

————, *Exploring the Lusitania* (Weidenfeld & Nicolson, 1995)

Bathe, B W, *British Warships 1845–1945* (HMSO, 1970)

Beanse, Alec, *The Brennan Torpedo* (Victorian Forts and Artillery, 2012)

Braun, Theodor, 'Die kindheit des fünfundfiebzigjährigen Torpedos', *Marine-Rundschau* (November 1935)

Breyer, Siegfried, *Battleships and Battlecruisers 1905–1970* (Macdonald and Jane's, 1979)

Branfill-Cook, Roger, *Moment of Destiny* (2nd edn E-book, 2012)

————, *X.1: The Royal Navy's Mystery Submarine* (Seaforth, 2013)

Brown, D K, *Warrior to Dreadnought* (Caxton, 2003)

————, *The Grand Fleet* (Caxton, 2003)

Budzbon, Przemyslaw, 'G5 Class MTBs', *Warship*, No 8 (Conway Maritime Press, 1978)

Bureau of Ordnance, Department of the Navy, *The Whitehead Torpedo USN 45c/M X 3.55m Mark I, Mark II, Mark III and 45c/M X 5m Mark I* (Naval Torpedo Station, 1898)

————, *The Schwartzkopff Torpedo USN* (Naval Torpedo Station, 1903)

————, *21-inch Submerged Torpedo Tubes* (Washington, June 1944)

————, *Torpedo Data Computer Mark 3, Mods 5 To 12 Inclusive* (June 1944)

————, *Torpedo Control Equipment, Torpedo Director Mark 27* (Washington, February 1947)

————, *21-inch Above Water Torpedo Tubes Mark 14 and Mods and Mark 15 and Mods, Description, Operation, and Maintenance* (Washington, November 1955)

Burt, R A, *British Battleships 1919–1939* (Arms & Armour Press, 1993)

Caruana, J, 'Decima Flotilla Decimated', *Warship International*, No 2 (1991)

Chinn, George M, *The Machine Gun*, vol 1 (reprint, Edwards Brothers, 1951)

Commander Destroyers Pacific Fleet, *Destroyer Torpedo Attack Instructions (Tentative)*, Destroyer Tactical Bulletin No 4–43

Compton-Hall, Richard, *Submarine Boats: The Beginnings of Underwater Warfare* (Conway Maritime Press, 1983)

————, *Submarine Warfare: Monsters and Midgets* (Blandford, 1985)

————, *Submarines at War 1914–1918* (Periscope Publishing, 2004)

Czarnecki, Joseph, 'Were the Best Good Enough? The Performance of Japanese Surface Forces in Torpedo Attack versus the expectations of the Decisive Battle Strategy', <http://www.navweaps.com/index_tech/tech-067.htm>

————, 'Torpedo Defense Systems of World War II' (2001), <http://www.navweaps.com/index_tech/tech-047.htm>

Doma-Mikó, István, *Inter Japán Magazin* (2013), <http://inter-japanmagazin.com/a-japan-kulonleges-tamado-alakulat/>

Dropsy, Christian, *Les Fortifications de Metz et Thionville* (Brussels, 1995)

Fock, Harald, *Z-Vor! Destroyers and Torpedo Boats 1914–1939* (Koehler, 2001)

Forester, C S, *The Man in the Yellow Raft* (Michael Joseph, 1969)

Friedman, Norman, 'Current and Future Torpedoes', in *Seaforth World Naval Review 2014*, ed Conrad Waters (Seaforth, 2013)

Friedman, Norman, Arthur D Baker III, Arnold S Lott and Robert F Sumrall, *Ship's Data # 3: USS Arizona (BB 39)* (Leeward Publications, 1978)

Fulton, Robert, *Torpedo War and Submarine Explosions* (William Elliot, New York, 1810; reprinted by William Abbatt in Extra No 35 of *The Magazine of History with Notes and Queries*, 1914)

Gardiner, Robert, and David Lyon, *The Campaign of Trafalgar 1803–1805* (Chatham, 1997)

Garze, William H, Jnr, Kevin V Denlay, and Robert O Dulin, Jnr, 'Death of a Battleship, A Re-analysis of the Tragic Loss of HMS *Prince of Wales*', <http://www.sname.org/communities1/resources/viewtechnicalpaper/?DocumentKey=33ea44bc-2156-4808-bae2-3303e0995ef9>

Gay, Franco, *Navi Italiane nella 2e Guerra Mondiale 4/I Incrociatori Pesanti Classe Trento* (Edizioni Bizzarri, 1975)

Gray, Edwyn, *A Damned Un-English Weapon* (New English Library, 1973)

————, *The Devil's Device* (Naval Institute Press, 1991)

————, *19th Century Torpedoes and Their Inventors* (Naval

Institute Press, 2004)

Green, William, and Gordon Swanborough, *Flying Colours* (Salamander, 1981)

Greger, René, *The Russian Fleet 1914–1917* (Ian Allan, 1972)

Grusonwerk, *Expériences de Tir, Rapport No 10, 22–27 septembre 1890, Magdeburg-Buckau* (Walter Ochs & Co, 1890)

Hackmann, Willem, *Seek & Strike* (HMSO, 1984)

Hackett, Robert D, and Sander Kingsepp, 'Shinyo! Battle Histories of Japan's Explosive Motorboats', <http://www.combinedfleet.com/ShinyoEMB.htm>

————, 'Sensuikan! HIJMS Submarine I-58: Tabular Record of Movement', <http://www.combinedfleet.com/I-58.htm>

Hansen, Hans Jürgen, *The Ships of the German Fleets 1848–1945* (Hamlyn, 1974)

Harvey, Frederick, *Instructions for the Management of Harvey's Sea Torpedo* (London, 1871)

Hogg, Ian, and John Batchelor, *Naval Gun* (Blandford, 1978)

Hovdet, Håvard, *Torpedo G7a Drawings*, <www.uboatarchive.net/G7A-Plans.htm>

Hovgaard, William, *Modern History of Warships* (Conway Maritime Press, 1978)

Howarth, Stephen, *Morning Glory* (Hamish Hamilton, 1983)

Jentschura, Hansgeorg, Dieter Jung, and Peter Mickel, *Warships of the Imperial Japanese Navy 1869–1945* (Arms & Armour Press, 1986)

Kennedy, Ludovic, *Pursuit, The Sinking of the Bismarck* (William Collins, 1974)

Kirby, G J, 'Torpedo History Articles', Parts 1 to 3, *JRNSS*, vol 27, nos 1 & 2 (1972)

Le Fleming, H, *Warships of World War 1, No 4 – Miscellaneous* (London, Ian Allan, nd)

Macintyre, Donald, *Narvik* (Pan, 1971)

Mearns, David, and Rob White, *Hood and Bismarck* (Channel 4 Books, 2001)

Milford, Frederick J, 'US Navy Torpedoes', *The Submarine Review* (The Naval Submarine League, Annadale, April 1996, October 1996, January 1997, October 1997)

Nordenfelt, Thorsten, *The Nordenfelt Machine Guns Described in Detail* (1884, reprint by The Naval and Military Press)

Northcott, Maurice, *Hood: Design and Construction* (Bivouac Books, 1975)

Nottelmann, Dirk, *Die Brandenburg-Klasse* (Mittler, 2002)

Okun, Nathan, *The Effects of Underwater Explosions* (1999), <http://www.navweaps.com/index_tech/tech-026.htm>

Osman, Yusuf, 'On the Trail of the Elusive Admiral, Admiral Sir Henry Felix Woods Pasha, (KCVO, Grand Cordon of Mecidiye and Osmaniye and Knight of the Saxe-Coburg Order)', <http://levantineheritage.com/testi39.htm>

Paloczi-Horvath, George, *From Monitor to Missile Boat* (Conway Maritime Press, 1996)

Pargeter, C J, *Hipper-Class Heavy Cruisers* (Ian Allan, 1982)

Parkes, Oscar: *British Battleships, A History of Design, Construction and Armament, 1860–1950* (Leo Cooper, 1990)

Pearl Harbor Navy Yard, 'USS *Nevada* Torpedo and Bomb Damage', Record Group 181, Pearl Harbor Navy Yard General Correspondence Files, 1941–45 (National Archives & Records Administration, San Bruno (San Francisco) Regional Branch; transcribed by Researcher@Large)

————, 'Salvage Officer Report, USS *West Virginia*, 15 June 1942' (Naval Historical Center)

Phelan, Keiren, and Martin H Brice, *Fast Attack Craft* (Macdonald and Jane's, 1977)

Polenov, L L, *Cruiser Aurora* (Leningrad Shipbuilding, 1987)

Poolman, Kenneth, *Escort Carrier 1941–1945* (Ian Allan, 1972)

Preston, Anthony, *Battleships of World War I* (Galahad Books, 1972)

Raven, Alan, and John Roberts, *Man-o'-war 1: County Class Cruisers* (RSV Publications, 1978)

————, *Man-o'-war 2: 'V' and 'W' Class Destroyers* (RSV Publications, 1979)

————, *Man-o'-war 3: Battleships Rodney and Nelson* (RSV Publications, 1979)

Roberts, John, *The Battleship Dreadnought* (Conway Maritime Press, 2001)

Ropp, Theodore, *The Development of a Modern Navy, French Naval Policy 1871–1904* (Naval Institute Press, 1987)

Ross, Al, *The Destroyer Campbeltown* (Conway Maritime Press, 1990)

Rössler, Eberhard, *The U-Boat* (Cassell & Co, 2001)

Schenk, Peter, *Kampf um de Ägäis* (Mittler & Sohn, 2000)

Sieche, Erwin F, 'SMS *Szent István*', *Warship International*, No 2 (1991)

Skulski, Janusz, *The Heavy Cruiser Takao* (Conway Maritime Press, 1994)

Slover, Eugene Lee, website, <www.eugeneleeslover.com/USNAVY/CHAPTER-12-J.html>

Stephenson, Parks, 'Capsizing of the USS *Oklahoma*' (2010), <http://i-16tou.com/okie/okie6.html>

Thomas, David, *Battle of the Java Sea* (Pan, 1971)

Tully, Anthony P, 'Shell Games at Surigao: The entangled fates of battleships *Fuso* and *Yamashiro*' (1999), <http://www.combinedfleet.com/atully06.htm>

US Naval Technical Mission to Japan, *Defenses of Tsushima and Entrance to Sea of Japan*, (January 1946); *Japanese Torpedoes and Tubes*, Article 2, 'Aircraft Torpedoes' (March 1946); *Japanese Torpedoes and Tubes*, Article 3, 'Above-water Tubes' (March 1946); *Japanese Torpedoes and Tubes*, Article 1, 'Ship and Kaiten Torpedoes' (April 1946), <www.fischer-tropsch.org/primary_documents/gvt_reports/USNAVY/USNTMJ%20Reports>

US Navy, War Damage Reports, <http://www.ibiblio.org/hyperwar/USN/rep/WDR/>

US Navy Torpedo Station, *Spar-torpedo Instructions* (1890)

Westwood, J N, *The Illustrated History of the Russo-Japanese War* (Regnery, 1974)

Whitley, M J, *Cruisers of World War Two* (Arms & Armour Press, 1996)

————, *Destroyers of World War Two* (Cassell & Co, 2000)

Specifications for Service Torpedoes

Notes: Diameters are standardised, rounded up in imperial measurements (inches). Year is when first designed, entry into service may have been later. Practice head may have been lighter than warhead. Whiteheads were used by many countries before the latter began producing designs of their own.

Dia	Type	Year	Warhead	Length	Weight	Propulsion and Controls	Speed Knots at Range
Whitehead Fiume Factory/Weymouth Factory/St Tropez Factory							
14in	Prototype Fusiform Austrian trials	1866	17.6lbs 8kg Wet gun-cotton	11ft 1^3/$_4$ins 3.4m	300lbs 136kg	Comp air 370psi, 26kg/cm^2; 2-cyl oscillating engine with cylinders at right angles, fed through reducing valve at 500psi; single 2-bladed prop; stabilising ribs top, bottom & sides; hydrostatic valve depth control with external wires controlling tail planes; adjustable fixed rudder	6.5kts 200yds/183m Continuing at lower speed to max 300yds/ 274m
14in	Prototype Fusiform Austrian trials	1867	14lbs 6.35kg	11ft 7in 3.53m	346lbs 157kg	As above	5.7kts 200yds/183m
16in	Prototype Fusiform Austrian trials	1867	67lbs 30.4kg	14ft 1in 4.9m	650lbs 295kg	As above	6.7kts 300yds/274m
14in	Prototype Fusiform Austrian trials	1868	40lbs 18.1kg Gun-cotton	11ft 7in 3.53m	346lbs 157kg	Comp air 700psi, 49.2kg/cm^2; 2-cyl V-twin engine; single 3-bladed prop; stabilising ribs top, bottom & sides; fixed horizontal bow planes; pendulum depth control; external wires to tail planes; adjustable rudder	7kts over 600yds./549m
16in	Prototype Fusiform Austrian trials	1868	67lbs 30.4kg Gun-cotton	14ft 1in 4.9m	650lbs 295kg	As above	7kts over 600yds./549m
14in	Standard Fusiform RN trials	1870	17.6lbs 8kg Gun-cotton	13ft 10^1/$_2$in 4.23m	346lbs 157kg	2-cyl comp air 700psi, 49.2kg/cm^2; single 3-bladed prop; stabilising ribs top & bottom; pendulum depth control; internal wires to tail planes; adjustable rudder	7.5kts 600yds/549m
16in	Standard Fusiform RN trials	1870	67lbs 30.4kg Gun-cotton	14ft 0in 4.27m	650lbs 295kg	As above	Around 7kts 1000yds/914m
16in	Fiume Standard	1871				As above	7kts 1000yds/914m
14in	Fiume Small	1871	26.5lbs 12kg	14ft 0in 4.27m		As above	16.5kts 800yds/732m
14in	Fiume Mark 1	1875	26.5lbs 12kg	14ft 6in 4.42m	529lbs 240kg	Balance chamber & pendulum relocated behind air flask; 1000psi, 70.3kg/cm^2; Brotherhood 3-cyl radial engine with slotted piston and exhaust ports in lower cylinder walls. Modified in 1877 with servo-actuation of horizontal rudders	18kts 600yds/549m
14in	Fiume Mark 2	1876	30lbs 13.6kg	14ft 6in 4.42m	594lbs 269.4kg	2-bladed contra-rotating propellers; omission of fins top and bottom	20kts 600yds/549m
14in	Fiume Mark 3	1876	58lbs 26.3kg	13ft 3in 4.04m	554lbs 251.3kg	As above	21kts 600yds/549m

15in	Fiume, in Bronze or Steel	1882	74lbs 33.6kg	18ft 9½in 5.73m	904.5lbs 410.3kg	As above	23.5kts
		1882				Air flask pressure 1500psi, 105.5kg/cm²	
14in	Fiume Short	1882	88lbs 40kg	11ft 0in 3.35m	435lbs 197.3kg	Built for Russia	21kts 600yds/549m
		1883				Semi-rounded nose adopted	
12in	Fiume Baby for small boat use	1883	33lbs 15kg				
14in	Fiume Mark 4	1885	58lbs 26.3kg	14ft 9in 4.2m	660lbs 299.3kg		23.5kts 600yds/549m
18in	Fiume Mark 1	1890	198lbs 90kg	16ft 7in 5.05m	1136lbs 515.3kg	First 18in torpedo; comp air; cold running; 3-cylinder radial engine; 3-bladed contra-rotating propellers	30kts 800yds/730m
18in	Fiume Mark 2	1891	187lbs 84kg	16ft 7in 5.05m	1136lbs 515.3kg		29.5kts 800yds/732m
		1895				Gyroscope introduced	
		1897				4-bladed contra-rotating propellers introduced	
14in	Weymouth Mark I	1898	110lbs 50kg Wet gun-cotton 1916 changed to amatol	14ft 11½in 4.56m	706lbs 320.2kg	Gyroscope	30kts 600yds//549m 29kts 750yds//686m
27.5in	Fiume for Japan	Circa 1900					
18in	Fiume Mark 3	1905	220lbs 100kg		1609lbs 729.8kg	For small boat use	29kts 2190yds/2002m
18in	Fiume Mark 3H	1907	253lbs 115kg		1620lbs 734.8kg	First heater engine	34kts 4370yds/3996m
188in	Mark 5 Weymouth	1908	199lbs 90kg Wet gun-cotton	17ft 0in 5.182m	1452lbs 659kg	4-cyl comp air, wet heater; 4-bladed contra-rotating props; 3-speeds, set before entering tube; gyro control	40kts 1000yds/910m 36kts 2000yds/1830m 27kts 4000yds/3660m
21in	Fiume	1908				First 21in torpedo	
18in	Fiume	1908	253lbs 115kg		1654lbs 750.2kg	First designed for dry heater	42kts 6560yds/6000m
18in	Fiume	1913	220lbs 100kg		1742lbs 790kg	First wet heater (steam torpedo); 2-cylinder side-by-side engine	44kts 6560yds/6000m
21in	Weymouth Mark 2	1914	225lbs 102kg		2794lbs 1267.3kg		29kts 10,000yds/9144m

Great Britain & British Dominions – Royal Navy, Royal Air Force, Royal Engineers
RL (Royal Laboratories); RGF (Royal Gun Factory); RNTF (Royal Naval Torpedo Factory Greenock, later Alexandria); RANTF (Royal Australian Naval Torpedo Factory)

16in	RL Mark I*	1872	26lbs 11.8kg		530lbs 240.4kg	1872 2-cyl V-twin engine; 1874 3-cyl radial Brotherhood engine; 1875 contra-rotating 2-bladed propellers	12kts 600yds/549m
14in	RL Mark I*	1876	32lbs 14.5kg	14ft 6in 4.42m	525lbs 238kg	First wet heater (steam torpedo); 2-cylinder side-by-side engine	44kts 6560yds/6000m
14in	RL Mark II	1879	34lbs 15.4kg	14ft 7in 4.45m	575lbs 260.8kg	First to be carried in side cradles	19kts 600yds/549m
14in	RL Mark III	1881	34lbs 15.4kg	14ft 7in 4.45m	578lbs 262kg		20kts 600yds/549m

14in	RL Mark IV	1883	60lbs 27.2kg	14ft 6in 4.42m	630lbs 285.8kg	Semi-rounded nose introduced	23kts 600yds/549m
14in	RL Mark V	1885	60lbs 27.2kg	14ft 6in 4.42m	654lbs 296.7kg		25kts 600yds/549m
12in	BABY for small boat use	1886	33lbs 15kg				
14in	RL Mark VI	1886	60lbs 27.2kg	14ft 6in 4.42m	648lbs 293.9kg		25kts 600yds/549m
14in	RL Mark VII	1887	70lbs 31.75kg	15ft 0in 4.57m	707lbs 320.7kg		27kts 600yds/549m/549m
14in	RL Mark VIII	1888	65lbs 29.5kg	15ft 0in 4.57m	708lbs 321kg	3-bladed contra-rotating propellers	26kts 600yds/549m
18in	RGF Mark I	1890	188lbs 85.3kg	16ft 7in 5.05m	1213lbs 550.2kg		30kts 800yds/732m
14in	RGF Short for small boat use	1890	85lbs 38.5kg	12ft 5in 3.78m	861lbs 254.5kg		28kts 800yds/732m
24in	Brennan	1890	200lbs 90.7kg	22ft 0in 6.7m	2240lbs 1016kg	Wire-wound drums; 3-bladed contra-rotating propellers; 2000yds/1829m of wire carried	25kts short range 22kts 1000yds/914m 20kts 1600yds/1463m
18in	Mark II	1892	188lbs 85.3kg	16ft 7in 5.05m	1227lbs 556.6kg		30.5kts 800yds/732m
14in	Mark IX	1893	77lbs 35kg	15ft 0in 4.57m	726lbs 329.3kg	4-bladed propellers fitted in 1897	27.5kts 600yds/549m
18in	Mark III	1894	171lbs 77.5kg	16ft 7in 5.05m	1213lbs 550.2kg		30.5kts 800yds/732m
18in	Mark IV	1895	171lbs 77.5kg	16ft 7in 5.05m	1218lbs 552.5kg	3-cyl radial engine; 1899 fitted with 4-cyl radial, 56bhp engine; gyroscope in the later production	30.6kts 800yds/732m
18in	Mark V River & Tribal DD	1895	296lbs 134kg	16ft 7in 5.05m	1353lbs 614kg	Nickel steel air flask 2200psi, 154.7kg/cm^2	30.6kts 800yds/732m
14in	Mark X A/c use 1910	1897	77lbs 35kg		762lbs 345.6kg	Gyroscope	30kts 800yds/732m
18in	Mark VI	1905	200lbs 90.7kg	17ft 1in 5.2m	1490lbs 675.9kg	Comp air; cold running	41kts 1000yds/910m 28.5kts 4000yds/3700m
21in	Mark I Beagle class DD	1908 Modified: 225lbs 102kg Wet gun-cotton	Mk I 200lbs/91kg Short: 17ft 10^1/$_2$in 5.45m Long: 23ft 1^1/$_4$in 7.04m	Short: 2100lbs/953kg Long: 2800lbs/1270kg	Wet heater; 2100psi/148kg/cm^2	S: 50kts 1000yds/910m 30kts 7500yds/6850m L: 50kts 1000yds/910m 30kts 12,000yds/11000m Mod: 50kts 2000yds/1820m 30kts 10,800yds/9900m
18in	Mark VI*H	1908	200lbs 90.7kg	17ft 1in 5.2m	1490lbs 675.9kg	First wet heater (steam torpedo) in service	Max 45kts Max 6000yds/5486m
18in	Mark VII	1909	320lbs 150kg TNT			Comp air; 4-cyl radial engine; first torpedo designed for wet heater	41kts 3000yds/2700m 30kts 6000 – 7000yds /5500–6400m
18in	Mark VII*						35kts 5000yds/4600m 29kts 7000yds/6400m
21in	RGF Long	1909	280lbs 127kg	23ft 1^1/$_2$in 7.05m	2863lbs 1298.6kg	4-cyl radial wet heater engine	Max 50kts Max 12000yds/10973m

21in	Mark II Mark II* BB & BC from 1914	1910	280 lbs/127kg Wet gun-cotton Then: 400 lcs 181kg TNT Last: 515 lbs 234kg TNT			4-cyl radial wet heater engine	45kts 3000yds/2700m 35kts 4000yds/3600m 30kts 5500yds/5000m Later in WWII: Subs: 35kts 5000yds/4570m DD: 29kts 8000yds/7300m
18in	Mark VIII Subs & a/c	1913	320lbs 150kg TNT			Comp air; wet heater	35kts 2500yds/2300m 29kts 4000yds/3650m
21in	Mark IV Mark IV*	1916	515lbs 234kg TNT	22ft 7½in 6.896m	3206lbs 1454kg	Burner cycle	35kts 8000yds/ 29kts 10,000yds/9150m 25kts 13,500yds/12,350m WWII submarines: 40kts 6000yds/5500m 35kts 9500yds/8700m
18in	Mark IX for a/c	1917	250lbs 113.4kg		1077lbs 488.5kg		29kts 2000yds/1829m
21in	Mark V A & B Class DD Kent Class CA	1917		23ft 4in 7.1m		Wet heater; Kent-class version had strengthened tail assembly to allow for launch from high weather deck	40kts 5000yds/4570m 25kts 13,500yds/12,340m
24.5in	Mark I Rodney & Nelson BB	1923	743lbs 337kg TNT	26ft 7in 8.103m	5700lbs 2585kg	Oxygen-enriched air; later converted to comp air only	35kts 15,000yds/13,700m 30kts 20,000yds/18,300m
21in	Mark VII London class	1925	740lbs 336kg TNT	25ft 6in 7.77m	4106lbs 1862kg	Oxygen-enriched air; later converted to comp air only	35kts 5700yds/5200m
21in	Mark VIII submarines	1927	Mark VIII: 750lbs 340kg TNT Mk VIII** early: 722lbs 327kg torpex Mk VIII** late: 805lbs 365kg torpex		3452lbs 1566kg	Comp air; burner cycle semi-diesel engine	Mark VIII: 40kts 5000yds/4570m Mark VIII** early: 45.6kts 5000yds/4570m Mark VIII** late: 41kts 7000yds/6400m
21in	Mark IX Surface ships		750lbs 340kg		3731lbs 1692.4kg		Max 40kts Max 14,000yds/12,800m
18in	Mark XI	1934	465lbs 211kg TNT		1540lbs 698.5kg	Comp air; burner cycle	35kts 2500yds/2300m
18in	Mark XII	1935	388lbs 176kg TNT	16ft 3in 4.95m	1548lbs 702kg	Comp air; burner cycle	40kts 1500yds/1400m 37kts 3500yds/3200m
18in	Mark XIV	1938	375lbs 170kg TNT		1630lbs 740kg	Comp air; wet heater	45kts 1650yds/1510m 41kts 2950yds/2700m
18in	Mark XV A/c & MTBs	1942	545lbs 247kg torpex	17ft 3in 5.26m		Also built at the RANTF; burner cycle semi-diesel 4-cyl radial engine, with separate steel cylinder heads, 225bhp weighing 130lbs (59kg)	40kts 2500yds/2300m 33kts 3500yds/3200m
18in	Mark XVI Project	1943				Electric	
21in	Mark XI	1943	710lbs 322kg			Electric	
18in	Mark XVII A/c	1944	600lbs 270kg torpex	17ft 3in 5.26m			40kts 2500yds/2300m
21in	Mark 12 Ferry/ Fancy	1952	750lbs 340kg torpex			HTP	28kts 5500yds/5000m

18in	Mark 30	1954		8ft 0in 2.4m	646lbs 293kg		19kts 830yds/760m 12.5kts 3000yds/2700m
21in	Bidder Mk 20 E for escorts Mk 20S for subs	1960	196lbs 89kg torpex	21ft 2¼in 6.46m	1810lbs 821kg	Electric; passive homing	20kts 12,000yds/11,000m
21in	Mark 21 Pentane						
21in	Mark 22 Vickers PV						
21in	Mark 23 Grog	1971					
21in	Mark 24 Tigerfish	1974		21ft 2in 6.45m	1650lbs 748.4kg	2-speed electric motor driving contra-rotating propellers; initial wire guidance on launch; final approach using onboard 3-D sonar and computer	40kts 12,000yds/10,973m
12.75-in	Sting Ray	1985		7ft 11in 2.4m		Electric motor; magnesium/silver chloride seawater battery	
21in	Spearfish	1987		27ft 10in 8.48m	4400lbs 1996kg	Sundstrand gas turbine fuelled by HAP (hydroxyl amine perchlorate) mixed with OTTO II fuel; axial flow pump-jet propulsor	Max reputedly 70kts Max reputedly 70,000yds/64,000m

Germany

14in	Schwartzkopff Fusiform	1876	31lbs 14kg Gun-cotton	14ft 9in 4.5m	602lbs 279.4kg	3-cyl comp air 1500psi, 105.5kg/cm² with single 2-bladed propeller; pendulum depth control; adjustable rudder; phosphor-bronze body	17kts 440yds/400m
14in	Schwartzkopff	1883	44lbs 20kg		581lbs 264kg	As above, with 2-bladed contra-rotating propellers	21kts 640yds/585m
14in	C35/91	1891	90lbs 40.5kg	15ft 7in 4.75m		3-cyl engine; comp air 1371psi; bronze torpedo with or without gyroscopes	27kts 547yds/500m
18in	C45/91 Bronze	1891	193lbs 87.5kg	16ft 9in 5.11m		As above but pressure 1428psi	27kts 1094yds/1000m
18in	C45/91 Steel	1891	265lbs 120kg	16ft 10¾in 5.15m		As above	27kts 1640yds/1500m
14in	Schwartzkopff	1898	125lbs 56.7kg	15ft 1in 4.6m	728.4lbs 330kg	3-cyl engine; comp air 1350psi; bronze torpedo; sold to US Navy	
18in	C/03	1903	325lbs 147.5kg	16ft 10¾in 5.15m		C/03 AV: 3-cyl 2143psi heater C/03 AVK 2357psi heater C/03 D: wet heater (steam); 2143psi	AV: 26kts 3280yds/3000m AVK: 27kts 3828yds/3500m D: 27kts 5468yds/5000m
18in	Schwartzkopff	1905	264.5lbs 120kg				30kts
18in	C/06	1906	269lbs 122kg	18ft 6½in 5.65m		C/06 AV: 2286psi; 4-cyl heater C/06 AVK: 2500psi; 4-cyl heater C/06 D: 2286psi; 4-cyl steam	AV: 27kts 3940yds/3600m AVK: 27kts 4590yds/4200m D: 27kts 6450yds/5900m
19.7in	G/6	1906	353lbs/160kg G/6 D 362lbs/164kg	19ft 8¼in 6m		As above	AV: 27kts 5470yds/5000m AVK: 27kts 6000yds/5500m D: 27kts 9200yds/8400m
19.7in	G/7	1907	430lbs 195kg	23ft 7.02m		4-cyl 2428psi; steam	27kts 10,700yds/9800m
23.6in	H/8	1908	463–550lbs 210–250kg	26ft 3in 8m		8-cyl; 2428psi; steam	27kts 15,300yds/14,000m
19.7in	G/7***	1914	440lbs 200kg	23ft 7.02m	2491lbs 1130kg	4-cyl; steam	36kts 11,700yds/10,700m

18in	G 125	1914	308lbs 140kg			steam	36kts 6560yds/6000m
18in	Aircraft torpedo	1917	350lbs 160kg		1680lbs 762kg		35kts 1640yds/1500m
	G/7?	1917				Prototype electric	28kts 2000yds/1830m
21in	G7a	1937	617lbs 280kg	22ft 9in 7.163m	3334lbs 1538kg	4-cyl 350bhp; steam	Max: 44kts Max: 15,310yds/14,000m
21in	G7e	1939	617lbs 280kg	22ft 9in 7.163m	3540lbs 1608kg	Electric 100ehp at 1700rpm	30kts 5470yds/5000m
18in Aircraft	LF5	1939	440lbs 200kg		1626lbs 738kg		30kts 2500yds/2300m
21in	G7ut	1942	617lbs 280kg	22ft 9in 7.163m	3814lbs 1730kg	Steinbarsch & Steinbutt; Walter HTP turbine 430shp	45kts 87,500yds/80,000m
21in	G5ut	194?		18ft 5.5m		Goldbutt Walter HTP turbine 390shp	45kts 41,500yds/38,000m
21in	DM1 Seeschlange (Sea Serpent) ASW	1971	220lbs 100kg	15ft 1$\frac{3}{4}$in 4.15m incl wire reel	3020lbs 1370kg	Electric; silver-zinc battery; wire-guided with passive homing	33kts 6560yds/6000m 20kts 13,100yds/12,000m
21in	DM2A1 Seal Anti-ship	1967	551lbs 250kg	21ft 5$\frac{3}{4}$in 6.55m	3020lbs 1370kg	As above	33kts 22,000yds/20,000m
21in	SST-3 Seal SST-4 Seal	1967 1975	573lbs 260kg	19ft 11in 6.08m	3116lbs 1414kg	Electric; silver-zinc battery; wire-guided; SST-4 has passive homing	35kys 12,000yds/11,000m 28kts 22,000yds/20,000m 23kts 40,000yds/37,000m
21in	DM2A3 DM2A4 Seehecht (Seahake)	1985 1999	573lbs 260kg PBX (hexogen- aluminium)	21ft $\frac{3}{4}$in 6.6m with 4 battery modules	3020lbs 1370kg	Electric; silver-zinc battery driving contra-props; optical fibre guided with passive homing; communication with launch submarine; optimised for littoral combat	A-3: 35kts 22,000yds/20,000m A-4: 50kts 88,000yds/50,000m

United States

14in	Fish torpedo 1st prototype Fusiform	1871	70–90lbs Gun-cotton	12ft 6in 3.81m	480lbs 218kg	2-cyl comp air; 4-blade prop; hydrostatic valve, stern planes; adjustable rudder	6–8kts 300–400yds/274–366m
14in	Fish torpedo 2nd prototype Fusiform	1872	70–90lbs Gun-cotton	12ft 6in 3.81m	480lbs 218kg	As above	8.5kts 1,300yds/1190m
14.2in	Howell	1889	100lbs 45.4kg Wet gun-cotton	132in 3.353m	580lbs 263kg	132lb flywheel spun up to 10,000rpm by external drive; variable pitch twin 3-blade props; pendulums controlled azimuth & depth	24–25kts 200yds/180m Then slower to maximum 800yds/730m
21in	Bliss-Leavitt Mark 1	1904	200lbs 91kg Wet gun-cotton	197in 5.004m	1500lbs 680kg	Single-stage turbine comp air @ @ 2250psi, 158.2kg/cm²; heater; single 4-bladed prop; Obry gyro	27kts 4000yds/3360m
21in	Bliss-Leavitt Mark 2	1905	200lbs 91kg Wet gun-cotton	197in 5.004m	1900lbs 862kg	2-stage turbines comp air @ 2250psi, 158.2kg/cm²; heater; contra-rotating contra-rotating 4-bladed props;	26kts 3500yds/3200m
21in	Bliss-Leavitt Mark 3		200lbs/ 91kg Wet gun-cotton	197in 5.004m	1500lbs 680kg	As above	26kts 4000yds/3660m
18in	Bliss-Leavitt Mark 4 Subs	1908	200lbs/91kg Wet gun-cotton	197in 5.004m	1547lbs 702kg	As above	30kts 2000yds/1830m Mod 1 29kts 3000yds/2740m
18in	Bliss-Leavitt Mark 6	1911	200lbs 91kg Wet gun-cotton	204in 5.182m	1800lbs 616kg	As above	35kts 2000yds/1830m

Diameter	Name	Year	Warhead	Length	Weight	Propulsion	Performance
18in	Bliss-Leavitt Mark 7 Mod 0 Submarines	1912	205lbs 93kg TNT	204in 5.182m	1588lbs 720kg	2-stage horizontal turbines comp air @ 2500psi, 175.8kg/cm^2; steam; contra-rotating 4-bladed props;	32kts 4000yds/ 3650m
18in	Bliss-Leavitt Mark 7 D Short: A/c	1917	200lbs 90kg TNT	120in 3.048m		2-stage horizontal turbines comp air @ 2250psi, 158.2kg/cm^2; steam; contra-rotating 4-bladed props	35kts 2000yds/1830m
18in	Bliss-Leavitt Mark 7 D Aircraft Mod A Mod 2A Mod 5A	1920	Mod A: 205lbs 93kg TNT 2A: 319lbs 145kg TNT 5A: 326lbs 148kg TNT or TPX	204in 5.182m	A: 1593lbs 723kg 2A: 1736lbs 787kg 5A: 1628lbs 738kg	As above	A: 31kts 3200yds/2926m 2A: 30kts 6000yds/5486m 5A: 35kts 3500yds/3200m
21in	Bliss-Leavitt Mark 8	1915 Mods 5, 6 & 8: 1923	Mods 0 to 2B: 321lbs/146kg Mods 3A & 3B: 385lbs/175kg Mods 0 to 2B: 321lbs/146kg Mods 3A & 3B: 385lbs/175kg Mods 5, 6 & 8: 466lbs 211kg TNT	256.3in 6.51m	2600lbs 1179kg	2-stage horizontal turbines comp air @ 2600psi, 182.8kg/cm^2; steam; contra-rotating 4-bladed props	Mods 0,1,2,2A & 2B: 27kts 10,000yds/9140m OR 27kts 12,500yds/11,430m Mods 3A & 3B: 27kts 13,500yds/12,340m Mod 8: 29kts 15,000yds/13,720m
21in	Bliss-Leavitt Mark 9 Short Mod 1 BB Mod 1B Subs	1915	Mod 1: 210lbs 95kg TNT Mod 1B: 395lbs/ 179kg torpex	196in 5.004m	Mod 1: 2059lbs 934kg 1B: 2377lbs 1078kg	2-stage horizontal turbines comp air @ 2800psi, 196.9kg/cm^2; steam; contra-rotating 4-bladed props;	Mod 1; 27kts 9000yds/8530m Mod 1B: 34.5kts 5500yds/5030m
21in	Mark 10 Submarines	1918	Mod 0: 400lbs 181kg TNT Mod 3: 497lbs 225kg TNT or 485lbs 220kg TPX	183in 4.953m	Mod 0: 2050lbs 930kg Mod 3; 2215lbs 1005kg	As above	Mod 0: 36kts 3500yds/3200m 30kts 5000yds/4570m
21in	Mark 11 DD, CA & CL	1926	500lbs 227kg TNT	271in 6.883m	Mod 0: 3511lbs 1593kg Mod 1: 3521lbs 1597kg	As above	46kts 6000yds/5500m 34kts 10,000yds/9150m 27kts 15,000yds/13,700m
21in	Mark 12 DD, CA & CL	1928	500lbs 227kg TNT	271in 6.883m	3505lbs 1590kg	As above	44kts 7000yds/6400m 34.5kts 10,000yds/9150m 27.5kts 15,000yds/13,700m
22.5in	Mark 13 A/c Mod 0 through Mod 12	1938	Mod 0: 404lbs 183kg or 392lbs 178kg TNT Mod 10: 603lbs /274kg TNT or 606lbs / 275kg TPX or 600lbs / 272kg HNX	Mod 0: 159in 4.089m Mod 10: 165in 4.191m	Mod 0: 1949lbs 884kg Mod 10; 2216lbs 1005kg	Turbines; steam; air gyro; Mod 0 had 'Fiume' tail, all later mods had 'RL' tail; shroud ring added from Mod 6; all later torpedoes had plywood nose drag ring and box tail added; gyro angle setting dropped from Mod 10	Mod 0: 30kts 5700yds/5210m Mod10: 33.5kts 4000yds/3660m
21in	Mark 14 Submarine	1930	660 lbs TPX 299kg	246in 6.25m	3209lbs 1456kg	Turbines; steam; air gyro	46.3kts 4500yds/4115m 31.1kts 9000yds/8230m
21in	Mark 15 DD	1934	825lbs TPX 374kg	288in 7.3m	3841lbs 1742kg	Turbines; steam; air gyro	45kts 6000yds/5486m 33.5kts 10,000yds/9144m 26.5kts 15,000yds/13,716m
21in	Mark 16 Submarine	1944	920lbs TPX 417kg	245in 6.2m	3922lbs 1779kg	Navol H2O2; alcohol fuel; turbines	46.2kts 11,000yds/12,802m

Diameter	Mark	Year	Warhead	Length	Weight	Notes	Performance
21in	Mark 17 Destroyer	1944	920lbs TPX 417kg	288in 7.3m	4600lbs 2086kg	Navol H2O2; alcohol fuel; turbines	46kts 18,000yds/16,459m
21in	Mark 18 Submarine	1943	575lbs TPX 261kg	245in 6.2m	3154lbs 1431kg	Electric with air gyro	29kts 4000yds/3660m
21in	Mark 19 submarine	1945		245in 6.2m	3154lbs 1431kg	Mark 18 Electric with electric gyro Abandoned in favour of the Mark 23	29kts 4000yds/3660m
21in	Mark 20 submarine	1945		245in 6.2m		Electric Abandoned in favour of the Mark 23	33kts 3500yds/3200m
22.5in	Mark 21 payload for Petrel missile	1945		161in 4m	2216lbs 1005kg	Mod 1 Electric; Mod 2 Turbine; acoustic homing	33.5kts 6300yds/5760m
21in	Mark 22 Submarine anti-ship	1945		246in 6.2m	3060lbs 1388kg	Electric; active acoustic homing (azimuth)	29kts 4000yds/3660m
21in	Mark 23 submarine					Single-speed version of Mark 14	46 kts 4500yds/4115m
19in	Mine Mark 24 FIDO	1942		84in 2.1m	680lbs 308kg	Electric; passive acoustic homing	12kts 4000yds/3660m
22.5in	Mark 25 aircraft			161in 4m	2306lbs 1046kg	High-temperature turbine; air gyro	40kts 2500yds/2286m
21in	Mark 26 submarine		900lbs TPX 408kg	246in 6.2m	3200lbs 1461kg	Electric; electric gyro; contra-rotating electric motors; seawater battery; vari. running depth	40kts 6000ys/:5490m
19in	Mark 27 Cutie	1945		90in 2.28m	720lbs 327kg	Electric; passive acoustic homing	12kts 5000yds/4572m
19in	Mark 27 Mod 4	1945		125in 3.18m	1175lbs 533kg	Electric; passive acoustic homing	16kts 6200yds/5670m
21in	Mark 28 Submarine	1945	600lbs 272kg	246in 6.2m		Electric; passive acoustic homing	19.6kts 4000yds/3660m
21in	Mark 29 Submarine	1945		246in 6.2m		Electric; passive acoustic homing	28kts 4000yds/3660m 21kts 12,000yds/10,973
10in	Mine Mark 30	1943	50lbs 22.7kg	90in 2.28m	265lbs 120kg		
21in	Mark 31 Destroyer	1945		246in 6.2m	3000lbs 1361kg	Electric; passive acoustic homing; contra-rotating electric motors; 2-speed	29kts 4000yds/3660m 20kts
19in	Mark 32 Mod 2 DD ASW	1951	107lbs 49kg HBX	83in 2.108m	700lbs 318kg	Electric; active homing	12kts 9600yds/8800m
21in	Mark 33 A/c & submarine	1949	550lbs 249kg HBX	156in 3.962m	1770lbs 803kg	Electric; electro-hydraulic controls; passive acoustic homing; cast cast aluminium hull	27kts 15,000yds/13,710m
19in	Mark 34 Aircraft ASW	1948	Mod 0: 116lbs 53kg Mod 1: 170lbs 77kg HBX	129in 3.175m	1150lbs 522kg	Electric; passive homing; 2-speed search/acquisition	17kts 3600yds/3300m
21in	Mark 35 A/c & sub & DD	1949	270lbs 122.5kg HBX	161in 4.089m	1770lbs 803kg	Electric; seawater battery; passive & active homing; pre-set search ceiling & floor; rh or lh circling search pattern	27kts 15,000yds/13710m
21in	Mark 36 Submarines	N/A N/A	800lbs 363kg HBX-1	246in 6.248m	4000lbs 1814kg	Electric; seawater battery; pattern runner	47kts 7000yds/6400m

Dia.	Name	Year	Warhead	Length	Weight	Notes	Performance
19in	Mark 37 Mod 0 Mod 1 Mod 2 Mod 3	1957 1960 1967 1967	330lbs 150kg HBX	135in 3.429m Mods 1 & 2/ 161in 4.089m	1430lbs 649kg Mods 1 & 2:1690lbs 766kg	Electric; seawater battery; passive acoustic homing in search mode; active homing in attack run. Mods 1 & 2: wire-guided. NT37 version replaced the battery with an OTTO fuel II engine	26kts 10,000yds/9140m 17kts 23,500yds/21,490m NT37: 36kts 15,000yds/13,710m
21in	Mark 38	N/A				Cancelled in favour of Mark 37	
19in	Mark 39	1956	130lbs 59kg HBX	133in 3.378m	1275lbs 578kg	Mk 27 Mod 4 with spool for wire-guidance	15.5kts 13,000yds/11,890m
12.75in	Mark 40 A/c & ASROC	N/A	300lbs 136kg HBX	105in 2.667m	1250lbs 567kg	Solid-propellant turning turbine to power pump-jet propulsor	80kts 2000yds/1830m
21in	Mark 41 Aircraft	1949				Aircraft dropped version of Mark 35	
21in	Mark 42 Submarine	N/A	800lbs 363kg HBX	245in 6.248m	4000lbs 1814kg	Navol fuel; non-homing	40kts 20,000yds/18,290m
10in	Mark 43	1952	54lbs HBX	92in 2.3m	265lbs	Electric; deep diving but only 6 minutes search capacity	21kts 4500yds/4115m
12.75in	Mark 44	1956	75lbs 34kg	8.2ft 2.5m	432lbs 196kg	Electric; 30ehp motor; seawater battery; active sonar; max depth: 910m/ft	30kts 6000yds/5490m 30kts 6000yds/5490m
19in	Mark 45 Astor later Freedom	1960	Nuclear warhead HBX			Electric; seawater battery; 160ehp motor	Max: 40kts Max: 15,000yds/13,710m
12.75in	Mark 46	1963	96.8lbs 43.9kg PBXN-103	102in 2.6m	508lbs 230kg	OTTO fuel II internal combustion reciprocating engine; max depth: 366m/1200ft	40kts 12,000yds/10,900m
21in	Mark 47	N/A				Cancelled in favour of Mark 48	
21in	Mark 48	1976	650lbs 295kg	230in 5.84m	3440lbs/ 1560kg ADCAP: 3695lbs/ 1676kg	OTTO fuel II swash-plate piston engine driving axial flow pump-jet propulsor; max diving depth 3000ft/914m	55kts 21miles/33,800m
12.75in	Mark 50 Barracuda	1974	100lbs 45kg Shaped charge	9ft 6in 2.9m	800lbs 360kg	Rankine cycle stored chemical energy (sulphur hexafluoride gas sprayed on block of lithium) generating steam; pump-jet propulsor; max depth: 580m/1900ft	40kts 15,000m
12.75in	Mark 54 Mako	2004	96.8lbs 43.9kg PBXN-103	107in 2.72m	608lbs 276kg	OTTO fuel II internal combustion reciprocating engine	40kts

Japan

Dia.	Name	Year	Warhead	Length	Weight	Notes	Performance
21in	Type 6	1917	484lbs 200kg	269in 6.83m	3157lbs 1432kg	Submarines; comp air; 4-cyl radial engine (Schwartzkopff-type)	36kts 7660yds/7000m 32kts 11,000yds/10,000m 26kts 16,400yds/15000m
24in	Type 8	1919	759lbs 345kg	331in 8.4m	5207lbs 2362kg	Destroyer & cruiser use; comp air; 4-cyl radial engine (Schwartzkopff-type)	38kts 11,000yds/10,000m 32kts 16,300yds/15,000m 28kts 22,000yds/20,000m
21in	Type 89	1929	660lbs 300kg		3677lbs 1668kg	Submarine use; comp air; 2-cyl double-acting reciprocating engine (Whitehead Weymouth-type)	45kts 6000yds/5500m 43kts 6500yds/6000m 35kts 11,000yds/10,000m
24in	Type 90	1930	825lbs 375kg		5743lbs 2605kg	Destroyer & cruiser use; comp air; 2-cyl double-acting reciprocating engine(Whitehead Weymouth-type) 2nd Class DD up to 1942	46kts 7660yds/7000m 43kts 11,000yds/10,000m 35kts 16,400yds/15,000m

Diameter	Type	Year	Warhead	Length	Weight	Notes	Performance
18in	Type 91	1931	Mod 1: 330lbs/150kg Mod 2: 450lbs/204kg Mod 3: 528lbs/240kg Mod 4 (Strng): 675lbs/306kg Mod 7 (Strng): 920lbs/417kg	207.7in 5.28m Mod 2: 216in/5.49m Mod 7 Strong: 225in/5.72m	Mod 1: 1728lbs/784kg Mod 2: 1840lbs/835kg Mod 3: 1872lbs/849kg Mod 4 Strg: 2030lbs/921kg Mod 7 Strg: 2320lbs/1052kg	Aircraft torpedo; comp air Mod 3 2560psi/180kg/cm²; Mod 3 Strong 2280psi/160kg/cm²; 8-cyl radial engine 210bhp; from Mod 2 1941 had 2 air-blast gyros, 1st controlled azimuth; 2nd corrected rolling, allowing for warhead to be filled with explosive; freewheeling props prior to water entry. Mod 2 version designed for the attack on Pearl Harbor known as 'gyorai' ('thunder fish'); Rubber nose protective shroud for protection on water entry & wooden tail fins.	Mod 1, 2, 3: 42kts 2200yds/2011m Mod 3 & 4 Strong: 42kts 1640yds/1500m Mod 7 Strong: 41kts 1640yds/1500m
21in	Type 92	1932	660lbs 300kg	354.5in 7.15m	5940lbs 1720kg	Submarine use; electric; 2 x 54-cell lead-acid batteries; 6-pole compound interpole motor	28–30kts 7660yds/7000m
24in	Type 93	1933	Mod 1: 1078lbs 490kg Model 3: 1716lbs 780kg	354.5in 9m	Mod 1: 5940lbs 2700kg Mod 3: 6160lbs 2800kg	Model 1: 100% pure oxygen; starting on air then changeover to oxygen; sea water diluent; 2-cyl double-acting reciprocating engine (Whitehead Weymouth-type) Model 2: experimental high-speed; higher rpm smaller-pitch propellers. Model 3: 1943; 1st air vessel removed, starting on carbon tetrachloride	Mod 1: 49kts 22,000yds/20,000m 40kts 35,000yds/32,000m 36kts 44,000yds/40,000m Model 2: 56kts 5470yds/5000m Model 3: 49kts 16,400yds/15,000m 40yds 27,300yds/25,000m 36kts 32,000yds/30,000m
21in	Type 94 Model 1	1934				Experimental oxygen torpedo for aircraft, designed 1934 but never produced; started on air; 8-cyl radial engine	48kts 3300yds/3000m
18in	Type 94 Model 2	1934	330lbs 150kg	208in 5.28m	1870lbs 848kg	Experimental oxygen torpedo for aircraft, designed 1934 but never produced; started on air; 8-cyl radial engine 250bhp	45kts 2200yds/2000m
21in	Type 95	1935	Modif 1: 891lbs 405kg Model 2: 1210lbs 550kg	281.5in 7.15m	Modif 1: 3660lbs 1665kg Model 2: 3800lbs 1730kg	Oxygen torpedo for submarines Prototype 1935 Modif 1: 1938; 100% pure oxygen; starting on air then changeover to oxygen; sea water diluent; 2-cyl double-acting reciprocating engine (Whitehead Weymouth-type) Model 2: 1943; starting on steering air	Modif 1: 49kts 9840yds/9000m 45kts 13,000yds/12,000m Model 2: 49kts 6000yds/5500m 45kts 8200yds/7500m
21in	Type 96	1942	891lbs 405kg	281.5in 7.15m	3660lbs 1665kg	Interim submarine torpedo introduced due to problems with Type 95 Mod 1: 38% oxygen not requiring air or carbon tetrachloride	48kts 4900yds/4500m
18in	Type 97	1937	770lbs 350kg	220.6in 5.6m	2156lbs 980kg	100% oxygen-fuelled torpedo for midget submarines; 1st air vessel unable to be checked or charged in tube; 100% pure oxygen; starting on air then changeover to oxygen; sea water diluent; 2-cyl double-acting reciprocating engine (Whitehead Weymouth-type).	45kts 6000yds/5500m
18in	Type 98	1942	770lbs 350kg	220.6in 5.6m	2000lbs 950kg	New version of Type 97 introduced due to problems with 1st air bottle: 38% oxygen not requiring air or carbon tetrachloride	45kts 6000yds/5500m
18-in	Type 01	1941				Experimental jet-propelled version of Type 91 Mod 3; kerosene fuel	30kts 320yds/293m

Diameter	Name	Year	Warhead	Length	Weight	Notes	Performance
18in	Type 02 Type 02 Special	1942	770lbs 350kg	Type 02: 220.5in 5.6m Type 02 Spl: 221in 5.61m	Type 02: 2200lbs 1000kg Type 02 Spl: 2150lbs 975kg	Type 02: For torpedo boats & midget submarines, produced 1944; comp air; 8-cyl radial engine (Whitehead-type); 6 tail fins Type 02 Special: 8 tail fins	Type 02: 39kts 3300yds/3000m Type 02 Special: 39kts 2190yds/2000m
18in	Type 04	1944	Mark 2: 670lbs Mark 4: 920lbs/417kg	Mark 2: 207.7in 5.28m Mark 4: 225in 5.72m	Mark 2: 2170lbs/ 984kg Mark 4: 2435lbs/ 1105kg	Strengthened simplified version of Type 91: max launch speed increased to 400knots; larger hydrostatic diaphragm; heavier pendulum	Mark 2 42kts 1640yds/1500m Mark 4: 41kts 1640yds/1500m
18in?	Type KR	1944				Experimental rocket-powered torpedo	
11in	Type 05	1945	132lbs 60kg	149.6in 3.8m	507lbs 230kg	For use on small torpedo boats: comp air; 5-cyl swash plate engine; 7hp	20kts 1650yds/1500m
23in	Type M		1654lbs 750kg	279.5in 7.1m	3430lbs 1556kg	Aircraft torpedo; experimental; comp air; 8-cyl radial engine 470bhp	50kts 2734yds/2500m
18in	Type QR	1945	450lbs 204kg	216in 5.49m	1840lbs 835kg	Modified Type 91 Mod 2 for ASW; designed to descend in spiral near where sub detected; 300yds/290m diameter of spiral; continued down to 320ft/100m	N/a
11.8in	Model 6	1945	220lbs 100kg	116.7in 2.96m	595lbs 270kg	Unpowered ASW torpedo with full-length wings; steel warhead and wooden body; spiral diving torpedo used in similar way to Type QR; intended to have proximity fuze	N/a
11.8in	Model 7	1945	485lbs 220kg	116.7in 2.96m	1100lbs 499kg	As above, but steel warhead and steel body	N/a
12.75in	Type 73 GRX-4		100lbs Kg Plastique HEAT	9ft 3in		Mitsubishi Rankine-cycle engine (sulphur hexafluoride & lithium catalyst); shrouded pump-jet; active/passive homing; max depth: 1900ft	41kts 6 nautical miles
21in	Type 89	1990s	267kg			Electric; silver oxide/zinc battery; wire-guided active/passive homing; Max depth: 900m/ft	55kts 39,000m 40kts 50,000m

Russia
The Imperial Russian Navy purchased and then manufactured Whitehead torpedo designs under licence.
The Soviet Navy recommenced torpedo production in 1927 with new designs.

Diameter	Name	Year	Warhead	Length	Weight	Notes	Performance
21in	53-27	1927	584.2lbs 265kg	22ft 11$\frac{1}{2}$in 7m	3770lbs 1710kg	First Soviet torpedo, based on a never-produced design of 1917; wet heater	45kts 3700m
18in	TAV Aircraft	1932	212lbs 96kg	17ft 0$\frac{3}{4}$in 5.2m	1413lbs 641kg	Based on Pattern 1910 torpedo; dropped by parachute (3 drogue chute), from height of 6500–9800 feet/2000m–3000m	29kts 3280yds/3000m
18in	TAN Aircraft	1932				Low altitude drop	
21in	53-36 Surface ships, MTBs, subs	1936	661.4lbs 300kg	22ft 11$\frac{1}{2}$in 7m	3748lbs 1700kg	Wet heater. Unsuccessful; only 100 built	43.5kts 4270yds/4000m 33kts 8750yds/8000m
18in	45-36N Novik Cl DD	1936	440.9lbs 200kg	18ft 8$\frac{1}{2}$in 5.7m	2061lbs 935kg	Wet heater; copied from Whitehead Italian torpedo purchased in 1932. Used from 21in submarine tubes with adaptors	41kts 3280yds/3000m 32kts 6560yds/6000m
21in	53-38	1938	661.4lbs 300kg	23ft 7$\frac{1}{2}$in 7.2m	3560.5lbs 1615kg	Wet heater: copied from Whitehead Italian torpedo purchased in 1932.	44.5kts 4270yds/4000m 34.5kts 8750yds/8000m 30.5kts 10,940yds/10,000m

18in	45-36NU	1939	626lbs 284kg	19ft 8$\frac{1}{4}$in 6m	2266lbs 1028kg	Update with larger warhead	41kts 3280yds/3000m 32kts 6560yds/6000m
21in	53-38U	1939	882lbs 400kg	24ft 3$\frac{1}{4}$in 7.4m	3803lbs 1725kg	Update with larger warhead	44.5kts 4370yds/4000m 34.5kts 8750yds/8000m 30.5kts 10,940yds/10,000m
18in	45-36AV-A High altitude 45-36AN Low	1939	441lbs 200kg	18ft 8$\frac{1}{2}$in 5.7m	2061lbs 935kg	Strengthened to increase survivability on water entry; low altitude torpedo 45-36AN set to single speed only	39kts 4370yds/4000m
21in	53-39	1941	699lbs 317kg	24ft 7$\frac{1}{4}$in 7.5m	3924lbs 1780kg	Modification of 53-38 torpedo with increased speed	51kts 4370yds/4000m 39kts 8750yds/8000m 34kts 10,940yds/10,000m
21in	ET-80 Submarines	1942	882lbs 400kg	24ft 7$\frac{1}{4}$in 7.5m	3968lbs 1800kg	First Soviet electric torpedo	29kts 4370yds/4000m
21in	ET-46	1946	992lbs 450kg	24ft 5$\frac{1}{4}$in 7.45m	3990lbs 1810kg	Electric; modified ET-80 using German technology from G7e	31kts 6600yds/6000m
21in	SAET-50 SAET-50M	1950	827lbs 375kg	24ft 5$\frac{1}{4}$in 7.45m	3638lbs 1650kg	First Soviet passive homing electric torpedo; homing range 600–800m/ yds SAET-50M with more powerful battery & own propeller noise screening system	SAET-50: 23kts 4400yds/4000m SAET-50M: 29kts 6600yds/6000m
21in	53-51	1951	660lbs 300kg	24ft 11$\frac{1}{4}$in 7.6m	4134lbs 1875kg	Kerosene comp air wet heater; 53-39 with new magnetic fuse & pattern running	51kts 4400yds/4000m 39kts 8750yds/8000m
21in	ET-56 Submarines	1956	660lbs 300kg	24ft 3$\frac{1}{4}$in 7.4m	4409lbs 2000kg	Electric; non-homing	36kts 6600yds/6000m
21in	53-56 53-56V 53-56VA	1956 1964 1966	882lbs 400kg	25ft 3in 7.7m	4409lbs 2000kg	Wet heater; 53-56 oxygen; others kerosene comp air; non-homing, except for 53-56VA acoustic wake-follower; 53-56V & 53-56VA only for export	-56: 50kts 8750yds/8000m 40kts 14,200yds/13,000m -56V: 50kts 4400yds/4000m 40kts 8750yds/8000m -56VA 29kts
21in	53-57	1957	672lbs 305kg	24ft 11$\frac{1}{4}$in 7.6m	4409lbs 2000kg	Non-homing; kerosene http, based on German WW2 Ingolin technology	45kts 19,700yds/18,000m
21in	53-58	1968	Nuclear warhead	24ft 11$\frac{1}{4}$in 7.6m		Non-homing Non-homing	
21in	SET-53 SET-53M ASW	1958 1964	220lbs 100kg	25ft 7in 7.8m	3263lbs 1480kg	Electric; SET-53: lead-acid battery; SET-53M: silver-zinc battery; passive acoustic homing, range 660yds/600m acoustic homing, range 660yds/600m	-53: 23kts 8750yds/8000m -53M: 29kts 15,300yds/14,000m
21in	53-61 ALLIGATOR 53-61M	1961 1969	672lbs 305kg			Kerosene HTP; acoustic wake-follower; 53-61M modified homing system	55kts 16,400yds/15,000m 35kts 24,000yds/22,000m
21in	SAET-60 SAET-60M Submarines	1961 1969	661lbs 300kg	25ft 7in 7.8m	4409lbs 2000kg	Electric; silver-zinc battery; passive acoustic homing	SAET-60: 2kts 14,200yds/13,000m SAET-60M: 40kts 16,400yds/15,000m
21in	53-65 53-65K 53-65M Submarines	1965 1969 1969	661lbs 300kg	3ft 6in 7.2m	4563– 4630lbs 2070– 2100kg	Kerosene HTP except 53-65K: kerosene oxygen turbine; acoustic wake-follower	53-65: 45kts 19,700yds/18,000m 53-65K: 45kts 20,800yds/19,000m 53-65M: 44kts 24,000yds/22,000m
21in	SET-65 Yenot-2	1965	452lbs 205kg	25ft 7in 7.8m	3836lbs 1740kg	Electric; silver-zinc battery; active sonar guidance range 880yds/800m	40kts 17,500yds/16,000m
21in	TEST-68	1969	220lbs 100kg	25ft 11in 7.9m	3307lbs 1500kg	Electric; silver-zinc battery; wire- guided with active-passive sonar homing, range 880yds/800m; max depth 200m/650ft	29kts 15,300yds/14,000m

Diameter	Name	Year	Warhead	Length	Weight	Details	Speed/Range
21in	TEST-71 TEST-71MKE TEST-3	1971 1973	452lbs 205kg	25ft 11in 7.9m	TEST-71: 3858lbs/ 1750kg TEST-71MKE: 4012lbs/ 1820kg	Electric; silver-zinc battery; wire-guided with active-passive sonar homing, range 880yds/800m; max depth 400m/1300ft	40kts 16,400yds/15,000m 35kts 27,300yds/25,000m
400mm 15.75in	MGT-1 Submarines	1961	176lbs 80kg	14ft 9in 4.5m	1124lbs 510kg	Electric; silver-zinc battery; passive sonar homing; defence weapon for subs against surface ships	28kts 6600yds/6000m
400mm 15.75in	SET-40 SET-40U	1962 1968	176lbs 80kg	14ft 9in 4.5m	1212lbs 550kg	ASW active/passive homer, detection range 660-880yds/600-800m	29kts 8700yds/8000m
600mm 25.6in	65-73	1973	Nuclear warhead	36ft 11m	8820lbs + 4000kg +	Kerosene HTP turbine; non-homing; anti-aircraft carrier & shore base weapon	50kts 54,700yds/50,000m
600mm 25.6in	65-76 Kit ('Whale')	1976	992lbs+ 450kg+	33ft 11m	8820lbs + 4000kg +	Kerosene HTP turbine; non-homing; 65-73 with conventional warhead	50kts 54,700yds/50,000m
21in	UGST	1990s	441lbs 200kg	23ft 7½in 7.2m	4850lbs 2200kg	OTTO fuel II; pump-jet propulsor; acoustic wake-follower with active/passive homing; max depth 500m/1650ft	Max: 50kts Max: 43,800yds/40,000m
21in	VA-111 Shkval ('Squall')	1977	1543lbs 700kg	26ft 10¾in 8.2m	5952lbs 2700kg	Solid-fuel supercavitating rocket; submarine last-ditch unguided defence torpedo; reputed to have later homing version	200kts 12,000–16,400yds/ 11,000–15,000m
21in	USET-80 Submarines	1980	440–661 lbs 200–300kg	25ft 11in 7.9m	4410lbs+ 2000kg+	Electric; silver-zinc battery; active/passive homing wake-follower; max depth 400m/1300ft	40–50kts 22000yds/20,000m
18in	RAT-52 Aircraft	1952	529lbs 240kg	12ft 7½in 3.897m	1382lbs 627kg	Solid-fuel rocket anti-ship torpedo, air range 1100yds/10,000m; airspeed 300–400kts	58–68kts 570yds/520m in water
18in	45-54VT 45-56NT Aircraft	1954 1956	441lbs 200kg	14ft 9in 4.5m	2100lbs 950kg	Kerosene wet heater engine; anti-ship torpedo dropped from up to 33000ft/10,000m by parachutes; non-homing; NT model dropped from lower altitude	39kts 4400yds/4000m
18in	AT-1 Helicopters	1962	154–353 lbs 70–160kg		1235lbs 560kg	Electric; silver-zinc battery; active/passive homing ASW torpedo acquisition range 550–1100yds/500–1000m	27kts 5500yds/5000m
21in	AT-2 A/c AT-2U Stand-off	1965 1973	176–331 lbs 80–150kg	15ft 9in 4.8m	2315lbs 1050kg	Electric; silver-zinc battery; active/passive homing ASW torpedo detection range 1100yds/1000m; AT-2U is payload of 85R Metel ASW stand-off missile	40kts 7700yds/7000m
400mm 15.75in	SET-72 SET-73	1972	132–220 lbs 60–100kg	14ft 9in 4.5m	1543lbs 700kg	Electric; silver-magnesium seawater battery; active/passive homing ASW	40+kts 870yds/8000m
18in	APR-1 Aircraft	1960s	176lbs 80kg	12ft 1½in 3.7m	1433lbs 650kg	Solid-fuel rocket ASW torpedo active/passive homing acquisition range 1400yds/1300m; max depth 420m/1400ft	870yds/800m
18in	VTT-1 T-67 Strizh Helicopters	1976	154lbs 70kg		1190lbs 540kg	Electric; silver-zinc battery; wire-guided with active/passive homing, acquisition range 550–1100yds/500–1000m; max depth 200m/650ft	28kts 5500yds/5000m
18in	AT-3 UMGT-1 A/c, heli, S/O	1981	132lbs 60kg	12ft 5½in 3.8m	1538lbs 698kg	Electric; silver-magnesium seawater battery; active/passive homing ASW acquisition range 1650yds/1500m; max dept 500m/1650ft; UMGT-1 was payload of 85RU Rastrub & RPK-6 Vodopak stand-off ASW missiles	41kts 8700yds/8000m
330mm 13in	Kolibri A/c & heli	1978	97lbs 44kg	8ft 10in 2.7m	542lbs 246kg	OTTO fuel II turbine; copied from US Mark 46 Mod 0: active/passive homing ASW acquisition range 1100yds/1000m; max dept 450m/1500ft	45kts 5500–8700yds/ 5000–8000m

350mm 13.78in	APR-2 A/c & heli	1980s	220lbs 100kg	12ft 2in 3.7m	1368lbs 575kg	Solid-fuel rocket ASW active/passive homing acquisition range 1650yds/1500m; max depth 600m/2000ft	62kts 1600–2200yds/1500–2000m
355mm 13.98in	APR-3 APR-3E A/c & heli	1990s 2014	168lbs/76kg -3E: 163lbs 74kg	10ft 6in 3.2m 3E: 12ft 1in 3.685m	992lbs 450kg -3E: 1157lbs 525kg	Solid-fuel pump-jet propulsor; ASW active/passive homing acquisition range 2200yds/2000m; max depth 800m/2600ft	75kts 113secs engine burn: 3570yds/3264m
400mm 15.75in	APSET-95 Aircraft	1995	132lbs 60kg	12ft 7in 3.845m	1587lbs 720kg	Electric	Max: 50kts Max: 33,000yds/30,000m

China

21in	Yu-1 Yu-1A	1971	880lbs 400kg	25ft 7in 7.8m	4409lbs 2000kg	Modified Soviet Type 53 wet heater Yu-1A passive sonar homing; used in version of CAPTOR mine; latest has active homing	Max: 50kts
18in	Yu-2	1970	440lbs 200kg	13ft 1½in 4m	1382lbs 627kg	Modified Soviet RAT-2; solid-fuel rocket; first unguided; later passive homing	Max: 70kts In air: 5470yds/5000m In water: 1094yds/1000m
21in	Yu-3Sturgeon ZhonguaXun)	1984	452lbs 205kg	25ft 7in 7.8m	3000lbs 1361kg	Electric; silver-zinc battery; active/passive homing; max depth 400m/1300ft	35kts 14,220yds/13,000m
21in	ET32	2014	420lbs 190kg	21ft 7¾in 6.6m		Export model of Yu-3 Sturgeon; max depth 350m/1150ft	35kts 14,220yds/13,000m
21in	Yu-4 Jia	1987	680lbs 309kg	7.75m	3913lbs 1775kg	Developed from Soviet SAET-50; electric; silver-zinc battery; active/passive homing;	40kts 16,400yds/15,000m
21in	Yu-5 Sub ASW	1989	880lbs 400kg	25ft 7in 7.8m		OTTO fuel II; wire-guided with active/passive homing; max depth: 400m/1300ft	50kts 32,800yds/30,000m
21in	ET34	1995		21ft 7¾in 6.6m		Electric; silver-zinc battery; wire-guided with active/passive homing; max depth: 300m/985ft	42kts 19,685yds/18,000m 40kts 21,870yds/20,000m Variable speed: 27,340yds/25,000m
21in	ET36	1998		21ft 7¾in 6.6m		As above	36kts 10,000m 25kts 27,40yds/25,000m Variable speed: 19,658–21,870yds/ 18,000–20,000m
21in	Yu-6	2005				OTTO fuel II; wire guided with passive/active homing, wake-follower; Loongson-1 onboard microprocessor	Max: 65kts final run in Max: 49,200yds/45,000m
21in	Yu-8					Electric version of Yu-8	

France
In the nineteenth century and during the Great War the French Navy utilised the range of Whitehead torpedoes manufactured at the Saint-Tropez factory.
During the Great War the Schneider torpedo factory produced armaments for the land combat at the front.

21in	1924V Submarines	1924	683lbs 310kg	21ft 9in 6.63m	3285lbs 1490kg	Compressed air, alcohol wet heater	44kts 3281yds/3000m 35kts 7655yds/7000m
21in	1924Q Surface ships	1924	694lbs 315kg	23ft 4¼in 7.12m	3792lbs 1720kg	Compressed air, alcohol wet heater	35kts Max 16,404yds/15,000m
15.75in 400mm	1926V Submarines 1926W MTBs 1926DA A/c	1926	317lbs 144kg	16ft 7½in 5.07m	1442lbs 654kg	Used by submarines to attack merchant ships & smaller warships, often combined in trainable mounts with 21in tubes; comp air, wet heater engine; unsuccessful in action	43kts 2187yds/2000m
21in	K2 Surface ship ASW	1956		14ft 5¼in 4.4m	2434lbs 1104kg	Gas turbine; Max depth 300m/984ft	50kts 1640yds/1500m
21in	L3 Surface ship ASW	1961 =		14ft 1¼in 4.3m	2006lbs 910kg	Electric; Max depth 300m/984ft	25kts 5468yds/5000m

21in	L4 Aircraft			10ft 3¼in 3.13m	1190lbs 540kg	Anti-surface ship & ASW; electric;	Max depth 300m/984ft 30kts 5468yds/5000m
21in	L5 Mod 1 Submarines			14ft 5¼in 4.4m	2204lbs 1000kg	Anti-surface ship & ASW; electric;	35kts
21in	L5 Mod 3 Submarines			14ft 5¼in 4.4m	866lbs 1300kg	Anti-surface ship & ASW; electric; Max depth 550m/1804ft	35kts 10,390yds/9500m
21in	L5 Mod 4 ASW	1976		14ft 5¼in 4.4m	2061lbs 935kg	Surface ship ASW; electric Max depth 500m/1640t	35kts 7655yds/7000m
21in	F17 Submarines	1988		17ft 7¼in 5.38m	2866lbs 1300kg	Anti-surface ship; electric	35kts
21in	F17 Mod 2 Sub ASW	1998		17ft 7¼in 5.38m	3108lbs 1410kg	Electric; Max depth 600m/1968ft	Max 40kts Max 21,872yds/20,000m
12.75in	MU90 Impact	2008		9ft 8½in 2.96m	650lbs 295kg	Fusion of French Murène programme & Italian WASS A290 programme; lightweight ASW torpedo; electric; pump-jet; max depth 1000m/ 3281ft	55kts Max 15,310yds/14,000m
21in	F21 Black Shark	2015		16ft 4¾in 5m	3307lbs 1500kg	Franco-Italian cooperation project; wire-guided; electric; silver oxide/ luminium battery; max depth 1000m/3281ft	Max 50kts Max 54,680yds/50,000m
Sweden							
400mm 15.75in	Torpedo 45 ASW for Littoral combat			9ft 4¼in 2.85m	705lbs 320kg	Electric; silver oxide/zinc battery with electrolyte cooling system; wire-guided active/passive homing; can be air-dropped without parachute	
21in	Torpedo 617			22ft 11½in 7m	4080lbs 1850kg	Anti-surface ship; wire guidance, passive homing; 2-speed	
21in	Torpedo 62	2014		19ft 8¼in 6m	3197lbs 1450kg	Thermal HTP turbine; wire-guided with active/passive homing	45kts + 50,000m+
India							
12.75in	Shyena	2012	50kg	2.75m	220kg	Electric; active/passive homing; max depth: 540m/ft	40kts+ Max: 12,000m
South Korea							
21in	White Shark Baek Sang Eo	2004		2.7m	1100kg	Electric; active/passive homing	40kts 30,000m
Italy							
14in	A37-256	1877	81.5lbs 37kg	14ft 4in 4.37m		Comp air; balance chamber & pendulum behind air flask; 1000psi, 70.3kg/cm^2; Brotherhood 3-cyl radial engine; servo-actuation of horizontal rudders; 2-bladed contra-rotating propellers; no fins top and bottom; imported from Fiume	22kts 850yds/777m
14in	B43-356	1879	95lbs 43kg	14ft 5in 4.39m		As above; torpedo body in bronze	22kts 850yds/777m
14in	B57-356	1885	125lbs 56.7kg	14ft 7in 4.45m		Torpedo body in bronze; 1500psi, 105.5kg/cm^2	24kts 1080yds/988m
18in	B90-450	1889	198lbs 90kg	16ft 3in 4.95m		Torpedo body in bronze; comp air; cold running; 3-cylinder radial engine; 3-bladed contra-rotating propellers	30kts 1100yds/1006m
18in	A60-450	1897	132lbs 60kg	16ft 3in 4.95m		Torpedo body in steel; gyroscope; 4-bladed contra-rotating propellers	32kts 850yds/777m
18in	A62-450	1897	137lbs 62kg	16ft 6in 5m		As above	31kts 2150yds/1966m
18in	A90-450	1898	198lbs 90kg	15ft 7in 4.75m		As above	34kts 2150yds/1966m

18in	A110-450	1898	242lbs 110kg	16ft 6in 5m		As above	34kts 2150yds/1966m
18in	A68-450	1905	150lbs 63kg	14ft 7in 4.4m			31kts 3250yds/2970m
18in	A90-450	1905	198lbs 90kg	16ft 3in 4.95m			31kts 3250yds/2970m
18in	A95-450	1906	210lbs 95.3kg	16ft 10in 5.1m			34kts 2150yds/1966m
18in	A100-450	1911	220lbs 100kg	15ft 7in 4.75m			34kts 2150yds/1966m
18in	A100-450	1912	220lbs 100kg	16ft 10in 5.1m			34kts 2150yds/1966m
18in	A100-450	1912	220lbs 100kg	13ft 5in 4.1m			38.5kts 2200yds/2011m
18in	A110-450	1913	243lbs 110kg	17ft 0in 5.2m			38kts 2200yds/2011m
18in	A115-450	1914	254lbs 115kg	17ft 0in 5.2m			41kts 3250yds/2970m
21in	A180bis-533	1916	397lbs 180kg	20ft 9in 6.3m			27kts 9750yds/8915m
21in	A180bis-533	1917	397lbs 180kg	20ft 9in 6.3m			25kts 9750yds/8915m
21in	W270-533.4 X 7.2 'F' Submarines	935	551lbs 250kg	23ft 7in 7.2m	3417lbs 1550kg	Built by Whitehead; wet heater engine	43kts 3300yds/3000m 28kts 10900yds/10,000m
21in	W270-533.4 x 7.2 Veloce Submarines	1935	595lbs 270kg	23ft 7in 7.2m	3748lbs 1700kg	Wet heater engine; streamlined head	50kts 3300–4400yds/3000–4000m 30kts 13,100yds/12,000m
18in	F200/450 x 5.46 Aircraft	1939	375lbs/175kg Later: 441lbs/200kg	17ft 11in 5.46m	1995lbs 905kg	Whitehead; wet heater engine; used by the Luftwaffe under the designation F5W	40kts 3300yds/3000m
18in	SI 200/450 x 5.36 Aircraft	1939	441lbs 200kg	17ft 7in 5.36m	2145lbs 973kg	Silurifico Italiano; wet heater engine; given Luftwaffe designation F5I	40kts 3300yds/3000m
18in	W200-450 x 5.75 Cagni class subs	1939	441lbs 200kg	18ft 10½in 5.75m		Wet heater engine; could be fired from 21in tubes with sub-calibre fittings	44kts 3300yds/3000m 30kts 8750yds/8000m
21in	SI 270-533.4 DD, CA & CL	1939	608lbs 276kg	24ft 3in 7.4m	3748lbs 1700kg	Built by Silurificio Italiano, Naples	46kts 4400yds/4000m 35kts 8750yds/8000m 29kts 13,100yds/12,000m Later versions: 48kts 4400yds/4000m 38kts 8750yds/8000m 30kts 13,100yds/12,000m
21in	SI 250-533.4 Submarines	1939	551lbs 250kg	23ft 7in 7.2m		Built by Silurificio Italiano, Naples	49kts 4400yds/4000m 38kts 8750yds/8000m
18in	SI 200/450 x 5.36 MAS	1939	441lbs 200kg	17ft 7in 5.36m	2050lbs 930kg	Built by Silurificio Italiano, Naples	44kts 2200yds/2000m
18in	W 200/450 x 5.25 MAS	1939	441lbs 200kg	17ft 2¾in 5.25m	1896lbs 860kg	Built by Whitehead	46kts 4400yds/4000m
50cm 19.7in	W120/500 x 2.6 Circular run aircraft	1939	265lbs 120kg	8ft 6½in 2.3m	772lbs 350kg	Built by Whitehead; dropped by parachute; electric; no depth control: ran in circles, spirals and curves; Luftwaffe designation LT350	13.5kts initial down to 3.9kts 16,400yds/15,000m

18in	Luftwaffe designation LT280	1939	198lbs 90kg		617lbs 280kg	Aircraft dropped circling torpedo; electric	13.5kts initial down to 3.9kts 13,100yds/12,000m
21in	Whitehead G-6E		661lbs 300kg	19ft 6in 5.9m		Electric; wire-guided; passive acoustic homer	
21in	Whitehead G-6EF Kangaroo			20ft 2in 6.1m		Electric; wire-guided; active sonar homing	
21in	Whitehead A-184		1212lbs 550kg	19ft 8in 6m	2860lbs 1297.3kg	Electric; optic fibre wire-guided with 2-way communication with launch vessel; active-passive acoustic homer controlling course and speed	17,000yds/15,545m
12.75in	Whitehead A-244/S			8ft 10in 2.7m		Electric; active-passive homer with countermeasures activation feature; self-adaptive search pattern	33kts 7000m+
12.75in	Whitehead A-290					Electric	50kts
21in	IF21 Black Shark	2015		16ft 4³/₄in 5m	3307lbs 1500kg	Franco-Italian co-operation project; wire-guided; electric; silver oxide/aluminium battery; max depth 1000m/3281ft	Max 50kts Max 54,680yds/50,000m

Index